Amherst, 16/11/82

To Monika,
all you need to know about <u>PP</u> (and more!)

from
Vince

PIERS PLOWMAN
a reference guide

A
Reference
Guide
to
Literature

Everett Emerson
Editor

PIERS PLOWMAN
a reference guide

VINCENT DiMARCO

G.K.HALL &CO.

70 LINCOLN STREET, BOSTON, MASS.

Library of Congress Cataloging in Publication Data

DiMarco, Vincent.
  Piers Plowman, a reference guide.

  Includes index.
  1. Langland, William, 1330?-1400? Piers the Plowman—
Bibliography. I. Title.
Z8482.4.D55   016.821'1   82-3137
ISBN 0-8161-8309-0   AACR2

This publication is printed on permanent/durable acid-free paper
MANUFACTURED IN THE UNITED STATES OF AMERICA

Contents

The Author

Vincent DiMarco, Associate Professor of English at the University of Massachusetts (Amherst), received his B.A. from the State University of New York at Buffalo, and his M.A. and Ph.D. from the University of Pennsylvania, where his dissertation was on Chaucer. He has coedited (along with Leslie Perelman) the Middle English Letter of Alexander to Aristotle, and has published essays on Chaucer, medieval drama, and Piers Plowman.

Preface

This reference guide presents an annotated list of writings about and records of the fourteenth-century Middle English alliterative poem, extant in three versions, which is generally known as Piers Plowman and which is widely attributed to an individual named William Langland. The entries, arranged chronologically and, within a given year, alphabetically by author, extend from the record of a bequest of 1395 (when the poet may still have been alive) through 1979.

Excluded from the bibliographical entries, except insofar as they enter into critical notices and discussions of the poem, are those political and religious tracts and treatises that derive from and contribute to the "Piers Plowman tradition" by invoking for their own ends the name or character of the virtuous laborer, Piers, or the concepts of Dowel, Dobet, and Dobest, in some general fashion without commenting directly on the poem or its author. Also excluded, but with the same qualification, are those works of poetry and prose that contain allusions to, echoes of, and imaginative elaborations upon the poem or the life of its author. Renderings of the poem into Modern English, translations of it into foreign languages, and selections from it printed in modern anthologies have been excluded, except when such works in their introductions or notes present critical commentary deemed worthy of admission. Only Masters theses that have led to publication have been included. Published, though often relatively inaccessible, foreign-language dissertations have been sought out and annotated whenever possible. Unpublished dissertations are listed with reference to their printed abstracts, and in only two cases (Döring, 1921.1, Devlin, 1928.5) where the abstract of an inaccessible, unpublished dissertation was not generally available have I composed my annotations on the basis of the abstract, rather than on personal examination of the dissertation. Similarly, though I include as a convenience to the reader without access to a major library many modern reprints and revised editions of earlier works, only in a small number of cases (signaled through appropriate cross-references) have I been unable to examine personally the earliest version of a bibliographical entry, and thus to comment when necessary on later, significant revision.

Preface

Because the aim throughout has been to present as objectively as possible the development and tradition of critical commentary on the poem and the extraliterary material from which some of that commentary derives, I mention literary histories and modern surveys only when they go beyond a mere recapitulation of others' work to contribute in noteworthy fashion to the evolving corpus of criticism. I have noted reviews of major works, but cannot claim the list of reviews is exhaustive. Those works, in the great majority of cases unpublished, that I have not been able to secure are marked by an asterisk.

The earlier entries in this guide, occasionally presenting verbatim the documentary and critical notices of the poem and its author in the period before reputable texts of the poem, take as their starting point the list of notices of Piers Plowman assembled by Skeat in Langland (1884.2) with a check of my own additions to Skeat's list afforded by the work of Marx (1931.5) and McGinnis (1932.13), both of which later works concentrate on the time before the eighteenth century. For work produced since Skeat's pioneering editions, my primary sources of bibliographical entries have been the MLA and MHRA bibliographies, YWES and CBEL, the review of scholarship on the poem by Bloomfield (1939.1), and the bibliographies furnished by Wells (1916.4); J.A.W. Bennett, in Langland (1969.22); Proppe (1972.20); and Colaianne (1978.4). In particular, the annotated bibliography of Dr. Colaianne, although it concentrates on the period 1875-1977 and differs significantly in format from the present work, has proven a valuable, late check for my modern bibliographical entries; however, I make the modest claim to have unearthed from all periods under discussion more than a few critical notices that have escaped previous bibliographies.

A brief introduction, concentrating on the critical concerns of the earlier, less well-noticed period of commentary, is followed by a table of manuscripts, which is largely derived from Skeat, in Langland (1886.1); Knott and Fowler, in [Langland] (1952.6); Kane, in [Langland] (1960.10); Donaldson (1966.2); and Kane and Donaldson, in [Langland] (1975.14); included are the sigla of which manuscripts are used throughout. This is followed by a list of abbreviations, the annotated bibliography, and an index. Line numbers mentioned in the annotations refer, except when noted, to Skeat's Clarendon Edition, Langland (1886.1).

In the preparation of this reference guide, I have had the benefit of research in the Beinecke and Sterling libraries of Yale University, the Frost Library of Amherst College, the Bodleian Library, Oxford, the British Library, and the Universitäts-Bibliothek of Albert-Ludwigs-Universität, Freiburg; I remember with pleasure and gratitude the kind cooperation of the staffs of these institutions. John Kendall, Eric Esau, and Meg Caulmare of the University of Massachusetts libraries assisted me cheerfully on a number of specific queries. I gratefully acknowledge the help, in large

Preface

things and small, furnished by my colleagues in the Department of English of the University of Massachusetts, Everett Emerson, Gary Aho, Dan Collins, Joseph Frank, James Freeman, Ernest Gallo, Paul Mariani, and Meredith Raymond, as well as that of Willi Erzgräber, Herbert Pilch, Irmgard Born, and Ursula Schaefer of the English Seminar of Freiburg University. But beyond all other acknowledgments, I am especially grateful to Dr. Elizabeth Brewer, whose command of European sources saved me from more errors than I wish to imagine.

I acknowledge the kind permission of the editors of <u>Anglia</u> to draw upon an essay published in that journal.

Introduction

To search through the early criticism and commentary on <u>Piers Plowman</u> and its author with the expectation of discovering such riches as present themselves to the student of Chaucer's early critical reception is largely to seek in vain. Not only does Langland find no enthusiastic praise from the pens of his contemporary poets and their immediate successors, but most of the familiar compliments so abundantly paid to Chaucer on the basis of his vivid powers of description, felicitous poetic diction, freshness of invention, freedom from prolixity, and variety of rhetorical and verbal effects are either virtually without analogue in early notices of <u>Piers Plowman</u> or are found in highly abbreviated fashion and recast into the particular context of the language of satire. A telling comparison suggests itself in Sir Brian Tuke's comments on Chaucer in Francis Thynne's edition (1532) and the nearly contemporary remarks on <u>Piers Plowman</u> by Robert Crowley in the <u>editio princeps</u> of the poem (1550.1). Whereas Tuke (speaking for the editor) praises along with Chaucer's "excellent lernyng in all kyndes of doctrynes and sciences," his "frutefulnesse in wordes" well adapted to matter and purpose, his "swete and pleasaunt sentences," "perfectyon in metre," "compendyousnesse in narration," "sensible and open style," and "sharpnesse or quycknesse in conclusion," the extent of what we might describe as Crowley's "literary" comments on Langland's poem is largely limited to the breezy assertions that once the unfamiliar device of alliteration is noted, "the metre shall be very pleasaunt to reade," and that the "somewhat darck" meaning of the poem's language may be understood by those who break the shell of its verbal structure to reach the kernel of its meaning within.

That this "kernel" of significance was understood by Crowley in the context of satire (or, as Crowley puts it, with the poet's intention "most christianlie [to] enstructe the weake, and sharplye rebuke the obstynate blynde") need not surprise us: the satiric voice is, as Derek Brewer has shown, one of the range of effects of a Gothic artist like Chaucer, an effect increasingly emphasized in critical reactions to medieval poetry in the fifteenth and sixteenth centuries. Indeed, it is on this particular point of appreciation primarily as satire that sixteenth-century estimation of Chaucer and

Langland would seem to merge, as witnessed by the false ascription of
the anti-Catholic Plowman's Tale to Chaucer and its confusion by
Leland (c. 1545.1), Milton (1642.1), Dryden (1700.1), and others with
Langland's poem. But what does, perhaps, surprise is the unanimity
of response to this one effect of Piers Plowman and the subordination
to satire of seemingly all other literary effects. Bale (1557.1)
sees "sub amœnis coloribus & typis" in the poem primarily the fervent spirit of a Wyclifite denouncing the blasphemies of the Roman
church; and indeed, Bale may once have thought (1548.1) that the work
was that of Wyclif himself. Crowley gives every reason to believe
that it was the prophetic satire of the poem that led to its publication. Selden (1622.2) finds its satire of the "infecting corruptions"
of the time not without attendant beauties of invention and judgment,
but clearly appreciates the poem first and foremost as satire. And
to Weever (1631.1), Piers Plowman deserves mention exclusively, it
would seem, as a book of "bitter inuectives."

It is not much of a simplification to say that until the rise
of antiquarian studies in the Restoration, such literary-critical
comments on the poem as one finds are grounded in an appreciation of
the poem as satire and seldom pass beyond this estimation. Whereas
so stern a moralist as Ascham could comfortably install Chaucer as
the "Englishe Homer" largely on the basis of his observance of the
unity of time and his lively description of outward and inward nature, and Googe could liken him to Ennius in his "so fine and filled
phrases," Langland's elevation to the company of classical writers by
Puttenham (1589.1) places him with the satirists Lucilius, Persius,
and Juvenal, and is accompanied by the writer's denunciation of his
"loose meetre, and his termes hard and obscure, so as in them is little pleasure to be taken."

If, however, the range of early critical commentary on Langland
is more narrowly conceived than that on Chaucer, emphasizing the
moral and didactic over the more readily pleasurable, this same emphasis would seem to have insulated Piers Plowman from the moral zeal
of those reformers and puritans whose mistrust of fictions led them
to view Chaucer's works as other than edifying literature, and to use
the phrase "a Canterbury tale" as one of abuse. Only Hanmer (1577.2)
appears to bemoan the reading of Piers Plowman along with other
imaginative literature instead of works of theology and ecclesiastical history; but Hanmer's examples of presumably frivolous or immoral
writing are described with so many salutary effects that his true
meaning is far from clear. His is a single, perhaps confused voice,
whose dissent is more than made up for by Prynne's defense (1633.1,
perhaps referring to the Plowman's Tale) of the "serious, sacred,
divine" nature of "Pierce the Plowmans tales and Dialogues," and the
inclusion of a copy of Langland's poem in the inventory of so staunch
a Puritan as Governor Thomas Dudley (1657.1).

Despite the generally high regard in which the sentence of
Piers Plowman was held by early commentators, there is reason to

believe that readers' knowledge of what the poem meant was decreasing. Turner's comments (1560-64[?].1) would seem at least an indictment of the Middle English as construed in Crowley's or Rogers's editions, and may thus describe a failing sixteenth-century knowledge of the language. To Webbe (1586.1), the poet's "dooinges" are "somewhat harshe and obscure"; to the author of the Arte of English Poesie (1589.1), the poet's "termes" are described similarly. Bolton (1618[?].1) mentions the poem in the context of Salust's supposed use of "outworn Words" stolen from Cato, in arguing for the use by historians of contemporary language; and Fuller (1662.1) saw the need to affix to his discussion of the poem and The Prayer and Complaint of the Plough-man (which he ascribes to the same author) a short glossary of obsolete Middle English words. Although no printed glossary devoted exclusively to Piers Plowman appeared until Whitaker's edition (1813.1), understanding of the poem may be said to have profited from the general antiquarian interest in glossaries and dictionaries incorporating "old words," as evidenced by Coles (1676.1), Hickes (1705.1), and Ruddiman[?] (1710.1), all of whom gloss words cited from the poem. By 1707 the anonymous author of the essay "Of the Old English Poems and Poetry," admitting that the language of England before Chaucer, as exemplified by Robert of Gloucester, was but "a confus'd Mixture of Saxon and the Norman Jargon," nevertheless asserts that the language of Piers Plowman (from which he quotes) "is much mended of what it was in Gloucester's Days."

This same essayist, while thus commending the state of Langland's language and the depiction of character the poem evinces, has no praise at all for Langland as a metricist, however. In this he is typical of the sixteenth and seventeenth centuries, which in general developed from the meager description of Langland's measure offered by Crowley ("three wordes at the leaste in euery verse which begyn with some one letter") either hopelessly vague and/or disparaging descriptions of Langland's metrical practices (e.g., Puttenham [1589.1], Selden [1622.2]) or uncritically complimentary evaluations, as those of Webbe (1586.1) and Meres (1598.1), both of whom saw the measure of the poem as quantitative. But lacking any indication of how these two writers applied such a method to the versification of the poem, one suspects that the term may have meant little more to them than that Piers Plowman was freed from the "barbarous" device of rhyme for which Chaucer during the same period had been more than once criticized. A more sophisticated metrical examination of Piers Plowman may be said to begin with Hickes (1705.1), who illustrated alliterative measure from the poem in the context of "Saxon" literary and linguistic antiquities, as did Percy (1765.1) in a highly influential essay that described the harmony of Langland's verse as dependent neither on quantity nor on rhyme. But Warton (1754.1) had pronounced against the constraints against naturalness of expression forced upon a poet seeking three alliterating syllables per line, and he repeated his argument in his great History of English Poetry (1774.2) in a way that makes clear his

feelings regarding Langland's failure to avail himself of the improvements in poetical language and versification already introduced
into the language. Yet at least one writer of the period, in a call
for a new edition of the poem (1787.1), sides with Langland against
these "discordant Gallicisms" brought to the language by Chaucer.

The eighteenth century offers the first glimmerings of a more
familiar kind of literary criticism of the poem, though it must be
admitted that far less attention was paid to Piers Plowman during
this period than to Chaucer and the romance. In her sensible anthol-
ogy of earlier English verse, Elizabeth Cooper (assisted by William
Oldys) praises along with the poem's satire and morality, the "rich
Imagination" and the "uncommon Spirit" with which its argument is
rendered. She sounds one other new theme of the period by calling
attention to the poem's lack of an overall unity of design in the
face of "every Vision seeming a distinct Rhapsody," a charge echoed
by Cibber (1753.1) and Warton (1754.1), the latter of whom notes,
however, the poem's humor, spirit, and imagination. Ellis (1801.1)
is the first to defend the poem's consistency of action and characterization against such charges, and does so in a surprisingly modern
appeal to the poetic device of the dream vision. Whitaker (1813.1),
who seeks likewise to show that the poem "was written after a regular
and consistent plan," nevertheless notes Langland's indistinct mixture of personifications and the appearance of allegorical characters
while Will is awake. The argument for unity of design was stoutly
denied by Campbell (1819.2).

As equally unsettled a critical verdict was rendered in the
first half of the nineteenth century concerning the worth and significance of the poem's allegory. Clearly, to Brydges (1800.1), the
poet's employment of allegory needed less a defense than his decision
to use alliterative measure; while to Milman (1855.4), allegory was
seen to mark a positive moral advance in mankind's development, and
to Morley (1864.1), it was the literary form best suited for embody-
ing the purest aspirations of mankind. Marsh (1862.1) saw the allegorical design as itself inconducive to an ordered and unified plan,
but he accepted without great demur the poet's decision to employ it
as the dominant mode of exposition. But Whitaker, as already noted,
was less happy with Langland's presentation of allegorical characters
in a narrative that fluctuated between dreaming and waking; and
D'Israeli (1841.1) saw allegory as proof positive of the primitive
conception of society that had nurtured the poem. Warwick (1861.1),
seemingly holding up the poem against an implied standard of realistic depiction, emphasized what he saw as the contrived and incongruous situations and depictions inherent to the allegorical form.
But rather more mixed critical assessments were rendered by Wright
(1842.3) who, in drawing a contrast between the tableaulike effect of
Piers Plowman and the more continuous and consistent allegorical
representation in a narrative like the Roman de la Rose, praised the
vigor and immediacy of Langland's presentation while at the same time
seeming to object to allegorical writings in general; and Schele de

Introduction

Vere (1853.1) who saw Langland's allegorical depiction as a mode
forced upon him by circumstances both literary and political, yet
succeeding nonetheless. His is a view that has won a minority of
adherents in our own day, for example, Cejp (1954.1 and 1955.1).

More of a consensus in the nineteenth century is voiced with
regard to the poet's religious orthodoxy. As opposed to what seems
on review too facile and uncritical a pronouncement by earlier writers of Langland's dissent, even heterodoxy, a more careful assessment
of his religious opinions, emphasizing his adherence to traditional,
orthodox beliefs, begins to be stressed around mid-century, by Wright
(1842.3), Craik (1844.1), and Milman (1855.4). Once again, however,
the pithy comments of Ellis (1801.1), distinguishing even more carefully between the explicit religious and political sentiments of the
poem and the extent to which they may have participated in and contributed to events and movements beyond their intention and control,
suggest a profitable line of inquiry that in the twentieth century
has been sounded most recently in Pearsall's denial (1978.12) of any
meaningful doctrinal connections of Langland and Wyclif at the same
time as he sees reflected in the poem the antisacerdotal bias of
late medieval popular religious movements.

Modern literary criticism of Piers Plowman may be said largely
to date from the Early English Text Society editions of the poem
(1867-84) of Walter W. Skeat, culminating in his Clarendon Press
Parallel Text Edition of all three versions (1886.1). Although important MSS were unknown to him, and although his editions can in no
rigorous sense be claimed to have established critical texts on
scientific, "Lachmannian" principles of genealogical descent, his
prodigious efforts resulted in the establishment of the text of all
three versions based on at least the comparison of readings from
many MSS, and the attempt roughly to classify extant MSS into family
groupings. The availability of these editions spurred more sophisticated work on the language and meter of the poem, though often, as
with Kron (1885.1) and Luick (1889.3), the mistaken opinion of Skeat
that MS. L (B-text) preserved the autograph text of the poem severely
limited the value of such researches; but Teichmann, as early as
1891, sensed the implications of Skeat's error in this regard and
pointed a better direction in textual studies of the B-version.
Skeat's copious and erudite notes may also be said to have encouraged
the efforts of numerous local antiquaries, amateur students of language and would-be philologists, often with bizarre results (e.g.,
Dowe [1873.3], Purton [1873.7], and Ffoulkes [1892.1]) that clearly
must have tried the patience of this great scholar. But a much more
valuable effect of Skeat's vast learning brought to bear on the poem
in his notes and commentary was a burgeoning interest in the literary
relations of Piers Plowman, in such researches of those of Brink
(1877.1), Jusserand (1893.1), and Snell (1899.2); in the attempt of
Hopkins (1895.3) to classify the sources of the poet's allusions; and
in the more specialized source and influence studies of Bellezza
(1894.1), Traver (1907.5), Manly (1908.6), and Owen (1912.5), the

last of whom surveyed the poem's place in the Continental allegorical literary tradition. This is a direction of scholarly investigation that has continued, of course, into our own day, perhaps best represented recently in the appreciation of the poem as illustrative of various genres by Bloomfield (1961.3) and by various studies of Salter and Pearsall, in the provocative study of Langland and Spenser by Anderson (1976.2), and in the parallels with Latin and French works recently advanced by Bourquin (1978.2).

Skeat's work, moreover, in its progressively stronger acceptance of the evidence of the poem as furnishing autobiographical details of the life of its author, may likewise be said to have initiated a long-lived critical controversy regarding the use of such references in the poem, and their bearing on the larger, more acrimoniously debated question of the authorship of the three versions, which Skeat himself never apparently doubted were largely the product of the same individual. As early as 1894, Hanscom warned against reading the poem as the autobiography of its author, a counsel that was shared by Jack (1901.1), Manly (1906.3), and Krog (1928.6), but ignored by Hopkins (1895.3), Bright (1928.2), and with direct reference to the authorship question as formulated by Manly, Mensendieck (1910.9). In recent times, the value and function of such "autobiographical" detail have been profitably discussed by Donaldson (1949.1) in his study devoted to the C-text poet, and by Kane, both in his treatment of the general question in relation to Langland and Chaucer studies (1965.12) and in his important investigation and reappraisal of the evidence in the authorship question (1965.13). The development of inquiry into the authorship question itself has been the subject of incisive and commendable reviews of scholarship, such as that of Bloomfield (1939.1), who called attention to a disconcerting difference of opinion among those who were otherwise allied in opposing single authorship; by Kane (1965.13), who concluded largely on the basis of the external evidence that there was no compelling reason to believe in multiple authorship; by Farris (1966.4), who considered the various contentions raised by Manly to have been satisfactorily dealt with in the course of time; and by Colaianne (1978.4), who briefly noted the inconclusiveness of the debate, as well as its ultimately salutary effect in focusing attention on the question of the poem's unity and coherence. Other, perhaps less objective recapitulations of the controversy are included in various studies contributing to the debate, included below with cross-references.

Although I think it fair to say that, seventy-five years after Manly's challenge to the accepted view initiated the controversy, the burden of proof still lies on the shoulders of those who deny single authorship, four aspects of the problem perhaps deserve mention. First, we may note that doubts of single authorship are not as recent a phenomenon as opponents of Manly's theories have sometimes made them appear, as can be substantiated in the unappreciated comments of Hearne and the provocative (though admittedly undeveloped) remarks of

Introduction

Ritson, not to mention those of Marsh (1860.1), at one time enlisted by Manly himself. Second, that although the text of the A- and B-texts presented by Skeat has been greatly improved upon by Kane (1960.10) and by Kane and Donaldson (1975.14), there is no consensus that these later editions represent authoritative critical texts and hence provide an unerring basis for studies of the original language, grammatical forms, and alliteration that Manly promised would vindicate his position. Third, that the evidence of such tests of internal evidence applied to Skeat's editions by Deakin, Blackman, Day, and others at the height of the controversy is of mixed value and of widely differing conclusion. And fourth, that as has been noted, the debate can in no way be said to have been concluded: Baugh (1948.1) asserted his dissatisfaction with the rebuttal of Manly's theory of the "lost leaf"; Fowler (1974.9) has recently reiterated his suspicions of the disposition among critics to link the A- and B-texts together through the assumption of single authorship in a way that does not do justice to the coherence of the A-text; and Covella (1972.5 and 1976.7) has seen verifiable differences of grammatical forms among the versions. Even the editor of what will become the Athlone Press edition of the C-text (Russell [1962.9]) has admitted that the retention in that version of scribal errors in the B-text weakens the case for single authorship; and he has suggested the possibility of the C-text representing an editorial, rather than authorial, revision, drawing upon materials left incomplete by the poet.

A major preoccupation of twentieth-century scholarship and criticism of the poem has been the elucidation of its thematic and structural unity in relation to theological thought. Comprehensive studies by Dunning (1937.3), Hort ([1938].5), Robertson and Huppé (1951.9), and Erzgräber (1957.3) draw with differing emphases on the patristic and scholastic traditions of commentary on Scripture and philosophical inquiry, while in more specialized studies such organizing principles have been detected in the poem as the Three Lives (variously explained by Wells [1929.1 and 1938.9], Coghill [1933.1], Meroney [1950.9], Dunning [1956.3], and Hussey [1956.6]); the figure of Piers (Coghill [1933.1] and Salter [1962.11]); the Trinity (Frank [1957.4]); the quest for Christian perfection (Bloomfield [1958.1]); the mystical identification with God (Vasta [1965.20]); the theme of spiritual regeneration and salvation (Lawlor [1962.4] and Frank [1957.4]); and the figure of the Dreamer and his visions (Gerould [1948.10], Salter [1962.11], Holleran [1966.7], Mills [1969.23], and Higgs [1974.11). In particular, the exegetical approach to the poem's meaning with recourse to the "four-fold" method of allegorical interpretation first suggested with reference to Piers Plowman by Coghill (1933.1), but later invoked by and henceforth associated with Robertson and Huppé (1951.9), has elicited objections both methodological and practical by Frank (1957.4), who considers the poem representative of personification allegory; Donaldson (1960.4), who feels that exegetical criticism is insensitive to the particular meaning and use of a figure or image in context; Salter (1968.13), who argues for the special applicability of figural allegory to Langland's poem; and Aers (1975.1), who claims that Robertson and Huppé's readings do not adequately take into account Christianity's essential historicism. In particular, the figural approach advocated by Salter has borne fruit in such studies as those of Ames (1970.3), Schroeder (1970.16), and Carruthers (1973.2). But without any systematic attempt to interpret major portions of the poem through the four levels of interpretation, sensitive and valuable "exegetical" readings of individual images and metaphors have been offered by such scholars as Kellogg, Kaske, and Hill; while the poet's debt to scholastic philosophy and psychology, earlier recognized by Sanderlin (1941.9), has recently been elaborated upon by such investigators as Harwood and Schmidt.

Studies such as these go far to answer the call of Bloomfield (1939.1) for further work on the intellectual backgrounds of the poem—a call which, with particular reference to the need of study of the C-text in its historical milieu, has been echoed by Fowler (1971.11). Perhaps taking the lead from such provocative researches as those of Salter (1962.11), Woolf (1962.16), and Muscatine (1972.18), the more recent work of Carruthers (1973.2) and Martin (1979.10) sees the poem in its time as an exploration of the spiritual uncertainties of its author, expressed in a form and mode that is itself a reflection of a late medieval crisis of values. These are sensitive and, in their way, comprehensive studies that enlarge and recast older, more narrowly focused critical concerns with autobiography, unity, and the function and value of Langland's allegory in a fashion that explores the sometimes disordered process of the poem, while respecting the sophistication of Langland's attempt through his poetry to understand, order, and make coherent his spiritual experience.

Table of Manuscripts

(line numbers from Kane [1960.10] and Kane and Donaldson [1975.14]0)

A-text

A   Bodleian Library MS. Ashmole 1468

Ch   Chaderton MS., Liverpool University Library F.4.8 (A-text to XI 313; then C-text from C XII 297)

D   Bodleian Library MS. Douce 323

E   Trinity College, Dublin, MS. D.4.12

H   British Museum MS. Harley 875

H^2 British Museum MS. Harley 6041 (A-text to XI; C-text from C XII 297)

H^3 British Museum MS. Harley 3954 (B-text to c. V 105; A-text V 106-XI)

J   Ingilby MS., Pierpont Morgan Library of New York MS. M 818

K   Bodleian Library MS. Digby 145 (A-text to XI; C-text XII 297-XXIII)

L   Library of the Honourable Society of Lincoln's Inn MS. no. 150

M   Library of the Society of Antiquaries of London MS. no. 687 (formerly the Bright MS.)

N   National Library of Wales MS. no. 733B (A-text to VIII 184; C-text from C IX)

P   Pembroke College, Cambridge (fragment containing parts of IV and VII)

R   Bodleian Library MS. Rawlinson Poetry 137

Table of Manuscripts

T Trinity College, Cambridge, MS. R.3.14 (A-text to XI; C-text from XII 297)

U University College, Oxford, MS. 45

V Vernon Manuscript, Bodleian Library MS. English Poetry a. 1

W The Duke of Westminster's Manuscript, Eaton Hall (A-text to XI; C-text XIII-XXIII)

Z Bodleian Library MS. 851 (appears to be a memorial reconstruction of the A-text up to the end of VIII; C-text from C XI)

B-text

Bm British Museum MS. Additional 10574 (C-text to II 131; A-text II 90-212; B-text III-XX)

Bo Bodleian Library MS. Bodley 814 (C-text to II 131; A-text II 90-212; B-text III-XX)

C Cambridge University Library MS. Dd.1.17

C^2 Cambridge University Library MS. Ll.4.14

Cot The Piers Plowman Manuscript, British Museum MS. Cotton Caligula A XI (C-text to II 131; A-text II 90-212; B-text III-XX)

Cr British Museum C 71.c.29, Robert Crowley's first impression of his 1550 edition, representing the text of a MS no longer extant

Cr^2 British Museum C 71.c.28, Robert Crowley's second impression of his 1550 edition, showing conflation of the text of Cr with that of another MS, also lost

Cr^3 British Museum C 122.d.9, Robert Crowley's third impression of his 1550 edition, perhaps incorporating correction from another manuscript.

F Corpus Christi College, Oxford, MS. 201

G Cambridge University Library MS. Gg.4.31

H British Museum MS. Harley 3954 (corresponding to A-text MS. H^3) (B-text to c. B V 105)

Table of Manuscripts

Hm   Huntington Library MS. HM 128 (formerly MS. Asbhurnham 130)

Hm^2 Huntington Library MS, HM 128 (fragments of B II and III copied from the same archetype as of HM)

L   Bodleian Library MS. Laud Misc. 581

M   British Museum MS. Additional 35287

O   The Piers Plowman Manuscript, Oriel College, Oxford, MS. 79

R   Bodleian Library MS. Rawlinson Poetry 38, four leaves of which are bound in British Museum MS. Lansdowne 398

W   Trinity College, Cambridge, MS. B.15.17

Y   Yates-Thompson MS, Newnham College, Cambridge

[Ht]   Huntington Library MS. 114 (formerly MS. Phillips 8252) (based on a B-text archetype, but heavily corrupted by the C- and A-text traditions)

S   Sion College MS. Arc. L.40 2/E (a B-text MS showing hundreds of unique unoriginal variants)

Ca   Caius College, Cambridge, MS. 201 (a transcript of Rogers's 1561 printing)

J   Bodleian Library MS. James 2 (a modern transcript of a few hundred lines of the B-version)

C-text

A   University of London Library MS. V. 17 (formerly the Sterling MS.)

B   Bodleian Library MS. 814 (corresponding with B-text MS. Bo; C-text through C III 128)

Ch   Chaderton MS., Liverpool University Library F.4.8 (corresponding with A-text MS. Ch; C-text after C XII 297)

D   Bodleian Library MS. Douce 104

D^2 Bodleian Library MS. Digby 145 (corresponding with A-text MS. K, C-text from C XII 297)

E   Bodleian Library MS. Laud Misc. 656

F   Cambridge University Library MS. Ff.5.35

Table of Manuscripts

G   Cambridge University Library MS. Dd.3.13

H^2 British Museum MS. Harley 6041 (corresponding with A-text
MS. H^2; C-text from C XII 297)

I   University of London Library Library MS V. 88 (formerly the
Ilchester MS.)

K   Bodleian Library MS. Digby 171

L   The _Piers Plowman_ Manuscript, British Museum MS. Cotton
Caligula A XI (corresponding with B-text MS. Cot;
C-text through C III 128)

M   British Museum MS. Cotton Vespasian B XVI

N   British Museum MS. Harley 2376

N^2 National Library of Wales MS. no. 733B (corresponding with
A-text MS. N; C-text from C XI)

O   British Museum MS. Additional 10574 (corresponding with
B-text MS. Bm; C-text to II 131)

P   Huntington Library MS. HM 114 (formerly MS. Phillips 8231)

P^2 British Museum MS. Additional 34779 (formerly MS. Phillips
9056)

Q   Cambridge University Library MS. Additional 4325

R   British Museum MS. Royal Library 18. B.XVII

S   Corpus Christi College, Cambridge, MS. 293

T   Trinity College, Cambridge, MS. R.3.14 (corresponding with
A-text MS. T; C-text from XII 297)

U   British Museum MS. Additional 35157

V   Trinity College, Dublin, MS. D. 4. 1

W   The Duke of Westminster's Manuscript, Eaton Hall (corresponding with A-text MS. W; C-text from C XIII)

X   Huntington Library MS. HM 143

Y   Bodleian Library MS. Digby 102

Table of Manuscripts

Z   Bodleian Library MS. 851 (corresponding with A-text MS. Z;
          C-text from C XI)

Ca   Caius College, Cambridge, MS. 669 (a seventeen-line fragment)

Sources and Abbreviations

ABR   American Benedictine Review

AM   Annuale Mediævale

AN&Q   American Notes and Queries

Archiv   Archiv für das Studium der Neueren Sprachen und Literaturen

Bilboul   Retrospective Index to Theses of Great Britain and Ireland 1716-1950. Edited by Roger R. Bilboul. Vol. 1, Social Sciences and Humanities. Santa Barbara and Oxford: Clio Press, 1975

CBEL   The New Cambridge Bibliography of English Literature. Vol. 1, 600-1660, edited by George Watson. Cambridge: Cambridge University Press, 1974

CE   College English

ChR   Chaucer Review

Comprehensive Dissertation Index 1861-1972. Vol. 29, Language and Literature A-L; vol. 30, Language and Literature M-Z. Ann Arbor, Mich.: Xerox University Microfilms, 1973

DA   Dissertation Abstracts. Abstracts of Dissertations and Monographs on Microfilm, 1952-June, 1969. [Ann Arbor, Mich.]: University Microfilms

DAI   Dissertation Abstracts International. Section A: Humanities and Social Sciences, July 1969-1980. [Ann Arbor, Mich.]: University Microfilms

DNB   Dictionary of National Biography. Founded in 1882 by George Smith. Edited by Leslie Stephen and Sidney Lee. 22 vols. London: Oxford University Press, [1921-22]

EA   Études Anglaises

ELH   [Formerly Journal of English Literary History]

ELN   English Language Notes

ES   English Studies

ESC   English Studies in Canada

Gabel and Gabel   Gernot U. Gabel and Gisela R. Gabel, Dissertations in English and American Literature. Theses Accepted by Austrian, French and Swiss Universities 1875-1970. Hamburg: G. Gabel, 1977

HLQ   Huntington Library Quarterly

Index to Theses   Index to Theses Accepted for Higher Degrees in the Universities of Great Britain and Ireland [1950-1977]. London: Aslib, 1953-1980

LSE   Leeds Studies in English

Literaturblatt   Literaturblatt für germanische und romanische Philologie

McNamee   Lawrence F. McNamee, Dissertations in English and American Literature: Theses Accepted by American, British and German Universities 1865-1964. New York and London: R.R. Bowker, 1968

MHRA   Modern Humanities Research Association (Annual Bibliography of English Language and Literature, 1920-1976

MLA   Modern Language Association (International Bibliography, 1969-79

MLN   [Formerly Modern Language Notes]

MLQ   Modern Language Quarterly

MLR   Modern Language Review

MP   Modern Philology

Sources and Abbreviations

MS	Mediaeval Studies
N&Q	Notes and Queries
NM	Neuphilologische Mitteilungen
PAPS	Proceedings of the American Philosophical Society
PMLA	Publications of the Modern Language Association (Annual Bibliography, 1921–68)
PQ	Philological Quarterly
REL	Review of English Literature
RES	Review of English Studies
SEL	Studies in English Literature
SP	Studies in Philology
STC	A Short-Title Catalogue of Books Printed in England, Scotland & Ireland and of English Books Printed Abroad 1475–1640. Compiled by A.W. Pollard and G.R. Redgrave. London: The Bibliographical Society, 1926; Second edition, Revised & Enlarged. Begun by W.A. Jackson & F.S. Ferguson[,] completed by Katherine F. Pantzer. Vol. 2, I–Z. London: The Bibliographical Society, 1976
TLS	Times Literary Supplement (London)
TSE	Tulane Studies in English
TSLL	Texas Studies in Language and Literature
VNL	Victorian Newsletter
Wing	A Short-Title Catalogue of Books Printed in England, Scotland, Ireland, Wales, and British America and of English Books Printed in Other Countries 1641–1700. 3 vols. Compiled by Donald Wing of the Yale University Library. New York: Columbia University Press, for the Index Society, 1945, 1948, 1951; Second edition, revised and enlarged. Vol. 1: A1– E2926. New York: Index Committee of the Modern Language Association, 1972

Sources and Abbreviations

YES   Yearbook of English Studies

YWES   The Year's Work in English Studies, edited for the English Association, 1919-1979

Writings about *Piers Plowman*, 1395-1979

1395

1 BRUGE, WALTER de. "Testamentum Walteri de Bruge Canonici Ebor."
In Testamenta Eboracensia or Wills registered at York.
Vol. 1. Publications of the Surtees Society, no. 4. London:
J.B. Nichols and William Pickering, 1836, p. 209.
   "Item lego Dominico Johanni Wormyngton unum ciphum
argenteum cum uno cooperculo, bibleam meam rubeo coreo cooper-
tam, unum librum vocatum Pers plewman, et unum alium librum
vocatum Pars Oculi, cum aliis tractatibus in uno volumine."
   This will was probated 30 September 1395. For the sig-
nificance of such early evidence of the poem in the north of
England, see B., 1898.1; Burrow, 1957.1; and cf. Wyndhill,
1431.1.

C. 1400

1 ANON. Ascription. MS. V (C-text), fol. 89^v.
   "Memorandum quod Stacy de Rokayle pater willielmi de
Langlond qui stacius fuit generosus & morabatur in Schiptoun
vnder whicwode tenens domini le Spenser in comitatu Oxoniensi
qui predictus willielmus fecit librum qui vocatur Perys
ploughman."
   Dated c. 1400 by N.R. Ker, A.I. Doyle, and F. Wormald,
and put forward by Kane (1965.13); the early date of this
ascription makes it of high value in the authorship question,
though Manly (1909.8), and Moore (1914.3) tended to derogate
its significance. The note was apparently first appreciated
by Sir Frederic Madden, who communicated its contents to
Thomas Wright, who first printed it (in part) in [Langland],
1842.3. For a discussion and reproduction of this ascription,
see Kane, 1965.13.

c. 1425

C. 1425

1   ANON. Explicit. MS. Ch, p. 202.
     "Explicit liber Willielmi de petro le plouȝman."
     Kane (1965.13, p. 34) describes this as "the only final
     explicit in any manuscript which designates an author, and the
     only rubric at any point in any version to name an author un-
     mistakably." This manuscript, unknown to Skeat, was dated by
     Knott and Fowler (1952.6) as "early fifteenth century."

1431

1   WYNDHILL, JOHN. "Testamentum domini Johannis Wyndhill Rectoris
     Ecclesiæ parochialis de Arnecliffe." In Testamenta Eboracen-
     sia: A Selection of Wills from the Registry at York. Vol. 2.
     Publications of the Surtees Society, no. 30. Durham, London,
     and Edinburgh: Surtees Society, 1855, p. 32.
     "Item do et lego Johanni Kendale unum librum Anglicanum
     de Pers Plughman." This will was drawn 16 September 1431 and
     probated 15 January 1433/34. See Burrow, 1957.1.

1433

1   ROOS, THOMAS. Will. In The Fifty Earliest English Wills.
     Early English Text Society, edited by F.J. Furnivall, o.s. 78.
     London: N. Trübner & Co., p. 2.
     Includes a bequest of "librum vocatum piers plowman."

1459-60

1   STOTEVYLE, THOMAS. "Inventatorum librorum Thomæ Stotevyle Anno
     Henrici VIti xxxviijo in oratio eiusdem Thomæ existente."
     In The Text of the Canterbury Tales. Vol. 1. Edited by J.M.
     Manly and E. Rickert. Chicago: University of Chicago Press,
     1940, p. 610.
     In an inventory found on a flyleaf of a MS of the Summa
     de penitentia of Raymond de Pennaforte, Petrus Plowman' is
     included along with some French romances and a copy of the
     Canterbury Tales. Stotevyle, of Dalham and Denham, Suffolk,
     made his will 20 December 1466; there is no date of probate
     recorded.

post 1546

1465

1 CHARLETON, Sir THOMAS. Inventory. In The Nobility of Later
   Medieval England (The Ford Lectures for 1953 and Related
   Studies), by K.B. McFarlane. Oxford: Clarendon Press, 1973,
   p. 238.
       Along with such items as "an engelysche boke the whiche
   was called Troles and a nod^r of Caunt^{r}bury tales," and an
   "englische booke calde Giles de regimeie principium," "j of
   perse plowman." McFarlane comments, "The library of a man of
   evident discrimination."

C. 1545

1 LELAND, JOHN. Commentarii de scriptoribus Britannicis. Edited
   by Anthony Hall. Oxford: e Theatro Sheldoniano, 1709,
   p. 423.
       ". . . sed Petri Aratoris fabula, quæ communi doctorum
   consensu Chaucero, tanquam vero parenti, attribuitur, in
   utraque editione, quia malos sacredotum mores vehementer
   increpavit, suppressa est."
       The poem is here for the first time confused with the
   Plowman's Tale, often attributed erroneously to Chaucer after
   it was printed with the Tales of Canterbury by Thynne in 1542.

Post 1546

1 BALE, JOHN. Index Britanniæ Scriptorum quos ex variis biblio-
   thecis non parvo labore collegit Ioannes Baleus, cum aliis.
   John Bale's Index of British and Other Writers. In Anecdota
   Oxoniensi. Medieval and Modern Series, edited by Reginald
   Lane Poole, part 9. Oxford: Clarendon Press, 1902, pp. 383,
   509, 510.
       "Robertus Langlande, natus in comitatu Salopie in villa
   Mortymers Clyberi in the cleyelande within viij. myles of
   Malborne hylles, scripsit Peers ploughman. li.i. In a somer
   seson   warme
   sonday whan sote was ye sunne.
   ex collectis Nicolai Brigan."
       "Uisio Petri Ploughman, edita per Robertum Langlande,
   natum in comitatu Salopie, in villa Mortymers Clybery in the
   cley lande within viij myles of Malborne hylles
   li.i 'In quodam estatis die cum sol caleret,' etc.
   ex collectis Nicolai Brigam."

post 1546

> Robertus Langlande, a Shropshyre man, borne in Claybery
> about viii myles from Maluerne hylles, wrote
> Peers ploughman,　　　　li.i　In a somer season whan set was
> 　　　　　　　　　　　　　　the sunne &c
> ex domo Guilhelmi Sparke."
> 　　"Robertus Langlonde, sacerdos (vt apparet) natus apud
> Clybery prope Maluernum montem, scripsit Peers plowghman opus
> eruditum as quodammodo propheticum.　Claruit A.D. 1369, dum
> Ioannes Chichestre pretor esset Londini.
> Ex Ioanne Wysdome medico."

For the sources of these remarks in Bale's autograph
notebook, see Moore, 1914.3, but cf. Kane, 1965.13.　A note
on the endpaper of MS. Hm, Hm^2, in what appears to be Bale's
hand, similarly reads "Robertus Langlande natus in comitatu
Salopie, in villa Mortymers Clybery in the claylande, within
.viii. myles of Malborne hylles, scripsit, peers ploughman,
li. i.// In a somer season whan set was sunne." See Bale,
1548.1 and 1557.1.

1548

1　BALE, JOHN.　Illvstrium maioris Britanniæ scriptorvm.　Wesel:
　　Theodoricum Platænum, fol. 157^r.
　　　　In a list of works attributed to "Ioannes Wicleuus,"
　　the following item appears:　"Petrum Agricolam.　li. I."
　　Cf. 1557.1.

1550

1　[LANGLAND, WILLIAM.]　The vision of Pierce Plowman, now fyrste
　　imprynted by Roberte Crowley, dwellyng in Ely rentes in
　　Holburne.　Anno Domini 1505 [a mistake for 1550, usually
　　overprinted and corrected].　Cum priuilegio ad imprimendum
　　solum.　117 leaves, not including title page or the printer's
　　address to the reader; 119 leaves total.　STC 19906.
　　　　The editio princeps, based on a (lost) MS of the B-text
　　related, according to Kane and Donaldson in [Langland]
　　(1975.10), to MSS. WHmS, but occasionally showing Crowley's
　　use of a C-text MS.
　　　　Crowley's preface, "the printer to the reader," asserts
　　the author to be "Roberte langelande, a Shropshere man borne
　　in Cleybirie.　aboute viii. myles from Maluerne hilles."
　　Since Crowley remarks upon his consultation with antiquaries
　　in order to discover the identity of the author, it is not un-
　　reasonable to conclude that his information here is dependent
　　upon Bale.　The poem was written between 1350 and 1409, during

1550

which time many, as for example Wyclif, cried out against the "worckes of darckenes. . . . There is no maner of vice, that reygneth in anye estate of men, whiche [Langland] hath not godly, learnedlye, and wittilye, rubuked." The meter of the poem is described as "three wordes at the leaste in euery verse which begyn with some one letter." The sense of the poem is "somewhat darcke, but not so harde, but that it maye be vnderstande of such as wyll not sticke to breake the shell of the nutte for the kernelles sake."

Crowley tends to downplay the prophetic aspects of the poem in favor of those providing moral correction for the individual Christian. Ascribes variation in the text of supposed prophecies among the MSS (C IX 351) to someone other than the author. Crowley's address is printed by Skeat, in [Langland], 1886.1; for a facsimile reprint of Crowley's first edition, see [Langland], 1976.12.

2   [LANGLAND, WILLIAM.] The vision of Pierce Plowman, nowe the seconde time imprinted by Roberte Crowley dwellynge in Elye rentes in Holbourne. Whereunto are added certayne notes and cotations in the mergyne, geuynge light to the Reader. And in the begynning is set a briefe summe of all the principall matters spoken of in the boke. And as the boke is deuided into twenty partes called Passus: so is the summary diuided, for euery parte hys summarie, rehearsynge the matters spoken of in euerye parte, euen in suche order as they stande there. Imprinted at London by Roberte Crowley, dwelling in Elye rentes in Holburne. The yere of our Lord MDL. cum priuilegio ad impremendum solum. 117 leaves, not counting prefatory material; 125 leaves total. STC 19907ᵃ.

In effect, the second edition (because reset and corrected) by Crowley, offering, as Kane and Donaldson (1975.10) say, "a conflated text based on a new manuscript (also lost) under constant comparison with the text of the first impression." This MS was apparently related to OC2; though Crawford (1957.2), noting the existence of six A-text lines after Prol 215, also posits correction by an A-text MS. Contains a summary of the Prologue and the individual passūs, and marginal notes.

3   [LANGLAND, WILLIAM.] The vision of Pierce Plowman, nowe the seconde tyme imprinted by Roberte Crowlye dwellynge in Elye rentes in Holburne Whereunto are added certayne notes and cotations in the mergyne, geuyng light to the Reader. And in the begynning is set a brefe summe of all the principal matters spoken of in the boke. And as the boke is deuided into twenty partes called Passus: so is the Summary diuided,

1550

for euery parte hys summarie, rehearsynge the matters spoken
of in euery parte. euen in suche order as they stande there.
Imprinted at London by Roberte Crowley, dwellyng in Elye
rentes in Holburne, The yere of our Lord, M.D.L. Cum
priuilegio ad imprimendum solum. 117 leaves, not counting
title page and prefatory material; 125 leaves total. STC
19907.
    Crowley's third impression, or edition; perhaps indi-
cating correction by another MS. For differences between
Crowley's impressions, and the possibility of another impression of the poem by him, see Crawford, 1957.2. The title
page and prefatory material of Crowley's third impression
were occasionally attached to copies of the first edition,
as in the case of Samuel Pepys's copy, reproduced in facsimile as [Langland], 1976.12.

1557

1   BALE, JOHN. Scriptorvm Illustriū maioris Brytannię quam nunc
    Angliam & Scotiam uocant. . . . Basel: Ioannem Oporinum,
    p. 474.
        Entry entitled Robertvs Langelande: "Robertus
Langelande, sacerdos, ut apparet, natus in comitatu Salopię,
in uilla uulgo dicta Mortymers Clibery, in terra lutea, octauo
à Maluernis montibus milliario fuit. Num tamen eo in loco,
inconditio & agresti, in bonis literis ad maturam ætatem
usque informatus fuerit, certo adfirmare non possum. ut
nequę, an Oxonij aut Cantabrigię illis insudauerit: quum apud
eorum locorum magistros, studia præcipue uigerent. Illud
ueruntamen liquido constat, eum fuisse ex primis Ioannis
Uuicleui discipulis unum, atque in spiritus feruore, contra
apertas Papistarum blasphemias aduersus Deum & eius Christum,
sub amœnis coloribus & typis edidisse in sermone Anglico pium
opus, ac bonorum uirorum lectione dignum quod uocabat
        Visionem Petri Aratoris, Lib. i. In aestiuo tempore cum
sol caleret.
Nihil aliud ab ipso editum noui. In hoc opere erudito,
præter similitudines uarias & iucundas, prophetice plura
prędixit quę nostris diebus impleri uidimus. Compleuit suum
opus anno Domini 1368, dum Ioannes Cicestrius Londini prætor
esset." (For a translation, see Hales, 1892.2.)
    There is no reference to "Petrum Agricolam" in the list
of Wyclif's works in this enlargement of 1548.1.

1558

1   BRERETON, RICHARD. "The inventorye of the goodes and cattals
    late of Richard Brereton esquyer." In <u>Lancashire and Cheshire
    Wills and Inventories from the Ecclesiastical Court, Chester</u>.
    Vol. 1. Chetham Society Publications, edited by Rev. G.J.
    Piccope, no. 33. Manchester: Chetham Society, pp. 174-75.
        Two copies of "Pyers Ploughman" valued at 8 d. and 6 d.,
    listed in this inventory from Ley, Cheshire.

1561

1   [LANGLAND, WILLIAM.] <u>The vision of Pierce Plowman, newlye
    impryntyd after the authours olde copy, with a brefe summary
    of the principall matters set before euery part called Passus,
    Wherevnto is also annexed the Crede of Pierce Plowman, neuer
    imprinted with the booke before. Imprynted at London, by Owen
    Rogers, dwellyng neare vnto great saint Bartelmewes gate, at
    the sygne of the spred Egle. The yere of our Lorde God, a
    thousand, fyve hundred, thre score and one. The .xxi. daye
    of the Moneth of Februarye. Cum priuilegio ad imprimendum
    solum</u>. 142 leaves (128 leaves in those copies found without
    <u>Pierce the Plowman's Crede</u>). STC 19908.
        Skeat, in Langland (1886.1), describes the text of <u>Piers
    Plowman</u> in this edition as a "careless reprint of Crowley's
    third issue," while Knott and Fowler, in [Langland] (1952.6),
    think it derives from "Crowley's second edition." The present
    writer's collations of Rogers's text with those readings that
    distinguish Crowley's second impression from his third impres-
    sion indicate that Skeat was correct.
        The prefatory material is taken almost verbatim from
    Crowley's remarks in [Langland] (1550.3), though Rogers makes
    an attempt to rearrange this material by preceding individual
    passūs with their relevant summaries. Rogers's text of the
    <u>Crede</u> is a reprint of its first edition by Reynold Wolfe
    (1553). For early annotations of a copy of Rogers's edition,
    see Anon., 1577.1.

1560-64[?]

1   TURNER, WILLIAM. Letter to John Foxe concerning his <u>Book of
    Martyrs</u>. In <u>The Works of Nicholas Ridley, D.D. Sometimes
    Lord Bishop of London, Martyr 1555</u>. Edited by Rev. Henry
    Christmas. Parker Society, no. 39. Cambridge: Cambridge
    University Press, 1841, p. 490.

1560-64[?]

> "Hoc me valde male habet, quod sanctissimi martyris
> domini Thorpii liber non sit ea lingua Anglice conscriptus,
> qua eo tempore quo ipse vixit tunc tota Anglia est usa. Nam
> talis antiquitatis sum admirator, ut ægerrime feram talis
> antiquitatis thesauros nobis perire; quo nomine haud magnam
> apud gratiam inierunt qui Petrum Aratorem, Gowerum et
> Chaucerum, et similis farinæ homines, in hanc turpitur mixtam
> linguam, neque vero Anglicam neque pure Gallicam, transtu-
> lerunt."

Foxe's Book of Martyrs was published in 1559; and
Turner, who had been deprived of the deanery of Wells in 1553,
was restored to his position 18 June 1560. He was suspended
for nonconformity in 1564. This, then, would appear to be a
criticism of one of the early editions of the poem. Skeat in
[Langland] (1884.2) ascribes this letter to Ridley.

1577

1   ANON. Annotations on the flyleaf of a copy of [Langland]
    (1561.1) printed by Silverstone, "The Vision of Pierce
    Plowman," N&Q, 2d ser. 6, no. 142 (18 September 1858):229-30.
        Sees the "divers maner of Englishinge" in Pierce the
    Plowman's Crede and Piers Plowman as suggestive of different
    authors. Takes the author of Piers Plowman to have lived
    c. 1350, and notes the mention of Wa[l]ter Brute in the Crede.
    Ascribes the Crede to Chaucer.

2   HANMER, MEREDITH. The Avncient Ecclesiasticall Histories of the
    First Six Hundred Yeares after Christ. London: Thomas
    Vautroullier, p. 409.
        Complains that instead of perusing works of divinity or
    ecclesiastical history, "many now adayes had rather rede the
    stories of Kinge Arthur: the monstrous fables of Garagantua:
    the Pallace of pleasure, though there follow neuer so much
    displeasure after: the Dial of Princes, where there is much
    good matter: the Monke of Burie full of good stories: Pierce
    Ploweman: the tales of Chaucer where there is excellent wit,
    great reading and good decorum obserued . . . Reinard the Fox:
    Beuis of Hampton: the hundred merry tales: skoggan:
    Fortunatus: with many other unfortunate treatises and amorous
    toies. . . ."

3   HOLINSHED, RAPHAELL. The Laste volume of the Chronicles of
    England, Scotland, and Irelande, with their descriptions.
    London: Lucas Harison, p. 1003.
        In a list of learned men temp. Edward III, which
    Holinshed (p. 1001) says he takes from Bale: "Robert

Langland, a secular Priest, borne in Salopshire, in Mortimers Cliberie."

1580

1   STOW, JOHN.   The Chronicles of England, from Brute vnto this
    present yeare of Christ 1580.   London: Ralphe Newberie,
    p. 387.   STC 23333.
            Entry for 1341/42:   "This yeare Iohn Malverne, fellowe
    of Oriall Colledge in Oxford, made and finished his booke
    entituled The Visions of Pierce Plowman."
            This false ascription, resting perhaps on no more than
    the mention of the Malvern Hills in the beginning of the poem
    (see Langland, 1867.3) was accepted and/or enlarged upon by
    Pits (1619.1), Wood (1674.1), Tanner (1748.1), [Percy]
    (1765.1), Warton (1774.2), Ellis (1801.1), and Guest (1838.1),
    though it was doubted by Ritson (1802.1).   To complicate mat-
    ters, it would appear that three different individuals are
    variously referred to by these writers, and that the accounts
    of Malverne, John (d. 1415?) and Malverne, John (d. 1422?) in
    the DNB fail correctly to identify the fellow of Oriel College
    taken for the author of Piers Plowman or, as in the case of
    Wood, for that author's alias.   A.B. Emden, A Biographical
    Register of the University of Oxford to A.D. 1500, vol. 2
    (Oxford: Clarendon Press, 1958) distinguishes John Malverne
    (Maleverne), a Benedictine associated with Worcester Cathedral
    and probably the author of the Continuation of Higden's
    Polychronicon (d. 1410) from John Malverne of Balliol College,
    physician to Henry IV and author of De remediis spiritualibus
    et corporalibus contra pestilenciam, who died in 1422, and
    from John Malvesore (Malvesoure, Malvesonere), fellow of
    Oriel College in 1389 and still in residence in 1394, who
    died October 1417.   For identification of the author with yet
    another John Malvern, see [Ffoulkes], 1892.1, but cf. Skeat,
    1893.2.

1586

1   WEBBE, WILLIAM.   A Discourse of English Poetrie Together, with
    the Authors iudgment, touching the reformation of our English
    Verse.   London: Iohn Charlewood for Robert Walley, pp. 103-4.
    STC 25172.
            "The next of our auncient Poets, that I can tell of, I
    suppose to be Pierce Ploughman, who in hys dooinges is some-
    what harshe and obscure, but indeede a very pithy wryter, and
    (to hys commendation I speake it) was the first that I haue

1586

seene, that obserued ye quantity of our verse without the
curiosity of Ryme."
Besides the poet "Pierce Ploughman," Webbe admits
knowledge of three other writers before Skelton, viz., Gower,
Chaucer, and Lydgate. Gower is praised for the delight and
knowledge his works afford; Chaucer, though his style is often
considered blunt and coarse to moderns, is said to have sati-
rized so learnedly and pleasantly "that none would call him
into question"; and Lydgate was preoccupied with "supersti-
tious and odd matters." Since Webbe writes with the purpose
of reforming English verse of the "infection" of rhyme, his
citation of "Piers Plowman" as writing quantitative verse is
especially interesting; though we can be sure he did not know
the poem at all well. For a modern reprint of Webbe's
treatise, see Webbe, 1870.4; and cf. Meres, 1598.1.

1588

1 FRAUNCE, ABRAHAM. The Arcadian Rhetorike or the Praecepts of
   Rhetorike made plaine by examples. Book 1, chapter 25 ("Of
   Polyptoton"). London: Thomas Orwin, Sig E 4². STC 11338.
      "He that made the booke called Pierce Plowman, maketh
   three or foure words in euerie line begin with the same
   letter, thus
      In a sommer season, when set was the sunne, &c."
   For a facsimile edition, see Fraunce, 1969.13.

2 H[ARVEY], I[OHN]. A Discorsive Problem concerning Prophecies,
   How far they are to be valued, or credited, according to the
   surest rules, and directions in Diuinitie, Philosophie,
   Astrologie and other learning. London: Iohn Iackson for
   Richard Watkins, p. 62. STC 12908.
      Writes in an exposé of ridiculous (and dangerous)
   prophecies: "For how easily might I heer repeat almost infinite examples of villanous attempts, pernitious uprores,
   horrible mischeefes, slaughters, blasphemies, heresies, and
   all other indignities, and outrages, desperately committed,
   and perpetrated through means of such inueterate, and new
   broched forgeries. . . . Neither shal I therfore neede to
   ransacke Pierce Plowmans satchell; nor to descant upon
   fortunes, newly collected out of the old Shepherds
   Kalender. . . ."

1589

1   PUTTENHAM, GEORGE[?]. The Arte of English Poesie. London:
Richard Field, pp. 20, 48, 120. STC 20519.
Writes in treating various genres of poetry and how
ancient poets received surnames: "There was yet another kind
of Poet, who intended to taxe the common abuses and vice of
the people in rough and bitter speaches, and their inuectiues
were called Satyres, and them selues Satyricques. Such were
Lucilius, Iuuenall and Persius among the Latines, & with vs
he that wrote the booke called Piers plowman."
Treating the "most commended" writers of the first ages
of English poetry, the writer later (p. 48) follows Chaucer
and Gower with Lydgate "and that nameless, who wrote the
Satyre called Piers plowman. . . ." This author "seemed to
haue bene a malcontent of that time, and therefore bent himselfe wholy to taxe the disorders of that age, and specially
the pride of the Romane Clergy, of whos fall he seemeth to be
a very true Prophet, his verse is but loose meetre, and his
termes hard and obscure, so as in them is little pleasure to
be taken." Elsewhere (p. 120) the author warns modern writers
against imitating Piers Plowman, Gower, Lydgate, or Chaucer,
"for their language is now out of vse with vs."
Authorship of this treatise has been attributed to
George Puttenham, Richard Puttenham, and John, Lord Lumley.
For a modern reprint, see Puttenham, 1970.14.

1595

1   MAUNSELL, ANDREW. The First Part of the Catalogue of English
printed Bookes: Which concerneth such matters of Diuinitie,
as have bin either written in our owne Tongue, or translated
out of anie other language. London: John Vvindet for Andrew
Maunsell, pp. 80–81. STC 17669.
Bibliographical notices of Owen Rogers's edition
(1561.1), Pierce plowman in prose, The Plowmans prayer and
complaint vnto Christ, and The Plowmans complaint of sundry
wicked liuers. For a modern reprint, see Maunsell, 1965.17.

1598

1   MERES, FRANCIS. Palladis Tamia. Wits Treasvry Being the Second
part of Wits Common wealth. London: P. Short for Cuthbert
Burbie, leaves 279^r, 279^v, 283^v. STC 17834.
"As Homer was the first that adorned the Greek tongue
with true quantity: so Piers Plowman was the first that

1598

obserued the true quantitie of our verse without the
curiositie of Rime." Compares "Piers Plowman," Lodge, Hall,
and others with Horace, Lucilius, Juvenal, and other classical
satirists.

Meres's work, in effect a "commonplace book in the
vernacular," is largely of interest for its "Comparative
Discourse of our English Poets," which describes those of
Shakespeare's plays known to the author. But his remarks on
Piers Plowman show no deep firsthand knowledge of the poem
and are largely derived from Webbe (1586.1) and Puttenham[?]
(1589.1). For a facsimile reprint, see Meres, 1938.7.

1614

1   CAMDEN, WILLIAM. Remaines, concerning Britaine: But especially
England, and the Inhabitants thereof. . . . Reviewed, cor-
rected, and encreased. London: Iohn Legatt for Simon
Waterson, p. 235. STC 4522.

Writes in treating apparel: "Neither was the Cleargy
cleare then from this pride, as you may perceiue by Pearce
Plowman. Albeit Polydor Virgill, and the late Archbishop of
Canterbury most reuerend D. Parker noteth that the Cleargy of
England neuer ware silke or veluet vntill the time of the
pompous Cardinall Wolsey, who opened that dore to pride among
them which hitherto cannot be shut." These remarks are not
to be found in the first edition of Camden's work (1605).

1618[?]

1   [BOLTON, EDMUND.] Hypercritica or a rule of Judgment for writing, or reading our History's. In Nicolai Triveti Annalium
Continuatio . . . et Edmundi Boltoni Hypercritica. Edited by
Anthony Hall. Oxford: e Theatro Sheldoniano, 1722. Addresse
the fourth, section 3 (unpaginated).

Arguing for the use of language closest to that of court
for the writing of history, Bolton approves of the language
of Spenser's Hymns, then continues: "I cannot advise the
allowance of other his [Spenser's] Poems, as for practick
English, no more than I can do Jeff. Chaucer, Lydgate, Peirce
Ploughman, or Laureat Skelton. It was laid out as a fault to
the charge of Salust, that he used some outworn Words, stoln
out of Cato his Books de Originibus. And for an Historian in
our Tongue to affect the like out of those Poets would be
accounted a foul Oversight."

12

1619

1 PITS, JOHN. <u>Relationvm Historicarum de Rebus Anglicis</u>. Paris:
Rolinvm Thierry & Sebastianvm Cramoisy, p. 878.
<u>1342</u> De Ioanne Maluernæo. Ioannes Maluernæus,
Miluernæum alij vocant, natione Anglus, Oxonij studijs
aliquando bonarum litterarum operam dedit, eratque ibi
Orialensis alumnus Colegij. Postea factus est ordinis S.
Benedicti Monachus Vvigorniensis. Scripsit magnum quoddam
opus visionum Anglicè, quod absoluisse perhibetur anno Domini
1342, cui operi titulum fecit
<u>Pierce Plovvmam</u>, quod opus in aliquibus Angliæ Biblio-
thecis adhuc MS reperiri ferunt. Scripsit prætereà
<u>Ad continuationem Polychronici, chronicorum, Librum</u>
<u>vnum</u>. MS Cantabrigiæ Collegio S. Benedicti. De alijs eius
scriptis aut gestis hactenus nihil invenio. Claruit anno
Domini præfato 1342, regnante apud Anglos Edvvardo tertio."

1622

1 PEACHAM, HENRY. <u>The Compleat Gentleman Fashioning him absolute</u>
<u>in the most necessary & Commendable Qualities</u>. . . . London:
Francis Constable, p. 95. <u>STC</u> 19502.
"After [Gower] succeeded <u>Lydgate</u>, a Monke of <u>Burie</u>, who
wrote that bitter Satyre of Piers Plow-man. He spent most
part of his time in translating the workes of others, hauing
no great inuention of his owne. He wrote for those times a
tollerable and smooth verse." For a modern edition, see
Peacham, 1962.8.

2 SELDEN, JOHN. "Notes on the Poly-olbion of Michael Drayton."
In <u>The Poly-olbion: A Geographical Description of Great</u>
<u>Britain</u>. London: Spenser Society, 1889, fol. 109.
In a note to Drayton's line (Seventh Song), "Whilst
Maluerne (king of Hills) faire Seuerne ouer-lookes," Selden
comments: "Hereford and Worcester are by these hils seauen
miles in length confined; and rather, in respect of the
adiacent vales, then the hils selfe, vnderstand the attribute
of excellency. Vpon these is the supposed vision of Piers
Plowma<u>n</u>, don, as is thought, by Robert Langland, a Shropshire
man, in a kind of English meeter: wch for discouery of the
infecting corruptions of those times, I prefer before many
more seemingly serious inuectiues, as well for inuention as
iudgement. . . ."
According to Meres (1598.1), Drayton's poem was already
begun in 1598, though the first part was not published until
1613, and the second part not until 1622.

1631

1 WEEVER, JOHN. <u>Ancient Fvnerall Monvments with in the vnited</u>
   <u>Monarchie of Great Britaine, Ireland, and the Ilands</u>
   <u>adiacent</u>. . . . London: Tho. Harper, sold by L. Sadler,
   p. 72. <u>STC</u> 25223.
         "In this Kings [Edward III's] raigne Robert Longland a
   secular Priest, borne in Shropshire, at Mortimers Cliberie,
   writ bitter inuectiues against the Prelates, and all religious
   orders in those days, as you may reade throughout this book,
   which he calls, the vision of Piers Plowman."

1633

1 PRYNNE, WILLIAM. <u>Histio-Maxtix. The Players Scovrge, or, Actors</u>
   <u>Tragædie</u>. London: Printed by E.A[llde] and W. J[ones] for
   Michael Sparke, p. 834. <u>STC</u> 20464.
         Among "dramatists" worthy to be read, lists John Bale,
   Skelton, and Nicholas Grimald, "which like <u>Geffry</u> <u>Chaucers</u> &
   <u>Pierce</u> the <u>Plowmans</u> <u>tales</u> and Dialogues, were penned only to
   be read, not acted, their subiects being al serious, sacred,
   divine, not scurrilous wanton or prophan, as al modern Play
   poëms are."

1642

1 [MILTON, JOHN.] <u>An apology Against a Pamphlet call'd A Modest</u>
   <u>Confutation of the Animadversions upon the Remonstrant against</u>
   <u>Smectymnuus</u>. London: Printed by E.G. for Iohn Rothwell,
   p. 33. <u>Wing</u> M 2090.
         "Which for him [Joseph Hall] who would be counted <u>the</u>
   <u>first</u> <u>English</u> <u>Satyr</u>, to abase himselfe to, who might have
   learnt better among the Latin, and Italian Satyrists, and in
   our own tongue from <u>the</u> <u>vision</u> <u>and</u> <u>Creed</u> <u>of</u> <u>Pierce</u> <u>plowman</u>,
   besides others before him, manifested a presumptuous under-
   taking with weak, and unexamin'd shoulders."
         Probably a reference to <u>Pierce the Plowman's Crede</u>. For
   a modern edition of Milton's <u>apology Against a Pamphlet . . .</u>
   <u>against Smectymnuus</u>, see Milton, 1953.4, where it is noted
   that elsewhere in his writings (<u>Of Reformation</u> [1641]), Milton
   quotes the <u>Plowman's Tale</u> as if it were Chaucer's.

Ante 1652[?]

1 BUCHANAN, DAVID. Davidis Buchannani de Scriptoribus Scotis Libri
   Duo, nunc primum editi. Edited by David Irving. Edinburgh:
   Balfour & Jack, for the Bannatyne Club, 1837, p. 9.
   "De Roberto Langland Robertus Langland, natione Scotus,
   professione sacerdos, vir ex obscuris ortus parentibus, pius
   admodum et ingeniosus, et zelo divinæ gloriæ plenus, inter
   monachos Benedictinos educatus in civitate Aberdonensi, vir
   utique erat in omni humaniore literatura insigniter doctus,
   et in medicina admodum clarus. Pium opus sermone vulgari
   scripsit cui, titulum imposuit,
      Visionem Petri Aratoris, lib. I.
      Pro Conjugio Sacerdotum, lib. I.
   Claruit anno Christi Redemptoris 1369, regnante Davido Secundo
   in Scotia."

1657

1 DUDLEY, THOMAS. "Will of Governor Thomas Dudley." New England
   Historical and Genealogical Register 12, no. 4 (October 1858):
   355.
      In a list of historical and religious writings compris-
   ing Gov. Thomas Dudley's library, "yͤ Vision of Pierc Plowman."
   This could be either the edition(s) of 1550 or that of 1561.
   Thomas Goddard Wright, Literary Culture in Early New England
   1620-1730 (New Haven: Yale University Press; London:
   Humphrey Milford; Oxford University Press, 1920), p. 39,
   comments: "This is perhaps the most curious item in all the
   lists of colonial books. It would cast much light upon colonial culture if we could know how [Dudley] came to own such a
   volume, and whether he ever read it."

1662

1 FULLER, THOMAS. "Shropshire." In The History of the Worthies
   of England. London: Printed by J.G.W.L. and W.G.
   "Shropshire," pp. 8-9 [the book is not continuously pagi-
   nated.] Wing F 2440.
      "Robert Langeland, forgive me, Reader, though placing
   him (who lived one hundred & fifty years before) since the
   Reformation: For I conceave that the Morning-star belongs to
   the Day, than to the Night. On which account this Robert
   (regulated in our Book not according to the Age he was in, but
   Judgement he was of,) may by Prolepsis be termed a Protestant.

1662

"He was born at Mortimers-Clibery in this County eight
miles from Malvern-Hills: was bred a Priest, and one of the
first followers of J. Wickliffe, wanting neither Wit, nor
Learning, as appears by his Book called, the vision of Pierce
Plough-man, and hear what Character a most Learned Antiquary
giveth thereof.
"It is written in a kind of English meeter, which for
discovery of the infecting corruptions of those times, I
preferre before many of the more seemingly serious Invectives,
as well as for Invention as Judgment.
"There is a Book first set forth by Tindal, since,
exemplified by Mr. Fox, called The Prayer and Complaint of
the Plough-man, which though differing in title and written
in prose, yet be of the same language, I must referre it to
the same Author. . . .
"It's observeable that Pitzæus (generally a perfect
Plagiary out of Bale) passeth this Langland over in silence:
and why? because he wrote in opposition to the Papal Interest:
Thus the most Light-finger'd Thieves will let that alone,
which is too hot for them. He flourished under King Edward
the Third, Anno Dom. 1369."
Biographical details clearly dependent on Bale; aesthetic evaluation drawn from Selden (1622.2). Contains a
short glossary of obsolete Middle English words.

1674

1   [WOOD, ANTHONY à.] Historia et Antiquitates universitatis
    Oxoniensis. Vol. 2. Oxford: e Theatro Sheldoniano, p. 106.
    Wood W 3385.
        "Johannes Maluernius, Wigorniensis, inter primos
    Collegii hujus Socios deprehenditur; is vero ad Regulam postea
    S. Benedicti Monachus Wigorniensis extitit. Scripsit, præter
    alia:
        Petri Aratoris Phantasmata: qui quidem Libellus in
    plerisque olim Bibliothecis reperiebatur, editus autem Lond.
    est an Dom. 1561. cujus è Passu decimotertio (ita enim opus
    partiri visum) liquet scriptorem hunc è vivis nondum exces-
    sisse cum in Prætoris Londinensis Munere versaretur Joh.
    Cicester, quod in an. MCCCLXIX. cadit.
        Continuationem Polychronici Chronicorum. MS in
    Biblioth. Coll. S. Benedicti Cantab. & alia.
        Robertus de Langland, Johan Malverne nonnullis appella-
    tur, fertur autem inter sui seculi Poetas maxime facetos
    excelluisse. Occurrit porro alius quidam Joh. Malverne
    Medicinæ Doctor qui Librum conscripsit. De remediis Spiri-
    tualibus & Corporalibus contra Pestilentiam. MS. inter cod.

Digb. nu 147. An is a Malvernio illo alienus fuerit, qui anno MCDXIV Canonicus S. Georgii, in Castro Windelsoriano reperitur, compertum no habemus." Not in the translation of Wood's History by John Gutch (1786).

1676

1 COLES, E[LISHA]. An English Dictionary. London: Samuel Crouch, Sig A 3b. Wing C 5070.
"I have not only retain'd, but very much augmented the number of Old Words. For though Mr. Blount (as he saies expressly) shunn'd them, because they grew obsolete; yet doubtless their use is very great: not only for the unfolding those Authors that did use them, but also for giving a great deal of light to other words that are still in use. Those that I call Old Words are generally such as occurr in Chaucer, Gower, Pierce Ploughman and Julian Barnes." For a facsimile reprint, see Coles, 1973.3.

1689

1 HICKES, GEORGE. Institutiones Grammaticæ Anglo-Saxonicæ et Mœso-Gothicæ. Oxford: e Theatro Sheldoniano, p. 28.
". . . sic in libro cui titulus The vision of Piers plowman
Cokes, and her knaves cryden hote pyes,
ubi obiter notetur, quod knave ab A. Sax. cyapa, proveniens, puerum, vel servum significat. A gen. sing. hire, venit her in moderno sensu." For a facsimile reprint, see Hickes, 1971.16.

1700

1 [DRYDEN, JOHN.] Fables Ancient and Modern; Translated into Verse From Homer, Ovid, Boccace, & Chaucer: with Original Poems. London: Jacob Tonson, Sig. *B 4a. Wing D 2278.
"As for the Religion of our Poet [Chaucer], he seems to have some little Byas towards the Opinions of Wickliff, after John of Gaunt his Patron; somewhat of which appears in the Tale of Piers Plowman: Yet I cannot blame him for inveighing so sharply against the Vices of the Clergy in his Age: Their Pride, their Ambition, their Pomp, their Avarice, their Worldly Interest, deserved the Lashes which he gave them, both in that and in most of his Canterbury Tales. . . ." Piers Plowman is here confused with the Plowman's Tale. For a modern edition of Dryden's work, see 1900.2.

1705

1 HICKES, GEORGE. Linguarum Vett. septentrionalium thesaurus
   grammatico-criticus et archæologicus. Vol. 1. Oxford: e
   Theatro Sheldoniano, pp. 4, 16, 17, 23, 25, 35, 38, 44, 57,
   62, 65, 71, 103, 105-7, 112, 121, 124, 132, 196-97, 217.
   The poem is quoted to illustrate various points of grammar, as well as such words as worth, but, forþi, myd, welaweye,
   mould, rink, gome, segge, leode, reuke, freke, girle, lynde,
   syr king, melleþ, and meten. Describes alliteration, and
   divides lines into verses. Skeat notes that Hickes (p. 196)
   identifies the author with Piers Plowman ("celebris ille
   satyrographus, qui se Pierce Plowman vocat"); but earlier
   (p. 25), Hickes identifies him thus: "Robertus Langeland,
   auctor XX satyrarum, quibus titulus The vision of Pierce
   Plowman. . . ."

1707

1 ANON. "Of the Old English Poets and Poetry. An Essay." The
   Muses Mercury: or, Monthly Miscellany 1 (June):127-39, esp.
   129-30.
        Considers the English language until Chaucer's time a
   "confus'd Mixture of Saxon and the Norman Jargon," as exemplified by Robert of Gloucester's Chronicle, which is unintel-
   ligible without a dictionary. Robert of Gloucester flourished
   500 years previous; more than 120 years after his death lived
   "Robert de Longland," a Shropshire man. Quotes from the confession of Sloth, corresponding to B V 392-425, loosely based
   on Crowley's text. Remarks that, despite the meter, the portrait of the character (whom he takes to be a jolly friar) is
   not ill drawn, "and will please the Curious, who will see that
   the English is much mended of what it was in Gloucester's
   Days." Notes the existence of ballads on Robin Hood and on
   "one of the Ralphs, Earls of Chester, each of which must be
   as old as that on Robin Hood; for the last Ralph was contemporary with that famous robber." Dates Chaucer as "about 70
   years after Longland."
        The author of this essay may have had access to manu-
   script sources, for Robert of Gloucester's Chronicle, from
   which he quotes four lines, was first edited by Thomas Hearne
   in 1724, though the Chronicle had earlier been drawn upon by
   such writers as John Stow, John Selden, John Weever, and
   Thomas Fuller.

1 HEARNE, THOMAS. "A Letter to Mr. Bagford, containing some
   Remarks upon Geffry Chaucer and his Writings." In <u>Robert of
   Gloucester's Chronicle</u>. Vol. 2. Edited by Thomas Hearne.
   Oxford: Theater, 1724, p. 605.
   "I have not found [the Plowman's Tale] in one of those
   [manuscripts] I have consulted at <u>Oxford</u>, which has made some
   think 'tis not <u>Chaucer's</u>, and this they believe confirm'd from
   the Style, which is different from his other Poems. <u>Mr. Pitts</u>
   confounds it with the Satyr, that is called <u>Piers Plowman</u>; but
   the Publishers have skillfully ascrib'd it to him, being war-
   ranted from a MS. in Mr. Stow's Library; though it must be
   confess'd, that 'tis not properly term'd a tale."

2 LELAND, JOHN. <u>Comentarii de scriptoribus Britannicis auctore
   Joanni Lelando Londinate ex autographo Lelandino nunc primus
   edidit Antonius Hall A.M. Coll. Reg. Oxon</u>. Oxford: e
   Theatro Sheldoniano.
   See Leland, c. 1545.1.

1 RUDDIMAN, THOMAS[?] "General Rules for Understanding the Lan-
   guage of Bishop Dowglas's Translation of Virgil's Aeneis."
   In <u>Virgil's Aeneis, Translated into Scottish Verse, by the
   Famous Gawin Douglas Bishop of Dunkeld. . . .</u> Edinburgh:
   Printed by Andrew Symson and Robert Freebairn, Sig. A2^v.
   "Our Author generally is pretty exact in his Quantities,
   and makes the Accent fall uniformly upon the same Syllables;
   except on the last of the Verse, which, even in the learned
   Languages the Poet was at liberty to use as he pleas'd. As to
   the Measures, or Number of Syllables in his Verses, which at
   first view may often appear not so constant and regular, it
   might be a sufficient Apology for him, that the same is ob-
   jected against <u>Chaucer</u>, <u>Gower</u>, <u>Langeland</u>, & the most celebrated Poets before or about his time; who took a greater
   freedom than is now allowed: But this seeming Inequality of
   their numbers, will in a great measure be accounted for by the
   many Contractions and Elisions, & the frequent Diareses or
   Divisions of Syllables; which cannot so easily be discover'd
   for want of these signs of Apostrophus or Diaresis, by which
   they are now distinguish'd."
   George Chalmers's <u>Life of Thomas Ruddiman</u> (1794), cited
   by William L. Alderson and Arnold C. Henderson, <u>Chaucer and
   Augustan Scholarship</u> (Berkeley, Los Angeles, and London:
   University of California Press, 1970), p. 258, states that

1710

this part of the collaborative edition was "undoubtedly written" by Ruddiman, who was likewise responsible for the glossary, which also cites Piers Plowman.

1719

1 HEARNE, THOMAS. Guilielmi Neubrigensis Historia sive Chronica
      rerum Anglicarum. Oxford: e Theatro Sheldoniano, p. 770.
          Mentions Pierce the Plowman's Crede, "which is altogether
      different from the Book in meeter commonly called Piers
      Ploughman, the Author whereof was Robert Langlande a Shrop-
      shire Man, born in Cleybirie about eight miles from Malvern
      Hills, and it was written in the Year of our Lord MIIIC and
      IX according to an ancient Copy mentioned in a MS. Paper
      shew'd me by my late very worthy and truly honest Friend
      Mr. John Urry Student of Christ-Church. There is no manner
      of Vice that reigneth in any Estate of Men which this Writer
      Robert Langelande hath not godlily, learnedly and wittily
      rebuked. And from hence, perhaps, it is that both this Book
      and Mr. Rawlinson's, and some other Satyrical Books, bear also
      the Name of Pierce the Ploughman."
          Clearly derived from Crowley's "the printer to the
      reader." Hearne's own copy of Crowley's first impression is
      now in the British Library.

1721

1 STRYPE, JOHN. Historical Memorials chiefly Ecclesiastical and
      such as Concern Religion and the Reformation of it, and the
      Progress made therein, under the Reign and Influence of King
      Edward VI. Vol. 2. London: John Wyat, pp. 266-67.
          Notice of Crowley's second impression, with descriptive
      remarks drawn almost verbatim from Crowley's "the printer to
      the reader."

1722

1 [BOLTON, EDMUND.] Nicolai Triveti Annalium Continuatio; ut et
      Adami Murimuthensis Chronicon, cum ejusdem Continuatione:
      quibus accedunt Joannis Bostoni Speculum Cœnobitarum, et
      Edmundi Boltoni Hypercritica. Omnia nunc primum edidit ē
      codicibus manuscriptis Antonius Hallius, S.T.P. Oxford:
      e Theatro Sheldoniano.
          See Bolton, 1618[?].1.

1724

1   ROBERT OF GLOUCESTER. <u>Robert of Gloucester's Chronicle</u>. Edited
    by Thomas Hearne. Oxford: Theater.
        See Hearne, 1709.1.

2   HEARNE, THOMAS. "Entry for 23 February 1724." In <u>Remarks and
    Collections</u>. Vol. 8, <u>1722-25</u>. Oxford Historical Society,
    no. 50. Oxford: Oxford Historical Society, 1907, p. 174.
        Quotes notes of antiquary William Fulman that <u>Pierce
    the Plowman's Crede</u> was written after <u>Piers Plowman</u>. Tenta-
    tively reiterates his belief that <u>Piers Plowman</u> was written
    after 1409, "and yet after all I have there insinuated
    [Hearne, 1719.1] that Pierce the Ploughman's Crede was so
    called, as other Satyrical Books were, in Imitation of the
    former, so that I still am of the opinion & believe that
    Pierce Plowmans Vision is the oldest, tho' not as old as Mr.
    Fulman seems to take it."
        Hearne came upon Fulman's notes on <u>Pierce the Plowman's
    Crede</u> when he acquired Fulman's copy of Rogers's edition
    (1561.1) of <u>Piers Plowman</u> and the <u>Crede</u> from the library of
    Arthur Charlett. Cf. Hearne, 1725.1.

1725

1   HEARNE, THOMAS. "Entry for 14 July 1724." In <u>Remarks and Col-
    lections</u>. Vol. 8, <u>1722-25</u>. Oxford Historical Society,
    no. 50. Oxford: Oxford Historical Society, 1907, pp. 395-96.
        "In one of my letters to Mr Baker, I said somewhat con-
    cerning the Age of Piers Plowman. Mr Baker tells me (in the
    said Letter of the 8th of July, 1725) that in Mr. Strype's
    Ecclesiastical Memorials, Vol 2, p. 266, he finds this
    Account: 'The Book was very antient, written in the Reign
    of Edw 3rd, for in the 2^d side of the 68th leaf mention is
    made of a dear year, John Chichester being then Maior of
    London, which was in an. 1350.' This (says Mr Baker) he
    quotes from Rob. Crowley's Edition, which Mr Baker hath not,
    but hopes I may have it: and after--'By some of them (MSS) he
    learnt the Author's name was Langland, a Shropshire man, born
    in Cleybury, about 8 Miles from the Malvern Hills. And among
    the Antient Copies, one was noted to be written in the year
    MIIIICIX; which (says Mr Baker) must be meant of the age of
    the Copy, not the Author, who by this account must be older.
    'If you have (says he) Crowley's 2^d Edition, you can easily
    make a Judgment, for I write in the dark.' I have not Rob.
    Crowley's Ed. of Pierce Plowman, mentioned by Mr Baker. That
    which I have is the Ed. printed by Owen Rogers, 1561, in which

1725

Pierce the Ploughman's Crede is also printed. In p. 770 of
my Ed. of Guil. Neubrigensis I have fix'd the writing of
Pierce Plowman to anno 1409, by virtue of a MS Note shew'd me
by Mr Urry, and the MS. there mentioned seems to have been the
same noted in Strype [1721.1]. What to say, unless I could
see the MS., I know not. This is certain, that the Work hath
been much altered at different times. I saw a MS. of it
lately, in wch the difference from the print is so very great
that the Work seems to have undergone the same Changes with
Robert of Gloucester. In the Creed (Which I said is in the Edition I have) is mention (in C ii a) of Wicklef, who appeared
not till the end of K. Edward the third. And in C. iiii a is
a mention of Water Brut (or Walter Brute), who was later than
Wicklef. . . ."

Hearne's comparison of the different versions of Piers
Plowman with Robert of Gloucester's Chronicle is repeated in
an entry of his dated 6 August 1725 (Remarks and Collections,
vol. 8, p. 411) and in his notes on the flyleaves of Crowley's
edition of the poem, in which he identifies the MS. he has
seen as one "belonging to Peter Le Neve." It is worth noting
that Hearne, in his introduction to Robert of Gloucester,
stated his clear belief that the Chronicle had been twice revised, once by the author himself and another time most certainly by someone else, temp. Henry VI.

The MS. lent to Hearne by Le Neve, still in Hearne's
possession in 1732, was identified in a different context by
Cargill (1935.1) as MS. R (B-text), which Skeat (1886.1) considered a MS of the B-text in transition to the C-version.
And B.M. MS. Cotton Caligula A.XI, which Hearne used for his
edition of the Chronicle, also contained a copy of Piers
Plowman which, in the event he collated it, would likewise
have differed widely from the printed texts, in presenting
a "mixed" B-C-text.

1732-33[?]

1 SPENCE, JOSEPH. "Quelques remarques hist: sur les Poetes
   Anglois." First published in James M. Osborn, "The First
   History of English Poetry." In Pope and His Contemporaries:
   Essays presented to George Sherburn. Edited by James L.
   Clifford and Louis A. Landa. New York: Oxford University
   Press, 1949, pp. 230-50, esp. p. 244.
       "Ils [Chaucer's works] sont pleins de Descriptions &
   Caractéres: & il est peutêtre le premier qui ait fait des
   Contes Poëtiques, du stile qu'on appelle à present le stile
   Naif. Gower fût son Contemporain: mais il lui manque cette
   vivacité d'espirit, et cette force à dépeindre, que nous

voyons avec tant d'admiration dans tous les traits de ce pere
de notre Poesie Angloise.

"Dans le siécle quinziéme, a peine trouveroit on
quelqu'un qui ait réussi en poësie Angloise: si on excepte
l'auteur de Pierce le Labourer."

In his note to this passage, Spence comments: "Our
first Poetry was chiefly either of the Lyric or ye Satirical
kind: both of wch Fashions were probably deriv'd from y^e
Italians, as they receiv'd them from the Provencals. . . .
Figuiera . . . wrote always against ill Princes. . . . This
was the general Practice of the Provencal Poets in his time,
from 1200 to 1300; & so on, all ye while the Popes were settled at Avignon. Hence many things in Chaucer; Piers Plowman;
ye Mirrour for Magistrates, &c."

1737

1   [COOPER, ELIZABETH.] "Robert de Langland." In The Muses Library;
or a Series of English Poetry from the Saxons, to the Reign of
King Charles II. Vol. 1. London: J. Wilcox; T. Green;
J. Brindley; T. Osborn, pp. 7-19.

"The Author of the Satire, intitled, the Vision of Piers
the Plowman, and who may be truly call'd the first of the
English Poets. . . . I must own I can't read his Work, without
lamenting the unhappiness of a fluctuating Language, that
buries even Genius it self in its Ruins: 'Tis raising Edifices
of Sand, that every Breath of Time defaces; and, if the Form
remains, the Beauty is lost. This is the case of the Piece
before us; 'Tis a Work of great Length, and Labour; of the
Allegorick-kind; animated with a rich Imagination, pointed
with great Variety of just Satire, and dignify'd with many
excellent Lessons of Morality and Virtue: to say all in a
Word, if I may presume to say so much, Chaucer seems to have
this Model in his Eye; and, in his Pardoners Prologue, particularly, has a Feature or two nearly resembling the Speech
and Character of Sloth hereafter quoted."

Disagrees with Puttenham[?] (1589.1) that Langland wrote
after Chaucer, and places him temp. Edward III-Richard II.
"To this may be added; that the worst Writer, after Chaucer,
had some regard to Measure, and never neglected Rhymes:
Whereas this is generally defective in both; seldom affording
a perfect Verse, and using a Dialect hardly intelligible. But
of those enough! This work is divided into Twenty Parts; the
Arguments of which are wrote with uncommon Spirit; and several
Passages in it deserve to be immortal; But as to Conduct of
the Whole, I must confess it does not appear to me of a Piece;
every Vision seeming a distinct Rhapsody, and not carrying on

1737

either one single Action, or a Series of many. But we ought
rather to wonder at its Beauties, than cavil at its Defects;
and, if the Poetical Design is Broken, the Moral is entire;
which is, uniformly, the advancement of Piety, and Reformation
of the Roman Clergy."
Prints selected passages. Suggests Milton's acquaint-
ance in Paradise Lost, 2, 475 ff. with B XX 79ff. There is
reason to believe that William Oldys contributed largely to
this work; see DNB, 4, p. 1068.

2   [OLDYS, WILLIAM.] The British Librarian 2 (February):88. In The
British Librarian. London: T. Osborne, 1738, p. 88.
Paraphrases Webbe's remarks (1586.1) on the poet,
"Pierce Ploughman," in a notice of Webbe's Discourse on
English Poetrie.

1738

1   [OLDYS, WILLIAM.] The British Librarian. London: T. Osborne.
See [Oldys], 1737.2.

[1741]

1   [CAMPBELL, JOHN.] The Polite Correspondence: or Rational Amuse-
ment; being a Series of Letters, Philosophical, Poetical,
Historical, Critical, Amorous, Moral and Satyrical. London:
Printed and sold by John Atkinson and others, p. 271.
In an epistolary essay on Saxon verse, remarks on
alliteration thus: "Our Poets saw and copied this Beauty
very early. The first English Poet we have, I mean the Author
of the Satyr entitled, Pierce Plowman, uses it frequently as
in this Line.
"In a Somer Season, when set was the Sunne."
For a modern reprint, see Campbell, 1971.7.

1742

1   DART, JOHN. Westmonasterium, or the History and Antiquities of
the Abbey Church of St. Peter's, Westminster. Vol. 1.
London: James Cole; Joseph Smith; Tho. Bowles, Jer. Batley;
Tho. Taylor; John Bowles; Andrew Johnstone, p. 87.
Denies Chaucer's authorship of the Plowman's Tale, which
he ascribes to "a hot warm Incendiary as (pity it is, too many
Creatures of the State-Faction pretending Wickliff's Opinions
were) one Pierse Ploughman."

Ante 1744

*1   POPE, ALEXANDER. Note on Piers Plowman. In Pope's copy of
     Crowley's 1550 edition of the poem, according to the catalogue
     for the sale of the books of Dr. Benjamin Heath, recorded in
     Joseph Spence, Observations, Anecdotes, and Characters of
     Books and Men. Vol. 1. Edited by James M. Osborn. Oxford:
     Clarendon Press, 1966, p. 179.
          For Heath, see DNB, vol. 25, pp. 339-40. The catalogue
     mentioned is probably Catalogue of Books containing all the
     rare, useful, and valuable Publications to the present time to
     be Sold in April and May [1810] by Mr. Jeffrey, No. 11 Pall
     Mall, reissued later in the same year with prices and names of
     purchasers; see lot 1859. Osborn notes that the present loca-
     tion of Pope's copy of the poem, bearing his long note, is
     unknown.

1748

1   TANNER, THOMAS. Bibliotheca Britannico-Hibernica: sive, de
     scriptoribus, qui in Anglia, Scotia, et Hibernia ad sæculi
     XVII initium floruerunt, literarum ordine juxta familiarum
     nomine dispositis Commentarius. . . . London: Societas ad
     literas promovendas, pp. 465, 504-5.
          Devotes separate entries to Langland, Robertus and
     Malvernius, Johannes, although he treats them as the same
     person, in effect combining the biographies of Bale (1557.1),
     Stow (1580.1), and Wood (1674.1). Follows Wood in distin-
     guishing between this writer and Malvernius, Johannes, the
     author of De remedis spiritualibus et corporalibus contra
     pestilentiam. For a modern reprint, see Tanner, 1963.15.

1749

1   AMES, JOSEPH. Typographical Antiquities: Being an Historical
     Account of Printing in England with some Memoirs of our
     Antient Printers and a register of the Books printed by them,
     from the year MCCCCLXXI to the Year MDC. London: W. Faden,
     pp. 269-70, 306.
          Notices of Crowley's first impression (1550.1) and the
     edition of Rogers (1561.1). Owns a MS of the poem himself (to
     be identified as MS. O). For revisions of this work, see
     Ames, 1786.1, and Ames, 1819.1.

1753

1   CIBBER, [THEOPHILUS]. The Lives of the Poets of Great Britain
    and Ireland to the Time of Dean Swift. London: R. Griffiths,
    pp. 18-20.
        Disagrees with Cooper (1737.1) that Langland wrote be-
    fore Chaucer and considers them contemporaries. Critical
    estimation of the poem is a verbatim reproduction of Cooper.
    There is some reason to think that this work was largely the
    product of Robert Shiels. See DNB, vol. 4, pp. 362-63.

1754

1   WARTON, THOMAS. Observations on the Faerie Queene of Spenser.
    Vol. 1. London: R. & J. Dodsley; Oxford: J. Fletcher,
    pp. 88-89.
        Suggests that Spenser's Sheapheards Calendar was written
    partially in imitation of "the visions of Pierce Plowman." In
    a note to this passage, dates Piers Plowman after 1350, and
    describes it as consisting of "many distinct visions, which
    have no mutual dependance upon each other; so that the poem is
    not a regular and uniform whole, consisting of one action or
    design. The author seems to have intended it as a satire on
    almost every occupation of life, but more particularly on the
    clergy; in censuring whom, Wickliff had led the way not many
    years before. This piece abounds with humour, spirit and
    imagination; all which are drest to great disadvantage in a
    very uncouth versification, and obsolete language. It seems
    to be written without rhyme, an ornament which the poet has
    endeavour'd to supply, by making every verse to consist of
    words beginning with the same letter. This practice has con-
    tributed not a little to render his poem obscure and perplex'd,
    exclusive of its obsolete style; for to introduce his alliter-
    ation, he must have been often necessarily compell'd to depart
    from the natural and more obvious way of expressing himself.
    . . . From this it appears, that the example of Gower and
    Chaucer, who sought to reform the roughness of their native
    tongue, by naturalizing many new words from the Latin, French,
    and Italian, and who introduced the seven-lin'd stanza, from
    Petrarch and Dante, into our poetry, had little influence
    upon Langland, who chose rather to go back to the Saxon models,
    both for language and form of verse."
        Gives a specimen from the beginning of B Prol, and
    emends the text of the printed edition "sette was the sun" to
    "hotte was the sun" (on the basis of Bale's reading celeret
    [1557.1]). Accepts Chaucer's authorship of the Plowman's Tale
    and sees in it Chaucer's dependence on Piers Plowman.

1760-61[?]

1   GRAY, THOMAS. <u>Metrum: Observations on English Metre</u>. In <u>The</u>
<u>Works of Thomas Gray, with memoirs of his life and Writings by</u>
<u>William Mason to which are subjoined extracts philological</u>
<u>poetical and critical from the author's original manuscripts</u>
<u>selected and arranged by Thomas James Mathias</u>. Vol. 2.
London: Shakespeare Press for John Porter, pp. 37-39.
   The absence of rhyme in <u>Piers Plowman</u> suggests that the
introduction of rhyme after the Conquest was slow. Quotes the
beginning of B II and refers to Crowley's remarks on meter
(1550.1). "Pierce Plowman, a severe satire on the times,
written by Robert Langland in 1350, is wholly in such Saxon
verse without rhyme measure . . . and thus through the whole
poem, which is a very long one, with few exceptions, the
triple consonance is observed in every distitch."

1761

1   PERCY, THOMAS. Letter to Thomas Warton, June 1760. In <u>The</u>
<u>Correspondence of Thomas Percy and Thomas Warton</u>. Edited by
M.G. Robinson and Leah Dennis. Vol. 3, <u>The Percy Letters</u>,
edited by David Nichol Smith and Cleanth Brooks. [Baton
Rouge]: Louisiana State University Press, 1951, pp. 13, 15-16.
   "The versification of <u>Langland</u> in his <u>Pierce Plowman</u>, is
not peculiar to that poet: he is only one of the last English
Bards that has used it.--It is the very Metre of our Old Saxon
Poets: with this difference that he has written in one verse
at length, what is commonly found in them broken in two, after
this manner
           In a summer season,
           When set was the sunne
           I shope me into shroubs,
           As I a shepe were. &c
   "But with regard to the Saxon verse that it was the very
measure of <u>Piers Plowman</u>, will soon appear when my learned
Neighbor and Friend Mr Lye hath published his proposed Edition
and Translation of the Works of <u>Cædmon</u> the celebrated Saxon
Poet: A Work that will open an intire new field to Criticism
and Taste, and show that the Study of antiquities is not so
barren as is commonly supposed."
   "when <u>sette</u> was the sun."
   "Your conjecture is certainly right. Only I think it is
more probable that <u>Langlande</u> wrote
   --when <u>hette</u> was the sun."

1761

for so I find the word written (If I mistake not) in my
Ancient MS Collection of Old Ballads, in many places: See also
Gloss. ad G. Douglas."
    The edition of Cædmon proposed by Edward Lye (1694-1767)
never appeared. The glossary to the works of Gavin Douglas to
which Percy refers is Ruddiman, 1710.1.

1763

1 PERCY, THOMAS. Letter to Richard Farmer, 9 October 1763. In The
    Correspondence of Thomas Percy and Richard Farmer. Edited by
    Cleanth Brooks. Vol. 2, The Percy Letters, edited by David
    Nichol Smith and Cleanth Brooks. [Baton Rouge]: Louisiana
    State University Press, 1946, p. 51.
        "Inclosed I also send an attempt towards a Dissertation
    on the Metre of Pierce Plowman's Visions. This is only an
    incorrect proof, and contains even some capital mistakes,
    which I have removed in the Revise, as you will find, when
    you come to see it wrought off."

1764

1 EVANS, EVAN. Letter to Thomas Percy, 13 January 1764. In The
    Correspondence of Thomas Percy and Evan Evans. Edited by
    Aneirin Lewis. Vol. 4, The Percy Letters, edited by David
    Nichol Smith and Cleanth Brooks. [Baton Rouge]: Louisiana
    State University Press, 1957, pp. 56-57.
        In reply to a letter of Percy, 31 December 1763, in
    which was enclosed a draft of Percy's essay "On the Metre of
    Pierce Plowman's Visions" (see [Percy], 1765.1), Evans replies:
    "I never met with any traces of this method of writing [allit-
    eration] in English. Pierce the Plowman's Visions I never
    saw, but by your extracts from it, I find a faint resemblance
    of our cynghanedd or Symphonia consonantica in it. And as you
    say it is the prosody of the ancient Scaldi of the North, It
    is to me I own a discovery. For I always thought that method
    of writing peculiar to our nation and the Irish, who seem to
    have it in some measure. That the English had it very early
    I am persuaded by a passage in Giraldus Cambrensis, which I
    shall here quote at length as it gives great light to what
    you have advanced about the Metre of Pierce the Plowman."
    Evans then quotes from the edition of Giraldus Cambrensis's
    Cambriæ Descriptio by David Powel (1585), pp. 260-61.

1765

1 [PERCY, THOMAS.] Reliques of Ancient English Poetry: consisting
   of Old Heroic Ballads, Songs, and other Pieces of our earlier
   Poets (chiefly of the Lyric kind) Together with some few of
   later Date. Vol. 2. London: J. Dodsley, pp. 260-63.
         Langland did not invent any new mode of versification;
   rather, Piers Plowman is constructed by rules that governed
   ancient Icelandic poetry, Anglo-Saxon verse--rules "which were
   probably never wholly laid aside, but occasionally used at
   different intervals." Harmony of the verse depends neither
   on quantity of vowels nor on rhyme, but on alliteration, "a
   certain artful repetition of the sounds in the middle of the
   verses. . . . This was adjusted according to certain rules of
   their prosody, one of which was that every distich should contain at least three words beginning with the same letter or
   sound. Two of these correspondent sounds might be placed
   either in the first, or second line of the distich, and one in
   the other: but all three were not regularly to be crowded into
   one line." Feels that the irregularities of the old alliterative line notwithstanding, it closely resembles the French
   Alexandrine, which he takes as consisting of four anapests
   with a cæsura after the sixth syllable. States that both the
   French Alexandrine and the English "burlesque Alexandrine"
   (also consisting of four anapests) are derived from the alliterative verse of the "ancient Gothic and Francic poets."
   Percy names the author as "Robert Langland," a secular priest,
   born in Mortimer's Cleobury, and a fellow of Oriel College,
   Oxford, who flourished temp. Edward III-Richard II and "published" his poem shortly after 1350. The poem is divided into
   twenty passūs, a word which "seems only to denote the break or
   division between two parts, tho' by the ignorance of the
   printer applied to the parts themselves."
         Percy notes four Black Letter editions, and distin-
   guishes (incorrectly) between Crowley's second and third
   impressions ([Langland], 1550.2; 1550.3) on the basis of
   spelling of title page and foliation. He denies the ascription of Pierce the Plowman's Crede to Langland. Skeat corrects some of Percy's remarks on the alliterative measure in
   [Percy], 1868.2.

1774

1 MITFORD, WILLIAM. An Essay upon the Harmony of Language, in-
      tended Principally to Illustrate that of the English Language.
      London: printed by Scott for J. Robson, pp. 157-58.
           Quotes Percy's description (1765.1) of the alliterative
      measure of the poem. Cf. Mitford, 1804.1.

1774

2 WARTON, THOMAS. The History of English Poetry from the Close of
the Eleventh to the Commencement of the Eighteenth Century to
which are prefixed two dissertations. I. On the origin of
Romantic Fiction in Europe. II. On the Introduction of Learning into England. Vol. 1. London: J. Dodsley and others,
pp. 266-87, 306-7.
The author was Robert Longlande, a secular priest and a
fellow of Oriel College, Oxford, who flourished in 1350, but
who alludes to the (very recent) siege of Calais. The poem
is ". . . a satire on the vices of almost every profession:
but particularly on the corruptions of the clergy, and the
absurdities of superstitions. These are ridiculed with much
humour and spirit, couched under a strong vein of allegorical
invention. But instead of availing himself of the rising and
rapid improvements of the English language, Longlande prefers
and adopts the style of the Anglo-Saxon poets. . . . But this
imposed constraint of seeking identical initials, and the af-
fectation of obsolete English, by demanding a constraint and
necessary departure from the natural and obvious forms of expression, while it circumscribed the powers of our author's
genius, contributed also to render his manner extremely per-
plexed, and to disgust the reader with obscurities."
Calls attention to the prediction of the suppression of
the abbeys, and confesses his surprise that this "prophecy"
seems original to the poem. The poem's references to the
Antichrist suggest the author knew the Old French Roman
d'Anticrist of Huon de Meri; the humorous satire of monks
seeking donations are written "in a strain which seems to have
given rise to Chaucer's Sompnour's Tale." Pierce the Plowman's Crede is by another hand; and the Plowman's Tale is
written in imitation of Piers Plowman and attributed to
Chaucer: "But it has Longlande's alliteration of initials:
as if his example had, as it were, appropriated that mode of
versification to the subject, and the supposed character which
supports the satire."

1775

1 CHAUCER, GEOFFREY. The Canterbury Tales of Chaucer, to which
are added an essay upon his language and versification; an
introductory discourse; and notes. Vol. 4. Edited by Thomas
Tyrwhitt. London: T. Payne, pp. 73-75.
"Such was, in general, the state of English Poetry at
the time when Chaucer made his first essays. The use of Rime
was established; not exclusively (for the Author of the
'Visions of Pierce Ploughman' wrote after the year 1350 without Rime), but very generally; so that in this respect he
[Chaucer] had little to do but to imitate his predecessors."

30

In his note to this passage, Tyrwhitt dates the poem from
fol. 68 of Crowley's edition, though the reference is in
error, as John Chichester was mayor of London in 1369-70.
Tyrwhitt also cites the fable of belling the cat in suggesting that "the author wrote at the very end of the reign of
Edward III, when Richard was become heir apparent." On the
basis of an ascription in MS. Cotton Vesp. B.xvi, Tyrwhitt
declares the author's Christian name to be William, not
Robert.

Notes that the printed editions are so faulty that
Langland himself would have difficulty in recognizing his own
work; and agrees with Hickes (1705.1) and Percy (1765.1) regarding versification: "Each of his [Langland's] verses is in
fact a distich, composed of two verses, after the Saxon form,
without Rime, and not reducible to any certain Metre. I do
not mean to say, that a few of his Verses may not be picked
out, consisting of fourteen or fifteen syllables, and resembling the metre used in the Ormulum; and there are still more
of twelve and thirteen syllables, which might pass for very
tolerable Alexandrines: but then, on the other hand, there is
a great number of his verses . . . which cannot, by any mode
of pronunciation, be extended beyond nine or ten syllables; so
that it is impossible to imagine, that his verse was intended
to consist of any determinate number of syllables. It is as
clear that his Accents, upon which the harmony of modern
Rythms depends, are not disposed according to any regular
system. The first division of a verse is often Trochaic, and
the last Iambic; and vice versa. The only rule, which he
seems really to have prescribed to himself, is what has been
taken notice of by his first Editor, viz. 'to have three
wordes at the leaste in euery verse whiche beginne with some
one letter.'"

1778

1   CHATTERTON, THOMAS. Miscellanies in Prose and Verse. London:
    Fielding & Walker, p. 137.
        Anecdote of Chaucer: "After Chaucer had distributed
    copies of the tale of Piers Plowman, a Fransiscan friar wrote
    a satiric maumery upon him; which was acted at the monasteries
    in London, and at Woodstock before the court. Chaucer not a
    little nettled at the poignancy and popularity of the satire,
    meeting his antagonist in Fleet-street, beat him with his
    dagger; for which he was fined two shillings, as appears by a
    record of the Inner Temple, where Chaucer was a student."
        For a facsimile edition, see Chatterton, 1971.8.

1778

2   CHAUCER, GEOFFREY. The Canterbury Tales of Chaucer, to which are
       added an essay upon his language and versification; an intro-
       ductory discourse; and notes. Vol. 5. Edited by Thomas
       Tyrwhitt. London: T. Payne, p. v.
            Dates Piers Plowman after 1362, on the basis of "the
       great storm of wind, alluded to in fol. xx.b. 1.14," which he
       takes to refer to 15 January 1362.

3   WARTON, THOMAS. The History of English Poetry from the Close of
       the Eleventh to the Commencement of the Eighteenth Century to
       which are prefixed two dissertations. I. On the origin of
       Romantic Fiction in Europe. II. On the Introduction of Learn-
       ing into England. Vol. 2. London: J. Dodsley and others,
       p. 179n.
            Referring to B V 402, identifies "Randall of Chester" as
       Ranulph Higden, supposed author of the Chester mystery plays.
       Cf. [Ritson], 1782.1.

1781

*1   HENRY, ROBERT. The History of Great Britain from the First In-
       vasion of It under Julius Caesar. Edinburgh and London.
            See Henry, 1789.1.

1782

1   [RITSON, JOSEPH.] Observations on the Three First Volumes of the
       History of English Poetry in a Familiar Letter to the Author.
       London: J. Stockdale & R. Faulder, pp. 12, 21.
            Denies Warton's assertion (1774.1) that the Romance of
       Alexander was written in imitation of Piers Plowman. Ques-
       tions the ascription of Piers Plowman to Langland: "There is,
       I can assure you, more reason against Longlands title to the
       authorship of Piers Plowman than you are aware of." Rejects
       Warton's identification (1778.3) of "Randall of Chester" in
       favor of the crusader Randall Blundeville, earl of Chester.

1786

1   AMES, JOSEPH. Typographical Antiquities: or an Historical
       Account of the Origin and Progress of Printing in Great
       Britain and Ireland: Containing Memoirs of our ancient
       Printers, and a Register of Books printed by them From the
       Year MCCCCLXXI to the Year MDC. Begun by the late Joseph
       Ames . . . Considerably augmented, both in the Memoirs and

Number of Books by William Herbert. Vol. 2. London: printed
for the editor, and sold by T. Payne & Son, Benjamin White,
L. David, . . . and the rest of the Booksellers of Great
Britain and Ireland, pp. 758-60, 876.
    Notices of Crowley's first and second impressions
(1550.1 and 1550.2) and Rogers's edition (1561.1). Herbert
describes his own copies as a pure first impression, and a
copy of what is essentially a first impression with the title
page and prefatory material of the second impression attached.
Finds corroboration of Percy's contention (1765.1) of a third
impression in variant readings on the last leaf of Herbert's
own copy. See Ames, 1819.1.

1787

1   W., T.H. Letter. Gentleman's Magazine 57, no. 5, part 2
(November):945-56.
    Calls for a new edition of the poem, "which hath suf-
fered greatly both from licentious and negligent transcribers,
and from careless and unskillful printers." Although Langland
cannot bear comparison with Chaucer for wit, pleasantry, and
discrimination of character, his work is a "greater fund of
materials to elucidate the progress of the Saxon tongue, which
Chaucer is accused of vitiating with discordant Gallicisms."

1789

1   HENRY, ROBERT. The History of Great Britain from the First In-
vasion of It by the Romans under Julius Caesar. 2d ed.
Vol. 4. Dublin: printed for P. Byrne & J. Jones, pp. 447-48.
    "About the middle of the [fourteenth] century an attempt
was made to revive, or at least to imitate the alliterative
poetry of the Anglo-Saxons without rhyme, by Robert Langlande,
a secular priest of Oxford, in his famous allegorical satire
against persons of all professions, called The Vision of
Pierce Plowman. This poem abounds with the boldest personifications, the keenest satire, the most expressive descriptions, and the most singular versification. . . ."

1798

1   JEFFERSON, THOMAS. "An Essay Towards Facilitating Instruction in
the Anglo-Saxon and Modern Dialects of the English Language.
For the Use of the University of Virginia." In The Writings
of Thomas Jefferson. Vol. 18. Edited by A.E. Bergh.
Washington: Thomas Jefferson Memorial Assoc., 1904, p. 368.

1798

"The full alphabet of Roman characters was first used about the beginning of the sixteenth century. But the expression of the same sounds, by a different character did not change these sounds, nor the language which they constituted; did not make the language of Alfred a different one from that of Piers Ploughman, of Chaucer, Douglas, Spenser, and Shakespeare, any more than the second revolution, which substituted the Roman for the English black letter, made theirs a different language from that of Pope and Bolingbroke. . . ."
    This essay was first printed in 1851. An entry in Jefferson's hand, Pierce Plowman's visions. 8vo., suggests he may have owned an early edition of the poem; though the spelling of the title and his description of the volume as an octavo has suggested to E. Millicent Sowerby that the book referred to may well be Percy's Four Essays, as Improved and Enlarged in the Second Edition of the Reliques of Ancient English Poetry (1767), the last essay of which is "On the Metre of Pierce Plowman's Visions." See Thomas Jefferson, Catalogue of the Library of Thomas Jefferson, vol. 4, compiled, with annotations by E. Millicent Sowerby (Washington: Library of Congress, 1955), p. 517.

1800

1   PHILLIPS, EDWARD. Theatrum Poetarum Anglicanorum. Edited by Sir S.E. Brydges. Canterbury: J. White, p. 4.
    Phillips's work was originally published in 1675; it did not mention Langland or Piers Plowman. In this enlargement of Phillips's work, Brydges praises the satire of the poem and its "strong vein of allegorical invention," then goes on to echo the criticisms of the alliterative style of the poem voiced by Warton (1774.2).

1801

1   ELLIS, GEORGE. Specimens of the Early English Poets, to which is prefixed an Historical Sketch of the Rise and Progress of the English Poetry and Language. Vol. 1. London: printed by W. Bulmer for G. & W. Nicol & J. Wright, pp. 147-68.
    The reputed author is Robert Langland, a secular priest born in Mortimer's Cleobury and a fellow of Oriel College. The poem is described as a "long moral and religious discourse, and as such, is full of good sense and piety; but it is farther rendered interesting, by a succession of incidents, enlivened sometimes by strong satire, and sometimes by the

keenest ridicule on the vices of all orders of men, and particularly of the religious." The allegorical characters and
the incoherencies that result from their dialogues are defended on the basis of Langland's use of the dream vision.
Although the metrical harmony of alliterative lines is limited,
the modern reader quickly becomes accustomed to the device.
The fact that a "sensible and zealous" writer like Langland employed
alliteration in a work of religious instruction indicates that alliterative measure had "maintained a successful
struggle against the Norman ornament of rhyme." The obscurities of diction, censured by Warton (1774.2), are perhaps best
to be explained as the fault of copyists, rather than of the
author. The poet's religious beliefs are orthodox, yet the
emphasis in the poem is on the "principles of rational liberty," prophetic of "those bolder tenets which, for a series
of years, were productive only of national restlessness and
misery, but which ultimately terminated in a free government
and a reformed religion."

1802

1   [RITSON, JOSEPH.] Bibliographia Poetica: A Catalogue of Engleish
    Poets of the Twelfth, Thirteenth, Fourteenth, Fifteenth, and
    Sixteenth Centurys, with a short account of their works.
    London: G. & W. Nicol, pp. 26-31.
        From the MS rubric, "Visio Willelmi de Petro Ploughman,"
    Ritson concludes that Wille refers either to a personification
    of the mental faculty or to the author himself. Considers the
    author a Londoner by residence if not by birth, and doubts his
    connection with Oriel College, as had been suggested by Selden
    (1622.2). Describes the poem as ". . . a kind of religious
    allegorical satire; in which Pierce the ploughman, the prin-
    cipal personage, seems to be intended for the pattern of
    Christian perfection, if not, occasionally, for Jesus Christ
    himself."
        Ritson defends the possibility, against Tyrwhitt
    (1775.1), that Crowley's text is in the main accurate. Com-
    paring variant readings from the MSS at his disposal, con-
    cludes it "highly probable that the author had revised his
    original work, and given, as it were, a new edition; and it
    may be possible for a good judge of ancient poetry, possessed
    of a sufficient stock of critical acumen, to determine which
    was the first, and which the second."
        At least four of the MSS. Ritson consulted were of the
    A-text (MSS. H, H[3], L, and V). These MSS along with the
    printed editions seemed to him to differ markedly from the

1802

text as found in such MSS as D, M, N, and R, all of the C-text.
Had Ritson collated further, he would doubtless have distinguished the A-text from the B-text in the printed editions.
That Ritson at one time strongly suspected a third text is
clear from a manuscript entry in his own hand, quoted by
Donaldson (1949.1): "The differences as well between the
printed copies on the one hand and most if not all the MSS.
on the other, as between the MSS. themselves is very remarkable. Of the latter indeed there appears to be two sets, of
which the one has scarcely 5 lines togr. in common with the
other."

1804

1   MITFORD, WILLIAM. An Inquiry into the Principles of Harmony in
     Language, and of the mechanism of verse modern and antient.
     2d ed. London: T. Cadell & W. Davies, pp. 155-69.
          Alliteration, which cannot produce poetical measure,
     was used by Langland "as a meer ornament for the amusement of
     the ear." Nevertheless, the poem can be harmonized in four-
     foot verses, as becomes obvious when rhyme is added. Lang-
     land's lines are deficient sometimes by the lack of syllables,
     sometimes by an excess; hence, the modern reader will want to
     pronounce silent -e's, or move accents, or elide.

1807

1   BYRON, LORD GEORGE GORDON NOEL. Entry for 30 November 1807 in a
     memorandum book. In Letters and Journals of Lord Byron with
     Notes of his life. Vol. 1. Edited by Thomas Moore. London:
     John Murray, 1830, pp. 100-101.
          "In my list of English, I have merely mentioned the
     greatest;--to enumerate the minor poets would be useless, as
     well as tedious. Perhaps Gray, Goldsmith, and Collins, might
     have been added, as worthy of mention, in a cosmopolite ac-
     count. But as for the others, from Chaucer down to Churchill,
     they are 'voces et præterea nihil;'--sometimes spoken of,
     rarely read, and never with advantage. Chaucer, notwithstand-
     ing the praises bestowed on him, I think obscene and contempt-
     ible: he owes his celebrity merely to his antiquity, which he
     does not deserve so well as Pierce Plowman, or Thomas of
     Ercildoune."

1810

1   TODD, HENRY J.   Illustrations of the Lives and Writings of Gower
    and Chaucer collected from authentic documents.   London: F.C.
    and J. Rivington, T. Payne, Cadell & Davies, and R.H. Evans,
    pp. 240, 241, 245, 254, 261, 270, 327, 345, 349, 369, 373,
    388.
        The poem is used to illustrate such topics as the func-
    tion of limitours, love days, the dress of a Sergeant of Law,
    the behavior of physicians and sommoners, and the practice of
    telling tales on pilgrimages, and such words as chese,
    goleardeis, hovyth, rekkeles, rought, and vernicle.

1813

1   [LANGLAND, WILLIAM.]   Visio Willĩ de Petro Plouhman Item Visiones
    ejusdem de Dowel, Dobet, et Dobest or, The Vision of William
    concerning Piers Plouhman and the Visions of the same concern-
    ing the Origin, Progress, and Perfection of the Christian
    Life. ascribed to Robert Langland, a secular priest of the
    County of Salop., and written in, or immediately after, the
    year 1362. Printed from a MS contemporary with the Author,
    collated with two others of Great Antiquity, and exhibiting
    the original text; together with an introductory discourse, a
    perpetual commentary, annotations, and a glossary. By Thomas
    Whitaker. . . . London: John Murray, xlviii + 421 + 31 pp.
        The first edition of the C-text, based on MS. P, with
    unsystematic collations from MS. Ht (B-text) and MS. O (C-
    text). Whitaker believes that Crowley's text (1550.1) is from
    a bad, late MS representing the poet's revised text, and that
    MS. P faithfully preserves the author's original version.
        Considers the poem to have been written at a time of
    rampant excesses among the clergy but also at a period when
    the national intelligence had risen, as witnessed by the
    poem's satire, a mode that presumes considerable generaliza-
    tion and abstraction. Langland is praised for his acute moral
    sense, his indignation concerning the abuses of both public
    and private life, and his keen sarcastic humor. His allegory
    had the virtue of making real people of his personifications
    but also, occasionally, the vice of mixing personifications in-
    distinctly. Moreover, Langland's "casuistry is sometimes
    miserably perplexed, and his illustrations very unhappy. . . .
    He often sinks into imbecility, and not infrequently spins out
    his thread of allegory into mere tenuity." Although the re-
    formers of the sixteenth century claimed him as one of their
    own, his beliefs were orthodox: he did not, for example,
    accept Wyclif's predestinarian notions, and his persona refers

1813

to himself as a <u>Lollere</u> only in the sense of an idle wanderer.
The meter of the poem is identical to that of the poetry of
the Junius MS., reducible, in general, to "a kind of dactilics
or their opposites, anæpestics."

Summarizes the poem at some length (pp. xix-xxx) in an
effort to prove "that it was written after a regular and consistent plan." Nevertheless, notes such apparent inconsisten-
cies as Will encountering abstract personifications while
awake, and an ending of the poem, "singularly cold and com-
fortless," that leaves the enquirer "still remote from the
object of his search, while Antichrist remains triumphant, and
not a single hint is given at his final destruction, or the
final and universal domination of his great antagonist." For
review of this edition, see [Wright], 1834.1, and the remarks
of Skeat in Langland, 1873.5.

1814

1   GRAY, THOMAS. <u>The Works of Thomas Gray, with Memoirs of his life</u>
<u>and writings by William Mason to which are subjoined extracts</u>
<u>philological poetical and critical from the author's original</u>
<u>manuscripts selected and arranged by Thomas James Mathias</u>.
Vol. 2. London: Shakespeare Press for John Porter.
See Gray, 1760-61[?].1.

1816

1   JEFFERSON, THOMAS. Letter to Joseph Milligan, 6 April 1816. In
<u>The Writings of Thomas Jefferson</u>. Vol. 14. Edited by A.E.
Bergh. Washington: Thomas Jefferson Memorial Assoc., 1904,
p. 463.
"Had the preposterous idea of fixing the language been
adopted by our Saxon ancestors, of Pierce Plowman, of Chaucer,
of Spenser, the progress of ideas must have stopped with that
of the language."

1819

1   AMES, JOSEPH. <u>Typographical Antiquities; or the History of</u>
<u>Printing in England Scotland and Ireland. . . . Begun by the</u>
<u>late Joseph Ames, . . . Considerably augmented by William</u>
<u>Herbert, . . . and now greatly enlarged, with Copious Notes,</u>
<u>. . . by the Rev. Thomas Frognall Dibdin</u>. Vol. 4. London:
Longman, Hurst, Rees, Orme, & Brown, pp. 328-30, 546-47.

Notices of the editions of Crowley and Rogers, taken
from Ames (1786.1). Dibden adds that he would have availed
himself of many of Herbert's manuscript memoranda and additions to his interleaved copy respecting the author of the
poem, had not such material been superseded by Whitaker's
researches (1813.1).

2   CAMPBELL, THOMAS. "An Essay on English Poetry." In Specimens of
    British Poets; with Biographical and Critical Notices and An
    Essay on English Poetry. Vol. 1. London: John Murray,
    pp. 64-69.
         In modern pronunciation, the poem sounds as if written
    in a cadence alternating between anapestic and dactylic,
    though Mitford (1804.1) found it predominately anapestic.
    Some of Langland's verses, however, cannot be reduced to any
    perceptible meter. Even with allowance made for its anti-
    quity, Langland's style is vulgar, "and seems to indicate a
    mind that would have been coarse, though strong, in any state
    of society." Praises the originality of the poem, however:
    Langland "employs no borrowed materials; he is the earliest of
    our writers in whom there is a tone of moral reflection; and
    his sentiments are those of bold and solid integrity. The
    zeal of truth was in him; and his vehement manner rises to
    eloquence, when he denounces hypocrisy and imposture. The
    mind is struck with his rude voice, proclaiming independent
    and popular sentiments, from an age of slavery and supersti-
    tion, and thundering a prediction in the ear of the papacy,
    which was doomed to be literally fulfilled at the distance of
    nearly two hundred years."
         Follows Whitaker's edition (1813.1), but does not agree
    with Whitaker that the poem is unified: the appearance of
    visionary personages is often "sufficiently whimsical"; and
    if the poem has a design, "it is the most vague and ill-
    constructed that ever entered into the brain of a waking
    dreamer."

3   CAMPBELL, THOMAS. An Essay on English Poetry. Boston: Wells &
    Lilly, pp. 60-61.
         Campbell's remarks on Langland in an edition of his
    Essay (1819.2) published separately in the same year.

1823

1   HONE, WILLIAM. Ancient Mysteries Described, especially the
    English Miracle Plays, Founded on Apocryphal New Testament
    Story, Extant among the Unpublished Manuscripts in the British
    Museum. . . . London: printed for William Hone, pp. 124-26.

1823

        Extracts quoted and paraphrased from Whitaker's edition (1813.1), illustrating Christ's Descent into Hell. For a modern reprint of this work, see Hone, 1969.14.

1824

1   WARTON, THOMAS. <u>The History of English Poetry from the Close of</u> <u>the Eleventh to the Commencement of the Eighteenth Century</u>. Vol. 2. Edited by Richard Price. London: Thomas Tegg, pp. 101-2, 478, 481-510.
        Price's notes supplement Warton (1774.2) by referring to Tyrwhitt's dating of the poem (1775.1) and his argument for William being the author's Christian name. Price collates MS. H^3 (A-text) with Crowley's text for a passage printed by Warton and concludes that "Crowley's MS. appears to have been a very excellent one." Collation of Whitaker's text (1813.1) with MS H^2 (A-text) leads to the discovery that "another and a third version was once in circulation; and if the first draught of the poem be still in existence, it is here perhaps that we must look for it. For in this the narrative is considerably shortened, many passages of a decidedly episodic cast . . . are wholly omitted; others . . . but slightly sketched." Corrects portions of Whitaker's text through collation with MS. M (C-text) and MS. N (C-text).

1825

1   JEFFERSON, THOMAS. Letter to J. Evelyn Denison, 9 November 1825. In <u>The Writings of Thomas Jefferson</u>. Vol. 16. Edited by A.E. Bergh. Washington: Thomas Jefferson Memorial Assoc., p. 131.
        Suggests modernizing Anglo-Saxon: "Strip it of these embarrassments, vest it in the Roman type which we have adopted instead of our English black letter, reform its uncouth orthography, and assimilate its pronunciation, as much as may be, to the present English, just as we do in reading Piers Plowman or Chaucer, and with the contemporary vocabulary for the few lost words, we understand it as we do them." These sentiments are echoed in Jefferson, 1825.2.

2   JEFFERSON, THOMAS. Postscript to "An Essay on the Anglo-Saxon Language." In <u>The Writings of Thomas Jefferson</u>. Vol. 18. Edited by A.E. Bergh. Washington: Thomas Jefferson Memorial Assoc., p. 390.
        "But if, as I believe, we may consider [Anglo-Saxon] as merely an antiquated form of our present language, if we may throw aside the learned difficulties which mask its real

1832

character, liberate it from these foreign shackles, and proceed to apply ourselves to it with little more preparation
than to Piers Ploughman, Douglas, or Chaucer, then I am per-
suaded its acquisition will require little time or labor. . . ."

1826

1 RYAN, RICHARD. <u>Poetry and Poets: Being a collection of the</u>
<u>choicest Anecdotes relative to the Poets of Every Age and</u>
<u>Nation. . . .</u> Vol. 2. London: Sherwood, Gilbert & Piper,
pp. 108-9.
A notice of "Roberte Langlande," drawn from Warton
(1774.2).

1830

1 BYRON, LORD GEORGE GORDON NOEL. <u>Letters and Journals of Lord</u>
<u>Byron with Notes of his life.</u> Vol. 1. Edited by Thomas
Moore. London: John Murray.
See Byron, 1807.1.

1832

*1 [LANGLAND, WILLIAM.] <u>The vision and the creed of Piers Plough-</u>
<u>man, newly imprinted.</u> [<u>With notes and a glossary by Thomas</u>
<u>Wright.</u>] 2 vols. London: W. Pickering.
Source: <u>National Union Catalogue</u>, vol. 315, p. 247.
See [Langland], 1842.3.

2 RICHARDSON, CHARLES. <u>A New Dictionary of the English Language.</u>
Vol. 1. London: William Pickering; New York: William
Jackson, pp. 51, 52, and passim.
Quotations illustrating meaning from the works of
"Gloucester, Brunne and Peers' Plouhman" are listed first.
"Then follow Wiclif, supported whenever possible, by an early
translator of the Bible; next, in rank and order, Chaucer and
Gower, free, as the great patriarchs of our speech, from any
intermixture with their successors." Hopes that the "uncouth
aspect" of the three earliest works cited will not "repulse
all literary readers from a perusal of the quotations."

1833

*1   [LANGLAND, WILLIAM.] <u>The vision and the creed of Piers Ploughman</u>,
      <u>newly imprinted</u>. London: n.p.
            Source: <u>National Union Catalogue</u>, vol. 315, p. 247.
      See [Langland], 1842.3.

1834

1   [WRIGHT, THOMAS.] "The Visions of Piers Plowman." <u>Gentleman's</u>
      <u>Magazine</u>, n.s. 1 (April):385-91.
            A review of Whitaker's edition (1813.1). Whitaker was
      correct in basing his edition on one MS, but selected his base
      MS for the wrong reasons and had access to only three MSS.
      There are two distinct classes of MSS and two widely different
      versions of the text. Whitaker erroneously believed he was
      presenting the poem in its first version; he assumed that the
      poem was later revised by the author. The reviewer has in-
      spected seven MSS: W, C, T, C^2, G (B-text), G (C-text), and
      F (C-text). Of these, the reviewer believes that the first
      five give the text of one version, the last two that of the
      other version, printed by Whitaker. Considers MS. W the best
      copy of the poem and collates a portion with Whitaker's text.
      Wright is incorrect in his classification of MS. T; it is
      clearly a mixed A-C-text that could have indicated to him the
      existence of a <u>third</u> version, the A-text, noted by Price
      (1824.1).

1836

1   ANON. <u>Testamenta Eboracensia or Wills registered at York</u>.
      Vol. 1. Publications of the Surtees Society, no. 4. London:
      J.B. Nichols; and William Pickering.
            See Bruge, 1395.1.

1837

1   BUCHANAN, DAVID. <u>Davidis Buchanani de Scriptoribus Scotis Libri</u>
      <u>Duo, nunc primum editi</u>. [Edited by David Irving.] Edinburgh:
      Balfour & Jack, for the Bannatyne Club.
            See Buchanan, ante 1652[?].1.

1838

1   GUEST, EDWIN. <u>A History of English Rhythms</u>. Vol. 2. London:
    William Pickering, pp. 162-65.
        Defends the unity of the poem, but asserts that "the
    execution of the work is certainly superior to its concep-
    tion." Tries to reconcile the conflicting biographical no-
    tices of the author by Bale (1557.1), Holinshed (1577.3),
    Stow (1580.1), and Wood (1674.1): Robert changed his name to
    John when he entered the monastery at Worcester. Langland was
    his name from the obscure farm where he was born; Malvern, the
    name of an important ecclesiastical center, was taken by him
    when he entered religion. Since Cleobury lies on the borders
    of Worcestershire, Wood's error in making him a native of that
    shire is understandable. Wille is not merely, as Ritson
    (1802.1) contended, a personification of the mental faculty,
    but a persona of the poet. Guest refers to two versions, that
    is, that printed by Whitaker (1813.1) and that identified by
    Price (1824.1). Agrees that this latter version, despite the
    lateness of MS H^2, shows an earlier version of the poem.

1841

1   D'ISRAELI, I. <u>Amenities of Literature consisting of Sketches and
    Characters of English Literature</u>. Vol. 1. London: Edward
    Moxon, pp. 293-305.
        The style of the poem, bearing no resemblance to that of
    Chaucer or Gower, suggests the poem may be earlier than their
    works; though it is possible that the author disdained their
    exotic fancies, Latinisms, Gallicisms, and Italianisms, and
    trivial rhymes, "that in every respect he might remain their
    astonishing contrast, with no inferiority of genius." Rejects
    the charge of Warton (1774.2) that Langland affected obsolete
    English. Criticizes the structure of the poem as "a heap of
    rhapsodies, without any artifice of connexion or involution of
    plot, or any sustained interest of one actor more than another
    among the numerous ideal beings who flit along the dreamy
    scenes." Sees the extended allegory as the "rudest" and "most
    insupportable" of poetic fictions, the product of an early
    period of society in which a poet was concerned more with "the
    passions of mankind than with individuals." Considers the
    episode of belling the cat proof that the author's emphasis on
    passive obedience to higher powers was motivated by prudence
    rather than a sense of duty.

1841

2   RIDLEY, NICHOLAS. The Works of Nicholas Ridley, D.D. Sometime
    Lord Bishop of London, Martyr 1555. Edited by Rev. Henry
    Christmas. Parker Society, no. 39. Cambridge: Cambridge
    University Press.
        See Turner, 1560-64[?].1.

                                1842

1   [BROWNING, ELIZABETH BARRETT.] "The Book of the Poets. Scott,
    Webster, & Geary." Athenæum (London), 4 June, p. 498.
        In a survey of English poets contained in a review of an
    anthology: "Then [after Layamon] Robert Langlande, the monk,
    walking for cloister 'by a wode's syde,' on the Malvern Hills,
    took counsel with his holy 'Plowman,' and sang of other vi-
    sions than their highest ridge can show. While we write, the
    woods upon those beautiful hills are obsolete, even as
    Langlande's verses; scarcely a shrub grows upon the hills!
    but it is well for the thinkers of England to remember rever-
    ently, while, taking thought of her poetry, they stand among
    the gorse,--that if we may boast now of more honored locali-
    ties . . . still our first holy poet-ground is there." These
    remarks were continued in Browning (1842.2) and collected in
    Browning (1871.1).

2   [BROWNING, ELIZABETH BARRETT.] "The Book of the Poets (Second
    Notice)." Athenæum (London), 11 June, p. 520.
        "Yet Langlande's 'Piers Plowman,' and Chaucer's 'House
    of Fame,' and Lydgate's 'Temple of Glass,' and the 'Pastyme of
    Pleasure,' by Stephen Hawes, are the four Columnar Marbles,
    the four allegorical poems, on whose foundation is exalted
    into light the great allegorical poem of the world, Spenser's
    'Faery Queen.'" Reprinted: Browning, 1871.1.

3   [LANGLAND, WILLIAM.] The Vision and the Creed of Piers Ploughman
    newly imprinted. 2 vols. Edited by Thomas Wright. London:
    William Pickering, xlix + 629 pp.
        On the basis of a note in MS. V (see c. 1400.1), Wright
    is not convinced of the traditional name of the author. Dates
    the poem 1362 or soon thereafter. The author was well
    acquainted with the satiric poems attributed to Walter Map;
    the poem shows the familiar satire directed against church and
    society now carried over into the vernacular. Combination of
    satire and allegory is a literary fashion established by the
    Roman de la Rose. In Piers Plowman, however, "the allegory
    follows no systematic plot, it is rather a succession of pic-
    tures in which the allegorical painting sometimes disappears
    altogether, than a whole like the Roman de la Rose, and it is

                                44

on that account less tedious to the modern reader, while the
vigorous descriptions, the picturesque ideas, and numerous
other beauties of different kinds, cause us to lose sight of
the general defects of this class of writing. Piers Ploughman
is, in fact, rather a succession of dreams, than one simple
vision." The author was neither a sower of discord nor a
heretic. The style of the MSS suggests the poem was not popular among the nobility. Compares the beginning of the poem in
this edition to that of Whitaker (1813.1); concludes that his
own text "was the one published by the author, and that the
variations were made by some other person, who was perhaps
induced by his own political sentiments to modify passages,
and was gradually led on to publish a revision of the whole."
Sees this "revision" as moderating the sentiments and the expression of the original. Rehearses criticisms of Whitaker's
edition (1813.1) as found in 1834.1. This edition based on
MS. W, "the best and oldest" of the MSS. The text is accompanied by notes and a glossary. For a revised edition, see
[Langland], 1856.1.

1844

1   CRAIK, GEO[RGE] L. Sketches of the History of Literature and
    Learning in England from the Norman Conquest to the Accession
    of Elizabeth. Vol. 1. London: Charles Knight & Co.,
    pp. 238-52.
        Praises Wright's edition (1842.3) and criticizes that of
    Whitaker (1813.1) as presenting a text "widely differing from
    the common one, and which has evidently no claim to the pref-
    erence with which [Whitaker] has honoured it."
        Describes the elementary form of verse in the poem as
    demanding four accented syllables, two in each half-line; but
    while each accented syllable in the first half-line is usually
    preceded by one or two unaccented syllables, and usually only
    one of those in the second half-line is so preceded, the sec-
    ond half-line is usually shorter. Moreover, it appears the
    general rule that in the second half-line only the first
    accented syllable should alliterate, though exceptions are
    common.
        Sees nothing of "Anti-Romanism" in Langland, and judges
    his anticlericism to be no more virulent than that of Chaucer
    and other popular writers of the fourteenth century. For
    Chaucer, the "puritanism" is one of the forms of the poetry;
    for Langland, "the poetry is principally a form or expression
    of the puritanism."

1847

1847

1   WINSTON, CHARLES. <u>An Inquiry into the Difference of Style Observ-</u>
    <u>able in Ancient Glass Paintings, Especially in England; with</u>
    Hints on Glass Painting. Vol. 1. Oxford and London: James
    Parker & Co., pp. 408-14.
        Extracts from the poem are brought forward to illustrate
    the practice of introducing armorial bearings on glass, and to
    show how figures in medieval glass-paintings may be considered
    as portraits.

1853

1   SCHELE De VERE, M. <u>Outlines of Comparative Philology</u>. New York:
    G.P. Putnam & Co., pp. 168-69.
        Finds that Robert Langland shows an astonishing famil-
    iarity with the forms and character of Anglo-Saxon language
    and poetry. That <u>Piers Plowman</u> is the "most obscure work of
    his age" is due more to the state of confusion and transition
    in which Langland found the language than it is to his own
    mode of thought. And the vehicle of veiled allegory was no
    doubt dictated by the necessity of the author to conceal his
    meaning from civil and ecclesiastical enemies. But the poem
    shows his overcoming of the difficulties involved in imitating
    earlier poetic models, the alliterative measure, and the un-
    couth Midland dialect. Notes that the Mercian dialect, which
    Langland apparently preferred, "appears visibly changed in the
    successive MS. copies that were made during the lifetime of the
    author, and thus show how, within the limits of one genera-
    tion, the language was improved and developed."

1855

1   ANON. <u>Testamenta Eboracensia: A Selection of Wills from the</u>
    <u>Registry at York</u>. Vol. 2. Publications of the Surtees
    Society, no. 30. Durham, London, and Edinburgh: Surtees
    Society.
        See Wyndhill, 1431.1.

2   DENTON, W. "Peart as a Pearmonger." <u>N&Q</u>, 1st ser. 11, no. 283
    (7 April):274.
        Correction of Wright's gloss (1842.3) of <u>peart</u>, defined
    here correctly as "open," "clear," or perhaps "straight-
    forward."

3   DENTON, W. "Piers Plowman's Visions." N&Q, 1st ser. 11, no. 285
     (14 April):280.
          Seeks allusions in works other than Piers Plowman to the
     practice of lesser nobility seeking privileges of citizenship
     through becoming apprentices (as explained by Wright, in
     [Langland], 1842.3, note to line 2979). Requests Sir Henry
     Ellis to publish his notes to the poem, which were used by
     Wright.

4   MILMAN, HENRY HART. History of Latin Christianity; including
     that of the Popes to the Pontificate of Nicolas V. Vol. 6.
     London: John Murray, pp. 536-44.
          Whereas Chaucer gives the voice of the court, the castle,
     and the city, and Wyclif that of the university, Langland of-
     fers that of a humble parson or secular priest. Neither a
     disciple nor a precursor of Wyclif, Langland believes in the
     Creed and reverence to the saints, apparently even in the Real
     Presence and Transubstantiation. Transcends his age in his
     moral feeling, his distrust of the efficacy of merely outward
     observances, his emphasis on reason and conscience as the
     guides of the soul, and his constant appeal to the simplest
     and plainest Christian truths. His satire condemns the clergy
     who fail to live up to their obligations. He is antipapal,
     yet can admire an ideal pope.
          Milman praises Langland as a poet and notes the low in-
     cidence of French words in the poem. Sees the poet's use of
     allegory as a reflection of "the awakening moral sense of men,
     weary of the saints, and angels, and devils, delight[ing] in
     those impersonalities of the unchristian vices and Christian
     virtues." Considers the end of the poem to be neither the
     actual nor the intended conclusion: Langland may have broken
     off in despondency and left the poem unfinished; or may have
     been prevented from finishing; or, less probably, the end may
     have been lost.
          Milman in general depends on the text of the "learned"
     Whitaker (1813.1), although he refers to Wright's edition
     (1842.3). His comments are excerpted by Skeat, in Langland,
     1886.1.

1856

1   [LANGLAND, WILLIAM.] The Vision and Creed of Piers Ploughman
     edited, from a contemporary manuscript, with a historical
     introduction, notes, and a glossary, by Thomas Wright. 2d ed.
     rev. 2 vols. London: John Russell Smith, xl + 621 pp.
          The introduction and text are a reprint of [Langland],
     1842.3; the notes and glossary are revised.

1857

1857

1 PICCOPE, G.J., ed. <u>Lancashire and Cheshire Wills and Inventories</u>
   <u>from the Ecclesiastical Court, Chester</u>. Vol. 1. Chetham Society Publications, no. 33. [Manchester]: Chetham Society.
   See Brereton, 1558.1.

1858

1 ANON. <u>New England Historical and Genealogical Register</u> 12, no. 4
   (October).
   See Dudley, 1657.1.

2 SILVERSTONE. "The Vision of Pierce Plowman." <u>N&Q</u>, 2d ser. 6,
   no. 142 (18 September):229-30.
   See Anon., 1577.1.

1860

1 MARSH, GEORGE P. <u>Lectures on the English Language (First Se-</u>
   <u>ries)</u>. New York: Charles Scribner; London: Sampson Low,
   Son & Co., pp. 111, 124, 168, 422.
         Shows through comparison of the <u>General Prologue</u> and
   <u>Piers Plowman</u> that Langland used words of Latin and French
   derivation in a proportion at least as large as did Chaucer.
   Finds that Chaucer's style, judged by either an Anglo-Saxon
   or a modern English standard, is as idiomatic as that of
   Langland. Concludes from the differences in grammar, vocabulary, and orthography of the texts presented by Whitaker
   (1813.1) and Wright (1842.3) "that it is quite unreasonable
   to refer the two recensions to one writer, and it is by no
   means improbable that both are unlike the author's original."
   Marsh's doubt of single authorship was enlisted by Manly
   (1916.3). Regarding Marsh's remarks on Langland's vocabulary,
   see Marsh, 1862.1.

1861

1 [WARWICK, W.] "Medieval English Literature (No. 1): Piers
   Plowman." <u>National Review</u> 13 (October):273-308.
         <u>Piers Plowman</u> is the earliest major medieval work of any
   value, written by a "truly original" author about whom not
   much can be known for certain, but who probably was a monk and
   was educated at a university. The poem's subject is the condition of society; its aim--in which it transcends mere

satire--is to reform society through exposure of its misdeeds,
moral and religious exhortation, and exposition of scripture.
The plan of the work is exceedingly faulty, and the poem is
filled with the incongruities and forced resemblances inherent
to allegory. The poem's development is needlessly obscure and
complicated, its conclusion unsatisfactory. The figure of
Piers Plowman in particular points up the limitations of the
work: he appears as an allegorical reformer, and "is continually on the scene doing or saying something," but his
effect on the action is slight; "and, indeed, there is hardly
any action in the poem, in the critical sense of action."

1862

1 MARSH, GEORGE P. The Origin and History of the English Language,
and of the Early Literature it Embodies. New York: Charles
Scribner, 295-338.
        The poem was written 1360-70, probably by a clerk who
voiced sentiments "almost universally felt, though dimly ap-
prehended," and thus prepared the nation for the message of
Wyclif. The author knew the works of Walter Map, but his poem
is original in the sense that the American Declaration of
Independence, voicing popular sentiment, is nevertheless the
original work of Jefferson. Because of the poem's popular
subject matter, copyists took a license with the text that
they did not take with the work of Chaucer or Gower; this
scribal rather than authorial revision probably accounts for
the variations in the poem among the MSS.
        The poem shows little unity of plan. This is no defect,
however, since it takes the form of a calm allegorical exposition of religious and social life, designed to reveal the true
causes of evil and secure their correction through the force
of moral influence rather than violent resistance. Nevertheless, the poem is well calculated to "suggest opinions which
itself did not openly profess"; and its readers might have
been expected to recognize the need for stronger measures of
reform. Notes the humor in the poem, which is a fruit of a
society's development beyond warfare and hunting. The poem
shows little knowledge of romance literature, but exhibits a
proportion of Anglo-Norman vocabulary as large as Chaucer's,
proving that a large infusion of French words had by this time
been incorporated into the common language of England, instead
of being first introduced by the poets. Cf. Marsh, 1860.1.

1864

1   MORLEY, HENRY. <u>English Writers</u>. Vol. 1, <u>The Writers before</u>
     <u>Chaucer</u>. London: Chapman & Hall, pp. 757-67.
             The poem is not strictly the work of an active follower
     of Wyclif, though written by a man of Wyclif's mind. The poet
     is one of vivid imagination, who blends the Anglo-Saxon poetic
     manner with fourteenth-century courtly taste and speaks in
     well-sustained and often subtle allegories, "always embodying
     the purest aspirations." The argument of the poem is summa-
     rized at length.

1866

1   [LANGLAND, WILLIAM.] <u>Parallel Extracts from Twenty-nine Manu-</u>
     <u>scripts of Piers Plowman, with Comments, and a proposal for</u>
     <u>the Society's three-text edition of this poem</u>. By the Rev.
     Walter W. Skeat. Early English Text Society, o.s. 17.
     London: N. Trübner, 16 pp.
             Prints a specimen text (Wright, 1856.1, lines 1508-29)
     as found in twenty-nine MSS. Demonstrates the existence of
     three separate texts, referred to as "Vernon," "Crowley," and
     "Whitaker," respectively. Indicates major variations of the
     "Crowley" and "Whitaker" versions, and includes a table to
     show the variation in the arrangement of passūs. This work is
     superseded by its revised and enlarged edition, [Langland],
     1885.2.

1867

1   ANON. "Notes on Books, Etc." <u>N&Q</u>, 3d ser. 12, no. 301
     (5 October):280.
             Notice of Skeat's edition of the A-text; see [Langland],
     1867.3.

2   HOSKYNS-ABRAHALL, JOHN. "William de Langland: Stacy de
     Rokayle." <u>N&Q</u>, 3d ser. 11, no. 280 (11 May):388.
             Answer to Skeat (1867.5): Shipton under Whichwode is
     four miles NNW of Burford, seven miles SSW of Chipping Norton.
     See also Hoskyns-Abrahall, 1868.1.

3   LANGLAND, WILLIAM. The Vision of William concerning Piers
     Plowman, together with Vita de Dowel, Dobet, et Dobest,
     Secundum Wit et Resoun, by William Langland (about 1362-
     1380 A.D.) Edited from Numerous Manuscripts, with Prefaces,
     Notes and a Glossary, by the Rev. Walter W. Skeat, M.A.
     Vol. 1, The "Vernon" Text; or Text A. Early English Text
     Society, o.s. 28. London: Trübner, xliii + 158 pp.
         The first edition of the A-text, based on MS. V to A
     XI 180, and on MS. T from A XI 181-303. Besides these two
     MSS, Skeat has made use of A-text MSS. H, U, H^2, D, and A; he
     has chosen to reject from consideration for establishing the
     text MSS. L, H^3, and K. MSS. T, H, and U are collated as far
     as they go; D for the Prol, I-IV, and selectively afterwards;
     H^2 up until II 146, then sporadically, then throughout IX, X,
     and XI; MS. A supplies occasional readings.
         Describes the poem as taking no less than five different
     shapes in the MSS, representing three separate authorial ver-
     sions of the poem. He reviews the scant evidence noticed by
     earlier writers of the first version, the "Vernon" or A-text,
     and describes the ten MSS of the A-text known to him. Con-
     cludes that the A-text contained no more than eleven passūs,
     though three of the A-text MSS supplement this version with
     the C-text. The insufficiency of these scribal attempts to
     conclude a poem left unfinished by its author is seen clearly
     in the failure to reconcile different systems of numbering the
     passūs as well as in the difference in the arrangement of sub-
     ject matter in the two versions. But the evidence of the MSS
     suggests also that what we call the poem is in fact two dis-
     tinct works, with different titles and separate prologues:
     The Vision of William concerning Piers the Plowman and Vita de
     dowel, dobet, et dobest secundum wit de resoun. The argument
     for authorship is briefly reviewed, and the name William
     Langland accepted as most probable. The A-text was almost
     certainly begun in 1362, the Vita de dowel, dobet, et dobest
     perhaps begun late that same year or early 1363. The mention
     of John Chichester as mayor of London dates the composition of
     the later passūs of the B-text post 1370, perhaps as late as
     1375-76. The C-text was probably written 1379-80. That most
     of the revised versions are due to the author is apparent from
     the high quality of the poetry and the author's peculiar style.
     The text of this edition is reprinted, and the prefaces and
     notes revised and included, in Langland, 1886.1. This edition
     of 1867 was reprinted as [Langland], 1968.6.

1867

4 MORRIS, R., ed. Specimens of Early English. Selected from the
   Chief English Authors A.D. 1250-A.D. 1400 with Grammatical
   Introduction, Notes, and Glossary. Oxford: Clarendon Press,
   pp. 249-90.
        Selections from the poem printed from MS. V (A-text),
   included here as the first sizable printing of the A-text;
   though the notes give no idea of Morris's thoughts on the
   number of different versions of the poem.

5 SKEAT, WALTER W. "William de Langland: Stacy de Rokayle." N&Q,
   3d ser. 11, no. 276 (13 April):296.
        Queries the location of "Schiptone under Whichwode,"
   mentioned in annotation of MS. V (C-text). See Anon.,
   c. 1400.1, and Hoskyns-Abrahall, 1867.2.

6 SKEAT, WALTER W. "Lucifer." N&Q, 3d ser. 12, no. 293
   (10 August):110.
        Early literary attestations, including that of A I
   109 ff., of Lucifer as Satan, often with his habitation in
   the north. Reprinted: Skeat, 1896.2.

1868

1 HOSKYNS-ABRAHALL, JOHN. "The Author of 'Piers Plowman.'"
   Athenæum (London), 27 June, p. 902.
        Supplements his earlier identification of Shipton under
   Whichwode (1867.2) with references in the area to Langley
   Farm, Little Langley, and Langley Wood.

2 [PERCY, THOMAS.] Bishop Percy's Folio Manuscript. Ballads and
   Romances. Vol. 3. Edited by John W. Hales and Frederick J.
   Furnivall. London: N. Trübner & Co., p. xxxix.
        In his comments on Percy's remarks on the alliterative
   measure of Piers Plowman, Skeat rejects Percy's contention
   that the anapest is the basis of the English alliterative line
   and the French Alexandrine.

3 SKEAT, WALTER W. "William Longland, the Author of 'Piers
   Plowman.'" Athenæum (London), 13 June, pp. 832-33.
        Identification of the poet's surname from B XV 148, "I
   have lyved in lond quod I My name is Longe-wille." (Wright's
   edition, [1842.3], had read quod he.)

1869

1   PUTTENHAM, GEORGE. The Arte of English Poesie. (June?) 1589.
     Edited by Edward Arber. English Reprints, vol. 7. London:
     published by the editor.
          See Puttenham[?], 1589.1, and Puttenham, 1970.14.

2   LANGLAND, WILLIAM. The Vision of William concerning Piers the
     Plowman, together with Vita de Dowel, Dobet, et Dobest,
     Secundum Wit et Resoun, by William Langland (about 1362-
     1380 A.D.). Edited from Numerous Manuscripts with Prefaces,
     Notes and a Glossary, by the Rev. Walter W. Skeat, M.A.
     Vol. 2, The "Crowley" Text; or Text B. Early English Text
     Society, o.s. 38. London: N. Trübner, lvi + 427 pp.
          An edition of the B-text, based on MS. L and under com-
     parison with MSS. R, W, Y, M, O, C^2, Hm, C, Bo, Bm, Cot, F,
     and Cr. Skeat in general prints from MS. L, which he consid-
     ers to be probably the author's autograph, marked for correc-
     tion in his own hand, with the chief additions to the text
     from MS. R. He separates eleven of the MSS into subgroups as
     follows: LR; YCBoBmCot; OC^2; WCr; and as regards the rela-
     tionships of the other MSS, Skeat does not commit himself.
          Dates the B-text 1376-77 on the basis of the added im-
     portance the fable of belling the cat receives if Richard were
     already to have ascended the throne; a seeming reference
     (B III 299-349) to the royal jubilee; another one to the out-
     cry against John of Gaunt in 1377; and the absence of any
     reference to the papal schism.
          Notes the high degree of agreement among MSS of the
     B-text, terming it from the standpoint of "integrity" of the
     text the best of the three versions. Notes the mixture of
     dialectical forms of MS. L (and presumably of the speech of
     the author), but does not attempt to place the dialect con-
     clusively. Offers a convenient table of allusions to the
     author himself, to places, and to historical events found in
     the poem; a summary of the argument and corrections to
     Wright's second edition, [Langland], 1856.1. The text of the
     poem is accompanied by a running paraphrase, and is followed
     by critical notes on various readings of the MSS and the chief
     results of collation with Crowley's first edition (1550.1).
     An appendix prints a short glossary to the poem, found in
     MS. C^2. For explanatory notes to the Prologue and first
     seven passūs, see Langland, 1869.3, later expanded in
     Langland, 1885.2 and Langland, 1886.1. Skeat's edition of
     the B-text is reviewed by [Pearson], 1870.2. Edition re-
     printed 1972.10.

1869

3   LANGLAND, WILLIAM. The Vision of William concerning Piers the
    Plowman by William Langland (or Langley) According to the
    Version Revised and Enlarged by the Author about A.D. 1377.
    Edited by the Rev. Walter W. Skeat. Oxford: Clarendon Press,
    xlviii + 211 pp.
        An edition with introduction, selected bibliography,
    explanatory notes, and glossary to the Prologue and passūs
    I-VII of the B-text. This text has passed through ten edi-
    tions (tenth edition, 1923, often reprinted).

4   SKEAT, WALTER W. "Final -e in Early English." N&Q, 4th ser. 3,
    no. 62 (6 March):215-16.
        The scribe of MS. C (B-text) shows attention to final -e
    in his transcription of the poem, a fact that is worthy of
    note in alliterative poetry, where one syllable more or less
    in a line is seldom of consequence. Reprinted: Skeat, 1896.2.

5   SKEAT, WALTER W. "Did Adam and Eve Fall into the Sea?" N&Q,
    4th ser. 3, no. 64 (20 March):275.
        Adam and Eve's falling into the "sea" of this world
    (B VIII 40) is noted with reference to a similar idea ex-
    pressed by Phillipe de Thaon. Reprinted: Skeat, 1896.2.

6   SKEAT, WALTER W. "An Error in Fabyan's Chronicles." N&Q, 4th
    ser. 4, no. 86 (21 August):152-53.
        The reign of Edward III is wrongly calculated in
    Fabyan's Chronicle. In his edition of the A-text (1867.3),
    Skeat had declared incorrect Langland's reference to 1370 as
    Chichester's year of mayoralty; here he corrects the error.
    Reprinted: Skeat, 1896.2.

                                1870

1   LOWELL, JAMES RUSSELL. "Chaucer." North American Review 111,
    no. 228 (July):155-98 (Langland treated on pp. 179-82).
        Piers Plowman is the best example of popular poetry,
    containing all the simpler elements of poetry "but still in
    solution, not crystallised around any thread of artistic pur-
    pose." The poem is seen as possessing a "surly honesty,"
    preferring the "downright to the gracious," and employing
    speech "as a tool" rather than as "a musical instrument."
    Compared with Chaucer, Langland is diffuse, garrulous, and
    full of rustic shrewdness, rather than bonhomie.

1871

2 [PEARSON, CHARLES HENRY.] "Contemporary Literature." North
    British Review, o.s. 52 (n.s. 13) (April):211-322 (A review
    article by various hands; Pearson is responsible for the sec-
    tion on Piers Plowman, pp. 241-45).
        Skeat's edition of the B-text (1869.2) seems "almost
    flawless." Agrees with Skeat's rejection of any Oxford con-
    nection with the author. Suggests, however, that the accounts
    of Bale (1557.1) mentioning Cleobury Mortimer (Shropshire) and
    that of the annotation of MS. C (C-text) mentioning Shipton
    under Whichwode (Oxfordshire) can be reconciled: The poet's
    surname was probably Langley, rather than Langland, which is a
    name not found in the Midlands. Forming part of the manor of
    Acton Burnel in Shropshire are two hamlets, Langley and
    Ruckley, the latter of which was written Rokele in the four-
    teenth century. The Langleys in Oxfordshire connected with
    Wychwood forest are documented from 1213 to 1362, though there
    is nothing to connect subsequent heirs to the Langley Oxford-
    shire holdings with an Shropshire family. Hence it would ap-
    pear that the Langley identified in MS. C was a subtenant of
    the Burnels. Langleys at Langley are shown to be ·connected
    with the Burnels and with the Rokesly family at Ruckley; and
    Burnels were connected with Shipton under Whichwode through
    marriage with the Despensers, one of whom, Hugh le Despenser,
    seized the manor there.

3 SKEAT, WALTER W. "The Sun: Its Gender." N&Q, 4th ser. 5,
    no. 107 (15 January):75.
        The sun is almost always feminine in early English lit-
    erature, as exemplified in B XVIII 56. Reprinted: Skeat,
    1896.2.

4 WEBBE, WILLIAM. A Discourse of English Poetrie. 1586. Edited
    by Edward Arber. Early English Reprints, vol. 12. London:
    published by the editor.
        See Webbe, 1586.1.

                              1871

1 BROWNING, ELIZABETH BARRETT. Life, Letters and Essays of
    Elizabeth Barrett Browning. Vol. 2, The Book of the Poets.
    New York: James Miller.
        Collects and reprints with minor revisions [Browning],
    1842.1 and 1842.2 and her subsequent essays on the English
    poets.

1871

2   LOWELL, JAMES RUSSELL. "Chaucer." In <u>My Study Windows</u>. Boston:
     J.R. Osgood & Co., pp. 205-62 (Langland treated on pp. 228-38).
             Reprinted: Lowell, 1966.9. An expanded version of
     Lowell, 1870.1. Langland has as much tenderness as Chaucer,
     as much interest in life's variety and contempt for hypocrisy,
     and almost an equal sense of fun. But he is more diffuse and
     garrulous. It is the difference between rustic shrewdness
     and refined <u>bonhomie</u>, sly fun and broad, deep humor.

1873

1   ADDIS, JOHN. "Chaucer's Ploughman and Piers Ploughman." <u>N&Q</u>,
     4th ser. 11, no. 275 (5 April):280-81.
             Questions whether Chaucer took the Plowman of the
     <u>General Prologue</u> from <u>Piers Plowman</u>, for the plowman was a
     traditional type of the good man from as early as Ælfric's
     <u>Colloquy</u>.

2   ADDIS, JOHN. "Piers the Plowman." <u>N&Q</u>, 4th ser. 12, no. 292
     (2 August):96.
             The notion that the author was a priest seems to have
     arisen from his scriptural knowledge; but there are many
     lapses in this. Cites the Letter of John Ball as support that
     <u>shepe</u> in B Prol 2 means "shepherd."

3   DOWE, WILLIAM. "Piers the Ploughman." <u>N&Q</u>, 4th ser. 12, no. 300
     (27 September):252.
             Relates <u>shepe</u> (B Prol 2) to OE <u>scop</u> and words in other
     languages denoting "poet." Relates <u>Piers Plowman</u> to the Irish
     <u>Forus Folamain</u>, meaning a "dissertation or history by a
     teacher or priest."

4   "F." "Piers Plowman's Hot Pies and Pigs." <u>N&Q</u>, 4th ser. 11,
     no. 278 (26 April):342.
             Comparison of B Prol 225-26 with Jonson's <u>Bartholomew
     Fair</u> shows that in 1641 pigs and hot pies were still cheap
     fare, but that geese were no longer mentioned as such.

5   LANGLAND, WILLIAM. <u>The Vision of William concerning Piers the
     Plowman, together with Vita de Dowel, Dobet, et Dobest,
     Secundum Wit et Resoun, by William Langland (about 1362-
     1393 A.D.)</u>. Edited from Numerous Manuscripts, with Prefaces,
     Notes, and a Glossary, by the Rev. Walter W. Skeat. Vol. 3,
     <u>The "Whitaker" Text; or Text C</u>. Early English Text Society,
     o.s. 54. London: N. Trübner & Co., cxxviii + 536 pp.
             An edition of the C-text, based on MS. P (the same MS
     used by Whitaker, 1813.1). Besides P, Skeat describes the

following MSS.: E, Z, I, T, H^2, D^2, Bo, O, L, M, F, S, G, K, D, Y, N, V, R, P^2, and W. He separates the MSS into five sub-classes thus: PEZSGVR (subclass a); IYDTH^{2}D^{2}BoOL (subclass b); K (subclass e); M (subclass d); and F (subclass e). He considers the text of subclass b a slightly earlier form than that of subclass a; c an intermediate form between a and b; d closer to a than to b; and e varying widely from both a and b. MSS N, P^2, and W are not classified. MS. P is collated with E, I, M, F, and S throughout, and with Bo, T, K, and G occasionally.

Whitaker's edition and its limitations are described in detail, though Whitaker himself is praised for his enthusiasm and diligence. The poem is dated by Skeat as between 1393 and 1398 on the basis of what he takes to be an allusion to out-spoken criticism of Richard II by his subjects in C IV 203 ff., and the fact that the poem appears to have been written before Richard the Redeless, dated 1399, and assumed by Skeat also to have been Langland's work.

Agreement of MSS of the C-text is not as close as that of MSS of the B-text, and the C-text in general is inferior to the B-text in vigor and compactness. But the C-text is the fullest of Langland's versions, the most carefully finished, and is evidently intended as a final form of the poem, as is indicated in the minute corrections in the last two passūs. We may prefer the B-text, but we must remember that the C-text is the "best possible commentary upon it."

Skeat prints a table of allusions in the poem, to the author himself, to places, and to circumstances; and he re-marks on the addition in this version of an interesting auto-biographical passage, while certain allusions to places and events have been changed or expunged. He tabulates the divi-sion into passūs of the three versions and lists the passages original to the C-text. The argument of the poem is summa-rized, and the text presented with both a running paraphrase and side-note references to the A- and B-texts, Langland, 1867.3 and 1869.2. The text is followed by critical notes, largely concerned with Whitaker's readings. The volume also contains Skeat's edition of Richard the Redeless and The Crowned King, the latter of which is included as representing an early imitation of Piers Plowman. Explanatory notes to the C-text are to be found in Langland, 1885.2 and 1886.1. The Early English Text Society editions are reviewed by Lounsbury (1875.2) and Jusserand (1879.1). This edition of the C-text reprinted: Langland, 1978.13.

1873

6   LECHLER, GOTTHARD. <u>Johann von Wiclif und die Vorgeschichte der
    Reformation</u>. Leipzig: Verlag von Friedrich Fleischer;
    London: Williams & Norgate, pp. 244-55.
        Stresses the popular aspects of the poem--the integrity
    of the peasant, the use of the husbandman as an image of the
    Redeemer, the employment of the native alliterative measure.
    Finds the importance of the poem in its satire of the sins of
    the clergy of all levels, which had the effect of advancing
    the work of reform. Admits, however, that the author was
    neither a heretic nor a revolutionary. Translated as Lechler,
    1878.1.

7   PURTON, WILLIAM. "Piers the Plowman." <u>N&Q</u>, 4th ser. 11, no. 286
    (21 June):500-501.
        Argues that Prol 1-4 means that the author put on
    "sheep's clothing," that is, his monk's frock, and that he
    went out like a hermit who was unholy of works.

8   PURTON, WILLIAM. "Piers the Plowman." <u>N&Q</u>, 4th ser. 12, no. 303
    (18 October):309-11.
        Suggests Langland was a friar, since there was an
    Augustinian foundation at the Woodhouse, within three miles of
    Cleobury Mortimer, within his time; and because friars, like
    Will, wore russet and were more antipapal, more on the side of
    popular causes, than the priests. Calls attention to the ham-
    lets of Upper and Lower Langley near Cleobury Mortimer.

9   SKEAT, WALTER W. "Piers the Plowman." <u>N&Q</u>, 4th ser. 12, no. 288
    (15 July):11.
        In a reply to Purton (1873.7), argues for "shepherd"
    rather than "sheep," though admits the latter is possible.
    Reminds readers that the poet was dressed like a hermit, not
    like a monk. Cites the authentic C-text reading (Prol 2)
    "shepherd" in support of his argument.

10 SKEAT, WALTER W. "Piers the Plowman." <u>N&Q</u>, 4th ser. 12, no. 303
    (18 October):309.
        The "absurdities" and "nonsense" of Dowe (1873.3) are
    unmasked.

11 SKEAT, WALTER W. "Piers the Plowman." <u>N&Q</u>, 4th ser. 12, no. 304
    (25 October):338.
        Thanks Purton for his local notes (see 1873.8); asserts
    that it is certain from the poem that Langland was not a
    friar.

1874

1   BERNARD, EMIL. Grammatical Treatise on the Language of William
     Langland preceded by a sketch of his life and his poem Piers
     the Plowman. Dissertation, Rheinische Friedrich-Wilhelms-
     Universität zu Bonn. Bonn: Carl Georgi, 94 pp.
          Study of the language of the poem, based on Skeat's
     Early English Text Society editions (Langland, 1867.3, 1869.2,
     and 1873.5). Accepts Skeat's arguments on the chronology and
     dialect of the texts, and assembles a "biography" of the poet
     from allusions in the poem: Langland was the son of a free
     man or franklin, probably took minor orders, married a woman
     named "Kytte," had apparently studied the law, and so on.
     Describes Langland's language with reference to vowels, conso-
     nants, inflections, pronouns, numerals, adverbs, and verbs.
     Stresses the "peculiar quaintness" of Langland's style and
     form: whereas Chaucer's polished language was intended for
     refined ears, Langland writes for the comprehension of all.
     His language for the most part is pure and simple and without
     coarse expressions. But because he wishes to improve national
     morals, he sometimes describes the vices he would warn his
     audience against.

1875

1   GREEN, J.R. A Short History of the English People. London:
     Macmillan & Co., pp. 248-51.
          Sees the poem as a reflection of the social and religious
     awakening of the age, in particular of the misery of the
     peasant and the protest of Lollardry. Comparison of Piers
     Plowman and the Tales of Canterbury reveals the "social chasm"
     that separates rich and poor in fourteenth-century England.
     Langland lacks the human sympathy of Chaucer, his delight in
     the world around him, and his delicate irony. Occasional
     flashes of common sense and Hogarthian humor relieve the
     cumbrous allegory of Piers Plowman. Langland seems devoid of
     hope; the conclusion of the poem is one of terrible despair.

2   LOUNSBURY, THOMAS R. "Langland's Vision of Piers Plowman." New
     Englander 34, no. 2:274-85.
          Review of Skeat's editions (Langland 1867.3, 1869.2,
     1873.5). Considers Skeat's work to have superseded all pre-
     vious editions of the poem. Agrees with Skeat regarding the
     chronological series A-text, B-text, C-text, though he would
     not extend the possible date of composition of the B-text much
     beyond 1377. Sees the poem as an unequaled representation of
     the social and political conditions of the times, full of

1875

striking juxtapositions of high thoughts and everyday details,
composed by one whose seriousness, earnestness, aversion to
even the occasion of sin, and occasional intolerance are puri-
tanical. Langland makes explicit the cynicism that one can
often infer from Chaucer, and seems to have lost sight of
those recuperative forces operating to counteract the forces
of destruction in his society. The defects of the poem are
the product of its form as a series of visions, its tiresome
allegory, and its quaint expression produced by the constraint
of alliteration. Cf. Warton, 1774.2.

3 PURTON, WILLIAM. "The Author of Piers the Plowman." N&Q, 5th
ser. 3, no. 74 (29 May):422-24.
       Aims to substantiate Purton (1873.8): C XII suggests
that Langland was associated with the friars; he could have
resided at Woodhouse without taking orders, had he been rich.
"W." found after the poet's signature in some MSS probably
stands for "Woodhousie."

1877

1 BRINK, BERNHARD ten. Geschichte der Englischen Literatur.
Vol. 1, Bis zu Wiclifs Auftreten. Berlin: Verlag von Robert
Oppenheim, pp. 440-60.
       Compared with Richard Rolle, Langland seems more humane
and socially oriented; yet unlike Dante, he has no comprehensive theory of life. Langland was familiar with scripture and
the work of the Fathers, and was acquainted with Juvenal,
moralists like Dionysius Cato, the Roman de la Rose, Tournoi-
ment de l'anticrist, Grossteste's Castel d'amour, and the
works of medieval preachers and satirists. The revisions of
the poem reflect the progress of religious agitation; the B-
text in particular increases prophetic passages dealing with
apocalyptic and reformational topics. Though Langland nowhere
utters an unorthodox doctrine, he is one with Wyclif in his
ethical concern and his distinguishing of the Church of Christ
from its outward form. The reformers of the sixteenth century
were correct, therefore, in seeing him as a forerunner of the
Reformation. Translated as Brink, 1883.1.

2 LANGLAND, WILLIAM. The Vision of William concerning Piers
Plowman, together with Vita de Dowel, Dobet, et Dobest, and
Richard the Redeles. Edited by Walter W. Skeat. Part 4,
section 1, Notes to Texts A, B, and C. Early English Text
Society, o.s. 67. London: N. Trübner & Co., 512 + *137-
*144 pp.

Notes to Langland, 1867.3, 1869.2, and 1873.5, incorporating much of the material in the notes of Langland, 1869.3.
In two sections, with the first section devoted to the explanatory notes (based on C-text lines, but collated with A- and
B-lines); a table of the division into passūs according to
page numbers in the editions of Wright (1842.3), Whitaker
(1813.1), and Skeat (1869.2 and 1873.5); and various indices
treating subjects and words discussed in the notes, books referred to by the editor, quotations made by the author arranged by source, and works the author appears to have known
well. Pages *137-*144 supplement Langland, 1866.1, by printing (with notes) newly discovered lines of A XII from MS. R.
For the second section of the present work, see Langland,
1884.2.

3   MORLEY, HENRY. <u>Illustrations of English Religion</u>. London,
Paris, and New York: Cassell, Petter & Galpin, pp. 77-102.
Interpretive summary of the poem, which Morley sees as
addressed to the whole English nation, regarding the material
condition of the country insofar as this topic concerned its
spiritual life. The poem is praised as a fervent expression
of the Christian task to bring men to God in advocating both
love as the fulfillment of the Law, and labor. Langland is a
Christian reformer in the truest sense, in that he seeks to
strengthen the power of the clergy by the improvement of those
who are untrue to their vocation. Considers Langland orthodox
in doctrine, but ready to expose a wicked life, be it of pope
or peasant.

4   ROSENTHAL, FRIEDRICH. <u>Die alliterierende englische Langzeile im
XIV. Jahrhundert</u>. Dissertation, Leipzig. Halle: E. Karras,
vi + 46 pp.
Description of the alliterative form of <u>Piers Plowman</u>
and seven other poems, including <u>Pierce the Plowman's Creed</u>,
<u>Richard the Redeless</u>, <u>The Crowned King</u>, and <u>Sir Gawain and the
Green Knight</u>. With regard to <u>Piers Plowman</u>, tabulates deviations from the normal alliterative pattern in all three versions under the following categories: more than two alliterating letters in the first half-line; more than one alliterating letter in the second half-line; absence of the first alliterating letter; absence of the second alliterating letter;
absence of the third alliterating letter; lines in which there
are two different alliterating letters; lines in which words
beginning with <u>h</u> alliterate with words beginning with a vowel,
and where <u>s</u> alliterates with <u>sch</u> or <u>sh</u>, <u>v</u> with <u>f</u>, <u>v</u> with <u>w</u>,
<u>f</u> with <u>w</u>, <u>c</u> (or <u>k</u>) with <u>ch</u>, <u>g</u> with <u>c</u> (or <u>k</u>); and lines without
any alliteration. Substantially reprinted: Rosenthal,
1878.2. Skeat, in Langland 1884.2, reproduces Rosenthal's
tables, with minor corrections.

1878

1878

1 LECHLER, GOTTHARD. John Wiclif and His English Precursors.
  Translated by Peter Lormier. London: C. Kegan Paul & Co.
      A translation, with additional notes, of Lechler,
  1873.6.

2 ROSENTHAL, F. "Die alliterierende englische Langzeile im
  14. Jahrhundert." Anglia 1:414-59.
      See Rosenthal, 1877.4.

3 ROSSETTI, WILLIAM MICHAEL. Lives of Famous Poets. A Companion
  Volume to the Series Moxon's Popular Poets. London:
  E. Moxon, Son, & Co., p. 3.
      Judges that there was not a single authentically great
  English writer of prose or poetry before the time of Chaucer
  and his older contemporary William Langland. Mentions
  Langland along with Chaucer, "not indeed as indicating that
  Langland shares with Chaucer in so great a splendour, but in
  order that we might not leave unmentioned the writer who,
  before Chaucer's prime, and in so close proximity to him and
  to the influences which moulded him, had already succeeded in
  distancing all predecessors, and in leaving a lasting bequest
  to his posterity of English readers, and to ours."

1879

1 JUSSERAND, J.J. Review of Walter W. Skeat's Vision of William
  Concerning Piers the Plowman, by W. Langland. Notes to Texts
  A, B and C. Revue critique d'histoire et de littérature,
  n.s. 7:313-19.
      Amidst general praise of Skeat's editions and notes
  (Langland, 1867.3, 1869.2, 1873.5, and 1877.2), takes issue
  with Skeat's dating of the B-text after the accession of
  Richard II. Interprets the cat in the fable of belling the
  cat as Edward III at the time when the Black Prince was either
  dead or dying, and sees Richard, the heir presumptive, as the
  "younger cat" whose coming is feared by one of the rats. Excesses of Edward implicitly alluded to include the poll tax of
  1377 and his encouragement of Parliament in 1377 to reverse
  the reforms of the Good Parliament of 1376. Langland writes
  in the hope that Edward III will restore good relations with
  the Commons. Moreover, the C-text does not make any direct
  allusion to Richard II; and if Langland appears to have introduced criticisms of the new government, they are criticisms
  that fit equally well the days of Edward III. The criticisms

made here are responded to by Skeat in Langland, 1884.2; also cf. Jusserand, 1933.4.

1880

1   HOPKINS, GERARD MANLEY. Letter to Robert Bridges, 5 September 1880. In The Letters of Gerard Manley Hopkins to Robert Bridges. Edited by Claude Colleer Abbott. Oxford: Oxford University Press, 1935, pp. 107-8.
    In a response to correspondence of Bridges either lost or destroyed, apparently treating the meters of lines longer than ten syllables, Hopkins writes: "So far as I know triple time is in English verse a shy and late thing. I have not studied Piers Ploughman and so cannot pronounce how far triple time is boldly employed in it; at least it must have been suggested. But on the Romance side of our versification triple time appeared, I think, late. It may have been suggested by Piers Ploughman's rhythm, as I have said, but partly I conjecture it arose from a simple misunderstanding or misreading of Chaucer and the verse of that date and thereabouts." Judges that Chaucer's final -e was misread as a syllable to be counted in the scansion, and led, as a result, to the doggerel verse of Ralph Roister Doister, for example. Suggests that the older poetry should be read as couplets with a pause dividing each line, on either side of which there are two or three or perhaps even more stresses, and in a rhythm that varies from iambic to anapestic. Feels that the cæsura had come into English versification on the one hand from Piers Plowman and on the other from French Alexandrines and ten-syllable lines. See Hopkins, 1882.2.

2   LANIER, SIDNEY. The Science of English Verse. New York: Charles Scribner's Sons, pp. 163-66.
    Sees the predominant measure of the poem in a bar ⅜♪♪♪, with the rhythmic accent at the second time-unit of the bar instead of at the first, as it is in Old English poetry. Reprinted: Lanier, 1945.3.

1881

1   MULLINS, J.B. "Visio Willelmi de Petro Ploughman." N&Q, 6th ser. 3, no. 62 (5 March):186.
    Queries whether all copies of Whitaker's edition of the poem (1813.1) lack pp. 265-66. See Skeat, 1881.3.

1881

2 SKEAT, WALTER W. "Langland, or Langley, William." Encyclopædia
   Britannica. Vol. 14. 9th ed. New York: Henry G. Allen &
   Co., 1888, pp. 285-86.
        Suggests that "Langland should rather be Langley" on the
   strength of Pearson's argument (1870.2). Describes the contents of the poem and its history in print. Sees the general
   plan of the poem as somewhat vague, but the author's execution
   of it vivid and remarkable. The author's objects are to describe the life of the poor classes; to inveigh against clerical abuses; to represent the miseries caused by pestilence and
   hastily contrived marriages; and to denounce lazy workmen,
   sham beggars, and the abuses of the law courts. The allegorical personages are mouthpieces of the author himself. The
   poem is alliterative, but not very regular, "as the author's
   earnestness led him to use the fittest words rather than those
   which merely served the purpose of rhythm." The date of this
   entry is supplied by Skeat himself in the course of the
   article.

3 SKEAT, WALTER W. "Vision Willelmi de Petro Ploughman." N&Q,
   6th ser. 3, no. 65 (26 March):254-55.
        In response to Mullins (1881.1), Skeat quotes his de-
   scription of Whitaker's edition in Langland, 1873.5: sheet Ll
   ends with p. 265; sheet Mm begins with p. 267.

                              1882

1 BAYNE, THOMAS. "Piers Plowman." N&Q, 6th ser. 6, no. 142
   (16 September):225-26.
        Notes untrustworthy and/or ambiguous references to "Piers
   Plowman" as author of the poem.

2 HOPKINS, GERARD MANLEY. Letter to Robert Bridges, 18 October
   1882. In The Letters of Gerard Manley Hopkins to Robert
   Bridges. Edited by Claude Colleer Abbott. Oxford: Oxford
   University Press, 1935, p. 156.
        "So far as I know--I am enquiring and presently I shall
   be able to speak more decidedly--it [sprung rhythm] existed in
   full force in Anglo saxon verse and in great beauty; in·a de-
   graded and doggerel shape in Piers Ploughman (I am reading
   that famous poem and am coming to the conclusion that it is
   not worth reading); Green was the last who employed it at
   all consciously and he never continuously; then it dis-
   appeared. "

1883

1   BRINK, BERNHARD ten. Early English Literature (to Wiclif).
     Vol. 1. Translated by Horace M. Kennedy. New York: Henry
     Holt & Co., 1883, pp. 352-67.
         A translation of Brink (1877.1). For a modern reprint
     of this translation, see Brink, 1974.5.

2   PEACOCK, EDWARD. "Remarks on Prof. Skeat's Notes on 'Piers the
     Plowman.'" N&Q, 6th ser. 7, no. 172 (14 April):284-85.
         Citations of the practice, mentioned in the poem, of
     feeding bread to horses (C IX 192); the proverb "naked as a
     needle" (C XV 105); the legend of the Seven Sleepers (C XVI
     272); and the continued use of the word organs for organ.

1884

1   JUSSERAND, J.J. Les Anglais au moyen âge. La vie nomade et les
     routes d'Angleterre au XIVe siècle. Paris: Hachette, passim.
         The poem is used to illustrate the social history of
     eating habits, tavern recreation, laxity of religious disci-
     pline, late medieval scepticism concerning crusades, and so
     forth. Translated as Jusserand, 1889.2.

2   [LANGLAND, WILLIAM.] The Vision of William concerning Piers
     Plowman, together with Vita de Dowel, Dobet, et Dobest, and
     Richard the Redeles. Edited by Walter W. Skeat. Part 4,
     section 2: General Preface, Notes, and Indexes. Early Text
     Society, o.s. 81. London: N. Trübner & Co., lxxvii +
     513-910 pp.
         Contains general preface; indices of proper names and
     subjects, glossary, manuscripts, first lines of the passūs;
     notices of the poem by various authors; additions and correc-
     tions for Langland, 1867.3; 1869.2; 1873.5; 1877.2 and the
     present work; lists of errata; and a general index.
         In the preface, after describing the various parts of
     his edition, describes the form of the poem as it exists in
     the three versions, in MSS that combine the A- and C-texts
     and the B- and C-texts, and in MSS that show an intermediate
     form of the poem, for example, MS. H³ (A-text). Suggests that
     in its earliest form the A-text terminated with A VIII (as in
     MSS. H and I); that another form of the poem is recognizable
     from the MSS that omit A XII; that yet another form contains
     A XII in whole or in part; that the A-text may have been ampli-
     fied in the process of its revision into what later became the
     B-text; that beside the B-text in its commonest form, an

amplified B-text is in evidence in MS. R; that MS. I may show
the earliest draft of the C-text; and that besides the C-text
in its usual form, we encounter MSS that show a mixture of
versions. States that the author of the A-text wrote three
distinct visions (Field of Folk, Holy Church, and Lady Meed;
Deadly Sins and Piers Plowman; Vita de Dowel, Dobet, Dobest),
and afterwards called the poem by the name of his favorite
character. Piers in this version is "no more than the type
of the ideal honest man." The B-text retains the first two
visions, but reduces the third and changes it into what might
be called the vision of Wit, Study, Clergy, and Scripture. To
this is added the new visions, extending all the way to the
vision of Antichrist. Langland has realized in the course of
this revision that the true guide to God the Father was Jesus
Christ, "who must therefore be his true Piers." This identity
is first hinted at in B XIII 123-32, then signaled more directly in B XV 190-206 and B XVI 17-53; and "Piers becomes
incarnate in the form of Jesus" in B XVI 94. After Christ's
Ascension, a new Piers, Peter, begins the succession of His
deputies on earth; Langland wishes to emphasize the fact that
the popes, who often claimed to be merely the successors of
Peter, ought rather to have become the true successors of
Peter's master. The poet's name is probably William Langland,
and though Pearson's argument (1870.2) is strong, it relies on
the unlikely substitution of the rare name Langland for the
more common Langley.

Supplements earlier remarks (1869.2) with a comprehensive account of the poet's life, drawn from the poem itself.
Rejects the opinion of Jusserand (1879.1) that C II 72-75
proves the author was a religious, and argues instead that the
passage refers to entry into the Church through baptism. Also
tends to value less than Jusserand the author's confessions
regarding his earlier idle and misspent life in the face of
his careful and diligent revision of his composition.

Quotes comments on the poem from D'Israeli (1841.1),
Marsh (1862.1), Milman (1855.4), and Morley (1877.3)--the last
of which is enlisted in opposition to Whitaker's description
(1813.1) of the end of the poem as one of disappointment and
gloom.

Reiterates his previous description of the language of
the B-text MSS as that of the dialect of the poet, and notes
the mixture of Western and Midland forms in the C-text, as
well as a number of Northern forms in the B-text. Offers the
chief rules of alliterative verse as practiced by Langland as
follows: two or more strong syllables per half-line; within
these strong syllables two rhyme letters in the first half-
line, and one in the second half-line, with the alliterative
pattern set by the rhyme-letter of the first strong syllable

1884

of the second half-line, and with vowels expected to rhyme with vowels, and special consonant clusters (e.g., sp, ch, str) frequently rhyming with identical clusters. To illustrate the alliterative patterns of the three texts, prints the tables of Rosenthal (1877.4) with minor corrections.

With regard to MSS (Index III), Skeat's researches enlarge his earlier investigations in Langland (1866.1). Printing A III 67-77 from forty-five MSS (not all of which he has fully collated), Skeat suggests the following MSS classifications:

A-text: subclass a: VH; subclass b: R, E, U, J(?), D, A, L; mixed text, partly A-text, subclass c: T, H^2, W(?); amplified A-text, subclass d: H^3; mixed text, partly A-text subclass d: K.

B-text: subclass a: L, M(?), R; subclass b: Bo, Bm, Cot; subclass c: O, C^2; subclass d: Cr, Hm, W; subclass uncertain: Hm^2; subclass e: F; subclass f: Ht.

C-text: subclass a: Z, S, G, V, R, N; mixed text, partly C-text, subclass b: I; subclass b, beginning C XII 297: T, H^2, D^2; mixed text, partly C-text, subclass b(?) from C XIII 1: W; mixed text, partly C-text, subclass b only near the beginning, as far as C III 128: B, O, L: subclass c: K; subclass d: M; subclass e: F; subclass doubtful: P^2. As in Langland, 1873.5, Skeat considers C-text subclass c intermediate to subclasses a and b; subclass d closer to a than to b; and subclass e as varying considerably from both a and b.

Describes the previously unavailable MSS. W and I, and prints a passage from A XII of MS I (containing a few unique lines) that he sees as proof the A-text was meant to conclude with passus XII.

With these classifications of the MSS ought to be compared Langland, 1867.3, 1869.2, and 1873.5, representing earlier stages of his investigations. This index of manuscripts was printed separately as Langland, 1885.2; but cf. Skeat's later classifications, under the influence of Kron, 1885.1, in Langland, 1886.1.

3   MARSHALL, EDWARD H. "Byron on 'Piers Plowman.'" N&Q, 6th ser. 10, no. 245 (6 September):169.
    Reply to Skeat, 1884.4; sees Byron, 1807.1.

4   SKEAT, WALTER W. "Byron on Chaucer." N&Q, 6th ser. 10, no. 244 (30 August):169.
    Queries the source of Byron's remarks on Langland and Chaucer, as quoted by D'Israeli (1841.1).

1884

5   SKEAT, WALTER W.   "'Piers Plowman' and Dryden."   N&Q, 6th ser.
    10, no. 244 (30 August):169.
        Queries the source of D'Israeli's remark (1841.1). that
    Dryden borrowed "one very striking line" from Piers Plowman.

                              1885

1   KRON, RICHARD. William Langleys Buch von Peter dem Plfüger.
    Untersuchung über das Handschiftenverhältnis, den Dialekt, die
    Unterschiede innerhalb der drei Redaktionen sowie über Entste-
    hungszeit und Verfasser. Erlangen: Verlag von Andreas
    Deichert, 129 pp.
        Describes the MSS and attempts to devise stemmae for all
    three texts, although accepts Skeat's contention (1869.2) that
    MS. L (B-text) is the poet's autograph, and hence derives all
    other extant B-text MSS from this MS. Considers the poet's
    dialect as basically West Midlands with exceptions noted in
    his forms for the third person singular present indicative and
    second person singular past indicative. Presents an analogue
    of the Rat Parliament from MS. Bibliothèque Nationale 7616; and
    interprets the cat as Edward III, the kitten as the pretender
    Richard. Dates the B-text before June 1377, and sees no ref-
    erences in the poem to John of Gaunt. Sees the references to
    the king in the C-text as likewise to Edward, though composed
    under the reign of Richard.

2   [LANGLAND, WILLIAM.] Parallel Extracts from Forty-five Manu-
    scripts of Piers Plowman, with Notes upon Their Relation to
    the Society's Three-Text Edition of This Poem. Edited by
    Walter W. Skeat. 2nd ed. rev. Early English Text Society,
    o.s. 17. London: Kegan Paul, Trench, Trübner & Co., 34 pp.
        A separate publication, almost verbatim, of Index III
    of Langland, 1884.2, intended to supersede Langland, 1866.1.

                              1886

1   LANGLAND, WILLIAM. The Vision of William concerning Piers the
    Plowman in Three Parallel Texts together with Richard the
    Redeless. Edited by Walter W. Skeat. 2 vols. Oxford:
    Clarendon Press, viii + 628, and xciii + 484 pp.
        Vol. 1 presents the three texts parallel. drawn from
    Skeat's earlier editions (Langland, 1867.3, 1869.2, 1873.5),
    though supplementing 1867.3 in A XII with lines from M.S. R
    (see Langland, 1877.2), and the text of Richard the Redeless.
        Vo. 2 offers introductory material, notes, glossarial
    index, and index to proper names and subjects, largely

reproducing Skeat's earlier work. With regard to the classification of MSS, however, Skeat adopts the results of Kron
(1885.1) which, not differing greatly from Skeat's own work
in Langland, 1884.2, are the product of a more careful examination of the MSS that Skeat felt were not worth collating
completely. His classification is as follows:

A-text; group $\underline{a}$: V, H; group $\underline{b}$: R, U, J, E; group $\underline{c}$:
T, H^2, W, L, K: group $\underline{d}$: Ď, H^3, A.

B-text; group $\underline{a}$: L, M, R: group $\underline{b}$: W, Cr, Hm, Hm^2;
group $\underline{c}$: O, C^2, G, $\overline{Y}$; group $\underline{d}$: F, Ht: group $\underline{e}$: C; group $\underline{f}$:
Bo, Bm, Cot.

C-text; group $\underline{a}$: P, E, N; group $\underline{b}$: I, D, Y (partly T,
H^2, W, D^2; also B, O, L); group $\underline{c}$: Z; group $\underline{d}$: K, M, F;
group $\underline{e}$: S, V, G, R; group $\underline{f}$(?): P^2.

For reviews of this edition, see Anon., 1887.1; Anon.,
1887.2; Bradley, 1887.3; and Garnett, 1887.4. For a modern
reprint of this edition, see Langland, 1969.22.

1887

1   ANON. Review of Langland, 1886.1. <u>N&Q</u>, 7th ser. 3, no. 57
        (29 January):99–100.
            Skeat's Clarendon edition (1886.1) praised as the
        "standard and definitive" edition of a poem equally important
        for the study of the history of the language, for the reli-
        gious thought of pre-Reformation England, and for its social
        customs and antiquities.
            Takes exception to two notes: <u>jangle</u>, "to gossip," is
        a derivation of <u>jangleur</u> rather than related to Dutch <u>janken</u>,
        "to howl"; and <u>bytelbrowed</u> (C VII 198) probably means "pro-
        jecting brows," rather than brows that jut out over the eyes.

2   ANON. Review of Langland, 1886.1. <u>Athenæum</u> (London), 19 March,
        pp. 380–81.
            A highly favorable review of Langland, 1886.1, which is
        commended over Skeat's "justly praised" Early English Text
        Society editions. Notes that Skeat has come to reject
        Pearson's argument (1870.2) that the poet's name was <u>Langley</u>,
        but suggests that Pearson's conclusions follow inescapably
        from Skeat's premises. Suggests that Stacy de Rokayle had a
        son named William Langley, who was wrongly identified by the
        annotator of MS. V (C-text) with the poet, whom he notwith-
        standing correctly designated as <u>Langland</u>. If this recon-
        struction is valid, Skeat's statements as to the poet's
        parentage lose their foundation.

1887

3   BRADLEY, HENRY. Review of Langland, 1886.1. <u>Academy</u> 31,
        no. 769 (29 January):70-71.
            Admits high praise for Skeat's Clarendon edition. Sug-
        gests that Langland's reputation as a writer has been over-
        inflated, and that it is "simply absurd" to compare him with
        Chaucer, for the allegoric mode has little if any dramatic
        reality and Langland's didactic purpose is stronger than his
        poetic form. Nevertheless, the poem offers an unparalleled
        opportunity for study of the intellectual and moral life of the
        times.
            Skeat's proposed development of Piers's identity is seen
        as imprecise: Piers represents the ideal humanity under the
        aspect of the honest workman, presented in a context in which
        the service of man is the only acceptable service of God. As
        the poem develops, Langland sees this theme realized in Jesus
        Christ; yet the C-text wisely alters or removes much of the
        identification of Piers and Christ, and by so doing clarifies
        the allegory of the Tree of Charity scene (C XIX), where
        Christ fights on behalf of Piers. Accepts Skeat's ascription
        of <u>Richard the Redeless</u> to Langland.

4   GARNETT, JAMES M. Review of Langland, 1886.1. <u>American Journal</u>
        <u>of Philology</u> 8, no. 31:347-55.
            Generally high praise for the parallel-text edition,
        though Garnett would have wanted one text, for example, the
        C-text, published with notes, preface, and glossary in an even
        handier format.
            Wishes more information on the poet's dialect and, while
        accepting that Langland's dialect probably is best represented
        by the MSS of the B-text that show predominantly Midlands
        forms with an admixture of Southern forms, notes that the
        prevalence of Southern forms in the C-text suggests that the
        poet may have produced the final version after returning from
        London to Worcestershire. Wishes more attention paid to the
        question of the authorship of <u>Richard the Redeless</u>, though he
        thinks Skeat's ascription of the poem to Langland is probably
        correct.

5   TEICHMANN, EDUARD. <u>Die Verbalflexion in William Langleys Buche</u>
        <u>von Peter dem Pflüger</u>. Dissertation, Tübingen; published in
        <u>Bericht über die Realschule mit Fachlassen (frühere königliche</u>
        <u>Gewerbeschule) zu Aachen</u>, 55 pp.
            An analysis of the inflexions of the verbs in the three
        texts of the poem under the following criteria: a form iden-
        tical in all three texts indicates the language was variable
        in this respect; when the B-text shows a form different from
        A-text or C-text, the B-text form is suspect if the A- and/or
        C-text form demonstrates organic development from Old English;

if the form in the B-text is sometimes attested by the A-text
and/or C-text but these texts elsewhere show a new form, then
that new form is probably scribal in origin; and when the B-
text and C-text use two different forms of the verb with some
consistency, and the form seen in the C-text is confirmed in
most cases by the MSS, it is reasonable to assume that the
author's language had changed in the interim.

6   WANDSCHNEIDER, WILHELM. Zur Syntax des Verbes in Langleys
    Vision of William concerning Piers the Plowman, together with
    Vita de Dowel, Dobet and Dobest. Dissertation, Kiel.
    Leipzig: Fr. Richter, 83 pp.
        A catalogue and investigation of the variety of uses in
    the B-text to which the poet puts the verb to be; modals;
    various formations of the present, present perfect, preterite,
    and pluperfect tenses; imperatives, infinitives, present and
    perfect participles; and the subjunctive.

1888

1   MORRIS, WILLIAM. "Feudal England." In Signs of Change: Seven
    Lectures Delivered on Various Occasions. London: Reeves &
    Turner, pp. 73-75.
        Distinguishes three kinds of poetry in fourteenth-
    century England, the courtly, the ballad, and the Lollard,
    the greatest example of the last being Piers Plowman, which
    is not a bad corrective to Chaucer, for at least in form the
    poem echoes popular concerns. But the poem seems to show the
    spirit of the rising middle class, and "casts before it the
    shadow of the new master that was coming forward for the work-
    man's oppression."

1889

1   GÜNTHER, ERNST. Englisches Leben im Vierzehnten Jahrhundert.
    Dargestellt nach "The Vision of William concerning Piers the
    Plowman" by William Langland. Dissertation, Leipzig.
    Leipzig: Hesse & Becker, 62 pp.
        Skeat's editions of the B- and C-texts (1869.2 and
    1873.5) are considered as representations of the life of the
    times. Categories of comparison are London, the house and its
    inhabitants, nobility and farmers, business and commerce, way-
    faring life, pilgrims and hermits, secular and religious
    clergy, the administration of justice, and education.

1889

2   JUSSERAND, J.J. English Wayfaring Life in the Middle Ages (XIVth
    Century). Translated by Lucy Toulmin Smith. London: T.F.
    Unwin, passim.
            A translation of Jusserand, 1884.1. Often reprinted.

3   LUICK, KARL. "Die englische Strabreimzeile im XIV, XV, und XVI
    Jahrhundert." Anglia 11:392-443, esp. 429-40.
            Accepting, with Skeat, MS. L (B-text) as the autograph
    of the author, declares that the work of "Langley" shows a
    peculiar metrical unevenness: at the beginning of the various
    passūs it is rhythmically smooth, but later the stressed
    syllables are often badly distributed in the verse-line and
    the rhythm almost lost. Suggests the poem is among the worst
    accentual verse of the fourteenth century: in the way that
    the author expected accents to fall on unstressed syllables,
    for example, he shows himself to have no real formal talents,
    and perhaps when he became excited, he abandoned form for
    expression. Nevertheless, Luick attempts to describe the poem
    metrically, according to the alliterative line-types he has
    devised.

4   MITCHELL, DONALD G. English Lands Letters and Kings. Vol. 1,
    From Celt to Tudor. New York: Charles Scribner's Sons,
    pp. 86-90.
            Appreciates Langland as representing "a popular seam in
    that great drift of independent and critical thought, which
    was to ripen into the Reformation." Terms the poem the
    "reasonably readable" production of an immature, crude, "yet
    sharper kind of John Bunyan." What Langland's poetry lacks
    in tenderness and sublimity, it makes up for in shrewdness and
    touches of "unwashed humor."

1890

1   KLAPPROTT, LUDWIG. Das End-e in W. Langland's Buch von Peter
    dem Pflüger, Text B. Dissertation, Göttingen. Göttingen:
    Louis Hofer, 48 pp.
            The historical final -e in Langland's time was unsteady
    in written prose and about to be silenced in spoken language.
    The unhistorical final -e always appears after a long accented
    vowel when the length of the vowel is not indicated by spell-
    ing or final position, and when a silent consonant is not the
    final letter. Final -e is a certain indication of length ex-
    cept when two consonants stand as the final sound, in which
    case final -e is ornamental. After a liquid or nasal, final
    -e fluctuates; shortening before d or a simple nasal (a ten-
    dency of Modern English) is apparently present. Historically

1892

correct final -e after short vowels, stressed or unstressed,
is beginning to disappear, though there are many exceptions,
for example, when a voiced consonant is the final sound.

1891

1 SKEAT, WALTER W. "Commence to (Said to Be Not an English
   Idiom)." N&Q, 7th ser. 12, no. 302 (10 October):294.
        Instance of this idiom is noted from C XV 203. Re-
   printed: Skeat, 1896.2.

2 TEICHMANN, EDUARD. "Zur Stabreimzeile in William Langland's
   Buch von Peter dem Pflüger." Anglia 13:140-74.
        The poet's dialect is apparently mixed, and spelling in
   the MSS is not systematic. MS. L (B-text) is the best single
   MS, though there is no firm reason to believe it is the poet's
   autograph (cf. Skeat, in Langland, 1869.2). Indeed, there is
   no reason to believe that the B-text is closer to the poet's
   language than the A- or C-text. The chief variable in the MSS
   is the final -e, the pronunciation of which cannot be deter-
   mined by the words bearing stress, only by the endings of
   lines. Lists lines the endings of which are clearly dissyl-
   labic, along with those apparent exceptions that can be explained with reference to the readings of the B- and C-texts,
   as well as doubtful cases.

1892

1 [FFOULKES, EDMUND SALISBURY.] A History of the Church of S. Mary
   the Virgin Oxford. London and New York: Longmans, Green &
   Co., pp. 164-76.
        Identifies the author of the poem with John of Malvern,
   prior of Great Malvern in 1435, since Great Malvern owned
   tenements in Longdon (Worcestershire) and Longdon equals
   Longedune or Longhille. Longe Wille is derived from villa
   which is written by the Germans as willa. John was merely a
   religious name. The A-text must have been written after 1381,
   and there is no evidence that the B- and C-texts were written
   before 1409, the date of at least one MS of the poem. Quotes
   and translates letters found in MS. Bodley 692 which he claims
   form part of the correspondence between the author, "Malvern,"
   and a Benedictine, discussing the revision and dispersal of
   the text. Criticized by Skeat, 1893.2.

1892

2   H[ALES], J[OHN] W. "Langland, William (1330?-1400?)." <u>DNB</u>.
    Vol. 23. Edited by Sidney Lee. London: Smith, Elder, & Co.,
    pp. 104-8.
        Rehearses the biographical information from the annota-
    tion to MS. V (c. 1400.1) and from Bale (1557.1); pronounces
    in favor of the theory of Pearson (1870.2), but finds some
    support for Bale's remarks in the existence of a hamlet called
    Langley close by Cleobury Mortimer, and concludes the poet may
    reasonably be assumed to have been born in southern Shropshire.
    Fills in the poet's biography from the details presented in
    the poem. Praises Langland for his vivid descriptions, as
    exact and realistic as Dante's, though lacking the Italian
    poet's greatness of conception and nobleness of poetic form.
    Sees in Langland's adoption of unrhymed alliterative measure
    a century after Layamon had admitted rhyme probably an
    independent and retrogressive step, "though we must remember
    that [Langland] knew his audience better than his modern
    critics can know it." Accepts the contention of Wright, in
    [Langland], 1842.3 and Skeat, in Langland, 1886.1, that
    <u>Richard the Redeless</u> was also his work.

3   SKEAT, WALTER W. "St Parnell." <u>N&Q</u>, 8th ser. 1, no. 1
    (2 January):10.
        Supplements note in Langland, 1886.1 to C V 111, by
    showing the stages of derivation of <u>Parnell</u> from <u>Petronilla</u>.
    Reprinted: Skeat, 1896.2.

4   SKEAT, WALTER W. "First Editions." <u>N&Q</u>, 8th ser. 1, no. 24
    (11 June):480.
        In the sixteenth century, the first edition of a work
    was as a rule the best, and later editions were mere reprints,
    as exemplified by Crowley's three "editions" of 1550. But of
    modern works, the first edition is usually the worst, though
    Wright's edition of the poem (1842.3) an exception. Reprinted:
    Skeat, 1896.2.

1893

1   JUSSERAND, J.J. <u>Les Anglais au moyen âge. L'épopée mystique de
    William Langland</u>. Paris: Libraire Hachette, 275 pp.
        A-text is dated 1362-63 on the basis of satire of abuses
    of provisors and praemunire (reflected in contemporary stat-
    utes); concern with crimes related to purveyance and main-
    tenance (denounced by the Commons in the Parliament of 1363);
    allusion to Peace of Bretigny (1360); and allusion to wind
    storm (apparently of 15 January 1362). Although retaining
    many of the allusions of the first version, the B-text can be

dated 1376-77 on the basis of the additions of the Rat Parliament, which Jusserand takes to refer to the Good Parliament of 1376, with Peter de la Mere, speaker of the Commons, represented as the "rat of renown," and the poet himself represented as the "wise mouse"; allusions to wars between the pope and Christian kings (which Jusserand takes as a reference to the activities of John Hawkwood, rather than, as did Skeat, to the Papal Schism); and the implication that the remaining days of the reigning monarch are few. Datable allusions in the C-text are few, but C IV 204, in its apparent reference to Richard as absolute monarch, suggests the time of the Parliament of 1398 that had virtually resigned all power over to the king, and voted the principal taxes for his lifetime.

In comparison with Chaucer, Langland is superior in the depiction of crowd and mass movement and in the communication of the power of Parliament. Langland often passionately supports the cause of Parliament, but criticizes the ambition of the Good Parliament. He favors the traditional division of classes, the virtue of mutual obligations, and the principle of common profit. Although his interest is mainly on things English, he favors peace with France and the peaceful conversion of the Saracens.

Langland attacks the abuses of the Church, not the institution. There is no proof of his leanings to Wyclif: his criticisms of the pope's encroachment on secular matters puts him on the side of the Commons. His worst criticism, in which he far outdoes Chaucer, is directed against churchmen of the lower ranks who sell the sacraments and deceive the simple.

The author was probably of low extraction, made free by having entered religion. Perhaps born 1331-32, he may have left Malvern for university, and later a career singing chantries, possibly at St. Paul's while he lived in nearby Cornhill. Opportunities for preferment were closed to him because of his low birth and marriage; and his life was marked by doubts, moodiness, depression, and a lack of will power.

His poem is best summarized by its sincerity, impetuousness, artlessness, and the ability to suggest in one striking image a whole complex doctrine. His sincerity, expressed in a deep aversion to all that is mere appearance or imposture, is especially noteworthy at the end of the Middle Ages when things were no longer believed so earnestly as previously.

Reviews citations of Piers Plowman in later literature, and sees in Piers's adoption by the rebels of 1381 proof that in some points Langland had expressed complementary opinions; yet the efforts of later religious reformers such as Bale (1557.1) and Fuller (1662.1) to make him a prophet of the Reformation are misguided.

1893

Suggests consideration of Langland in the context of medieval and later mystical literature, English and Continental; in particular, in his more fanatical aspects Langland is close to the German mystics, who were, of course, unknown to him. Langland's knowledge of the Pèlerinages of Deguilleville is perhaps seen in the device of a dream of a pilgrim seeking salvation who encounters various allegorical personages.

2   SKEAT, WALTER W. "'John of Malvern' and 'Piers the Plowman.'" Academy 43, no. 1089 (18 March):242.
A devastating criticism of [Ffoulkes], 1892.1.

3   TEICHMANN, EDUARD. "Zum Texte von William Langland's Vision." Anglia 15:223-60.
Finds it ill advised to rely so heavily as did Skeat (1886.1) on one MS, unless it can be proven that this MS was the author's autograph. Declares all extant versions of the poem are full of mistakes, and that the question of what MSS can be relied upon is undecided.
Criticizes Skeat for making use in his notes only occasionally of doubtful words elsewhere referred to. Assumes that the language of the poem in the extant MSS does not represent the work of the author who, writing in the alliterative tradition, would have been necessarily more careful in his grammatical forms.
Since the original language hasn't been preserved in the extant MSS, sees it important to investigate the unusual forms and mistakes in the three texts, especially those that fill out a half-line. Judges that the metrical laws governing the two half-lines differ: for the first half-line, there are two beats, the first of which is usually stressed more than the second; the number of syllables varies between five and nine; the position of the two stresses is variable, with the meter aiming at naturalness and clarity of thought and expression. For the second half-line, we should expect the alliterated syllable to be placed as close as possible to the first half-verse, the same alliteration to be maintained, and the half-line to be comprised of five to seven syllables. Illustrates these principles from the text, as well as suggests changes of Skeat's text, based on variants included in Skeat's (incomplete) notes.

1894

1 BELLEZZA, PAOLO. "Langland and Dante." N&Q, 8th ser. 6,
no. 136 (4 August):81-83.
Assumes Langland did not know Dante's works, but seeks
to find particular analogues. Both poets speak of heaven,
hell, and the world; both reproach ignorant clergy and the
vices of the papacy; both call for an ideal pope. Lady Mede
resembles the figure of False Worldly Happiness of Purg. IX,
6 and the allegorical she-wolf of Inf. I; the castle of human
wit of Inf. IV resembles the "courte as cleere as the sonne"
of B V 594 ff.

*2 HANSCOM, ELIZABETH DEERING. "The Vision of Piers Plowman."
Dissertation, Yale.
Source: Comprehensive Dissertation Index 1861-1972,
vol. 30, p. 245. See Hanscom, 1894.3.

3 HANSCOM, ELIZABETH DEERING. "The Argument of the Vision of
Piers Plowman." PMLA 9, no. 3 (September):403-50.
From a literary point of view, the poem is full of perhaps inexplicable problems: none of the texts is complete;
the last lines of A XII are probably spurious; the concluding
vision of the B- and C-text cannot be intended to end the
poem, for there has been no suggestion that Dobest will prove
inefficient; and the fact that the C-text closes at the same
point as the B-text suggests Langland died or abandoned the
poem before revising its end.
Langland is an acute observer, but lacks the quality
that perceives the relations of things; hence, his poem is a
succession of separate visions, a compilation of distinct
arguments, "of which the connection must be sought rather in
the probable intention of the writer than in the structure of
his work." The subject of the poem is the Christian life.
The question of Piers's identity is related to the progression of virtue implied in the Three Lives of Dowel, Dobet,
Dobest. Piers is the ideal English laborer who comes to be
identified with Christ not in B XVI (see Skeat, in Langland,
1886.1), but in B XVII 337, and who represents the Church of
Christ in the last vision.
Warns against reading the poem as the autobiography of
its author, and criticizes Jusserand (1893.1) for suggesting
that Langland would attack a custom (advancement of men of
servile birth through benefit of the clergy) that he has supposedly benefited from. Sees the poet as a social conservative, whose praise of the poor and arguments against riches
are in the main conventional, and who is unwilling to extend
his religious and social reflections to their logical

1894

conclusions. Later ages, however, accepted his premises, but
ignored his conclusions.

*4   HOPKINS, EDWIN M. "Character and Opinions of William Langland as
     Shown in the <u>Vision of William Concerning Piers the Plowman</u>."
     Dissertation, Princeton.
          Source: McNamee, vol. 1, pp. 155-56. See Hopkins,
     1895.3, for an abstract (under different title); and cf.
     Hopkins, 1894.5.

5   HOPKINS, EDWIN M. "The Character and Opinions of William
     Langland as Shown in 'The Vision of William Concerning Piers
     the Plowman.'" <u>Kansas University Quarterly</u> 2, no. 4 (April):
     233-88.
          Regarding scene and setting, with a few exceptions, the
     references of the A-text are to the country, indicating that
     Langland probably came to London about the time the A-text was
     written. Before, he had probably been a farmer, perhaps a
     vagabond. The vast majority of allusions to England outside
     London indicate acquaintance with the territory between
     Shropshire and London.
          Regarding content, Langland's attitude toward real and
     pretended science is less satirical than Chaucer's, though his
     attitude toward physicians is similar. Langland sees politi-
     cal and social questions largely in the context of a fivefold
     division of society--king, knights, clergy, commons, and plow-
     men--with each class possessing its own rights and duties.
     Piers himself was most probably a villein of the highest
     class with some property rights. Langland indignantly re-
     nounces the communistic principle in favor of one of reason-
     able equality. There is little novelty in his religious
     opinions, though he appears to attach little importance to
     Penance. His double conception of Christ as the Son of God
     and as Piers is full of inconsistencies; and Piers is best to
     be thought of as a man endowed with the spirit of Christ, or
     human nature in its highest form, until the end when he takes
     on the character of Christ. Langland's philosophical opinions
     show some traces of scholasticism in the curious questions
     posed in B X, C II, C XII, and C XV. It is uncertain whether
     he equates Anima with the soul or merely the vital principle.
     Wit is to him "the mind applied to the perception of truth,"
     conscience an intellectual faculty under divine direction,
     reason the "righteous judge which interprets and applies
     law."
          Regarding the form of the poem, the visions suggest that
     Langland's contemplative habits were productive of sluggish-
     ness.

1895

6   JUSSERAND, J.J. Piers Plowman: a Contribution to the History of
    English Mysticism. Rev. and enlarged by the author. Trans-
    lated by M[arion and] E[lise] R[ichards]. London: T. Fisher
    Unwin; New York: G.P. Putnam's Sons, 262 pp.
        A translation of Jusserand, 1893.1. For a modern re-
    print, see Jusserand, 1965.11.

7   JUSSERAND, J.J. Histoire littéraire du peuple anglais. Vol. 1,
    Des origines à la Renaissance. Paris: Firmin-Didot,
    pp. 383-414.
        Essentially a précis of Jusserand, 1893.1, adding no new
    facts and advancing no radically different interpretations.
    For an English translation, see Jusserand, 1895.4.

8   LOWELL, JAMES RUSSELL. "Criticism and Culture." Century Illus-
    trated Monthly Magazine 47, no. 4 (February):515-16.
        Piers Plowman is compared with Prometheus Bound: the
    primary object of both is dogma, not literature; and Langland
    stands in relation to Chaucer in a way analagous to Aeschylus
    in relation to Sophocles, that is, the "purely imaginative"
    versus "character and reflection."

1895

1   BELLEZZA, PAOLO. "Langland's Figur des 'Plowman' in der neuesten
    Englischen Literatur." Englische Studien 21:325-26.
        Cites the figure of the plowman in a speech by Macauley
    and in Tennyson's "Locksley Hall Sixty Years After."

2   COURTHOPE, W.J. A History of English Poetry. Vol. 1, The Middle
    Ages: Influence of the Roman Empire--the Encyclopaedic Educa-
    tion of the Church--the Feudal System. London: Macmillan &
    Co., pp. 200-247.
        The poem is discussed in the context of fourteenth-
    century chivalry and the church, both having declined from
    their earlier high ideals. The contents of the poem are de-
    scribed, with more attention paid to the "more interesting and
    artistic" Visio. Comparison with Dante's Commedia reveals
    Langland's conception of society is less symmetrical and logi-
    cal, but more practical. Both poets are orthodox Christians,
    yet both are willing to criticize individual popes. Both ad-
    vocate absolute monarchy, tempered by reason and religion.
    Langland is generally well disposed toward the feudal system,
    seeing avarice and ambition in ecclesiastical order the great-
    est cause of corruption. Dante's system is based on the meta-
    physical side of Catholicism, Langland's on the practical and

1895

ethical. Dante's allegory is philosophical, Langland's "merely a poetical vehicle of moral thought."

3   HOPKINS, EDWIN M. "The Education of William Langland." Princeton College Bulletin 7:41-45. (Abstract of thesis presented for the degree of Doctor of Philosophy, June 1894.)
Takes issue with Jusserand (1893.1) that Langland had a university education, for there is no reference to universities in the poem, and nowhere does the author show a great knowledge of grammatical theory and logic. Moreover, his knowledge of natural history appears to be dependent on the bestiaries.
Hopkins traces the approximately 475 allusions in the poem: almost nine-tenths are from the Vulgate, services of Church, works of the Fathers, and Latin hymns. The rest are from Legenda aurea (5); Disticha of Dionysius Cato (9); Historia scholastica of Peter Comestor (3); Compendium of Peter Cantor (2); works of Boethius (1); poetry of Juvenal (1); untraceable French sources (3 or 4). Langland's few direct references to authors are often incorrect. He probably had access to relatively few books, such as those that a priory, minster, or cathedral school might provide. He had a good memory, and doubtless knew people who had been to university, but shows no trace of the systematic grounding in knowledge that a university would have provided.

4   JUSSERAND, J.J. A Literary History of the English People. Vol. 1, From the Origins to the Renaissance. New York and London: G.P. Putnam's Sons, pp. 373-402.
See Jusserand, 1894.6.

5   SCHIPPER, J. Grundriss der englischen Metrik. Wiener Beiträge zur englischen Philologie. Vol. 2. Vienna and Leipzig: Wilhelm Braumüller, pp. 83-85.
Sees Piers Plowman, along with such poems as William of Palerne and Joseph of Arimathie, as exhibiting an accented syllable at the end of the hemistich, as well as secondary accents introduced more frequently than in the King Alisaunder fragments into the second hemistich. In Piers Plowman, in particular, the versification in many passages, especially in the beginning of various passūs, is regular, but in other passages the rhythm is scarcely intelligible, so long are the theses from the addition of unaccented syllables. As a rule, such extended verses are followed by normal lines tht reestablish the four-beat rhythm in unmistakable fashion. Translated as Schipper, 1910.13.

Writings about Piers Plowman, 1395-1979

1896

1   PETERSON, HANS C. A History of English Poetry from the Aesthetic
    Point of View. Part 1, "The Period from Langland to Spenser."
    Dissertation, Leipzig. Leipzig: Gustav Fock, 67 pp.
         Tabulates B Prol-III along with proportionate amounts of
    poetry by Chaucer, Lydgate, Surrey, Wyatt, Sackville, and
    Spenser according to criteria of subject matter (e.g., physi-
    cal strength, beauty, intellectual power, man subjected to
    external forces, etc.) and criteria of poetic technique (e.g.,
    emotionally charged diction, poetic phrases, figures of speech,
    etc.). Concludes that Langland's work is primitive: "The
    thirty-three effects show a dramatic spirit running through
    [the poem] that might have developed into something better had
    Langland possessed genius for poetic expression." Neverthe-
    less, Langland is praised for his depiction of types.

2   SKEAT, WALTER W. A Student's Pastime, Being a Select Series of
    Articles Reprinted from "Notes and Queries." Oxford:
    Clarendon Press, pp. 22-24, 49-50, 52, 54-55, 60-61, 311,
    316-17, 335-36.
         See Skeat, 1867.6, 1869.4, 1869.5, 1869.6, 1870.3,
    1891.1, 1892.3, and 1892.4.

1897

1   BELLEZZA, PAOLO. "Di alcune notevoli coincidenze tra la Divina
    Commedia e la Visione di Pietro L'Aratore." Rendiconti del
    Regio Instituto Lombardo di Scienze e Lettere, 2d ser. 29:
    1219-33.
         An expansion of Bellezza (1894.1), stressing such
    similarities between Piers Plowman and the Divina Commedia as
    the details and setting of the opening visions; the motif of
    the world as a wilderness; the imperative quality of the
    visions; the emphasis on charity; the descriptions of Sloth
    (B V 392 ff. and Purg. IV, 106 ff.); and Lady Mede (B II
    44 ff.) and Worldly Felicity (Purg. XIX, 7).

2   MACKAIL, J.W. "Piers Ploughman and English Life in the Four-
    teenth Century." Cornhill Magazine, n.s. 3 (July-December):
    42-58.
         The poem embodies an organized and consistent system of
    political and social realities, presenting a vivid picture of
    actual fourteenth-century life with imaginative insight, human
    sympathy, dramatic power, humor, and pathos. But the poem
    cannot rank with Chaucer's because of its form, its architec-
    tural deficiencies, and its defense of the oppressed. Piers

1897

Plowman partly fails "from want of that inhuman quality which
is inherent in nearly all great art."

1898

1   B., A.   "Zu W. Langland." Archiv 100:334.
        Citing Bruge (1395.1), notes how quickly the poem spread
    to the North.

2   HOPKINS, E.M.   "Notes on Piers Plowman. I: Who Wrote Piers
    Plowman?" Kansas University Quarterly 7, nos. 1 & 2 (April):
    1-26.
        Reviews all the testimony and commentary on the author's
    name, and concludes that the author was a devout, serious
    ecclesiast from the lower or middle class, well read but not
    broadly educated, whose Christian name was probably Robert and
    surname probably Langley, and who gave his name as Will in
    order to conceal his identity. He perhaps named himself
    Langland for the same reason, though it is more probable that
    he was not aware this name was in the poem; or Langland suc-
    ceeded Langley because of "an unhappy phonetic fate." Finds
    attractive the evidence brought forward by Skeat in Langland,
    1893.2, of a "Robertus Langeleye, alias Robertus Paterick,
    capellanus, London," who owned "unum messuag" and "quatuor
    shope in Les Flesshambles in Parochia Sancti Nicholai, unum
    tenementum in parochia Sancti Nicholai," and so on, were it
    not that this individual died in 1395, and the author of
    Richard the Redeless was flourishing in 1399.

3   SAINTSBURY, GEORGE. A Short History of English Literature.
    London: Macmillan & Co., pp. 131-38.
        Emphasizes the reflective, theological, and allegorical
    aspects of the poem over the dramatic and pictorial. Langland
    cannot be compared with Chaucer either for range, directness,
    or artistic sense. Pronounces Langland "intense, but narrow;
    pious, but a little Philistine," lacking in architectural
    skill, but a genius who was able to impress freedom and order,
    "swing and variety," on such an uncouth metrical form.

4   SCUDDER, VIDA D. Social Ideals in English Letters. Boston and
    New York: Houghton Mifflin Co., pp. 7-45.
        The poem is considered in its social context as invest-
    ing labor with a religious significance, glorifying poverty,
    and pleading for the brotherhood of man. Piers Plowman doubt-
    less inspired the ideals of the Peasants' Revolt, though it is
    quite possible that Langland, who presents no schemes for so-
    cial reconstruction, would have shrunk from the part his poem

played in the Revolt, just as he would have denounced the
Reformation. The poem may not be literature, for it lacks artistic selection and control. Compares it with the works of
Carlyle in its mixture of conservatism and radical, prophetic
qualities. But as opposed to Bunyan's Pilgrim's Progress,
Langland's vision is social, rather than individualistic.
    Sees Langland's social allegory guided by a spiritual at-
titude toward poverty and based on a sense that the only means
of social salvation lies in the voluntary action of believers.

5   SHUTE, HELEN W. "Piers Plowman." Archiv 100:155-56.
        Compares A I 38-39, B I 40-41, and C I 38-39. In the A-
    and C-versions, hit (39) refers to entire preceding line; that
    is the object; and saule (not measure, as Skeat contends in
    Langland, 1886.1) the subject of the verb. In B-version, Shute
    takes sueth as a form of the verb to see, and would translate
    the lines "For the fiend and thy flesh follow thee together;
    this and that seeth they soul and telleth it thee in thy
    heart."

                            1899

*1   HOPKINS, E.M. "Notes on Piers Plowman." Kansas University
         Quarterly 8:29-36.
             Source: CBEL, vol. 1, col. 536; Colaianne, 1978.4,
         p. 15, no. 37. A doubtful entry.

2   SNELL, F.J. The Fourteenth Century. Periods of European Litera-
         ture, no. 3. New York: Charles Scribner's Sons, pp. 379-86.
             In a general review of the author and the contents of
         the poem, suggests that Piers is Christ Himself, but that this
         interpretation was probably an afterthought of Langland's.
         Dowel is the godly life; Dobet is based on love; Dobest signi-
         fies ideal ministry. Psychomachy of the last vision reminds
         us of the Libro de Buen Amor; and there is a remarkable simi-
         larity of the concluding visions and the Castle of Persever-
         ance, both of which were inspired by Ephesians 6:12. Suggests
         also Langland's knowledge of Roman de la Rose, Tournoiment
         d'Anticrist, and Bozon's Castel d'amour.

                            1900

1   CAPES, W.W. A History of the English Church. Vol. 3, The En-
         glish Church in the Fourteenth and Fifteenth Centuries. Ed-
         ited by W.R.W. Stephens and William Hunt. London: Macmillan
         & Co.; New York: Macmillan Co., 139-40.

1900

       With no voice of revolution or dissent from the Church's beliefs and practices, Langland expresses in homely language the passionate impatience of the populace at the social evils of the time. But he believes that true royalty and priesthood are divinely sanctioned and should be supported by the loyalty of the people. Reason and conscience are mankind's guides, Scripture his ultimate standard; and moral tests, rather than ceremonal observances, are all-important.

2   DRYDEN, JOHN. Essays of John Dryden. Vol. 2. Edited by W.P. Ker. Oxford: Clarendon Press, pp. 246-73.
       Reprint of [Dryden], 1700.1.

3   MENSENDIECK, OTTO. Charakterentwickelung und ethisch-theologische Anschauungen des Verfassers von Piers the Plowman. Dissertation, Giessen. Leipzig and London: Verlag von Th. Wohlleben, 92 pp.
       Views the progress and development of the poem as an allegory of the author's moral and intellectual development. The A-text shows him learning to think independently, perhaps even suggesting that he studied at university. B IX shows him turning to God, rather than to the Church, for spiritual relief. He then determines the connection of ethical and religious principles, and recognizes that God's grace extends over all. Poverty and love are the highest principles of Dowel; Dobet is the realization of Dowel, showing that the ideal life is impossible in reality, though it once was possible for a few; Dobest, the founding of the Church and the Christian community, can only begin after Christ's death. By His death, Christ has saved mankind; this sacrifice is infinitely more valuable than Dowel, or whatever man can achieve.
       Langland believes that thetime of God's testing is passed; he hopes that the Church can be rebuilt, though he probably conceives of the pope rather like an Antichrist. Langland's emphasis on grace, rather than works, and his recognition of the degeneracy of the institutional aspects of the Church disqualify him from consideration as one of the Church's true and loyal sons.

1901

1   JACK, A.S. "The Autobiographical Elements in Piers the Plowman." JEPG 3, no. 4:393-401.
       With the exception of Wright [Langland], 1842.3), most editors and commentators accept the autobiographical basis of details in the poem; Skeat appears more certain, if anything, of autobiographical references in the poem in the time between his early English Text Society editions (1867.3, 1869.2, 1873.5) and his parallel-text edition (1886.1). With regard

to expressions of time, however, comparison of the three texts suggests a regard for alliteration, rather than a desire for accuracy, decides the choice of a given number, and that definite alliterative expressions are often used for indefinitely long periods of time. Similarly, the motifs of sleeping, dreaming, and wandering are all conventional to a medieval poet. Wandering in particular must be treated as a framework in which the poet connects the various parts of his story and imparts picturesqueness to the whole. He dreams, he awakes; and the search for what he has seen naturally takes the metaphor of physically moving about.

The poet probably didn't live in London, or if he did, he was most probably not the well-known character he represents himself as being in the figure of Long Will; for there is no mention of this author in chronicles or elsewhere. He may have been married, with a child, but just as possibly may not have been.

All the poem allows us to say of the author is that he was perhaps a student, though not a profound scholar. He was probably a priest, and an individual given to a quiet, meditative life. He may have lived in the country, where the courtly literary influences were not powerful; he may have known London. He apparently sympathized with the common people, though he may have feared persecution, or at least disliked publicity.

2   MOULTON, CHARLES WELLS, ed. The Library of Literary Criticism of English and American Authors. Vol. 1. Buffalo, N.Y.: Moulton Publishing Co., pp. 116-23.

Prints notices of the poem, including those of [Langland], 1550.1; Webbe, 1586.1; Puttenham[?], 1589.1; Selden, 1622.2; Fuller, 1662.1; [Percy], 1765.1; Warton, 1778.3; Henry, 1789.1; Ellis, 1801.1; Whitaker, 1813.1; Campbell, 1819.2; Guest, 1838.1; D'Israeli, 1841.1; Browning, 1842.1; [Langland], 1842.3; Milman, 1855.4; Schele DeVere, 1853.1; Marsh, 1862.1; [Langland], 1867.3; Lowell, 1870.1; Rossetti, 1878.1; Lanier, 1880.2; Morley, 1877.3; Mitchell, 1889.4; Scudder, 1898.4; and so on. Revised: Moulton, 1966.10.

1902

1   BALE, JOHN. Index Britanniæ Scriptorum quos ex variis bibliothecis non parvo labore collegit Ioannis Baleus, cum aliis. John Bale's Index of British and Other Writers. In Anecdota Oxoniensia. Medieval and Modern Series, edited by Reginald Lane Poole, part 9. Oxford: Clarendon Press.

See Bale, post 1546.1.

Writings about Piers Plowman, 1395-1979

1903

1   ERNLE, ROWLAND EDMUND PROTHERO. The Psalms in Human Life.
     London: E.P. Dutton & Co., pp. 107-9.
          Langland's frequent use of the Psalms is illustrated.

2   GARNETT, RICHARD, and GOSSE, EDMUND. English Literature: An
     Illustrated Record. Vol. I, From the Beginnings to the Age of
     Henry VIII. New York: Macmillan Co.; London: Macmillan &
     Co., pp. 95-101.
          Langland was perhaps the first English writer to assume
     formally the capacity of prophet, denouncing sins of society
     and encouraging men to a higher life; yet it would be diffi-
     cult to find anyone in this role less given to unreason and
     fanaticism. He is more constructive than Carlyle, more con-
     sistent than Ruskin, though lacking the eloquence of both.
     He is best to be described as a conservative reformer who
     lacks deep and surprising insight. Whereas Chaucer represents
     the interests of the aristocracy and middle class, Langland
     portrays the dissatisfaction of the lower and "the more think-
     ing" classes. He is a precursor of Wyclif; his Protestantism
     is "undeveloped," but his tendencies are wholly antisacer-
     dotal.
          His choice of alliterative measure is appropriate to his
     particular talents in depiction by "swift, forcible strokes";
     nevertheless, he shows the unfitness of alliterative measure
     for the higher grades of poetry, since alliteration is most
     well adapted to a monosyllabic language, and became more dif-
     ficult to handle as more long words came into use. (Vol. 1 of
     this four-volume coauthored work is solely the product of
     Richard Garnett.)

1904

1   SELLERT, FRIEDRICH. Das Bild in Piers the Plowman. Disserta-
     tion, Rostock. Rostock: Universitäts-Buchdruckerei von
     Adlers Erben, 152 pp.
          A catalogue and classification of images and figures in
     the three versions according to topics of content and expe-
     rience (animals, nature, the mineral world, parts of the body,
     the house and its furnishings, etc.) and according to their
     poetic expression (simile, personification, metonymy, etc.).
     Concludes that only a few of Langland's images are original:
     most are from the Bible, Patristic commentary, or Latin and
     vernacular proverbs. Langland and Chaucer share many images,
     but never exclusively; thus there is no reason to think that
     one depends on the other. Langland's images are at their best
     when they are of everyday life, at their worst when, depen-
     dent on the Church Fathers, they are wearily long-winded, un-
     clear, even occasionally tasteless.

1905

1   TOUT, T.F. The Political History of England. Vol. 3, The His-
    tory of England from the Accession of Henry III to the Death
    of Edward III (1216-1377). Edited by William Hunt and
    Reginald L. Poole. London, New York, and Bombay: Longmans,
    Green, & Co., pp. 423-24.
          Langland's representations are not so much of material
    suffering as of social discontent. He criticizes every class
    and, though no revolutionary, he is a ruthless denouncer of
    abuses, thoroughly filled with the spirit that animated the
    Peasants' Revolt. As such, he represents the modernity of his
    age more than does Chaucer.

1906

1   BAYNE, THOMAS. "Piers the Plowman." N&Q, 10th ser. 6, no. 134
    (21 July):46-47.
          Deplores the misidentification of Piers Plowman as the
    author of the poem in Southey's Sir Thomas More: or Colloquies
    on the Progress and Prospects of Society, as well as in modern
    references, for example, a translation of the Memoirs of the
    Lord of Joinville.

2   BRADLEY, HENRY. "The Misplaced Leaf of 'Piers Plowman.'"
    Athenæum (London), 21 April, p. 481.
          A correction and refinement of Manly (1906.3). Manly's
    solution is ingenious, but leaves us with the necessity of
    supposing that after relating the confessions of the Deadly
    Sins, the poet introduced at the end a new portrait, whose
    offenses, according to the medieval classification, belong to
    the sin of Covetousness. A V 236-59 belong after A V 145, at
    the end of the confession of Covetousness. The source of the
    confusion is not a MS in quires or gatherings, but the au-
    thor's loose sheets as handed to the first transcriber. One
    of such sheets, describing the confession of Wrath and the end
    of the confession of Envy, got lost; another, containing lines
    236-59, was misplaced. Believes that this theory strengthens
    Manly's argument that the B-text is not the work of the au-
    thor(s) of the A-text. Bradley's article is answered by
    Brown (1909.2). Reprinted: Furnivall, 1908.3.

3   MANLY, JOHN MATTHEWS. "The Lost Leaf of 'Piers the Plowman.'"
    MP 3, no. 4 (January):359-66.
          Reading the poem in its three versions consecutively,
    rather than in Skeat's parallel-text edition (1886.1), has
    convinced Manly that the three versions represent the work of

different authors; that in the A-text only the Prologue and
passus I-VIII are by the same hand, with the principal part
of Dowel, Dobet, and Dobest added by another; that A XII
101-12 as seen in MS. R (A-text) is by John But, who is also
responsible for at least half of that passus; and that the
apparently "autobiographical" details of the C-text should not
be taken as facts of the author's life. These arguments are
soon to be presented in detail by Manly (see Manly, 1908.6).
    Contends that A V 222-35 do not belong to the confession
of Sloth, but instead belong to the confession of Robert the
Robber, as part of either his confession or a confession suggested to him by someone else. Suggests a lacuna exists here
between A V 235 and 236, where originally there might have
been a transition from the personified abstractions to the
confession of Robert the Robber, as well as a less abrupt ending to the confession of Sloth. Posits a missing leaf which,
on the basis of many extant MSS of the poem, probably contained 60 to 80 lines (30 to 40 lines per side), and was already missing in the latest common ancestor of all extant MSS.
Manly notes the absence of Wrath from the catalogue of the
Deadly Sins, and assumes the description of this sin should
follow that of Envy, at A V 106. Between this point and line
235 are 129 lines which, after subtraction of spurious additions, leaves approximately what Manly thinks would be lost
from two leaves of a missing sheet. Supposes that the poet
responsible for the B-text noticed the omissions and attempted
to correct them by adding a declaration earlier in Sloth's
confession that Sloth had withheld wages, and by adding a
confession of Wrath. But this confession is "totally different in style from the work of A," and, indeed, more appropriate for Envy than for Wrath. Reprinted: Furnivall,
1908.3. See also Bradley, 1906.2; and Brown, 1909.2.

4   SAINTSBURY, GEORGE. A History of English Prosody from the
     Twelfth Century to the Present Day. Vol. 1, From the Origins
     to Spenser. London: Macmillan & Co.; New York: Macmillan
     Co., pp. 179-89.
         Compared with Anglo-Saxon verse, Piers Plowman is more
     regular in the length of lines, uniformity of alliteration,
     and correspondence of the hemistiches. Langland deliberately
     avoids the new metrical scansion, but when he does produce a
     rhythm it is not merely "rochaic," as in Anglo-Saxon verse,
     but often anapestic "triple time." His half-lines never run
     syllabically into one another, and are almost always divided
     by units of sense. Langland seems to avoid even accidental
     rhymes and assonanced syllables at the end of lines and uni-
     formly produces lines of approximately thirteen syllables.

His meter is appropriat :o the main uses for which he employs it: narrative including description, and argument including exposition. Nevertheless, the "poetical equipment" of the alliterative line, even in Langland, seems "poor and beggarly" after the ear is accustomed to the sweetness of rhyme and the charm of metrical verse.

5   STUBBS, CHARLES WILLIAM. The Christ of English Poetry. The Hulsean Lectures Delivered before the University of Cambridge MCMIV-MCMV. London: J.M. Dent & Co., pp. 65-120.

The spirit of Christian social liberty is preached by Langland in England, as it was by Dante in Italy. Langland believes that the only true revolution is a result of revelation, and that there is no social transformation possible except as the "application of a religious principle, of a moral development, of a strong and active common faith." Langland saw the same social ills as Dante, but unlike him did not reach a clear and comprehensive ideal of life. In his satire, Langland can be profitably compared to Carlyle; in his insistence that the full likeness to Christ is to be found in the plowman, Langland shows he appreciates humanity wherever it is found as being of infinite worth.

1907

1   BRADLEY, HENRY. "The Word 'Moillere' in 'Piers the Plowman.'" MLR 2 (January):163-64.

Rejects Skeat's definition (1886.1) as "woman, wife" in favor of "legitimate child, person born in wedlock," representing Old French muliere and Law Latin mulieratus. Notes that the author(s) of the A- and B-texts used this rare law term correctly.

2   HEARNE, THOMAS. Remarks and Collections. Vol. 8, 1722-25. Oxford Historical Society, no. 50. Oxford: Oxford Historical Society.

See Hearne, 1725.1.

3   MEAD, S. "'Wy' in Hampshire." N&Q, 10th ser. 7, no. 183 (29 June):508.

Quotes William Andrews's Bygone Hampshire with reference to Hampshire fairs apparently alluded to in B V 205, and queries the location of the modern "Wy." See Skeat, 1907.4.

1907

4   SKEAT, WALTER W.   "'Wy' in Hampshire."   N&Q, 10th ser. 8, no. 186
    (20 July):54.
            Answers Mead (1907.3) with reference to Skeat's note in
    Langland (1869.2), V 205: "Wy" refers to the modern Weyhill
    fair.

5   TRAVER, HOPE.   The Four Daughters of God. A Study of the Ver-
    sions of This Allegory with Especial Reference to Those in
    Latin, French, and English.   Dissertation, Bryn Mawr. Bryn
    Mawr Monographs, no. 6. Philadelphia: John C. Winston Co.,
    pp. 147-52.
            Langland's treatment of the theme of the Four Daughters
    of God (B XVIII; C XXI) is found in the context of the Harrow-
    ing of Hell, not the Incarnation (as in most Christian ver-
    sions) or the Creation (as in the Midrash). Doubts the in-
    fluence on Langland's version of the Castel d'amour (as
    suggested by Brink [1877.1]), since the situations are wholly
    different. Suggests the influence instead of Bernard's In
    festo annunciationis Beatæ Virginis or Bonaventure's Medita-
    tiones vitæ Christi. Sees only slight evidence of the influ-
    ence of the poem on the Castle of Perseverance (cf. Brink,
    1877.1), but notes perhaps an echo in the opening lines of
    Lydgate's "Poem on the Prospect of Peace."

1908

1   FISHER, A.W.   "A Note on Piers the Plowman."   MLN 23, no. 7
    (November):231-32.
            Elaborates Skeat's explanation (Langland, 1886.1) of
    B V 28-29 by suggesting that the "two staves" are to be ex-
    plained as for use by Felice and her husband Tom Stowe to beat
    their way home through the jeering crowd.

2   FLOM, GEORGE T.   "A Note on Piers Plowman."   MLN 23, no. 5 (May):
    156-57.
            Defends reed in C I 215, against Onions (1908.7), in
    the sense of the expression "to have one's own reed," meaning
    "when one arrives at one's own decision, forms one's own
    will," and so on.

3   FURNIVALL, F.J., ed.   Piers Plowman and Its Sequence Contributed
    to the Cambridge History of English Literature by John
    Matthews Manly.   Early English Text Society, o.s. 135b.
    Cambridge: Cambridge University Press; London: Kegan Paul
    & Co.; Henry Frowde, xvi + 42 pp.
            A reprint of Manly, 1908.6, with foreword by Furnivall,
    that includes Manly, 1906.3 and Bradley, 1906.2. Furnivall

1908

considers it "incontestably certain" that the "B and C re-
visers and enlargers of the A version of the poem, were not
the men who wrote that version, but wholly different persons."
Furnivall also believes with Bradley (1906.2) that sixty-two
of the lines apparently joined to the portrait of Sloth belong
instead to Covetousness. See Furnivall, 1910.4.

4   HALL, THEOPHILUS D. "Was 'Langland' the Author of the C-Text of
     'The Vision of Piers Plowman'?" MLR 4, no. 1 (October):1-13.
          Believes that strong internal evidence exists to chal-
     lenge the accepted view of the authenticity of the C-text,
     which had been ignored by sixteenth-century editors and sub-
     jected, in the opinion of Wright (1842.3), to interpolations
     by someone "perhaps induced by his own political sentiments to
     modify passages, and [who] was gradually led on to publish a
     revision of the whole."
          Hall notes many omissions of material in the B-text not
     carried over into the C-text, namely, in the opening of the
     poem (A-B Prol 5-10); in references to historical occurrences
     in the Hundred Years' War (B III 188 ff.); in the confession
     of Envy (B V); in the discourse of Wit (B IX) and of Dame
     Study (B X); and in the characterization of Haukyn (B XIII and
     XIV). Concludes that these omissions almost always result in
     more prosaic poetry and a loss of vividness. With regard to
     additions in the C-text, Hall notes the lack of alliteration
     in C I 94-124, a fierce diatribe against priests; an irrele-
     vant and inept insertion regarding the location of Hell in the
     North in C II (B III); and the "autobiographical" insertions
     in C VI (cf. B V) that make the author seem a hypocrite, for
     in B the argument concerns his justification of writing, not
     his idle loafing.
          With regard to structural changes, C VI (cf. B V) makes
     Langland's famous prophecy part of Reason's discourse; and in
     C X the poet's problem concerning the damnation of eminent
     heathens has become the problem of Recklessness, although the
     poet, or his persona, still receives the rebuke for such
     speculations. Concludes that the author of the C-text was
     more vehement in his denunciations and more stern, and was
     essentially a schoolman or moralist.
          In a note, states that this essay was written before
     Manly (1908.6), and although he agrees with Manly's ascription
     of the C-text to a different author and Manly's hypothesis
     concerning the "lost leaf" (see Manly, 1906.3), feels Manly
     does not do justice to the B-text poet's "power of pathos and
     the moral sublime," and questions Manly's contention of a
     second A-poet, beginning at the end of A VIII.

1908

*5   KOELREUTTER, MARIA. Das Privatleben in England nach den Dich-
      tungen von Chaucer, Gower und Langland. Dissertation, Zürich.
      Hall on the Saale: Druck von Ehrhardt Karras, 145 pp.
          Source: Gabel and Gabel, p. 9.

6   MANLY, JOHN M. "'Piers the Plowman' and Its Sequence." In The
      Cambridge History of English Literature. Vol. 2, The End of
      the Middle Ages. Edited by A.W. Ward and A.R. Waller.
      Cambridge: Cambridge University Press; New York: G.P.
      Putnam's Sons, pp. 1-42.
          The poem in its three versions is the work of five dif-
      ferent authors, as is proven by differences in diction, meter,
      sentence structure, methods of organizing material, use of
      rhetorical devices, the visualization of objects, interests of
      the authors, and treatment of social and theological questions
      --all of such a nature as to rule out single authorship.
          The A-text is composed of three visions, the first two
      of which are intimately connected and are distinguished by a
      unity of structure, directness of movement, and freedom from
      digression. The third vision, on the other hand, is charac-
      terized by the absence of "vitalised allegory," for the alle-
      gorical figures in this vision are of superfluous significance
      and, for the most part, merely indulge in debate, rather than
      contribute meaningful action. Moreover, clearness of phrasing
      and orderliness of thought is lacking in this part of the
      poem. A$_1$ (up to the end of A VIII) is not at all interested
      in casuistry or theological doctrine; A$_2$ indulges in scholas-
      tic methods of argumentation and is concerned with questions
      related to predestination. The similes of A$_1$ are all simple,
      whereas some of A$_2$ are elaborate. A$_2$ ceased work at XII 56,
      when Will and Anima-probate leave Scripture to seek Kind Wit;
      this is in opposition to Skeat (Langland, 1886.1) who con-
      tended that John But took up the poem no earlier than XII 99.
          The author of the B-text, who had before him as he wrote
      the three visions of the A-text, practically disregarded A XII
      and changed the preceding eleven passūs by insertions and ex-
      pansions; but he made for fewer verbal alterations than is
      commonly supposed, for many of his words are found among the
      so-called variant readings of A-text MSS. Of the nine prin-
      cipal insertions made in visions 1 and 2, six are mere elabo-
      rations of the A-text. Agrees with Jusserand (1893.1) that
      the B-poet seems often at the mercy of the associations of
      his diction. Topics alien to the main theme often intrude
      upon his writing, characters become mere mouthpieces of the
      author, dramatic consistency is often violated, and the unity
      and consistency of the visions are lost. The B-text may be
      unfinished, but the author, who lacks skill in composition and
      control of thought, probably couldn't have brought it to a

successful close. Nevertheless, the B-poet does have the
merits of sincerity and emotional power.

The very numerous changes and additions of the C-text
often defy explanation and, although occasionally supplying
better alliteration or eliminating an archaic word, sometimes
do harm to the style and thought. Examples of this are C XI
30-32, which presents a belief in astrology out of harmony
with the B-text, and C XI 51-55 and XVII 158-82, which appear
to be a rejection of the views of Bradwardine endorsed by the
B-text.

Lists a number of contexts in which the B-text seems to
have misunderstood the A-text, and the C-text seems to have
misunderstood the B-text, namely, B II 21 (the gender of
Lewte); B II 25 (False, instead of Wrong, the father of Mede);
B II 74 (B-poet shows he misunderstands the provinces of the
Deadly Sins by elaborating the feoffment); B Prol 11-16
spoiled in C-text; and segges of B Prol 160-66 changed in
C-text to syres.

Suggests that a careful study of the pronouns, verbs,
and meter will support his hypothesis of different authors.
He contends that the "autobiographical" details, largely in
the B- and C-texts, are fictional, that the names of Will's
wife and daughter are conventional, and that "Long Will, the
dreamer, is, obviously, as much a creation of the muse as is
Piers the Plowman." The A_1-poet may have been a monk or perhaps a layman and A_2-, B-, and C-poets probably clerics, perhaps from the secular clergy. John But was no doubt a scribe
or minstrel. Richard the Redeless was written by an imitator
of Piers Plowman, as can be demonstrated by numerous differences in diction, versification, and so on. The influence of
Piers Plowman was widespread, though it appears the poem imitated the Parlement of the thre Ages and Wynnere and Wastoure,
rather than vice versa. Allusions to "do wel and better" in
the letter of John Ball suggests that he had the poem itself
in mind and not merely a traditional allegory. And both Death
and Liffe and The Crowned King are related to Piers Plowman.
Reprinted: Furnivall, 1908.3.

7   ONIONS, C. TALBOT. "An Unrecorded Reading in 'Piers Plowman.'"
    MLR 3, no. 2 (January):170-71.
        On the basis of MS B^2 (C-text), would read reik (OED,
    s.v. raik) for reed in C I 215. Suggests that this northern
    form would prove a difficulty to southern scribes. See Flom,
    1908.2; but cf. Onions, 1908.8.

1908

8 ONIONS, C. TALBOT. "A Reading in Piers Plowman." MLN 23, no. 7
   (November):231.
        Desires Flom (1908.2) to document his assertion that the
   expression "to have one's reed" may be found in "Southern,
   Midland, and Northern M.E., and in Old Norse."

9 TUCKER, SAMUEL MARION. Verse Satire in England before the
   Renaissance. Columbia University Studies in English, ser. 2,
   vol. 3, no. 2. New York: Columbia University Press,
   pp. 70-79.
        The poem is a satire in the broadest possible sense; its
   allegorical form, lack of humor, and large constructive element make it a didactic poem which mounts a fairly complete
   criticism of its age. The allegorical vehicle is effective
   for satire only when personifications are made into genuine
   characterizations: this is true of the figures of Avarice,
   Gluttony, Piers, and for the most part, Lady Mede. Satire is
   essentially realistic, and allegory abstract; Langland's contribution is to adapt the abstract method to very real material. In general, Langland is more effective in the satire
   of various classes than in the personification of abstractions. He advances beyond his predecessors in the range of
   subject matter, characterization, attention to contemporary
   events. The only reform he envisions is "that wrought by
   love as an active principle." Langland drew from Jean de
   Meun for his satire of beggars and friars, but did not in-
   herit Jean's antifeminism. And unlike the Speculum stultorum,
   Piers Plowman contains no prologue designed to render a hidden
   meaning apparent.

1909

1 BRADLEY, HENRY. "The 'Lost Leaf' of 'Piers the Plowman.'"
   Nation 88 (29 April):436-37.
        A reply to Brown (1909.2). Contends that Brown's
   theory does not deal with the difficulty that the confession
   of Covetousness ends with merely a promise to deal honestly
   in the future, without any mention of restitution; that it
   posits the poet ending on the figure of Sloth, then going back
   to someone connected with Covetousness; and that it fails to
   recognize that the whole point of the introduction of Robert
   the Robber is to present someone who can't make restitution.
   Suggests instead that Langland's idea was to present first
   Covetousness and then an example of one who can't make restitution and whose situation is desperate unless God will accept his penitence.

With regard to the omission of Wrath, notes that Envy,
which he feels ought to have preceded Wrath, lacks both a profession of penitence and a promise of amendment; hence, part
of one and all of the next portrait are lacking.

2   BROWN, CARLETON F. "The 'Lost Leaf' of 'Piers the Plowman.'"
     Nation 88 (25 March):298-99.
          Aims at a simpler explanation than that of Bradley
     (1906.2): merely to move A V 236-41 (concerned with the dif-
     ficulty of making restitution) to immediately after A V 253
     means that the vow of Sloth would come to its conclusion at
     line 235; Robert the Robber would then be introduced at line
     236 and his prayer for mercy concluded with a vow. Lines
     247-59 then serve to dismiss Robert and prepare for the throng
     of nameless penitents who, like Robert, will seek St. Truth.
     Suggests these lines became misplaced, apparently like others
     in the A-text (e.g., II 37-39, which perhaps better belong
     after II 51), because they were added by the author at the top
     or bottom of the page and wrongly inserted by a scribe. With
     regard to the omission of Wrath, Brown notes that Manly
     (1906.3) has pointed out the omission of this sin elsewhere in
     the poem. Notes also that Hall (1908.4) had independently
     attributed the lines after V 236 to Robert's confession.

3   CHAMBERS, R.W., and GRATTAN, J.H.G. "The Text of 'Piers
     Plowman.' I: 'The A-text.'" MLR 4, no. 3 (April):357-89.
          Skeat's edition of the A-text (1867.3; 1886.1) is not a
     critical text, but a corrected version of MS. V. The impres-
     sion that the A-text is inferior in meter and style to the B-
     text is often founded upon readings in Skeat's A-text, whereas
     the B-reading often finds support in "variant" readings of
     other A-text MSS. In many of these cases, agreement of A-MSS
     readings with the B-text against the reading of MS. V (which,
     like its near relative, MS. H, is an edited text) proves V
     does not preserve the original reading. On the whole, MSS. TU
     represent a better textual tradition than VH, for they can be
     used to correct VH three times as often as vice versa. These
     two MS families incorporate almost all the extant texts; of
     the exceptions, MSS. D and L, though both corrupt, are inde-
     pendent enough of the two main lines of descent so as to con-
     stitute witnesses to the original readings where VH and TU
     disagree, and neither is clearly right or wrong.
          Manly (1908.6) had contended that many differences of
     the B-text from the A-text were eliminated on inspection of
     A-text variants; hence, a reviser, rather than the author, was
     to him responsible for preserving unoriginal readings. But
     the real text of A, founded mainly on TU and to a lesser

1909

extent on VH and the independent MSS, will be much closer in
form to the B-text.
Includes a critical text of A V 43-106, based on MS. T
with collations from MSS. R, U, E, H², D, K, W, L, A, V, and
H.

4   DEAKIN, MARY. "The Alliteration of 'Piers Plowman.'" MLR 4,
no. 4 (July):478-83.
Examines the alliteration in the three versions, taking
the alliterative pattern aa/ax as the norm and considering
deviations from this norm, such as increase in the number of
rhyme letters in either half-line, decrease in the number of
rhyme letters in either half-line, lines containing two rhyme
letters, extraordinary alliteration such as h alliterating
with a vowel, alliteration on a syllable bearing weak or secondary stress, and lines lacking alliteration. Tabulation
reveals that most deviations from the norm are very evenly
distributed or show fairly regular increase or decrease in
the successive versions. Finds nothing to strengthen Manly's
claim (1908.6) that an investigation of the alliteration
would prove his argument for multiple authorship.

5   KNOTT, THOMAS A. "The 'Lost Leaf' of 'Piers the Plowman.'"
Nation 88 (13 May):482-83.
Argues the value of Manly (1906.3) over Bradley (1906.2
and 1901.9) and Brown (1909.2). Bradley's suggestion of composition on separate sheets is not attested in medieval English literature; and Covetousness's confession is complete--
there is no need to make restitution. Moreover, Brown was
correct in pointing out the inconsistency in Bradley's
reconstruction between a vow to take a conventional pilgrimage
quickly followed by one to take a "highly spiritual" pilgrimage before seeing Rome. Bradley has dismissed Brown's objection that Robert the Robber belongs after Sloth as an example
of despair by claiming that there is no mention of wanhope in
Sloth's portrait; but he has f iled to take into account V
225. Reddite may be a speaker telling Robert to repent, as
did Repentence tell Envy and Gluttony's wife Gluttony.
Brown's argument fails, too, however; for V 59-60 indicate
Envy's portrait is not intentionally incomplete.
Counting the lines confirms that the number of lines
preceding the first break fill two quires of eight folios
each and the first two folios of the third quire. Then comes
the first break, containing the end of Envy and all of Wrath.
Then the inside two folios continue the 122 lines between the
breaks. Then comes the loss of another folio, containing perhaps more of Sloth and the introduction of Robert.

6   JUSSERAND, J.J.   "Piers Plowman the Work of One or Five." MP 6,
     no. 3 (January):271-329.
          The poem, in its various forms, represents the lifework
     of its author; hence, it was subject to long-term and irregu-
     lar revision, by which the poet added, emended, corrected
     mistakes, and sometimes failed to correct mistakes. Additions
     and corrections were placed in the margin, presumably, or on
     inserted slips or flyleaves, and for that reason it was often
     difficult to determine where they belonged in the text, as in
     the instance of Montaigne's revisions. The poet allowed in-
     complete texts of Piers Plowman to be circulated and perhaps
     had no control over their circulation. Yet the three visions
     are clearly part of one poem, for even the section devoted to
     Dowel, Dobet, and Dobest is anticipated by the end of passus
     VIII. All titles, colophons, marginal notes, and testimonies
     agree in calling the three forms of the work one work, written
     by one author. All MS notes and internal allusions attribute
     it to one author, although this author is variously named.
     Manly's five authors (see Manly, 1906.3, 1908.6) should be
     reduced to four with the exclusion of the "silly scribbler"
     John But who, unaware of the existence of the B-text, added
     a "senseless" ending. But Manly never acknowledges the im-
     probability of the premise on which his theory of multiple
     authorship rests: that each of the four authors must have
     died before the next wrote.
          Considers in turn Manly's alleged "proofs" of multiple
     authorship: the misplaced leaf; the fact that the third and
     fourth authors often seem not to understand what authors one
     and two meant; and the differences detected in the moods, feel-
     ings, ways of speaking, literary merit, meter, and dialect of
     various parts and versions. Regarding the misplaced leaf,
     agrees with Bradley (1906.2) that the proper place for Robert
     the Robber is after A V 145; Jusserand believes that the poet
     had left twenty-four lines in the wrong place in the A-text,
     perhaps because he had added them on a slip as an after-
     thought, allowing them to be misplaced by a scribe. The poet
     intended to transfer the lines when he wrote the B-text, but
     neglected to do so, just as many authors (e.g., Theodore
     Roosevelt) have read blatant mistakes in their proof and have
     not corrected them in revision. But the poet did correct his
     error in the C-text. Argues against Manly that the B-text's
     description of Sloth is in conformance with the conventional
     representation of that sin; that the confessions of the sins
     in the A-text are not always as bad, and those in the B-text
     not always as good, as Manly contends; that Leute in B II 21
     can be understood as feminine without any inconsistency; that
     making False, rather than Wrong, the father of Mede is in-
     tended by the poet as an improvement over the situation in

the A-text; that in elaborating upon feoffment in B II 74, the
poet is merely adding supplementary details (as he often does
in revision) which in no way impair the unity of the work; and
so on.

With regard to literary merit and mental power evinced
in the different sections and versions, concludes that the
differences are not as wide as Manly says exist between A_1 and
A_2, and that some of the same "incoherencies" are found in
both; that the narrative of A_1 is not interrupted more often
than that of A_2 for the introduction of the author's views;
and that both sections share the same antipathies. Likewise,
sees the A-text and the B-text equally dependent on the associations of the words the poet has used and equally forgetful
of the plan of the work. The author of the C-text appears to
be a better scholar than the author of A_2, but this is understandable, given the fact that he was by that time an older
man. By the criteria invoked by Manly, the two parts of Don
Quixote, Paradise Lost and Paradise Regained, and Robinson
Crusoe and its continuations would be declared not the work
of their respective authors.

Jusserand believes all the personal notes accord well
with one another and with the hypothesis of progressive versions written by the same author. Disagrees with Manly and
with Jack (1901.1) regarding the alleged "fictitiousness" of
the autobiographical references. Reprinted: Early English
Text Society, o.s. 139b, in Furnivall, 1910.4.

7   LONG, WILLIAM J. English Literature and Its Significance for the
    Life of the English-Speaking World. Boston, New York, Chicago,
    and London: Ginn & Co., pp. 81-83.
        The poem traditionally has been attributed to Langland,
    but is "now known to be the work of several different writ-
    ers." Considers the poem in its denunciation of the abuses
    that had entered into the medieval Church one of the greatest
    influences on the Reformation. Cf. Connolly, 1925.3.

8   MANLY, JOHN M. "The Authorship of Piers Plowman." MP 7, no. 1
    (July):83-144.
        A reply to Jusserand (1893.1 and 1909.6). Calls atten-
    tion to the "self-contradictory personality" of Langland as
    described by Jussèrand, and feels the poem is more influenced
    by foreign material than has been admitted. Doubts it con-
    tains unique democratic ideas, for matters of parliamentary
    debate were most probably circulating among the general popu-
    lace. Since the treatment given to social and political ques-
    tions changes in the three versions (e.g., C I 139 ff.),
    multiple authorship seems likely. Moreover, if social reform
    is characteristic of a single author working over a period of

years, it is hard to explain the absence of references to the
Peasants' Revolt in all versions.
Regarding the misplaced leaf, Manly can accept Jusserand's notions of the poet's adding new material on inserted
slips without thus committing himself to the theory of a single author. Jusserand had contended that Langland must have
allowed his work to be copied in various stages of incompletion, but Manly feels it is rash to assume that the endings of
any extant MSS represent a definite stage in compositon or
revision. Jusserand's contention that all MS notes and colo-
phons point to the work as being one poem by one author is
true only for the B- and C-texts, for there is no unmixed version of the A-text that treats Dowel as part of Piers Plowman.
Jusserand feels Bale's testimony (1557.1) is of great weight,
but Bale is often far from trustworthy about early authors
such as Chaucer and Wyclif. Jusserand is likewise wrong in
undervaluing John But, whose work shows that men continued
and modified texts which had come to them and whose continuation is supported by nineteen MSS.
Manly doubts Jusserand's reconstruction of the placement
of the passages dealing with Robert the Robber and the Deadly
Sins, for the C-poet's moving back the lines dealing with
Robert the Robber does not result in the smooth reading
Jusserand had claimed. Reiterates instances (see Manly,
1908.6, and cf. Jusserand, 1909.6) of the B- and C-poets'
misunderstanding of their predecessors' work. As regards
style, asks the reader to consider the sentences of the
various versions with respect to absolute length, number of
coordinate and subordinate clauses, and number of stressed and
unstressed syllables. Concludes that "the force of a large
number of important differences between two works cannot be
broken by showing that each difference has been found in works
undoubtedly by one author." Reprinted: Early English Text
Society, o.s. 139c, in Furnivall, 1910.4.

*9   OWEN, DOROTHY. "A Comparison of Piers Plowman with Some Earlier
     and Contemporary French Allegories." M.A. thesis, University
     of London.
          Source: Bilboul, vol. 1, p. 135. For a published ver-
     sion of this thesis, see Owen, 1912.5.

1910

1   BRADLEY, HENRY. "The Authorship of 'Piers the Plowman.'" MLR 5,
     no. 2 (April):202-7.
          A reply to Chambers (1910.2). Admits that Robert the
     Robber has some affinity to Sloth, but finds the evidence of

1910

the text supports its closer affinity to Covetousness. Suggests that moving V 236-59 back to after V 145 yields continuous sense, as the confession of Covetousness is thus brought
to a close in language appropriate to that sin but inappropriate to Sloth.

Calls attention to the testimony of John But which may
be worthless but perhaps may be valuable in suggesting that
the poem may have circulated in three parts: passūs I-V,
VI-VIII, and IX-XII. Hence, looks forward to Manly's arguments for separate authorship of A IX-XII. But warns against
arguments against single authorship based merely on the in-
feriority of a later production.

Speculates that Piers may be named from the ejaculation
Peter! with which the plowman first enters the poem; were this
true, Langland might well be considered the creator of the
ideal figure, rather than merely one who employed a name and
conception already current.

2   CHAMBERS, R.W. "The Authorship of 'Piers Plowman.'" MLR 5,
    no. 1 (January):1-32.
    An attempt to deal with various assertions of the
multiple-authorship question. Contends that Robert the Robber
is best understood as representing a class of men (see A Prol
43; VII 66) associated with vagabondage, ribaldry, and theft;
his confession is based on Sloth, linked with wanhope (as in
Chaucer's "Parson's Tale"). Hence, there is no reason to dis-
turb the order of the MSS as far as Robert is concerned.
Sloth's wicked winnings are not inappropriate, for all that
is gained through Sloth is won wickedly; and wicked winning is
associated with slackness in returning things borrowed, just
as Piers associates prompt returning with true winning.

Reference to Piers's wife and children (A VII), thought
by Manly (1909.8) to be a "palpable dislocation" of the A-text
passed over and allowed to stand in the B-text, is instead
integral to the passage in which it is found, which is an ad-
monition to work. Bradley's rearrangement of lines (1906.2)
separates the vow to seek Truth by nearly one hundred lines
from the crowds who cry for grace to seek him. Contends instead that only if the MSS refuse to make sense and the proposed rearrangement is utterly and immediately convincing can
such conjectural emendations be admitted and considered to be
certain evidence as to authorship.

Defends against Manly (1908.6 and 1909.8) the B-poet's
alleged "misunderstandings" of the A-text. Calls attention to
the fact that Manly's assertion that study of pronouns and the
verb to be will prove multiple authorship has yet to be carried out and that in his assertion, Manly may not have realized
that some of the forms of MS. V in the accepted text of the

A-version may not be original. Disagrees, finally, with
Manly's evaluation of the fictional status of Long Will, on
the strength of the poet's referring to himself in this
fashion in A IX 61-63 and IX 116-18. Moreover, in A VIII 42,
the "Wil" referred to is clearly the writer of the vision, not
the Dreamer. See Knott, 1917.3 and 1917.4.

3 DOBSON, MARGARET. "An Examination of the Vocabulary of the 'A.
     Text' of 'Piers the Plowman,' with Reference to Its Bearing on
     the Authorship." Anglia 33:391-96.
          Divides the A-text as follows: Ia: Prol-IV; Ib:
     V-VIII 131; II: VIII 132-XII 58. Subjects these divisions
     of the poem to various tests investigating relative richness
     of their respective vocabularies; words occurring in Ib and II
     that do not occur in Ia; words found in Ia that do not re-
     appear in Ib; and words found in Ia and Ib that aren't in II.
     With respect to adjectives, tests relative richness of the
     three parts in adjectives; adjectives common to two parts and
     not occurring in a third; and adjectives used in Ia which do
     not occur again in Ib and II. Also investigates different
     words used to express the same meaning; some words used to
     express different meanings; ethical words; and compound words.
     Concludes that most evidence tends to support the single-
     author theory.

4 FURNIVALL, F.J., ed. The Piers Plowman Controversy. Early
     English Text Society, o.s. 139b, c, d, e [,f]. London:
     Kegan, Paul, Trench, Trübner & Co.; London and New York:
     Henry Frowde, Oxford University Press, ii + 59 + 62 + 38 + 32
     [+ 202-207] pp.
          Reprints of Jusserand, 1909.6; Manly, 1909.8; Jusserand,
     1910.6; Chambers, 1910.2; and Bradley, 1910.1. Furnivall's
     foreword expresses the hope that Bradley's reply to Chambers
     (1910.2) (Bradley, 1910.1) will soon be made available in
     reprint. It is included, with a separate title-page, as The
     Authorship of Piers the Plowman contributed to The Modern
     Language Review by Henry Bradley and reprinted, by permission,
     for members of the Early English Text Society. Early English
     Text Society, o.s. 139f, pp. 202-7.

5 HALL, THEOPHILUS D. "The Misplaced Lines, Piers Plowman (A) V,
     236-41." MP 7, no. 3 (January):327-28.
          Replies to Manly (1909.8) in a defense of these lines as
     belonging to Robert the Robber: the lines are an afterthought
     prompted by the poet's sense of the defect of penitence with-
     out appropriate works. The lines deal with dishonesty, under
     the two aspects of dishonest trading and theft with violence;
     the former has been dealt with under Covetousness; the latter

1910

is exemplified in Robert. Suggests that Langland may have
died leaving the passage in a detached form.

6   JUSSERAND, J.J. "Piers Plowman, the Work of One or Five: a
     Reply." MP 7, no. 3 (January):289-326.
          A reply to Manly (1909.8), in which Jusserand responds
     to a number of points bearing on the authorship question.
     Argues that if the differences between versions and parts are
     as great as Manly claims, the authors of earlier parts would
     have protested the treatment accorded their work. Suggests
     that discrepancies as great as Manly has described exist be-
     tween poems certainly due to the same writer and cites in this
     regard Rabelais, Hugo, and so on. Argues that the absence of
     any reference to the Peasants' Revolt supports single author-
     ship. Regarding the testimony of Bale (1557.1), suggests that
     the importance of such testimony is in the fact that a con-
     tinuator would most probably sign his name to his production.
     With regard to Robert the Robber's unrevised misplacement,
     suggests it may be too much to demand complete consistency
     from an author who, like Langland, left incomplete lists of
     the Deadly Sins in all three versions. Argues that Manly is
     wrong in suggesting that the B- and C-texts introduce propor-
     tionately more personal sentiments than the A-text; that the
     revision of a good line into an inferior one suggests a re-
     viser different from the author. Regarding the "autobiograph-
     ical details," continues to believe that as long as nothing
     contradicts the explicit statement of the poem, "we are en-
     titled to take them for what they are given." Reprinted:
     Early English Text Society, o.s. 139d, in Furnivall, 1910.4.

7   MACAULEY, G.C. "The Name of the Author of 'Piers Plowman.'"
     MLR 5, no. 2 (April):195-96.
          Tradition favors Robert over William. It is easier to
     see how William could have arisen from the name of a persona
     of the poet than it is to accept Robert coming into being
     from the line "Thus i robed in russet · romed I aboute" (see
     1868.3).
          Notices that Bale's in terra lutea (1557.1) is connected
     with a false entymology of Cleobury (Cleybirie to Crowley,
     1550.1); and compares Bale's Index (Bale, post 1546.1), in
     the cley lande. Speculates on corruption in transmission from
     Brigham, Bale's source, since from Cleobury to the Malvern
     Hills is closer to twenty-eight rather than eight miles.

8   MENSENDIECK, OTTO. "Die Verfasserschaft der drei Texte des
     Piers the Plowman." Zeitschrift für vergleichende Literatur-
     geschichte 17:10-31.
          The differences noted by Manly do not necessarily mean
     multiple authorship; indeed, the differences between A_1, A_2,

B, and C are only understandable as the continuation and
development of the same author's writing. B XI offers in
effect the explanation of the unfinished state of A_1 by demonstrating how the author has come to know himself after a period of irresponsibility. The C-text shows these and other
events leading to different consequences; only one who had
experienced such events could interpret them differently in
these ways, with an accent on dogma wholly understandable
after the earlier autobiographical confessions.

9   MENSENDIECK, OTTO. "The Authorship of Piers Plowman." JEGP 9:
    404-20.
            Attempts to prove the A-poet's authorship of the B-text
    by showing how the B-text continues the autobiographical ex-
    periences and confessions of the A-text, with the various
    allegorical personifications representing the poet at particu-
    lar stages of his life and quest. In particular, with the
    friars supplying no good answers to the Dreamer's search for
    truth, he falls back on his own resources, with Truth in
    A IX 61 ff. representing the conventional opinion of an aver-
    age man, such as he would have entertained in his childhood.
    Wit (A IX 109 ff.) refers to his life in grammar school; Dame
    Study (A XI 1 ff.) represents the next step in his develop-
    ment, the studium generale. Introduction of Clergy (A XI
    104 ff.) indicates the poet had apparently not been admitted
    to the tonsure as a pupil of grammar, but later, after the
    tonsure, had embarked on the trivium and quadrivium. Clergy's
    wife, Scripture, is learning and scholarship as taught by the
    studium generale, with Clergy himself representing the cleri-
    cal skill leading directly to the clerical state and order.
    The argument among Clergy, Scripture, and the persona (A XI
    179 ff.) is only intelligible as the record of the poet's
    problems at this point in his life with the questions of de-
    terminism and free will. The B-text continues to depict the
    poet's struggles in these regards, with Imaginatif answering
    the earlier charge of the insufficiency of the Church's doc-
    trines by blaming the poet (B XII). These reproaches derive
    from the shame and remorse described in B XI 426 ff., and
    hence must be seen as the autobiographical record of the de-
    velopment of the author's character.

*10 PEEBLES, ROSE JEFFRIES. "The Legend of Longinus in Ecclesiasti-
     cal Tradition and in English Literature, and Its Connection
     with the Grail." Dissertation, Bryn Mawr.
             For the publication of this dissertation, see Peebles,
     1911.4.

1910

11 PREVITÉ-ORTON, C.W. Political Satire in English Poetry. Being
    the Members' Prize Essay for 1908. Cambridge: Cambridge
    University Press, pp. 18-22.
         The poem's political philosophy is compared unfavorably
    with that of the "Battle of Lewes." The poem is praised as a
    call to righteousness, but classed as prophetic, rather than
    political literature. It offers evidence of the approaching
    breakdown of the medieval polity, against which the author
    took refuge, like Dante, in the idea of the good ruler. Yet
    unlike Dante, the stress in Piers Plowman on inward religion
    shows the stirrings of the Reformation. Reprinted: Previté-
    Orton, 1966.13.

12 SAINTSBURY, GEORGE. Historical Manual of English Prosody.
    London: Macmillan & Co., p. 153.
         Sees Langland's poem as example of the greatest perfec-
    tion that can be expected in reverting to verse without rhyme.
    Describes his prosody as "a consistent medium, not so much
    dominated as permeated by a sort of anapæstic underhum of
    rhythm, but otherwise maintaining its independence." Consid-
    ers alliterative measure deficient in beauty and unsuited for
    many poetic subjects, but finds it "not unsuitable" for
    Langland's apocalyptic dreams and his occasional passages of
    mundane description.

13 SCHIPPER, JAKOB. A History of English Versification. Oxford:
    Clarendon Press.
         A translation of Schipper, 1895.5. For a modern reprint,
    see Schipper, 1971.26.

1911

1   CHAMBERS, R.W. "The Original Form of the A-Text of 'Piers
    Plowman.'" MLR 6, no. 3 (July):302-23.
         Examines the suggestions of Bradley (1910.1) that the
    A-text circulated in three installments (I-V, VI-VIII, IX-
    XII); that John But added his continuation without knowing of
    the B- and C-texts, or by regarding them spurious; and that
    the three works But refers to are the sections of the poem
    dealing with Piers (VI-VIII), the Field of Folk (I-V), and
    "that which is here written," that is, Dowel. Argues instead
    that no extant MS suggests publication by installments, and
    that the A-text begins VI and IX with clear links to what has
    gone before in a fashion that would be meaningless if parts of
    the poem had circulated separately. Even if this had at one
    time occurred, finds it hard to imagine this to have been the
    case by the time But wrote. Evidence of the MS relationships

opposes the view that But added to a MS containing Dowel only;
it appears that XII was an afterthought, added by the poet or
someone else. But's lines, which continue XII, must either be
subsequent to or contemporaneous with the addition of XII; and
the MSS that end at XI and those that contain XII, either with
or without But's continuation, descend from one original which
had both the Visio (I-VIII) and Dowel (IX-XI).

The "other works" mentioned by But could refer to the B-
text additions, generally dated from before But's continuation. As regards the extent of But's work, suggests either
all of XII, put together from one or two recollections of the
B-text and A XI, or A XII 89 ff., where the poem shifts from
Will's search for Dowel to the personality of Will himself.

2 GEBHARD, HEINRICH. Langlands und Gowers Kritik der kirchlichen
   Verhältnisse ihrer Zeit. Dissertation, Strasbourg. Hornberg:
   H. Niefer, iv + 193 pp.
   Langland and Gower criticize the Church from different
points of view: for Gower, such criticism is his reason for
writing, and hence the satire he presents is detailed; for
Langland, criticism of the Church is but a means to an end, an
attempt to find a truly Christian activity that speaks to his
personal needs. Both recognize the obligation to obey secular
institutions created by God; both recognize the historical
right of the pope, though Gower is more critical of papal
pronouncements, especially those related to the Church at war.
Langland challenges the orthodox teachings on predestination,
but Gower accepts these dogmas. Both accept Mary as mediatrix
of blessings. Both see no historical right in financial considerations brought to the sacrament of Penance. Both believe
faith without works is dead, but Langland questions the value
for salvation of prayers and masses by themselves. Gower is
easier on the value of pilgrimages and veneration of the
saints than Langland, whose opinion on images is close to that
of the reformers. Both authors follow Wyclif in denouncing
high ecclesiastical corruption as the work of the Antichrist,
though neither calls the pope the Antichrist. Both believe
that theology is not a science; both criticize the friars for
their scholasticism. Both value the contemplative over the
active life, though Gower is more detailed than Langland on
the failure of monks to live up to the ideals of monasticism.

3 KEILLER, MABEL M. "The Influence of Piers Plowman on the Macro
   Play of 'Mankind.'" PMLA 26:339-55.
   Argues that Mankind depends on Piers Plowman in respect
to the "central situation" (tilling a piece of ground); the
characters (Mercy corresponding to Piers and the Knight; the
Monk and his tormentors corresponding to the wasters of the

1911

Half-acre scene); and the setting, which is rustic in both, rather than martial, as in Lydgate's Assembly of Gods. Moreover, sees a similarity in the "general trend of thought," emphasizing labor and moderation in both works. Even Piers's Tearing of the Pardon in evident disgust is paralleled by Mankynd's feeling when he discovers his spade will not turn the earth.

4   PEEBLES, ROSE JEFFRIES. The Legend of Longinus in Ecclesiastical Tradition and in English Literature, and Its Connection with the Grail. Dissertation, Bryn Mawr, 1910. Bryn Mawr Series, no. 9. Baltimore: J.H. Furst Co., pp. 121-23.
    Notes that in B XVIII 78-100, Longinus is understood by the poet as "champion" of the Jews; acting in such a representative capacity, his conversion is more than a merely private incident.

1912

1   COULTON, G.G. "'Piers Plowman,' One or Five." MLR 7, no. 1 (January):102-4.
    As opposed to Manly (1906.3) and Bradley (1906.2), argues that the confession of Wrath in the B-text is appropriate, since wrathful quarrels among religious are frequent in the Middle Ages, and are often cited as inconsistent with the monastic ideal.

2   COULTON, G.G. "'Piers Plowman,' One or Five. MLR 7, no. 3 (July):372-73.
    Cites the Wyclifite adaptation of Bishop Thoresby's Instruction or Catechism for the People (the Lay Folk's Catechism), lines 1352 ff., describing the retention of ill-gotten gains in the context of Sloth. Manly (1906.3) had found this inappropriate to that sin.
    Notes the "remarkable parallelism" of the Wyclifite adaptation, lines 877 ff., with A VIII 160 ff. on the subject of indulgences.

3   KER, W.P. Medieval English Literature. Home University of Modern Knowledge, vol. 43. London and New York: Oxford University Press, pp. 106-9.
    As opposed to Pearl and Sir Gawain and the Green Knight, Piers Plowman lacks a single organizing thought; as opposed to Pilgrim's Progress, the poem is often confused in the variety of topics presented. The author is careless, and often employs a mechanical form of allegory "little better than verbiage." But the poem more than makes up for these

deficiencies in its comic scenes, sustained passages of rea-
soning, and larger structural harmonies. The fluctuating tone
of the poem and its consistent sociopolitical theory argue
against multiple authorship.

*4   KNOTT, THOMAS ALBERT. "An Essay towards the Critical Text of the
      A Version of <u>Piers Plowman</u>." Dissertation, Chicago, 33 pp.
           Source: <u>Comprehensive Dissertation Index 1861-1972</u>,
      Vol. 30, p. 245.

5   OWEN, DOROTHY L. <u>Piers Plowman: A Comparison with Some Earlier
      and Contemporary French Allegories</u>. London: University of
      London Press, xiii + 125 pp.
           Comparison of the poem with the following poems: <u>Li
      Romans de Carité</u>, <u>Le Songe d'Enfer</u>, <u>La Voie de Paradise</u>, <u>Le
      Roman de la Rose</u>, <u>Le Tournoiement de l'Anticrist</u>, <u>Le Pèleri-
      nage de Vie Humaine</u>, <u>Salut d'Enfer</u>, and <u>De Dame Guile</u>.
      Langland obviously knew French, as attested in his use of
      French phrases; but there is also the possibility he may have
      learned the language through his personal experience in the
      courts. There is no firm evidence that any of these alle-
      gories were to be found in English monasteries, but there is
      a strong probability that they may have been.
           With regard to the purposes of the poems under consid-
      eration, Owen concludes that <u>Piers Plowman</u> and various of the
      allegories share the intentions of delineating contemporary
      life from a satirical point of view; stating abstract ethical
      truths, presenting didactic instruction in sacred or secular
      learning, and embodying the personal experience of the writer.
      As regards setting, most of the French allegories noted
      used the dream form as does <u>Piers Plowman</u>, and considering the
      three <u>Pèlerinages</u> of Deguilleville as one poem offers a paral-
      lel to <u>Piers Plowman</u> in its continuous series of visions.
      But the dream vision is found in earlier Middle English lit-
      erature, and the <u>Parlement of the Thre Ages</u> in particular
      offers striking resemblances.
           In considering personification, contrasts the highly
      individualized "characters" of Langland's poem with the
      emphasis in the French allegories on the didactic element in
      the allegorical characterizations. Notes the frequent in-
      stances in the French allegories of incomplete lists of the
      Deadly Sins, but the frequency of the topic in medieval lit-
      erature precludes seeing the French poems as sources of
      Langland's Sins. With regard to allegorical action, notes the
      motifs of pilgrimage and quest, jousting and warfare, as com-
      mon to <u>Piers Plowman</u> and the French allegories. Specifically,
      pilgrimage and quest are used to give a framework to certain
      parts of the poem, and there are detailed descriptions in the

1912

works under consideration of allegorical journeys; but the
similarities between Piers Plowman and the French poems in
these regards may signal merely the use of common, conventional themes. Regarding jousting and warfare, the last
passus of Piers Plowman may show knowledge of Huon de Meri's
Tournoiement de l'Anticrist, as in both we see an attack of
Antichrist and the vices upon the virtues; armor of allegorical significance, sometimes used inconsistently; the wounded
tended by some allegorical persons; and the vices and virtues
recruited from human beings. Piers Plowman may also show
knowledge of the Roman de la Rose, for in the siege of the
castle in both poems (as opposed to the Tournoiement de
l'Anticrist), an attack on a building is substituted for a
tournament, and the position of the porters is important.
        With regard to allegorical devices, notes some simila-
ties, but no common details so strikingly similar as to justify the assertion of a source-relationship. Concludes that
much of the material considered was the common stock of alle-
gorists, probably supplied to French and English poets by
Scriptural commentary, the encyclopedic tradition, and so on.
The author of Piers Plowman is original, however, in his use
of common allegorical motifs; and the poem, unlike the French
allegories, seems often to represent the writer's mental and
spiritual experience.

                              1913

1   BRADLEY, HENRY. "Who Was John But?" MLR 8, no. 1 (January):
    88-89.
            Notes the rarity of the name in fourteenth-century
    England, as well as its occurrence in the Patent Rolls,
    identifying a King's messenger (fl. 1378-87). If this is the
    John But of A XII, if this person is responsible for A XI
    77-105 and not merely A XII 94-105, if he really is informed
    of Langland's death, and if the C-text was not finished
    earlier than 1387, then the C-text is not the work of the
    original author. Bradley concludes, however, that there is
    no way to prove the identity of this John But. Cf. Rickert,
    1913.4.

*2 HEMELT, FRANCIS JOSEPH. "The Seven Deadly Sins in English Liter-
    ature with Special Reference to the Piers Plowman." Disserta-
    tion, Johns Hopkins.
            Source: Comprehensive Dissertation Index 1861-1972,
    vol. 30, p. 245.

3   MOORE, SAMUEL. "Studies in Piers Plowman I: The Burden of
     Proof: Antecedent Probability and Tradition." MP 11, no. 2
     (October):177-93.
          Criticism of Jusserand (1909.6), Chambers (1910.2), and
     Mensendieck (1910.8 and 1910.9) for assuming that the burden
     of proof is on the shoulders of the proponents of the multiple-
     authorship theory; for antecedent probability offers no a
     priori proof of revision by a single author, and the "tradi-
     tion" of ascription to one author does not extend back earlier
     than Price (in Warton, 1824.1), who first recognized the ex-
     istence of all three versions. The arguments for single
     authorship made by Whitaker (1813.1), Wright (1842.3), and
     Skeat (1886.1) are considered less than compelling, if not
     entirely insufficient. See Moore, 1914.3; and cf. Kane,
     1965.12.

4   RICKERT, EDITH. "John But, Messenger and Maker." MP 11, no. 1
     (July):107-116.
          Develops the suggestion of Bradley (1913.1) and answers
     Chambers (1911.1). Accepts Bradley's identification of John
     But on the basis of A XII 78-82 which offer an accurate de-
     scription of the duties of a messenger and differentiate the
     duties of a messenger from those of a courier. Speculates
     that But steps in because Langland's poetry is being ascribed
     to other, perhaps ecclesiastical writers. The B-text was
     doubtless in circulation by the time But wrote; but he could
     have written in the first part of Richard's reign.

                              1914

*1   CHICK, E. "A Preliminary Investigation of the Pedigree of the
     B-text MSS of Piers Plowman." M.A. thesis, University of
     London.
          Source: Bilboul, vol. 1, p. 135. This material was
     drawn upon by Blackman, 1918.1.

2   JONES, H.S.V. "Imaginatif in Piers Plowman." JEGP 13, no. 4:
     583-88.
          Imaginatif is more than mere fancy, as Skeat (1886.1)
     suggests. Rather, it is the spokesman in the poem for Reason
     as a faculty consecrated to the service of God. It knows of
     future happenings; it suggests an accommodation of Kynde Witte
     to Clergy and the spiritual uses to which we should put the
     phenomena of the physical world. Below Reason, it modulates
     between the world of the senses and the intellectual world.
     Sketches the background of this concept in Platonic, neo-
     Platonic, and Aristotelian thought, as well as its use in

1914

medieval allegory and psychology (e.g., Richard of St. Victor).

3   MOORE, SAMUEL. "Studies in Piers Plowman. II: The Burden of
     Proof: The Testimony of the MSS; the Name of the Author."
     MP 12, no. 1 (May):19-50.
          Neither the texts of the extant MSS nor the external
     features of the MSS prove or disprove the contention that A_1
     and A_2 are the work of the same author; but the Visio is
     nevertheless complete in itself, and offers no evidence its
     author planned a continuation. The colophons suggest a
     unanimous regard of the A-version as consisting of two poems;
     and the colophon describing A_2 as "Vita de Dowel, Dobet, et
     Dobest secundum Wyt et Resoun" furnishes some evidence that
     the author of A_2 also wrote the B-version, for such a colophon
     is difficult to imagine if not by the author, and indicates
     that the author of A_2 did not execute all he had wished. The
     MSS give no evidence with regard to the authorship of the C-
     text. Moreover, the various references to Will in text and
     colophons furnish no evidence for deciding the question of
     single authorship; in particular, the lone reference of A_1
     (VIII 42 ff.) is most obscure and problematic.
          Concludes there is no evidence regarding the trust-
     worthiness of John But's information. Argues that the contra-
     diction between Brigham's note (one of the sources of Bale's
     information) and the annotation to MS. V (see c. 1400.1) can
     best be resolved by the hypothesis that in the fifteenth cen-
     tury the poem was ascribed to two different persons: Robert
     Langland, a Shropshire man, and an Oxfordshire man, the son of
     Stacy de Rokayle. Finds the theory of [Pearson] (1870.2) un-
     tenable, since Stacy de Rokayle's family had no connection
     with Shropshire.

1915

1   KNOTT, THOMAS A. "An Essay toward the Critical Text of the A-
     Version of 'Piers the Plowman.'" MP 12, no. 7 (January):
     389-421.
          Exposition of the genealogical method of establishing
     a text, with MS families, subfamilies, and so on, determined
     on the basis of common errors, deviations, and omissions, with
     due allowance made for coincidence and contamination, and the
     common possession of correct readings disregarded as of no
     value in discovering affiliations. After MS families are
     determined, the readings of the critical text can be decided
     upon through agreement versus disagreement of independent wit-
     nesses. In the event that, of three independent witnesses, no

reading can be dismissed as obviously unoriginal, probability
favors the tradition that has shown a smaller total number of
errors and deviations.

Knott distinguishes between the genealogical original of
all extant texts (not the author's original) and the critical
text. Determines three independent witnesses of the genealog-
ical original, $\underline{x}$, $\underline{y}$, and $\underline{z}$; of these, the "$\underline{x}$ tradition" is
represented in MSS. VH; the "$\underline{y}$ tradition" by MSS. TH^{2}DUREAH^3;
and the "$\underline{z}$ tradition" by the B-text. It is clear that $\underline{z}$ is an
independent line of descent, for none of the errors and omis-
sions of $\underline{x}$ or $\underline{y}$ show up in the B-text. The most reliable
textural tradition is the "$\underline{y}$ tradition"; though it is important to realize that the MSS that make up the "$\underline{y}$ tradition"
are subgrouped differently in three parts of the poem, that
is, Prol-I 183; II 1-VII 69 and VII 210-VIII 126; and VII 69-
VII 209. Criticizes Chambers and Grattan (1909.3) for the
failure to back up their classifications with evidence, even
from MSS that were accessible to them.

Knott's researches are continued by Fowler, 1949.2, and
Knott and Fowler in 1952.6; they are criticized by Kane in
[Langland], 1960.10, and see Chambers and Grattan, 1916.1.

2   KRAPP, GEORGE PHILIP. The Rise of English Literary Prose. New
    York: Oxford University Press, pp. 10-18.
        The free alliterative line of Langland is well suited to
    his somewhat rambling, "often turgid and colloquial" subject
    matter. His volubility of expression connects him with prose
    expression; often it is only a slightly unusual word order
    that distinguishes his verse rhythm from prose rhythm. Re-
    printed: Krapp, 1963.5.

3   MONROE, HARRIET. "Chaucer and Langland." Poetry 6 (April-
    September):297-302.
        Chaucer made rhyme and iambic measure English;
    Coleridge, Shelley, and Byron occasionally used four-stress
    meter, but not in imitation of earlier "Saxon" poetry. Now
    that Pound has consciously returned us to the older tradition,
    Langland may come into his own at last. As opposed to Chaucer,
    Langland was a great democrat and seer who "felt the miseries
    of the poor as the only fit subject for tragic passion."

1916

1   CHAMBERS, R.W., and GRATTAN, J.H.G. "The Text of 'Piers Plowman':
    Critical Methods." MLR 11, no. 3 (July):257-75.
        Defends the classification of Chambers and Grattan
    (1909.3) against Knott (1915.1) on the basis of the

1916

complicating factor of manuscript contamination and the com-
plexity of affiliations it causes. Skeat's editions are defended against the implicit criticism of Knott as representing
a necessary step in the establishment of a text; for beginning
with a sense of the intrinsic superiority of some readings
over others, Skeat recognized the necessity of determining
provisionally readings that ought to be adopted before clas-
sifying MSS by families. Skeat did not use MS. T because,
without a good edition of the C-text, he could not know if the
A-text of this mixed A- and C-text MS was pure (it was). R,
the next best MS, was not discovered until after his edition
was published. And the next best MS is V, which is what he
used.

2   GÖRNEMANN, GERTURD. Zur Verfasserschaft und Entstehungsge-
schichte von "Piers the Plowman." Dissertation, Marburg;
published in Anglistische Forschungen, no. 48. Heidelberg:
Carl Winters Universitätsbuchhandlung, 120 pp.
   Claims that the authorship question has yielded so few
results because both sides support hypotheses with hypotheses,
and too often Skeat's pronouncements have been accepted uncritically. Internal evidence argues for a terminus a quo of
1370 (Fable of the Rats added later) and a terminus ad quem of
June 1376, when the Black Prince was still alive. Consistency
of temporal allusions suggests one version of the poem, as is
also suggested by the fact that individual MSS of one "version" differ as greatly as do MSS of different "versions."
Asserts that the differences between the "versions" can only
be satisfactorily explained by scribal variations from a common original. Görnemann's thesis is reviewed by E. Björkman,
Anglia Beiblatt 27 (1916):275-77; and B. Fehr, Literaturblatt
für Germanische und Romanische Philologie 36 (1916):174. Her
arguments are answered in Krog, 1928.6.

3   MANLY, JOHN M. "The Authorship of Piers the Plowman." MP 14,
no. 5 (September):315-16.
   Brings forward the remarks of Marsh (1860.1) in support
of the theory of multiple authorship.

4   WELLS, JOHN EDWIN. A Manual of the Writings in Middle English
1050-1400. New Haven: Yale University Press; London:
Humphrey Milford, Oxford University Press, pp. 244-70.
   Describes the three versions of the poem and summarizes
modern scholarship from Skeat to Knott (1915.1); concludes
that the authorship question will be settled "only after extended discussion of very complicated evidence, the bases for
which are not now generally accessible." Sees the formal
deficiencies of the poem, born of the poet's enthusiasm and

and imagination, as the origin of much of its tremendous poetic force. Suggests the poet employs allegory not "as a fashionable or graceful medium," but as one naturally appropriate and blended throughout with realism and the concrete. Assumes the author is a cleric, though not a scholar; a reformer, but not a revolutionary. The poem is considered an unmatched exposé of the abuses in church and state which nevertheless espouses a singularly conservative philosophy. "Its remedy is through neither physical violence nor asceticism, the favorite modes of the period. It offers no definite code of life, no formulated programme for perfect conduct. It foresees no millennium."

1917

1 HANFORD, JAMES HOLLY. "Dame Nature and Lady Life." MP 15, no. 5 (September):313-16.
    Suggests that the author of Death and Liffe was influenced in his conception of Dame Liffe by A X 27-34, which associates Life and Nature. The later poet develops this character according to the description of Nature in Alanus de Insulis's De planctu naturæ (Prose II and Prose III). For an expanded study of the influence of Piers Plowman on Death and Liffe, see Hanford and Steadman, 1918.2.

2 HEMINGWAY, SAMUEL B. "The Two St. Pauls." MLN 32, no. 1 (January):57-58.
    B XV 235-36, like the Prologue to Chaucer's "Pardoner's Tale," lines 443-46, refer to Paul the Hermit, rather than Paul the Apostle.

3 KNOTT, THOMAS A. "Observations on the Authorship of 'Piers the Plowman': A Reply to R.W. Chambers." MP 14, no. 9 (January): 147-74.
    Claims that Chambers (1910.2) has offered a mutiliated version of Manly's arguments on the misplaced leaf (Manly, 1906.3), often substituting the views of Bradley (1906.1). Argues furthermore that Chambers errs in thinking Sloth is to be understood as idleness; more properly, it is the "exceeding disinclination to do good," only one of whose effects is idleness. Wanhope is a result of Sloth, not of idleness. Robert the Robber is clearly an exemplification of Robbery, who stresses his life of crime and begs Christ to have mercy on him, for alone he has no expectation of gaining a means of restitution. "To win" in A V 236-41 does not mean "to be the passive, idle recipient of a bare living," but "to earn a bare living by hard toil." Outside of the B-text, whose author

1917

inherited a textual problem the history of which was unknown
to him, no one attributes "wicked winnings" to Sloth. For a
continuation of this study, see Knott, 1917.4.

4   KNOTT, THOMAS A. "Observations on the Authorship of 'Piers the
    Plowman'--Concluded." MP 15, no. 1 (May):23-41.
        Disagrees with Chambers (1910.2) that A V 54-58 is inco-
    herent because it is inappropriate to Lechery; instead, sees
    in these lines the conventional medieval notion that over-
    indulgence in food and drink leads to that sin. Asserts that
    the mention of Piers's wife and children in A VII 71-74 (taken
    into the B-text) clearly interrupts Piers's remarks; the lines
    are probably, as Manly suggested, an interpolation taken into
    the text by a scribe, and were neither noticed nor corrected
    by the author of the B-text. Asserts, moreover, that since
    the Deadly Sins are presented in A V to show how all sinners
    ought to repent, there is good reason to believe that the A-
    text author included Wrath, and that the original version of
    Envy featured a repentence. Knott believes the dialect of A_1
    can be distinguished from that of A_2 and B, on the basis of
    the use of ben, beth versus arn, and heo versus she. Knott's
    remarks on dialect are contested by Chambers (1919.2) and
    Fowler (1952.1).

5   TRISTRAM, E.W. "Piers Plowman in English Wall-Painting."
    Burlington Magazine 31, no. 175:135-40.
        Notes a painting of Christ as a plowman (with tools
    forming His nimbus) in the Church of Ampney S. Mary's,
    Gloucestershire, from not later than 1400. Finds representa-
    tions of laborers gaining the reward of heaven, as well as a
    companion piece, the depiction of St. George and the Dragon as
    a lesson for the rich, variously represented in Sussex and
    Suffolk.

1918

1   BLACKMAN, ELSIE. "Notes on B-text MSS. of 'Piers Plowman.'"
    JEGP 17, no. 4:489-546.
        A classification of most of the extant B-text MSS (Bm,
    Cot, J, Ht, Hm, and a sixteenth-century reprint of Roger's
    edition are either unimportant to this study or inaccessible),
    now that it is clear that MS. L can no longer be thought of
    as the poet's autograph from which all other extant texts
    descend. The classification is based on four passages:
    Prol-II; VIII-IX; XII (the beginning of the B-poet's original
    work); and XVIII (the middle of his original work).

1919

Identifies three MSS groups and one independent MS wit-
ness as follows: λ: LMRF; γ: WCr; ω: CBoYOC^{2}G^2 (where G^2
corresponds with VIII-XX of MS. G); and G^1 (MS. G Prol-VII).
MS. L is the best of its family but, as in the case of MS. W
(also the best of its group), cannot receive criticism or support from other related MSS. Y and O, however, the best MSS
of their family, can be corrected by each other and by other
family members and thus give a good idea of their ancestor.
G^1 frequently stands apart from all B-text MSS in readings
that sometimes appear to be genuine.

As regards the value of particular MSS, Blackman sees W
and L as nearly equal in determining the text, with W slightly
inferior, but with the agreement of these two MSS conclusive.
When the reading of W and L differs, agreement of one with the
other group establishes a probability of correctness. G^1 is
probably independent, but until fully collated ought to be
used merely for corroborative purposes.

In her remarks on the establishment of the B-text, assumes that the C-text is derived from the B-text, that the
B-text is derived from the A-text, and that the C-text was
not contaminated by the A-text. Hence, where the A-text
agrees with the C-text against the B-text, the accepted B-text
must be faulty.

2   HANFORD, JAMES H., and STEADMAN, JOHN M., eds. "Death and Liffe:
An Alliterative Poem." SP 15, no. 3 (July):221-94, esp.
246-55.
     The poet of Death and Liffe drew for his account of the
contention of these two figures on C XXI 26-35, 64-70, where
the conception of a debate is clearly implied. Similarly,
Death's assaults on Life's children derives from the account
of the ravages of Death in C XXIII 69 ff. The introductory
vision of Death and Liffe is similar to the Visio, but more
essential inspiration is offered by Wynnere and Wastoure and
the Parlement of the Thre Ages. The figure of Lady Life shows
affinities with Anima of Piers Plowman, but a more direct
model would seem to be Natura in De planctu naturæ (see
Hanford, 1917.1).

1919

1   BAUM, PAULL FRANKLIN. "The Fable of Belling the Cat." MLN 34,
no. 8 (December):462-70.
     Lists Oriental and Western versions of the fable. The
earliest Oriental version is found in the Old Syriac Kalilah
and Dimnah (c. 570), the earliest Western version, in Odo of
Cheriton's Fabulae (c. 1220). Langland may have received the

1919

fable through oral sources, or he may have found it in a MS of
Odo's work or in "some other of the various collections that
contained it."

2 CHAMBERS, R.W. "The Three Texts of 'Piers Plowman,' and Their
   Grammatical Forms." MLR 14, no. 2 (April):129-51.
        Evidence for single authorship is afforded by the name
   Will found in A_1, A_2, B, C, and John But's additions, since
   the conventions of fourteenth-century dream allegory argue
   that this is the name of the author. Similarly, the accusa-
   tions of an earlier dissolute life don't make sense unless by
   the same author. Concerning the learning of the author
   evinced in the poem, A_1, A_2, B, and C all quote the Psalter,
   then Matthew, then Luke in a descending order of frequency.
   And the B- and C-texts sometimes carry over without correction
   mistranslations from the A-text.
        Regarding the dialect, Chambers argues against Manly
   (1908.6) and Knott (1917.4) that the reconstructed archetype
   of all extant texts will show that the A-, B-, and C-versions
   all used both ben and arn, she and heo, and church as well as
   kirk. Moreover, since the use of heo and kirk is definitely a
   provincialism, the use of such in a poem for Londoners would
   be especially extraordinary if the poem were by three or more
   authors. An abridged form of this essay is included in Erdman
   and Fogel, 1966.3.

3 POWELL, C.L. "The Castle of the Body." SP 16, no. 2 (April):
   197-205.
        The allegory of the Castle of the Body (A X 1 ff.) is
   shown as being similar to that of the early thirteenth-
   century Sawles Warde with respect to the inhabitants of the
   two houses (Wit and Inwit), the fact that the opponents without are led by the Devil, the governing power of the house,
   and the value placed on the soul. Dowel, the owner of the
   castle, is compared with "ure lawed" of Sawles Warde.
   Powell's argument is discounted by Cornelius, 1930.4.

1920

1 HUXLEY, ALDOUS. "Chaucer." London Mercury 2, no. 8 (June):
   179-89, esp. 180-81.
        Langland is appalled by the wickedness about him; the
   inspiration of the poem is the religious indignation of the
   prophet. "But to read Chaucer one would imagine that there
   was nothing in fourteenth-century England to be indignant
   about." Reprinted: Huxley, 1923.3.

116

1921

2   LEONARD, WILLIAM ELLERY. "The Scansion of Middle English Allit-
        erative Verse." University of Wisconsin Studies in Language
        and Literature 11 (Studies by Members of the Department of
        English, no. 2):58-104, esp. 72-80.
            Compares Piers Plowman with Gamelyn, both of which he
        considers to be composed in seven-stress lines. Finds that
        Piers Plowman preserves more consistently the alliterative
        tradition and has a larger percentage of secondarily stressed
        syllables at the end of the second half-line.

3   MUIR, RAMSAY. A Short History of the British Commonwealth.
        Vol. 1. London: George Philip & Son; Liverpool: Philip,
        Son & Nephew, p. 141.
            The poem is noted for its "remarkably democratic"
        spirit, as the representation of a time of intellectual fer-
        ment in which people were discussing the organization of the
        nation with greater and greater dissatisfaction.

4   WEDEL, THEODORE OTTO. The Mediæval Attitude toward Astrology
        particularly in England. Yale Studies in English, vol. 60.
        New Haven: Yale University Press, pp. 120-22.
            The attitude of the C-text regarding astrology appears
        to be an amelioration of that of the A- and B-texts, as a com-
        parison of A II 152 ff. and B X 207 ff. with C XV 28 ff. sug-
        gests. This is, however, a difference of opinion that does
        not prove separate authorship. Reprinted: Wedel, 1968.19.

1921

*1 DÖRING, ERNST HERMANN GEORG. "Die Personennamen in Langlands
        Piers the Plouhman." Dissertation, Leipzig (handwritten).
        Abstracted in Jahrbuch der Philosophischen Fakultät zu
        Leipzig für das Jahr 1921, pp. 50-52.
            Langland's names are classified under first names and
        family names. First names are generally drawn from the Bible,
        legend, history, and so on, and usually appear in forms de-
        rived from the French (Edmund and Edward are the only two
        English first names used). Regarding family names, Chichester
        and Stowe are the only two place-names that appear without de
        as family names. Family names formed from professions always
        include the article; and these names from professions are from
        Old French and Old English with the Old French names predomi-
        nating. Langland does not include names formed on the basis
        of personal characteristics.

1921

2   KNOWLTON, E.C. "Nature in Middle English." JEGP 20, no. 2:
      186-207, esp. 197-200.
          The treatment of Nature (Kinde) in Piers Plowman is
      unique among Middle English and Old French sources in making
      the equation of Kinde with God. As Kinde, God is shown to be
      interested in the welfare of the soul (A X) and to have pun-
      ished man for his lechery with disease. The conception of
      Nature in Piers Plowman is related to the allegorical figure
      of Life in Death and Liffe. Cf. Hanford, 1917.1, and Hanford
      and Steadman, 1918.2.

1922

1   ANON. "Notes on Sales." TLS, 11 May, p. 312.
          Lists four copies still in circulation of Crowley's
      first edition ([Langland], 1550.1) on vellum, with information
      regarding one of the copies that was sold at Sotheby's July
      1881. See also Gordon, 1965.8.

2   BANNISTER, ARTHUR T. "William Langland's Birthplace." TLS,
      7 September, p. 569.
          Brings forward Langlands, attested from 1719, on the
      western slope of the Malvern Hills, as Langland's birthplace.
      Cites local tradition that the "bourn" of the opening vision
      is a stream issuing from Primeswell, now called "Pewtress'
      spring"; and the "tour" is the Herefordshire Beacon. Supple-
      mented by Bright, 1928.2.

3   CHADWICK, D. Social Life in the Days of Piers Plowman.
      Cambridge: Cambridge University Press, xiii + 125 pp.
          In general, Chadwick finds that Langland's picture of
      society is a gloomy one, for his intent is to expose corrup-
      tion rather than to entertain. His loosely connected allegory
      allows Langland to attack abuses without naming names.
      Chadwick accepts the theory of single authorship, and feels
      that the poet's biography can be assembled from the personal
      references of the various texts.
          Regarding secular and religious clergy, Chadwick finds
      that Langland observes clear signs of decadence in the
      Church, especially the greed of prelates and of lesser offi-
      cials, due to the Church's wealth and the interest churchmen
      take in worldly matters. Langland's comments on pardons show
      a lack of confidence in the pope, but most often his target
      is papal policy, rather than doctrine. He feels that the
      priests' duties are preaching, teaching, and helping those in
      need of spiritual or physical aid. Langland was himself
      probably a clerk in lower orders, and he gives a sympathetic

account of the hardships of those in his position. He thinks the monks' business is to obey their rule, not to wander or amass wealth. Nuns are especially criticized, and friars are attacked on the basis of greed, immorality, lack of order and discipline, and simony.

Regarding secular government, Langland appears democratic concerning the necessary attributes of a good king; and he often mirrors the sentiments of Parliament, emphasizing in his revisions the dependence of the king on the will of the commons. He exposes the imperfections of the secular law and paints a decadent picture of knighthood.

Regarding country life, Langland shows that the old habits of hospitality are on the wane. He appears to know well the medieval methods of agriculture. Concerning town life, Langland emphasizes the respect due to a mayor as a royal deputy and intermediary between king and commons. He represents merchants in general in a bad light, describes various amusements rather well, and satirizes minstrels for the immorality of their performances. He distinguishes between minstrels who ought to be maintained and those who are evil or false.

With regard to the religion of the layman, Langland stresses the duties of each member of society to the Church. Baptism and penance are the sacraments he values most highly. He believes the righteous heathen can be saved; he is in a quandary regarding free will/determinism, but accepts the Church's teaching in this regard. He is widely read in the Bible as it is used in the Breviary.

With regard to the position of women, Langland repeats the conventional ecclesiastical satires on women, but perhaps does not completely believe such charges. The poem regards marriage as a purely business arrangement, however. Reviewed by Anon, TLS, 13 April 1922, p. 256; Bernhard Fehr, Anglia Beiblatt 34 (1923):87-89; C.L. Kingsford, English Historical Review 38 (1923):105-6; and Robert Lynd, New Statesman, 6 May 1922, pp. 19, 126, 128. Reprinted: Chadwick, 1969.7.

4   DAY, MABEL. "Alliteration of the Versions of 'Piers Plowman' in Its Bearing on Their Authorship." MLR 17, no. 4 (October): 403-9.

Divides the B-text into B_1 (B I-XI, or the revision of the A-text) and B_2 (B XI-XX, the B-text's original material), and finds that alliteration of prepositions and other normally unstressed words and syllables is more pronounced in B_2 than in A_1 and C and than in A_2 and B_1. Asserts that in different parts of the poem different prepositions alliterate. In regard to the Romance prefixes de- and re-, only in B_2 does the poet change the alliterating syllable in a single word from

1922

prefix to root syllable. Day considers the results of her research suggestive of five different hands in the composition
of the poem, not including John But.

1923

*1   ALLEN, B.F. "The Genealogy of the C Text Manuscripts of Piers
Plowman." M.A. thesis, London.
            Source: Bilboul, vol. 1, p. 135. Allen's researches
were substantiated and developed by Carnegy, 1934.2, and
drawn upon by Chambers, 1936.3.

*2   CARNEGY, F.A.R. "Problems Connected with the Three Texts of
Piers the Plowman." M.A. thesis, London.
            Source: Bilboul, vol. 1, p. 135. Part of this thesis
was published as Carnegy, in [Langland,] 1934.2.

3   HUXLEY, ALDOUS. On the Margin. London: Chatto & Windus,
pp. 203-7.
            Contains a reprint of Huxley, 1920.1.

1924

1   CHAMBERS, R.W. "Long Will, Dante, and the Righteous Heathen."
Essays and Studies 9:50-69.
            Explains the Pardon scene in terms of Piers's reaction
to the difference of the model pardon of the pope (which
reconciles indulgences with the Dreamer's idea of right conduct) and the abuses represented by the Priest. The Dreamer
decides in favor of Dowel, though he does not deny the pope's
power to grant pardons. The A-text ends with the large problems of predestination, salvation of the learned and righteous
heathen, and the efficacy of learning all unresolved. The B-
text supplies the reason for the period of time between the
questions and the attempts to answer them in the confession
of past misdeeds. Then Imaginatif, properly considered an
aid to Reason, explains the limitations of learning, the
proper hope in God's mercy, and the possibilities of the
salvation of the righteous heathen with reference to the same
line of the Psalm that the dreamer had recourse to in tearing
up the pardon.
            Chambers notes parallels with the Divina Commedia in
Beatrice's rebuke of the persona for his past life and the
questions concerning the fate of the heathens, Trajan and
Riphaeus. In both poems, the possibility of salvation of
righteous heathen is admitted. Much of the material of this
essay was incorporated in Chambers, 1939.3.

2 HUIZINGA, JOHAN. The Waning of the Middle Ages: A Study of the
   Forms of Life, Thought and Art in France and the Netherlands
   in the XIVth and XVth Centuries. [Translated by F. Hopman.]
   London: Edward Arnold & Co., p. 162.
         Mentions Piers Plowman as the first expression of the
   sanctity of productive labor in England, a country that became
   sensitive to economic matters earlier than the Continent. The
   reference to Piers Plowman is not in the original Dutch version, Herfsttij Der Middeleeuwen (Haarlem: H.D. Tjeenk
   Willink & Zoon, 1919). For a reprint of the English translation, see Huizinga, 1954.3.

3 THOMAS, P.G. English Literature before Chaucer. London: Edward
   Arnold & Co., pp. 141-48.
         The poem is discussed in the context of satiric English
   literature from "On the Evil Times of Edward II" (in which
   allegorical figures are used in satire of corrupt clergy and
   governmental officials) and Wynnere and Wastoure (which features the pleading of a case analogous to that concerning
   Peace and Wrong in Piers Plowman) to Richard the Redeless.
         The author of Piers Plowman is considered an impartial
   reformer who champions the cause of the common people as far
   as this position is consistent with loyalty to the sovereign.
   The author's religious position is conservative, despite his
   antipapal tone and denunciation of abuses of pilgrimages, indulgences, and services for the dead.

1925

1 BRIGHT, ALLAN H. "William Langland's Birthplace." TLS,
   12 March, p. 172.
         Contends that Nicholas Brigham (Bale's authority) is the
   sole authority for Langland's alleged birth at Clibery, and
   notes that all Brigham's works are lost. Suggests that
   Clibery was substituted for Lidbery (Ledbury), and that
   Langland never had anything to do with Cleobury Mortimer.
   Incorporated in Bright, 1928.2.

2 BRIGHT, ALLAN H. "William Langland's Early Life." TLS,
   5 November, p. 739.
         The Despensers held the Chase of Malvern at the time of
   the poet's birth. William, who never alludes to his mother,
   was illegitimate and hence could not use the name of his
   father, de Rokayle. C VI 63-88 shows in Langland's denunciation of the practice of elevating men of low estate to high
   office in the Church that he was arguing against his own best
   interests. He was educated at Malvern Priory, a foundation

1925

supported by the Despensers. He perhaps took up a small farm
in Longlands at the death of his father. William W. found in
later MSS stands for William Wycliffanus. Largely incorporated in Bright, 1928.2.

3 CONNOLLY, TERENCE L. An Introduction to Chaucer and Langland (A
Corrective of Long's History of English Literature). New
York: Fordham University Press, pp. 83-93.
     Defends Langland's orthodoxy against the Protestant
orientation of Long (1909.7). Langland satirizes abuses in
the lives of churchmen; he does not revolt against the authority of the Church. Penance and the other sacraments are
valued in the poem, and the Blessed Virgin Mary is reverenced
throughout. Argues, moreover, that Langland's beliefs in no
way harmonize with Wyclif's.

4 HITTMAIR, RUDOLF. "Der Begriff der Arbeit bei Langland." In
Neusprachliche Studien. Festgabe Karl Luick zu seinem sech-
zigsten Geburtstage dargebracht von Freunde und Schülern.
Marburg on the Lahn: N.G. Elwert'sche Verlagsbuchhandlung,
G. Braun, pp. 204-18.
     The practical strain exists in English literature much
earlier than on the Continent. Langland is not the first to
take up the subject of work, but his is the most important
early voice. His opinions are seen in the scenes with the
Plowman and Hunger, where he takes the side of the little man
but also sees the weakness of the working class. He decries
socioeconomic realities but wants the present social system
retained; and he asserts that reform must come from within.
As the poem proceeds, the labor question becomes less important than theological inquiries; but the theme of work holds
the poem together in the development of the lives of Dowel,
Dobet, and Dobest, for Langland insists that the religious
life requires work.

5 IIJIMA, IKUZO. Langland and Chaucer: A Study of the Two Types
of Genius in English Poetry. Boston: Four Seas Co.,
pp. 41-81.
     Describes the poem, with emphasis on its realistic
touches, but asserts that the poet's ideal and ethical standpoint toward his material is even more important. Sees
Langland essentially as a reformer who presents human ugliness
as evidence of social corruption; yet Langland believes in the
social system and, indeed, holds that the misdoings of the
king, the aristocrats, and the churchmen are responsible for
all social evils. Langland is radical, but not destructive;
democratic, but not revolutionary; very conservative, but not
autocratic. He aims to reform individuals, whereas Wyclif

122

wants to reform society. C XXIII shows that Langland is not
a communist. Instead, he can be thought of as a mystic, who
believes that the soul can unite with God in this life as
happens in B XVIII, and an idealist, who reacts to the imperfection of the real world in the light of the realization
of a perfect state or condition. Extends the comparison of
Langland and Carlyle, suggested by Scudder, 1898.4.

6 OWST, G.R. "The 'Angel' and the 'Goliardeys' of Langland's Prologue." MLR 20, no. 3 (July):270-79.
        In B Prol 123 ff., the "lunatic" is, as Skeat suggested,
   a representative of the poet himself; the "angel" speaking in
   Latin from on high, however, is meant to represent Thomas
   Brunton (Brinton), Bishop of Rochester, one of whose sermons
   (Sermo 69, MS. Harley 3760, fol. 186 ff.) decries the condition of the realm in the hands of corrupt ministers instead
   of wise counselors, calls for social justice and a sense of
   responsibility, and includes the exemplum of belling the cat.
   The "goliardeys' who responds is to be identified as Sir Peter
   de la Mare, spokesman of the Commons in the Good Parliament of
   1376.

                              1926

1 BRIGHT, ALLAN H. "William Langland's Early Life." TLS,
   9 September, p. 596.
        Brings forward notices of the activity of the de
   Rokayles, closely connected with the Despensers, 1327-31.
   Peter de Rokayle, taken to be the grandfather of the poet,
   was in rebellion with Hugh le Despenser in 1326 and made an
   attempt to rescue Edward II from Berkeley Castle that same
   year. The principal seat of the Despensers was Hanley Castle
   in Malvern Chase. At A III 117 ff., the poem describes leaving "longe lande" on the left and proceeding a mile to a
   court: this is Old Castle, the probable dungeon of the poem;
   but just 5 1/2 miles farther down the road is Hanley Castle.
   Asserts that an allusion to Richard's crossing into Ireland
   in XII 115 proves that John But wrote during April-September
   1399.

2 FAIRCHILD, HOXIE NEALE. "'Leyde Here Legges Aliri.'" MLN 41,
   no. 6 (June):378-81.
        Derives aliri (B VI 124) from on læghrycg, "on the ridge
   in a piece of grassy, untilled land." Thus, the faitours, when
   upbraided by Piers, laid their legs "aliri" perhaps by hiding
   their legs behind the slope of a ridge at the edge of a plowed
   field.

1926

3   OWST, G.R. <u>Preaching in Medieval England: An Introduction to</u>
    <u>Sermon Manuscripts of the Period c. 1350-1450</u>. Cambridge:
    Cambridge University Press, passim.
            The poem is considered as representing "nothing more nor
    less than the quintessence of English mediaeval preaching
    gathered up into a single metrical piece of unusual charm and
    vivacity." Sees the poet's ideas, symbolism, imagery, quota-
    tions from Scripture and French and Latin works, knowledge of
    law, conservative attitude toward authority, satire, and
    stress on love, good works, and the virtuous laboring poor
    all characteristic of sermon literature. In particular, sees
    the poem as illustrating such sermon topics and attitudes as
    the rivalry of parish priests and friar confessors, abuses of
    the pardoners, church decoration, and appeals to the visual.
    For the development of Owst's thesis concerning <u>Piers Plowman</u>,
    see Owst, 1933.8.

*4 SCHIFF, ELISABETH. <u>Studien zur Syntax Langlands</u>. Dissertation,
    Vienna.
            Source: Gabel and Gabel, p. 14.

                              1927

1   ADAMS, M. RAY. "The Use of the Vulgate in <u>Piers Plowman</u>." <u>SP</u>
    24, no. 4 (October):556-66.
            Examination of Biblical quotations in <u>Piers Plowman</u> sup-
    ports the theory of single authorship, since the same books of
    the Bible are relied upon in all three texts, and most of the
    Vulgate quotations are carried over from one version to an-
    other. Concludes from the internal evidence that the author
    was a priest, whose quotations from the Bible suggest he was
    probably in the lower orders, as they attempt to make the
    Church and the Bible more accessible to the common man. The
    majority of his quotations are from service books, the
    Breviary, and the Missal, though the exact contents of the
    Breviary he used cannot be determined.

2   BRETT, CYRIL. "Notes on Old and Middle English." <u>MLR</u> 22, no. 3
    (July):257-64, esp. 260-62.
            Takes <u>aliri</u> (B VI 124) to refer to the apparent twisting
    of a beggar's lower leg so that the calf appears to be in
    front. Explains the scene of the Angel and the Goliardeys
    (B Prol) wholly on internal evidence: the Angel stresses
    <u>pietas</u>, best construed as mercy; the Goliardeys stresses <u>jus</u>,
    or justice. The words of the Goliardeys are an argument
    against the Angel's speech and not, as claimed by Owst
    (1925.6), a reinforcement of it.

                              124

1928

3   DAY, MABEL. "Duns Scotus and 'Piers Plowman.'" RES 3, no. 11
     (July):333-34.
         The tree in B XVI is an imitation of a simile in Duns
     Scotus's De rerum principo, art. IV, no. 3, which compares the
     world to a tree ruled by God, part of the branches of which
     have dried up because of a gust of the wind of pride. Man's
     free will (Liberum Arbitrium) in the poem is represented in
     the Scotist conception of availing itself of the grace of the
     Holy Spirit. For the relevance of this "Scotist" conception to
     the authorship question, see Day, 1928.4.

4   K, A.R. "Parked." American Speech 2, no. 4 (January):215.
         Queries what appears to be the American usage of parked,
     "placed, put," in C VII 144.

5   STEWART, GEORGE R., Jr. "The Meter of Piers Plowman." PMLA 42,
     no. 1 (March):113-28.
         Denies that the meter of Piers Plowman has anything to
     do with that of Old English poetry, at least as has been de-
     scribed with reference to the types of Sievers. Sees dipodic
     verse pattern as able to reconcile the dominance of the pri-
     mary stresses of Langland's line with existence of numerous
     secondary stresses.

*6 THOMAS, G.A. "A Study of the Influence of Langland's Piers
     Plowman on Gower." Dissertation, Cornell.
         Source: Proppe, 1972.20, p. 90, no. 263; Colainanne,
     1978.4, 139, no. 578. In McGinnis, 1932.13, p. 2, I find this
     work referred to as Grace M. Thomas, "The After-History of
     Langland and Gower."

1928

1   BONSDORFF, INGRID von. "'Hankyn' or 'Haukyn'?" MP 26, no. 1
     (August):57-61.
         MS. L (B-text) reads Hankyn, which may be preferable to
     Haukyn, since it is recorded as a name borne by merchants
     (with whom the "actif man" is associated in B XII 267) in
     Hertfordshire, Essex, and the west country. Hankyn perhaps
     means "son of John," and this spelling, rather than English
     Jankin or Jenkin, might well be from the Low Countries.

2   BRIGHT, ALLAN H. New Light on "Piers Plowman." Preface by R.W.
     Chambers. Oxford: Oxford University Press, 93 pp.
         In his preface (pp. 9-22), Chambers reasserts the theory
     of single authorship, largely on the basis of arguments made
     previously; stresses the habit of fourteenth-century dream

1928

allegories not to distinguish the dreamer from the poet; and
notes that B XII 16-19 make no sense if construed in any other
way (see Chambers, 1919.2). Feels that the case for single
authorship is strengthened by Bright's work, but that
Langland's authorship of <u>Richard the Redeless</u> is not proven.
        Bright believes that the poet was born at Ledbury, which
is eight miles from the Malvern Hills, and not at Cleobury.
Speculates that the poet's father may have held some position
for the de Rokayles, who served the Despensers, the chief
lords of Malvern Chase, from Hanley Castle. The poet's mother
may have been a local, and the poet himself an illegitimate
who had been made "free" (C II 73) through ordination. He was
probably refused permission by his father to use his name
(C IV 365-70). He was sent to school at the Priory in Great
Malvern or in Little Malvern; lived at the Longland in Colwall
parish at the boundary of Ledbury parish; and was ordained
20 December 1348 as acolyte under the name Willelmus de
Colewell, at the parish church of Bromyard, by John de
Trillek, bishop of Hereford.
        "Longland" is a large arable field on the southern
boundary of Colwall, where it meets the parish of Ledbury.
This field is the model of the scene in A VII 1-7 where the
folk seek directions to St. Truth. The Field of Folk (A Prol
12 ff.) is located at a little brook called Promeswelle, near
the foot of the Herefordshire Beacon. The good knight of A
VII is identified as James de Brockbury, owner of the manor in
Colwall. Clergy of A XI-XII is probably Brockbury, since the
directions to Clergy are directions from Langland to Brockbury.
Scripture is Brockbury's second wife; Langland himself is
Study, for Langland tutored Scripture's stepchildren. The B-
and C-texts suppress many of these allusions. Langland may
have left for London 1355-56; for a time, he led an irregular
life (B XI 11 ff.); he later married, for this was allowed to
acolytes. C VIII 299-304 and B XIV 26-27 identify William as
Haukyn, but much of this is changed in the C-text.
        "Visio Willelmi W.," found in some MSS, identifies the
author as "Wiclefitæ." Langland was a conservative reformer,
a supporter of the Commons against the power of the crown as
well as against the claims of democracy. He would certainly
have repudiated his later reputation. B XIV 174-80, a prayer
for the poor, is suppressed in the C-text because the Peasants'
Revolt had occurred in the meantime.

3   COULTON, G.G. <u>Art and the Reformation</u>. Oxford: Blackwell,
        pp. 359-60, 398.
            Though Langland is an orthodox Christian, he is "as
    scornful as any Lollard" of the false spiritual pretenses used
    to elicit money for the building and adornment of churches.

Langland's belief in the salvation of the righteous heathen, typified by Trajan, is contrasted with that of Melchior Cano in his De locis theologicis (c. 1550).

4   DAY, MABEL. "The Revisions of Piers Plowman." MLR 23, no. 1 (January):1-27.
        Suggests there is evidence that the C-poet collated with A2 in revising the B-text. The B- and C-poets both used very good texts of the A-version; the B-poet's was of the type presented by MS. T, and the C-poet's of the type represented by MS. V. In three cases, the C-poet's copy of the A-text was corrupt. When the A- and B-texts agree, the C-poet seldom makes large alterations; where the B-text has treated the A-version freely, the C-poet often paraphrases and/or expands. Until the point where the B-text first seriously differs from the A-text, the C-poet gives more weight to the A-text reading; after that point, he values the B-text readings more.
        The paraphrases of the C-text often substitute weak generalities for the graphic details of the B-text, a characteristic that is at variance with the C-poet's vividness in his original passages. The C-poet is more insistent on regular aa/ax alliteration and often emends to achieve it. There are many instances of where the B- and C-poets had a bad text before them or misunderstood what was being revised. The C-text often corrects the inconsistencies introduced by the B-text's abstract revisions of the A-text; but in C XVII the C-poet's revisions confuse the Scotist conception of Liberum Arbitrium introduced by the B-poet. Moreover, the expansion of Piers into a more mystical conception is largely the work of the B-poet, but is sharply revised in the C-version. Such changes are considered as suggestive of multiple authorship. Day's notions of Liberum Arbitrium in the C-text are addressed by Sanderlin (1941.9). Her suggestions regarding use of the A-text by the C-text poet are denied by Chambers and Grattan (1931.2).

*5 DEVLIN, Sister Mary Aquinas. "The Date of the C Version of Piers the Plowman." Dissertation, Chicago.
        Abstracted: [University of Chicago] Abstracts of Theses, Humanistic Series, 4:317-20. Notes omissions in the C-text of the Peasants' Revolt (1381), the condemnation of Wyclif (1382), and the crusade of the Bishop of Norwich (1386). The additions of the C-text fit the period 1377-86; and the parallels of Piers Plowman and Usk's Testament of Love may be said to fix the terminus ad quem at 1388.

1928

6   KROG, FRITZ.   "Zur Verfasserschaftsfrage der Piers Plowman-
    Dichtung."   In Studien zu Chaucer und Langland. Anglistische
    Forschungen, no. 65.   Heidelberg: Carl Winters Universitäts-
    buchhandlung, pp. 116-74.
        Recapitulates the scholarship in support of single
    authorship, Manly's argument of multiple authorship (1909.8),
    and Görnemann's alternative hypothesis of scribal contamina-
    tion in descent from one original version (1916.2).
        Görnemann's argument that the differences between MSS
    are as great as or greater than differences between versions
    of the poem does not adequately take into account the notion
    of critical texts of the separate versions.   Her contention
    that the A- and C-texts are sometimes closer than the A- and
    B-texts and the B- and C-texts rests on selective evidence,
    and is not substantiated by close attention to A IX-XI, B
    VIII-X, and C XI-XII, for which Krog tabulates differences,
    omissions, and additions existing among the three versions.
    Similarly, Görnemann's use of the evidence of Chambers and
    Grattan (1909.3) that MSS of the TU family often agree with
    the B-text as opposed to A-text MSS of the VH family ignores
    the larger similarities and agreements of the A-text MSS.
    Krog shows that the A-text and the C-text are not directly
    related, and that the differences among the versions strongly
    indicate a chronological order of A-text, B-text, C-text.
    Reviewed by Elsie Blackman, MLR 25 (1930):344-45; Muriel B.
    Carr, MLN 44 (1929):538-41; Mabel Day, RES 5 (1929):212-13;
    J. Koch, Literaturblatt 50 (1929):cols. 19-24; and Hugo Lange,
    Englische Studien 65 (1929):82-84.

7   WINGFIELD-STRATFORD, ESMÉ.   The History of British Civilization.
    Vol. 1.   London: George Routledge & Sons; New York: Harcourt,
    Brace & Co., pp. 260-61.
        Langland was a medieval democrat but a Tory by today's
    standards in his principles of social charity as well as his
    insistence on a social hierarchy in which a poor plowman like
    Piers, for example, is not expected to better himself.

1929

1   WELLS, HENRY W.   "The Construction of Piers Plowman."   PMLA 45,
    no. 1 (March):123-40.
        The Visio is concerned with the life of the laity in its
    real and ideal aspects, the Vita with the world as seen by a
    thinker from the perspectives of learning, asceticism, and
    priestly responsibility.   There is, however, a certain degree
    of overlap, since the Vita at the end of the A-text is con-
    cerned with common attributes of laity and clergy such as the

1930

Ten Commandments, basic elements of the faith, and so on, but
the remaining section of the Vita is concerned in general with
the higher order of perfection required of the priesthood.
Both the Visio and the Vita are divided into three corresponding parts: Lady Mede parallels Dowel, in balancing questions
of secular and church government; the Deadly Sins parallel
Dobet, in regarding the inner life of the layman and the contemplative or religious life; and the Pardon parallels Dobest
in considering the honest labor of men and Christ's efforts to
cultivate souls with a mystical plan. Dowel is the active
life of intellectual studies and priestly duties; Dobet is the
contemplative life and the life of faithful hermits; Dobest is
the active life expressed in the corporate Church. The Three
Lives can likewise be seen as self-rule, self-obliteration,
and the care of souls, respectively, or lives under the pro-
tection of the Father, Son, and Holy Spirit. The Three Lives
are cumulative and include the preceding.

1930

1   BRIGHT, ALLAN H. "Langland and the Seven Deadly Sins." MLR 25,
     no. 2 (April):133-39.
          The differences in his treatments of the Deadly Sins are
     accounted for through Langland's evolving personal attitude
     toward them. The A-text indicates his intention that the sins
     will have a personal application; hence, Covetousness is
     emphasized, and Wrath--apparently not one of Langland's own
     sins--is omitted. The B- and C-versions introduce the depic-
     tion of the parson under Sloth, as representative of Langland's
     "London"--as opposed to his "Malvern"--period. Wrath is in-
     cluded, but the treatment of the sin is impersonal. The C-
     version, written in Langland's old age, renders impersonally
     the sins of Haukyn, a representative of Langland himself at
     the time he first went to London.

2   BRIGHT, ALLAN H. "Sources of Piers Plowman." TLS, 24 April,
     p. 352.
          Proverbs of B I 139 (and V 448), B XVII 315 ff., and
     B V 258 ff. are found in a MS of proverbs in the John Rylands
     Library, noticed by W.A. Panting [sic]. These proverbs are
     not in the A-version and are modified in the C-version. See
     Pantin, 1930.7.

1930

3 CAZAMIAN, LOUIS. The Development of English Humour. Part 1,
   From the Early Times to the Renaissance. New York: Macmillan
   Co., pp. 85-88.
        The poem shows very little, if any, borrowing from the
   French strain of lighthearted, cynical gaiety. The author is
   earnest and moral, yet "the quiet glow of a just perceptible
   slyness" is in evidence, along with a shrewd sense "of the
   other side of things," and irony. Appreciates the humor of
   the Angel speaking in Latin (B Prol 128-30) and Avarice's misunderstanding the word restitution (B V 232-40). Sees Langland's humor as based on his realistic powers, sense of contrasts, and fund of experience. Reprinted (from the edition
   of 1951): Cazamian, 1965.4.

4 CORNELIUS, ROBERTA D. The Figurative Castle. A Study in the
   Mediaeval Allegory of the Edifice with Especial Reference to
   Religious Writings. Dissertation, Bryn Mawr. Bryn Mawr:
   Bryn Mawr, pp. 26-36.
        The Castle of Kynde (A X 1 ff.; B IX 1 ff.) is consid-
   ered in the context of Latin and vernacular writing on the
   Wardens of the Soul. Langland's identification of Anima as
   "lyf" finds support in Augustine On the Psalms (PL, XXXVII,
   col. 1776) and On Genesis, XXXVII, 22 (PL, XXXIV, col. 496).
   Inwit is not, as Skeat thought, Conscience, but rather
   Intellect. Only two of the five Wardens correspond to senses;
   Langland may have had a Patristic source in mind for adapting
   the conventional pattern and introducing good works, industry,
   and good speech. Discounts the suggestion of Powell (1919.3)
   that the episode in Piers Plowman is dependent on Sawles Warde,
   for the most important and dramatic aspects of the incident in
   Sawles Warde--the arrival of the messengers and their dialogue
   with the daughters of "ure lauerd"--are not taken over by
   Langland. Also discounts the dependence of Gavin Douglas's
   use of the same allegory in King Hart, though admits Douglas
   may have known Piers Plowman.

5 COULTON, G.G. The Medieval Scene. London: Cambridge University
   Press, pp. 157-63.
        Piers Plowman is a better index to the "mind of the
   multitude" in the Middle Ages than is the Divina Commedia.
   Langland's poem shows the medieval emphasis on privilege side
   by side, and perhaps even above, the law. Langland has little
   sympathy with social disorder and insists on the dignity of
   honest poverty and hard work. The poem demonstrates the
   growth of a simple mystic religion among the people.

1931

6   OAKDEN, J.P. Alliterative Poetry in Middle English: The Dia-
     lectical and Metrical Survey (The Ward Bequest). Manchester:
     Manchester University Press, pp. 186–87.
          Statistical proportions of varying types of alliteration
     in the three versions, ranging from type aa/ax (the most com-
     mon: 65.2 percent, 70.3 percent, 72.1 percent, respectively)
     and type aa/aa (the next most common: 7.45 per cent, 7.57
     percent, 8.9 percent, respectively) all the way down to such
     infrequent patterns of alliteration as type ab/ab (.3 percent,
     .2 percent, .2 percent, respectively) and type ab/ba (.1 per-
     cent, .09 percent, .07 percent, respectively). Lines lacking
     alliteration are found to be in the following proportions:
     .8 percent, .7 percent, .9 percent. This work was completed
     by Oakden, 1935.9.

7   PANTIN, W.A. "Medieval Collection of Latin and English Proverbs
     and Riddles from the Rylands Latin MS. 394." Bulletin of the
     John Rylands Library 14, no. 1 (January):81–114.
          Proverbs in this MS with analogues in B I 139 (and V
     448), VII 315 ff., and B V 258 ff. are noticed by Bright
     (1930.2). Pantin himself draws attention (p. 101, correspond-
     ing to fol. 13, nos. 20–22) to the similarity of a MS entry to
     A V 14–20, describing the "great wind" of 15 January 1362, an
     allusion in the poem first pointed out by Tyrwhitt (1775.1).

1931

*1   BURESCH, FELIZITAS. Die Sprache William Langlands im Verhältnis
     zu derjenigen Chaucers. Dissertation, Vienna.
          Source: Gabel and Gabel, p. 14.

2   CHAMBERS, R.W., and GRATTAN, J.H.G. "The Text of 'Piers
     Plowman.'" MLR 26, no. 1 (January):1–51.
          The B-poet used a MS of the A-version that was better
     than any extant; the C-poet likewise used such a MS of the
     B-version. In numerous instances in the B-text (e.g., V
     335–37; XIX 178–80; XIX 231), the right B-reading can be re-
     stored only on comparison with the C-text. Occasionally the
     reading of all B-MSS (and hence the archetype of all extant
     texts) is wrong, but the C-poet relied on a text of the B-
     version that was free of such errors. The B-MSS are on the
     whole well written, yet are descended from a common archetype
     that contained many errors. A-MSS are perhaps derived from
     something nearer the author's original.
          The genealogical method allows us to arrange MSS of
     Piers Plowman into families, based on common errors; yet we
     must remain aware of the possibility of contamination, as well

as accidental coincidences, since scribes often trusted their
memory of lines without going back to the text as often as
accuracy would have demanded. Moreover, scribes apparently
felt free, once they had retained a general sense of the
lines, to substitute synonyms, and so on.

The work of Görnemann (1916.2) is hampered by the fact
that she relied on Skeat's collations which, while generally
accurate, are far from complete.

Disagrees with Day (1928.4) that the A-text was collated
with the B-text by the C-text poet, on the grounds of a priori
improbability and the fact that the C-text does not reinsert
any of the characteristic passages canceled by the B-poet or
changed in his revision of the A-text. In particular, the
principle of <u>durior</u> <u>lectio</u> strengthens the case for <u>dune</u>,
rather than <u>doom</u> in A II 183; and the reading of the B-text
here goes back no further than the archetype. Contends that
the C-poet is not as unwilling as Day suggests to change a
reading common to the A- and B-versions; and that the distri-
bution of alliterating prepositions in different sections of
the poem is more uniform than Day suggests if the relative
length of these sections is taken into account.

3   DAY, MABEL. "'Din' and 'Doom' in 'Piers Plowman.' A, II, 183."
    <u>MLR</u> 26, no. 3 (July):336-38.
        Stands by her earlier assertion (1928.4), against
    Chambers and Grattan (1931.2), that the original reading was
    <u>dome</u> on the basis of the corresponding passage in B II 205
    which has <u>dome</u> in a context where <u>dune</u> is impossible. Hence,
    if <u>dune</u> were the original reading, <u>dome</u> in the B-text is a
    deliberate alteration by the reviser, rather than a scribal
    error.

4   GAFFNEY, WILBUR. "The Allegory of the Christ-Knight in <u>Piers</u>
    <u>Plowman</u>." <u>PMLA</u> 46, no. 1 (March):155-68.
        The allegory of Christ as a knight jousting with Satan
    (B XVI, XVIII, and XIX) is linked to earlier tradition repre-
    sented by an Old French poem of Nicholas Bozon, sermons, and
    the <u>Ancrene Riwle</u> (the earliest occurrence). The closest
    analogue appears to be the poem of Bozon, for only here and
    in <u>Piers Plowman</u> is it emphasized that Christ took on the arms
    of human nature secretly, and only in these two works is the
    rescue of the captive connected with the Harrowing of Hell.
    But if he knew Bozon's version, Langland completely omitted
    the espousal motif, concentrating instead on the combat of
    Christ and the Devil "for mankynde sake." Gaffney's use of
    the <u>Ancrene Riwle</u> is criticized by Le May, 1932.12. See also
    St-Jacques, 1967.6.

1932

5   MARX, KITTY. <u>Das Nachleben von Piers Plowman bis zu Bunyan's</u>
     <u>The Pilgrim's Progress (1678)</u>. Dissertation, Freiburg in
     Breisgau. Quakenbrück: Handels-Druckerei C. Trute, vi +
     66 pp.
          Echoes of and allusions to <u>Piers Plowman</u> in poetry,
     drama, and political and religious pamphlets; accounts of
     early editions; accounts of early literary critics of the
     poem and of antiquaries.

1932

1   BRYNE, Sister Mary of the Incarnation. <u>The Tradition of the Nun</u>
     <u>in Medieval England</u>. Dissertation, Catholic University of
     America. Washington, D.C.: Catholic University of America,
     pp. 168-69.
          Cites Langland's satiric mention of nuns' immorality and
     covetousness in the context of conventional medieval satire
     against nuns. Notes that Langland's satire of nuns' conten-
     tiousness repeats the charge of Nigellus Wireker's <u>Speculum</u>
     <u>stultorum</u>.

2   BURDACH, KONRAD. "Der Dichter des Ackermann aus Böhmen und seine
     Zeit." In <u>Vom Mittelalter zur Reformation: Forschungen zur</u>
     <u>Geschichte der Deutschen Bildung</u>. Vol. 3, part 2. Berlin:
     Weidmannsche Buchhandlung, pp. 140-371.
          Argues that the influence of <u>Piers Plowman</u> on the
     <u>Ackermann aus Böhmen</u> (c. 1400) is due to the Wyclifite move-
     ment in Prague and Bohemia. Both poems assume that the origi-
     nal, pure nature of the human being, typified in Adam, stands
     in close relation to God; and that being realizes itself in
     work, belief in God, and simple love freed from the thought of
     profit. Both poems likewise describe ethical/religious goals
     distant from the <u>vita contemplativa</u>. Langland's poem does not
     seek to change the Church in radical fashion; rather, it seeks
     to emancipate human personality from scholastic logic and
     dialectic, to strengthen the practical individual will. The
     scenes of Haukyn versus the Learned Doctor, and the Dreamer
     before Clergy and Scripture suggest the poet's high estimation
     of the piety of the unlearned. Piers represents the divine
     attributes of mankind in proper relationship to his Creator
     and to society; he does not stand for God in the poem, and the
     line "Petrus id est Christus" is best to be taken as referring
     primarily to St. Peter, the servant of God. At the end of the
     poem, Piers stands for the ideal pope who is desperately
     needed in a world whose church has been corrupted. Believes
     that the central questions of the poem, those regarding

1932

poverty and work, are largely answered by the common medieval
doctrine of solicitude, as derived from and interpreted in the
Epistle of James.

3   CARGILL, OSCAR. "The Date of the A-Text of 'Piers Ploughman.'"
     PMLA 47, no. 2 (June):354-62.
          Allusion to the Great Wind of 13 January 1362 offers
     only a terminus a quo of the A-text, and most of the accounts
     of the windstorm were written years later. Reading the poem
     as an historical allegory suggests it was composed as late as
     1376 during the time of the Good Parliament. In particular,
     the Castle of Caro suggests the lay political party founded by
     John of Gaunt in opposition to William Wykeham. John of Gaunt
     himself may be represented in the poem by Wrong, since the C-
     text links Wrong to Satan and connects him with the north, and
     Gaunt had considerable holdings in the north of England, as
     did Alexander Neville and William Latimer. Latimer is prob-
     ably false, described as a traitor in A II 99-100. Lady Meed
     represents Alice Perrers; Guile is Adam de Bury; Simony per-
     haps Simon Sudbury, archbishop of Canterbury, and an eccle-
     siastical tool of Gaunt. Peter de la Mare is represented by
     Truth; Conscience, who has brought great plunder to Calais, is
     the Black Prince, who sided with Commons and Wykeham against
     Gaunt. Wykeham in June 1376 became a member of a council to
     aid the king. Fixes the terminus ad quem June 1376, since the
     Black Prince was dead on 8 July of that year.

4   COGHILL, N.K. "The Secentenary of William Langland." London
     Mercury 26, no. 151 (May):40-51.
          Praises Langland for his "intensity of tone," of both
     calm, and noisier, "Hogarthian" satire; his power to imagine
     and to organize images that develop his complex thought in a
     psychological rather than logical plan; his double awareness
     of the practical world and the kingdom of God; and his power
     to invent characters like Piers, who, though seldom in view,
     are nevertheless "spiritually alive."

5   COGHILL, N.K. "Langland, the 'Naket,' the 'Nauȝty,' and the
     Dole." RES 8, no. 31 (July):303-9.
          Argues that nauȝty in B VI 226 (replacing naket in A VII
     212) means "reprehensibly worthless," rather than "having or
     possessing naught; poor, needy." Suggests this is consistent
     with the B-poet's general habit of trying to make the sense of
     the A-text more clear and emphatic: here the revision empha-
     sizes the surprising idea of the A-text that even the "out of
     work stalwarts," and not just the deserving poor, ought to be
     maintained on some kind of dole. The B-reviser, who usually
     improves the alliteration of the A-text, here is willing to

sacrifice alliteration to emphasize the idea; but no conclusions regarding the authorship question can be drawn from
this. For the significance of the C-poet's attitude on this
topic, see Day, 1932.8.

6   CORNELIUS, ROBERTA D.   "'Piers Plowman' and the 'Roman de
        Fauvel.'"   PMLA 47, no. 2 (June):363-67.
        Suggests Langland's knowledge of the Roman de Fauvel
(c. 1310), although there is no record of the French poem in
England in the fourteenth century. Fauvel, in the sense of
"hypocrisy," is first used in French literature in this poem
and with the same meaning first used in English literature by
Langland. Moreover, in both poems, a character (Fauvel and
Fals, chiefly abetted by Favel) attempts to wed a double-
natured woman (Fortune, Lady Mede); there is a long journey
undertaken for this purpose (to the Macrocosm, to London); and
the wedding is prohibited because the woman is too noble.

7   DAY, MABEL.   "'Mele Tyme of Seintes,' 'Piers Plowman,' B, v,
        500."   MLR 27, no. 3 (July):317-18.
        St. Patrick's Purgatory relates how the blessed awaiting
entry to Paradise are fed once a day by a light shining from
Heaven. The Gospel of Nicodemus connects this light with that
of the ninth hour when Christ harrows Hell. Piers Plowman
links the feeding of the patriarchs with the Harrowing, but
the B-text relates that Christ dies at midday. The OED, however, shows that the Middle Ages used noon to mean the ninth
hour.

8   DAY, MABEL.   "Piers Plowman and Poor Relief."   RES 8, no. 32
        (October):445-46.
        A postscript to Coghill (1932.5): the C-poet seems to
differ radically from the B-poet on the attitude toward the
idle vagabonds, and clearly distinguishes, in C IX 279-90,
those who ought to be helped from those who should be left
unaided. This difference may be due either to the conservatism of an aging author or to the indignation of a different
reviser to ideas that were uncongenial to him.

9   HASELDEN, R.B.   "The Fragment of Piers Plowman in Ashburnham No.
        CXXX."   MP 29, no. 4 (May):391-94.
        The fragment of the B-text in MS. Hm (fols. 96^r-97^v;
96^v blank) was originally a part of the complete text of the
poem as found on fols. 114^r-206^r of the same MS [HM2] and not,
as Skeat had contended, a distinct production. The argument
is from the physical makeup of the MS, a production of three
separate scribes, rather than from textual evidence.

1932

*10 HJORT, G. "Piers Plowman as a Work of Moral Theology." Disser-
     tation, Cambridge.
          Source: Bilboul, vol. 1, 135. See Hort, [1938].5.

11 JAMES, STANLEY B. "The Mad Poet of Malvern: William Langland."
     Month 159 (February):221-27.
          Langland is compared with Jacopone da Todi: both were
     deranged, became vagabonds and/or unlicensed preachers, and
     produced masterpieces. Langland's mind was perhaps unhinged
     by one of the calamities of the fourteenth century--the plague,
     the Avignon Captivity, the Peasants' Revolt. Langland, "liv-
     ing in the death-chamber of a whole civilization," could not
     blind himself to realities. He was, perhaps, not as mad as
     he let others think, though if he were sane, his essential
     sanity was of an extreme sort that borders on insanity. Mak-
     ing a hero of a plowman was intended as a message for England,
     "drunk with blood" of the Hundred Years' War. Langland's
     message for today lies in the fact that although he saw abuses
     in the realm, his loyalty never swerved from pope and king;
     and he was no communist.

12 Le MAY, Sister Marie de Lourdes. The Allegory of the Christ-
     Knight in English Literature. Dissertation, Catholic Univer-
     sity of America. Washington, D.C.: Catholic University of
     America, pp. 10-16, 40.
          Criticizes Gaffney (1931.4) for not noting the funda-
     mental differences in the allegorization of Christ as a knight
     in Piers Plowman and the Ancrene Riwle, that is, that His de-
     piction in the earlier poem is in the outworn amour-courtois
     tradition, whereas that in Piers Plowman is wholly in the
     sense of a noble, valiant warrior.

13 McGINNIS, MYRTA ETHEL. "'Piers the Plowman' in England, 1362-
     1625: A Study in Popularity and Influences." Dissertation,
     Yale, 360 pp.
          Catalogues early references to, allusions to, and echoes
     of the poem in early literary criticism and documents of po-
     litical and religious controversy.

14 SULLIVAN, Sister Carmeline. The Latin Insertions and the Maca-
     ronic Verse in Piers Plowman. Dissertation, Catholic Univer-
     sity of America. Washington, D.C.: Catholic University of
     America, xii + 104 pp.
          Lists Latin quotations that are extraneous to the text,
     Latin quotations syntactically articulated with the text, and
     macaronic lines of the poem under five headings: those occur-
     ring in all three texts; those found in but two of the ver-
     sions of the poem; those found in only one version; those

found in the extended passages of the B- and C-versions beyond that corresponding with A XII; and those found in
passages of the A-, B-, or C-text that represent elaborations
in one of the texts over the others.

Regarding the poet's use of Latin quotations, concludes
that differences between the quotations in the three texts are
never very striking; that the very numerous Scriptural quotations are always used with an ethical, never merely poetical
value; that no inference as to the general knowledge of Latin
at the time is deducible from Langland's quotations; and that
the poet is familiar with religious literature.

With regard to the macaronic lines, concludes that Latin
words are often introduced for alliterative purposes; that
Langland uses the Latin name when referring to a book of the
Bible or to a particular verse or psalm; that he often uses
the Latin word to refer to names of prayers, parts of the
Divine Office, the Mass, and so on; that the various epithets
applied to Christ are given in Latin; and that Langland's
allegorical materials are in most instances verses from
Scripture.

15 TROYER, HOWARD WILLIAM. "Who is Piers Plowman?" PMLA 47, no. 2
   (June):368-84.
   Skeat's description (1886.1) of Piers in the Visio as
"no more than the type of an ideal honest man" and in the Vita
as "the .true guide to God the Father [who] had already come to
men in the person of Jesus" is insufficient. The medieval
mind emphasizes the duality of nature in Jesus Christ; and the
distinction between the Son of God and Piers as man is made
definite in the poem. Also evident is the medieval disposition of mind to consider diverse variants within a common
symbol: Piers is allegorically a symbol of mankind; morally,
the perfect laborer, the charitable lord, the righteous magis-
trate and the conscientious pope; and anagogically, Christ who
guides mankind to God as a revelation of mankind's redemption.
Piers as a character (B V; VI; VII; C XVI; B XVI; B XIX) and
Piers either alluded to or referred to is examined in light of
these multiple symbolic values.

In particular, the Pardon scene may become intelligible
when we consider Piers as a man who tears the Pardon in an
act symbolic of the futility with which the author associated
atonement by one's own life in an age of easily acquired pardons; but at the same time, praised by the merchants for pur-
chasing the Pardon, Piers stands for Christ who gave His life
for mankind's pardon. Likewise, Piers as a guide to the Tree
of Charity, and as the person who shakes the patriarchs out of
the tree into the power of the Devil, shows that Piers represents both Christ and Adam--for man brought death into the

1932

world, and a greater Man conquered death. Reprinted in Blanch, 1969.4.

1933

1 COGHILL, NEVILL K. "The Character of Piers Plowman Considered from the B Text." Medium Ævum 2:108-35.
The character of Piers Plowman successively embodies the cumulative ideas of Dowel, Dobet, and Dobest, rather than representing a man, either individual or in the aggregate. Piers first appears after spiritual advice is given to the "field full of folk," but there is still a need for practical advice. The Tearing of the Pardon shows in one sense the insufficiency of the simple life of action, and prophesies (B VII 117-20) Piers's transformation into Dobet. When he returns to the poem (B XVI), Piers is no longer a simple and ignorant farmer, but a teacher, healer, and sufferer who corresponds to the clerkly life of Dobet that includes, but goes beyond, the active virtues of Dowel. Piers is primarily of this world; hence, he disappears from the poem when Christ, Who "lives" Piers in the Incarnation and Crucifixion, "puts off" humanity to harrow Hell after His death. Piers returns in the opening lines of XIX still as Dobet; he becomes Dobest at XIX 177 after the episode of Doubting Thomas, where Christ is still humanly embodied. From this point, identification with Christ ceases, to be replaced by identification with one to whom Christ has delegated power: this is the embodiment of Dobest, the life of episcopal authority. Hence, Piers parallels Christ in living the Three Lives successively. The allegory of Piers in particular and the poem in general is an organic one, in which one identity becomes more meaningful while remaining visibly the same.

2 DAWSON, CHRISTOPHER. "William Langland." In The English Way: Studies in English Sanctity from St. Bede to Newman. Edited by Maisie Ward. London and New York: Sheed & Ward, pp. 159-94.
Langland is the most Catholic of English poets, writing in a time of social and religious upheaval. Chaucer represents what England has learned from Continental culture; Langland speaks in the language of the common people and the old Teutonic measure. His realism, often melancholy in spirit, transforms allegorical representations into individuals and offers the first utterance in English literature of the sentiments of the poor. Yet he is a conservative reformer, whose ideals paralleled those of the commons and were as far from

class hatred as they were from a sentimental pity for the
unfortunate.
     Langland sees true religion as consisting of works of
charity that will have the effect of renewing both Christianity and the state. Compared to the more learned, the more
political, and the consciously literary Dante, Langland's
savior is a plowman who, because he works for the poor who
stand close to God, comes to stand for Christ; Dante's is
figured as a Messianic emperor. Langland agrees with Wyclif
only where Wyclif agrees with popular opinion. The concluding
battle with the Antichrist foretells the coming apostasy of
sectarianism and heresy. Reprinted: Dawson, 1934.5 and
1954.2.

3   HJORT, G. "Theological Schools in Medieval England." Church
    Quarterly Review 116 (July):201-18.
         Study of the poem prompts the question of how Langland
    could have learned theology if he did not go to university.
    Determines that cathedrals in medieval England supported
    theological schools, the masters of which were chancellors of
    the cathedrals or their deputies. The matter taught in such
    schools was the Bible, the Sentences of Peter Lombard, canon
    law, and perhaps pastoral theology. The pupils were the min-
    isters of the cathedrals and some clergy-at-large. Disputed
    by Coulton, 1934.4.

4   JUSSERAND, J.J. What Me Befell: The Reminiscences of J.J.
    Jusserand. London: Constable & Co., pp. 46, 72, 97, 153,
    221.
         Among incidental references to Piers Plowman, an account
    of Skeat's acceptance of the interpretation of the allusions
    in Jusserand, 1879.1 (cf. Langland, 1884.2). Also mentions
    Jusserand's discussing Piers Plowman with President Theodore
    Roosevelt 7 January 1903.

5   KIRK, RUDOLF. "References to the Law in 'Piers the Plowman.'"
    PMLA 48, no. 2 (June):322-27.
         The author or authors of Piers Plowman seem to show
    greater legal knowledge in the B- and C-texts than in the A-
    text (although there is no significant increase in such knowl-
    edge from the B- to the C-text). Legal words in the B- and
    C-texts are more technical than in the A-text, and the laws
    alluded to in the last two versions are no longer laws that
    the common man could have been expected to know. If the poem
    is the work of one author, Skeat may have been correct in sup-
    posing that the author had read law in the time between the
    first two versions.

1933

6   MOHL, RUTH. The Three Estates in Medieval and Renaissance Liter-
        ature. New York: Columbia University Press, pp. 102-4.
            Piers Plowman is not "estates literature" in the strict-
        est sense of the term, for Langland is not content with the
        mere enumeration of all classes. Instead, he introduces
        various classes whenever he wants and in any order he chooses.
        Estates does not appear, yet all major classes are introduced
        and described. C III 30 ff., describing Lady Mede's marriage,
        is the nearest he comes to an enumeration of the estates. Re-
        printed: Mohl, 1962.6.

*7 NISHIWAKI, JUNZABURO. Langland. Kenkyusha English and American
        Men of Letters. Tokyo: Kenkyusha.
            Source: Saito, 1966.17.

8   OWST, G.R. Literature and Pulpit in Medieval England. A
        Neglected Chapter in the History of English Letters and of the
        English People. Cambridge: Cambridge University Press,
        pp. 56-109, 548-93, passim.
            The prototype of Langland's "Toure of Truth" and "Castel
        of Care" is to be found in homiletic tradition, as is the mix-
        ture of allegorical and realistic representations of the
        Deadly Sins. Even the "alternating personalities" of some of
        the sins--Sloth is a layman, then a parson, then a layman;
        Pride is masculine, then feminine in the C-text--is dependent
        on the method of the homiletic tradition that deals in turn
        with several ramifications of a vice. The Debate of the Four
        Daughters of God is also described in the homiletic tradition,
        in which, as was extremely common in France, the figure of
        Mede is linked to the tradition of the "Devil's Daughters."
        Satire of the court at Westminster, of churchmen, lawyers,
        medieval quacks, and vices of the tavern are shown to be popu-
        lar subjects of the homilists.
            Disagrees with Ker (1912.3) and Huizinga (1924.2) re-
        garding the allegedly original, even supposedly unique value
        put on labor in the poem, and finds instead that here too the
        poem mirrors homiletic thought: it is assumed that all must
        work in one's own office and station, and not to work, or to
        take upon oneself the duties and responsibilities of a class
        different from one's own, is to produce social disharmony.
        Moreover, the poem shares with the tradition of sermon litera-
        ture a recognition of the social aspects of sin and an aware-
        ness that social ills testify to man's unregenerate nature.
        Even the praise for the virtues of honest toil, which is at
        the center of the conception of Piers, is found in the homi-
        letic tradition, though the emphasis of that tradition falls
        more usually on the satiric deviations from the ideal. Pages
        576-89 of this study present an expanded version of Owst,
        1925.6.

9   SMITH, A.H.   "Robin Hood."   MLR 28, no. 4 (October):484-85.
         Possible antedating of the earliest reference to Robin
     Hood (B V 402) by a reference to the "stone of Robin Hode" in
     a document of 1322, the Monkbretton Cartulary. This evidence
     is discounted by Dobson and Taylor, 1976.8.

                              1934

*1   BUSAN, WILLIAM F. "The People of Piers Plowman." Dissertation,
     Boston College.
         Source: Comprehensive Dissertation Index 1861-1972,
     vol. 30, p. 245.

2   CARNEGY, F.A.R.   An Attempt to Approach the C-Text of Piers the
     Plowman. London: University of London Press, 83 pp.
         Prints part of Carnegy, 1923.2, without alteration, in
     presenting a provisional C-text corresponding to Skeat's
     passūs III-V; not an edition in the full sense, but taking
     account of differences in meaning and normalizing abnormal
     spellings in the base MS, and partially recording dialectical
     differences in the notes. Accepts, with Allen (1923.1), the
     division of the C-text MSS into two groups: t (MSS. TH^2) and
     y (the remaining MSS). Divides the y-group into two sub-
     families, i (MSS. UDYIP^{2}OLBD^2) and p (MSS. PERMQSFKGN). Finds
     the t-group much closer to the original C-text, and the i-
     subgroup much closer to t than is p. The p-subgroup, which
     Skeat considered the "last word" of the author on the C-text,
     is in reality a sophisticated recension of the text. The p-
     subgroup occasionally agrees with the B-text against the i-
     subgroup, but there are more than a few instances where p
     "improved" its original, tampered with alliteration and meter,
     and expanded lines from the original C-text. Much more numer-
     ous than p's agreements with the B-text are the instances of
     the i-subgroup receiving support from the B-text against the
     reading of the p-subgroup. MSS of the i-subgroup show many
     errors which are almost always due to scribal carelessness and
     hence almost always allow for the recovery of the original.
     Lists some examples of contamination of i-MSS by A- and B-text
     readings. Reviewed by Anon., TLS, 20 September 1934, p. 639;
     Elsie Blackman, MLR 29 (1934):492-93; and Mabel Day, RES 12
     (1936):103-5.

3   CARNEGY, FRANCIS A.R.   The Relations between the Social and
     Divine Order in William Langland's "Vision of William concern-
     ing Piers the Plowman." In Sprache und Kultur der Germanischen
     und Romanischen Völker. Anglistische Reihe, vol. 12.
     Breslau: Verlag Priebatsch's Buchhandlung, 47 pp.

1934

The aim of the poem is to solve the problem of how mankind may attain salvation. Piers alone is capable of guiding
the pilgrims because through his honest and faithful labor he
has found the way to truth. Langland's attitude on the
fourteenth-century labor problem is similar to Wyclif's:
servants must perform their duties even for sinful lords, but
masters are exhorted to treat their servants with humility.
Piers serves his master Truth in this fashion, though the
trial of Lady Mede shows that masters are often oppressive;
and the Half-acre scene shows that laborers seldom live up to
the ideal. Hunger's "solution" is insufficient, since it is
founded on force. Insufficient also is the Pardon, which is
superfluous for Piers (who already embodies right labor) and
for the others (to whom it is given with reservations that are
shown to be very seldom fulfilled).
    The proper relations of master and servant are not to be
attained through Dowel, which is nothing more or less than
"fiat voluntas tua" or "dilige deum et proximum tuum." Piers
obeys these precepts; he has been guided to Truth by conscience that teaches a man to love, and after the Tearing of
the Pardon, he relies entirely on "fiat voluntas tua" as directed by Patience to Activa Vita. Thus the solution of the
problem of salvation and the solution of the labor problem are
much the same thing; for in work, properly understood, lies
salvation. Work must be centered in Christ and involve the
complete abnegation of the self. Dobet shows the practical
working out of Dowel, that can be brought about only by
Christ's Incarnation and Crucifixion. Dobest is the perfect
rule of the Church on earth. Reviewed by Harry Caplan, MLN
51 (1936):561-62; and Nevill Coghill, Medium Ævum 4 (1935):
47-49.

4   COULTON, G.G. "Theological Schools in Medieval England." Church
    Quarterly Review 118 (April):98-102.
        Contends that Hjort (1933.3) overestimates the propor-
    tion of students who went to theological schools to those who
    studied at university. Argues that Langland was an intelli-
    gent clerk who, because clerks attend priests and give the
    responses when the priests say Hours, could have achieved
    great facility in quoting from the Breviary.

5   DAWSON, CHRISTOPHER. Mediaeval Religion (The Forwood Lectures
    1934) and Other Essays. New York: Sheed & Ward, pp. 155-95.
        Contains a reprint of Dawson, 1933.2, slightly revised,
    under the title "The Visions of Piers Plowman." Reprinted:
    Dawson, 1954.2.

1935

6   KROG, FRITZ. "Autobiographische oder typische Zahlen in Piers
Plowman?" Anglia 58:318-32.
        Accepts from Bright (1928.2) that the name of the poet
was William Langland, son of Eustace de Rokayle, who lived in
Longland, between Great Malvern and Ledbury. Criticizes
Bright, however, for imbuing the numbers 7 (as in "seuen ʒer,"
A IX (66) and 15 (as in "fiftene wynter," A VI 33) with auto-
biographical, rather than merely conventional importance.
Notes the inconsistency in the characterization of the second
wife of Clergy, who is supposedly modeled on James de
Brockbury.

7   LUCAS, F.L. "Two Poets of the Peasantry--Langland and Hesiod."
In Studies French and English. London: Cassell & Co.,
pp. 28-76.
        Langland's allegory is muddled, and his theology has be-
come nothing more than "mythology"; yet he is a vivid artist
who can be appreciated for his style, especially for the
homespun quality of his comparisons. Compared with Hesiod,
who also described peasant life in his Works and Days,
Langland's personifications are pale, and his religious con-
victions perhaps are less accessible to the modern reader.

1935

1   CARGILL, OSCAR. "The Langland Myth." PMLA 50, no. 1 (March):
36-57.
        The "mansed prest of þe march of Yrlonde" of B XX 220
(C XXIII 221) refers to Walter de Brug[g]e, a notorious
prelate. The memorandum of MS. V (C-text) represents de
Brug[g]e's attempt to find out about the author who had
attacked him. B XV 148 shows how "Longland" came into being,
though "Long Will" finds support elsewhere in the poem.
"Robert" evolved as Skeat (1886.1) suggested. The detail of
the Malvern Hills was suggested by the poem. Mortymers
Cleobury is not eight miles from the Malvern Hills--obviously
this was a detail added by an amateur. Cleobury is to be explained by Bale's "in Clayland"; though it must be remembered
that Bale's authorities are not authoritative. Brings forward
records of William de Rokayle linked in 1353 to Essex and
Norfolk, where the deRokeles and the Buts are often joined; and
of William Rokell, nominated for an auditing position by
Thomas Brunton, bishop of Rochester (and the "angel" of the
B-text Prologue). Cargill's attribution of MS. V is doubted
by Brooks, 1951.1.

1935

2   CHAMBERS, R.W.   "The Manuscripts of Piers Plowman in the
        Huntington Library, and Their Value for Fixing the Text of
        the Poem." Huntington Library Bulletin 8 (October):1-27
        (R.B. Haselden and H.C. Schulz, "Note on the Inscription in
        HM 128," pp. 26-27).
            MS. Hm (B-text) is closely allied with MSS. W and Cr;
        all three derive from a common original. W is on the whole
        better than Hm, which is about the equal in value of Cr,
        though much closer in spelling to the original. MS. [Ht]
        (B-text) is a member of the second and largest group of B-MSS
        (COBoCotBmYC^2). The product of an inaccurate transcriber,
        this MS is derived from one heavily interpolated with the
        C-text.
            MS. P (C-text), formerly used by Skeat (1873.5) and
        Whitaker (1813.1), is one of the best of its class, though it
        shows peculiarities of spelling that can't be close to the
        original. Of the C-text MSS, however, the p-subgroup is not
        as good as the i-subgroup; and one of the MSS of the i-
        subgroup, unknown to Skeat, is MS. X, which ought to serve as
        the basis of a new critical edition of the C-version. In a
        concluding note, Haselden and Schulz show that the note on the
        inside cover of MS. HM, "Robert or William Langland made pers
        ploughman," was not written before the early sixteenth cen-
        tury. For MS. [Ht], see Russell and Nathan, 1963.9. Parts of
        this article dealing with MS. X were reprinted with additions
        in Chambers, 1936.3. For MS. X, see also Bennett, 1948.2.

3   COGHILL, NEVILL.   "Two Notes on Piers Plowman: I. The Abbot of
        Abingdon and the Date of the C Text II. Chaucer's Debt to
        Langland." Medium Ævum 4 (June):83-94.
            Records of tenants seeking justice against the Abbot of
        Abingdon (B X 317-30) establish the date of the C-text as
        1393-94. In this scene, the king is Christ, whose coming is
        the Second Advent. The Abbot of Abingdon stands for any abbot
        lax in the government of his abbey. Cayme, besides referring
        to Cain, stands for the Antichrist. Langland's deletion of
        references to Abingdon in the C-text may have been prompted by
        the fact that the author has discovered at the time of this
        version that the peasants are still oppressed. Chaucer is
        likely to have read Piers Plowman. His debt is one of idea,
        rather than phrase, yet all the lines of Chaucer's portrait
        of the Plowman with the exception of the first and the last
        are paralleled by Langland. Coghill's researches on the abbot
        of Abingdon are supplemented by Hall, 1959.5.

1935

4   COGHILL, NEVILL. Introduction to <u>The Vision of Piers Plowman</u>.
    Translated by Henry W. Wells. New York: Sheed & Ward,
    pp. vi-xxix.
        Though admits that there can be no absolute certainty
    that the Dreamer autobiographically represents the author,
    Coghill assembles the poet's biography from references in the
    poem in a fashion consistent with Bright (1928.2). Sees Lang-
    land's use of the alliterative style as somewhat deficient:
    "The number of his stresses borders upon uncertainty; it is
    usually clear where he means his stresses to fall, but often
    the unstressed syllables demand more emphasis and attention
    than would have been permitted in the classic times of alliter-
    ation." Pronounces the poem one of the great Christian works
    about humanity, but one that differs from Chaucer's <u>Troilus</u>
    <u>and Criseyde</u>, for example, in viewing all human relationships
    as functions of a relationship with God, with eternal conse-
    quences. Outlines the fourfold method of analysis, as con-
    cerned, respectively, with the story, its meaning on earth,
    its moral meaning, and its meaning in Heaven; and asserts that
    all of these meanings are to be found in the poem, sometimes
    singly, sometimes interlinked; "but on all four planes the
    poem is complete, and all undertanding of it must move
    poetically among them all." Analyzes the poem as an inquiry
    judged by Christian criteria into the nature of the good life,
    based on the conformity of man with God, as perceived in the
    Trinity.

5   HOPKINS, GERARD MANLEY. <u>The Letters of Gerard Manley Hopkins to</u>
    <u>Robert Bridges</u>. Edited by Claude Colleer Abbott. Oxford:
    Oxford University Press.
        See Hopkins, 1880.1 and 1882.2.

6   JAMES, STANLEY B. "The Neglect of Langland." <u>Dublin Review</u> 196
    (January-March):115-32.
        Accounts for the neglect of Langland noticed by Dawson
    (1934.5) by the incompatibility of Langland's poem with the
    romantic reaction to industrialization and "puritan" values
    that led to reawakened interest in Chaucer and Arthurian lit-
    erature. But in the twentieth century, the values of <u>Piers</u>
    <u>Plowman</u>--sobriety, industry, the ability to view the world
    <u>sub specie</u> æternitatis--are particularly desirable.

7   JAMES, STANLEY B. <u>Back to Langland</u>. London and Edinburgh:
    Sands & Co., 167 pp.
        <u>Piers Plowman</u> is Dantesque in conception but flawed in
    execution, for in the poem the divine and human elements in
    Christ have become divorced and are not presented as belonging
    to the same person. Langland's failure is important, since it

1935

reflects on the breaking up of the earlier medieval synthesis;
yet we can now return to Langland for rediscovery of the medi-
evalism that integrated religion, thought, and social practice. Medieval Christianity was the source of the traditions
of nonconformity as well as post-Reformation Catholicism; and
Langland shows us both the puritan, homiletic strain and the
humanizing influences.

Langland is orthodox in his religious beliefs, satiric
in a more kindly than stern or morbid sense, and not a reformer, for he presents no social program. Piers is everyman,
and represents the bond of unity between every member of the
community and every class. That he is an idealized peasant
shows Langland's awareness of the spiritual and moral superiority of the type, a new kind of "knight" for the end of the
Middle Ages.

The poem appeals to the popular taste in that it manifests the popular conception of religion in its most sincere
form, eschewing theological subtleties and emphasizing the
practical character of Christianity. Langland is "supremely
English," yet with bonds as a member of the Universal Church;
and rather than inhibiting his insularity, his Catholicism
legitimizes it. He shows how false is the antithesis between
Catholicism and loyal nationalism. Reviewed by Anon., TLS,
9 May 1935, p. 303.

8   KELLOGG, ELEANOR H. "Bishop Brunton and the Fable of the Rats."
     PMLA 50, no. 1 (March):57-69.
          Brunton's Sermo 69 was delivered 18 May 1376, probably
     in London, and perhaps to the convocation that met in connec-
     tion with the Good Parliament. The poet of the B-text could
     hardly not have known of such a controversial address; and
     May 1376 should be considered a terminus a quo for this part
     of the poem.

9   OAKDEN, J.P. Alliterative Poetry in Middle English. A Survey of
     the Traditions. With assistance from Elizabeth R. Innes.
     Publications of the University of Manchester, no. 236. English
     Series, no. 22. [Manchester]: Manchester University Press,
     pp. 55-58.
          Describes the poem as not an isolated work in the allit-
     erative school. Praises the author for his realistic powers
     of description, especially of the "evils and sufferings and
     the aspirations of the common life of the times", and for his
     moral indignation, which prohibits any neat and tidy poetic
     form. Accepts the description of Piers's function in the poem
     made by Troyer (1932.15). Finds Langland to be a "great
     thinker, constructive and intense," neither a pessimist nor a
     foolish optimist, confident of the inherent goodness of human

nature, yet aware that the gladness of Easter will have to
give way to the coming of the Antichrist.

10 WIEHE, HEINRICH. Piers Plowman und die sozialen Fragen seiner
Zeit. Dissertation, Münster. Emsdetten (Westphalia): Heinr.
& J. Lechte, 73 pp.
     Langland was not a revolutionary, though he has often
been taken for one. Social criticisms, in fact, form a relatively small part of the poem in its three versions and are
mostly confined to the A-text. The author is largely ignorant
of the social situation of the nobility, and he is not concerned to resolve social confusion, except through God's law.
He has a friendly respect for knighthood as part of the social
hierarchy; but he is concerned with knights only theoretically
except when they threaten the Christian ideal of world order.
     The poet is a cleric who wants to purify the Church, and
who thus attacks the sins which the higher and lower clergy
fall prey to rather than the clergy themselves. He sees law
as a moral rather than social problem. He supports the equality of the commons (the landed gentry, in opposition to farmers
and agricultural laborers) versus the king, as long as consti-
tutional law is preserved. The poet is not an uncritical
spokesman for farmers and laborers; he sympathizes with their
poverty and their cruel treatment at the hands of overlords,
but not with them as a class. Langland's key to social questions is that everyone must do his own work and be responsible
to God. He does not urge the poor and oppressed to take
measures to better their lot; rather, he advocates reform from
within and charitable actions on the part of the powerful.
Social harmony is created by God and cannot be changed by man.

1936

1 DAY, MABEL, and STEELE, ROBERT. Mum and the Sothsegger. Edited
from the Manuscripts Camb. Univ. Ll.IV.14 and Brit. Mus. Add.
41666. Early English Text Society, o.s. 199. London: Oxford
University Press, pp. xiv-xix.
     Similarities of phrasing of Piers Plowman and Mum and
the Sothsegger (known to Skeat and others as Richard the
Redeless) are largely confined to the earlier parts of Piers
Plowman, and there is no evidence that the C-text influenced
the other poem. Although both authors are social critics who
emphasize the proper duty of lawyers to help the poor, criticize immoral clergy, and employ the dream vision, such are
common elements in medieval literature. Langland is an impersonal prophet with a "divine sympathy" for hardships of the
poor; the author of Mum and the Sothsegger has a more absolute

1936

conception of kingship and was perhaps a member of the lesser
gentry. Moreover, the detailed description of landscape in
Mum and the Sothsegger finds no analogue in Piers Plowman.

*2   DUNNING, T.P. "Interpretation of Text of Piers Plowman." M.A.
     thesis, National University of Ireland.
        Source: Bilboul, vol. 1, p. 135.

3   [LANGLAND, WILLIAM.] Piers Plowman: The Huntington Library
     Manuscript (HM 143) Reproduced in Photostat. Introduction by
     R.W. Chambers and Technical Examination by R.B. Haselden and
     H.C. Schulz. San Marino, Calif.: Henry E. Huntington Library
     and Art Gallery, 1-23 + 1-26 + fols. 1-106^V.
        Chambers's introduction (pp. 1-23) draws upon the work
     of Allen (1923.1), Carnegy (1934.2), and Chambers (1935.2) for
     the relationship of the C-text MSS. MS. X, discovered after
     Carnegy's researches, is the best MS. of the i-subgroup, and
     shares a common source with MSS. UDIP^2. The worst fault of
     MS. X is its omission of words, which can be remedied from
     other sources. Haselden and Schulz (pp. 1-26, second section)
     offer the results of examination with ultraviolet light,
     microscopes, and so on, of erasures and emendations invisible
     to the unaided eye. The MS. (preliminary pages, fols. 1-106^V,
     and endpapers) is reproduced in photostat.

4   LEWIS, C.S. The Allegory of Love. A Study in Medieval Tradi-
     tion. London: Oxford University Press, pp. 158-61.
        The poem is viewed as primarily a moral poem featuring
     "estates satire," that is traditional, conventional, conserva-
     tive, and unoriginal in its moral and political message.
     Langland is a learned poet, writing for a clerical audience.
     He is exceptional in the moments of sublimity (e.g., the
     Harrowing of Hell, the vision of Middle Earth) to which he
     sometimes aspires, and in his power to "render imaginable what
     before was only intelligible," as in the account of the In-
     carnation, C II 149 ff. He lacks Chaucer's variety and fine
     sense of language. "But he can do some things which Chaucer
     cannot, and he can rival Chaucer in Chaucer's special excel-
     lence of pathos." Often reprinted; see Lewis, 1977.10.

*5   STÜDL, JOHANN. Der Versmass in Langlands "The Vision of William
     concerning Piers the Plowman." Dissertation, Vienna.
        Source: Gabel and Gabel, p. 14.

1937

6   TRAVERSI, D.A. "Revaluations (X): The Vision of Piers Plowman."
    Scrutiny 5, no. 3 (December):276-91.
            Comparison of selections from the original with corre-
    sponding translations by Henry Wells (see Coghill, 1935.4)
    shows the degree to which changes in language and cultural
    conditions tone down the immediacy of personal experience and
    the direct statement of personal emotion. These particular
    characteristics of Langland are seen as stemming from a tradi-
    tion of preaching in which the tendency toward abstraction and
    allegory is joined with the popular instinct for realistic de-
    scription, expressed in the common idiom. Like Shakespeare,
    Donne, and Hopkins, Langland freed his poetic language from
    "scholarship gone to seed" and foreign influence of thought
    and meter. Langland's expression of his deepest feelings
    through the simplest images that are almost transparent
    vehicles for the underlying emotion is contrasted with
    Spenser's "pale" abstractions. Reprinted, revised, in
    Traversi, 1954.8, and abridged, in Alpers, 1969.1.

1937

1   BENNETT, H.S. Life on the English Manor. A Study of Peasant
    Conditions 1150-1400. London and Cambridge: Cambridge
    University Press, 1937, passim.
            The poem is used to illustrate such topics as the ig-
    norance of local clergy, the difficulties of the common-field
    system, methods of plowing, observance of holydays among
    laborers, details of household dwellings (e.g., the absence
    of chimneys), domestic occupations, tavern entertainments,
    and the villeins' practice of gaining freedom by entering the
    Church.

2   CHAMBERS, R.W. "Incoherencies in the A- and B-Texts of Piers
    Plowman and Their Bearing on the Authorship." London Mediaeval
    Studies 1:27-39.
            The Pardon scene becomes intelligible if we assume that
    the writer of the A-text knew the Glossa ordinaria on the line
    from the psalm Piers quotes: "Si ambulavero in medio umbre
    mortis, non timebo." When the priest impugns the ideal par-
    don, Piers responds with an assurance from Scripture, ex-
    plained in the Gloss, that the righteous through faith will be
    rewarded in the future life. The B-text shows Imaginatif re-
    ferring to "the gloss" on the same line. Similarly, the B-
    text offers another explicit explanation for what is implicit
    in the A-text, in the perfectly coherent confession of Sloth,
    in which that sin laments he has withheld wages and forgotten
    to restore what he has borrowed. Hence, his vow of restitu-

1937

tion follows naturally. Concludes that "we have no right to
assert that what is explicit in B cannot have been implicit in
the mind of A, though not expressed in the A-text."

3   DUNNING, T.P. Piers Plowman: An Interpretation of the A-Text.
     London, New York, and Toronto: Longmans, Green & Co., ix +
     214 pp.
          An analysis of the A-text in light of fourteenth-century
     thought. Assumes from MSS notes and colophons that the A-text
     is composed of two distinct poems, the Visio and the Vita;
     assumes also that since the poem is moral in tone and written
     by an orthodox Catholic, it is explicable with recourse to the
     works of the Fathers and Thomas Aquinas in particular.
          The theme of the Visio is the proper use of temporal
     goods; yet Langland differs from Dante in stressing this one
     aspect of the moral law while making clear the necessity of
     fulfilling the entire moral law. The Visio is divided thus;
     Statement of the theme (Prol-I); Vision of Lady Mede (II-IV);
     Vision of Repentance and Piers Plowman (V-VIII 129); and
     Epilogue (VIII 130-end).
          In the Prologue, Langland treats sin in its material
     element, stressing the sins of the concupiscible appetite.
     Holy Church, who presumes a knowledge of catechism, explains
     in passus I the purpose and use of temporal goods in the
     divine plan and points the way to Truth, which is defined in
     terms of the moderate use of temporal goods and the obligation
     to part with some earthly goods out of charity for fellowmen.
     The Vision of Mede elaborates man's duties to himself in re-
     gard to the use of temporal goods. All society is shown to
     be filled with the perversion of temporal goods; and the sins
     of the concupiscible appetite are feoffed to Mede and False.
     Theology objects to Mede's marriage because Mede, considered
     in the general sense of "gain," may be ordained to a good end.
     Only Conscience can judge how temporal goods are to be used in
     accord with the law of God; he shows that Mede means "gain in
     excess," though the king is not concerned. The Vision of Mede
     ends with the hope of Reason and Conscience helping to rule
     both the realm and the individual.
          The Vision of Repentance and Piers Plowman elaborates on
     the second part of passus I. The folk's search for Truth cor-
     responds to the Dreamer's request in I 81-82. Piers is the
     conventional medieval ideal of the just man, seen here as the
     idealized laborer. Takes issue with Carnegy (1934.3) that the
     Half-acre scene shows that salvation consists of the faithful
     performance of labor, for the plowing episode is meant to pre-
     cede the pilgrimage itself. The chief concern of this passus
     is the provision of bodily sustenance, not the duty or excel-
     lence of labor. Passūs VI and VII illustrate the medieval
     theory of private property, summed up as "private possession

and common use." The Pardon scene shows that Piers realizes
that God, not man himself, provides for man's material needs,
and that therefore Piers need not concern himself so much
about them. Piers believes the priest, who has interpreted
the Pardon correctly, and Piers rebukes him on the grounds of
abstinence.

The Vita in the A-text is probably a finished poem, as
Skeat thought before he discovered the "third passus" (which
he called passus XII), for the development of the poem "can be
considered progressive only in so far as each new speaker provides further material for the Dreamer's consideration," and
the line of thought points to Wit's explanation of the Three
Lives as the most acceptable to the Dreamer. The Visio defines the life of the plowman against the love of things of
the world, whereas the Vita defines it against the abuse of
Study and Learning. Yet there is no continuity in the "field
full of folk," proportion of material action to allegory, or
characterization of Piers. The B-poet's "lack of constructive
ability," seen in the additions he makes to the material of
the A-text, is strongly suggestive of multiple authorship.

Reviewed by B.A., Catholic World 147 (1938):246-47;
J.B., Oxford Magazine (17 February 1938):428-29; J.A.W.
Bennett, Medium Ævum 7 (1938):232-36; Nevill Coghill, MLR 33
(1938):577-78; A.G., Studies 26 (1938)):699-700; J.R. Hulbert,
MP 36 (1938):101; H. Koziol, Englische Studien 73 (1939):
263-66; and Fr. Krog, Anglia Beiblatt 49 (1938):202-5.

4 GLUNZ, H.H. Das Abendland: Forschungen zur Geschichte euro-
   päischen Geisteslebens. Vol. 2, Die Literarästhetik des euro-
   päischen Mittelalters: Wolfram--Rosenroman--Chaucer--Dante.
   Edited by Herbert Schöffler. Bochum-Langendreer: Verlag von
   Heinrich Pöppinghaus o.H.-G, pp. 520-39.

   Declares that the origins of the text and the relation
of the versions of the poem are not established, though the
similarity of Langland's idea of perfection to Joachim of
Flora's notion of the "Third Adam" suggests the possibility of
Joachistic writings in England before the time of the poem.
Sees the originality of the poem in its natural, sharp depiction of social faults. Divides the poem into four great
visions (the Visio and the Three Lives) focused on the figure
of Piers, which present a fourfold solution to mankind's problem based on reform of the state by strong, virtuous rulers
(if not the king, then someone else, like the plowman); the
moral reform of the individual; reform of society through
social love; and purification of the world in the chiliastic
sense. The poem is seen as a contemporary Bible, in which the
poet has substituted Piers, a man, for God. The theme of

1937

man's taking his religious fate into his own hands is viewed
as a poetic theme with analogues in Renaissance literature.
Reprinted: Glunz, 1963.2.

5   GRAVES, ROBERT (with KEMP, HARRY and RIDING, LAURA). "Politics
    and Poetry." Epilogue 3 (Spring):6-53.
        Piers Plowman is the first English political poem with
    literary pretensions. Langland is not a leveler: he believes
    in a strong king, church, and knightly class as a "national
    front against the depredations of the bourgeoisie." The poem
    is a semimystical tract intended to be committed to memory.
    As opposed to Chaucer, Langland makes no separation between
    his political opinions and his poetic energies. Reprinted:
    Graves, 1949.4.

6   KITTNER, HEINZ. Studien zum Wortschatz William Langlands.
    Dissertation. Halle. Würzburg: Verlag wissenschaftlicher
    Werke Konrad Triltsch, xiii + 131 pp.
        Presents the forms, meaning, etymology, and extent of
    use in the fourteenth century of Langland's vocabulary in all
    three versions of the poem, arranged according to etymological
    origins. Includes a list of words in the poem never used by
    Chaucer (perhaps because Langland was a preacher); a compari-
    son of Langland's vocabulary to that of Trevisa, Wyclif, and
    Gower; and a list of words first used in literature by
    Langland. Reviewed by R. Kaiser, Archiv 174 (1938):255; and
    Fr. Krog, Anglia Beiblatt 49 (1938):232-34.

1938

1   ASHTON, J.W. "'Rymes of . . . Randolf, Erl of Chestre.'" ELH 5,
    no. 3 (September):195-206.
        Examines appearances of Ranulf de Blundeville, Earl of
    Chester (alluded to in C VIII 9-12), in Sir Launfal and
    sixteenth-century drama. Munday's John a Kent and John a
    Cumber may give a hint of the genesis of once popular legends
    of this figure; Ranulf's association with the Welsh perhaps
    romantically elaborated upon his reputation as a warrior
    against the French and Saracens.

2   COULTON, G.G. "The Peasant Saint." In Medieval Panorama.
    London and Cambridge: Cambridge University Press, pp. 534-54.
        In a general analysis of the poet and poem, describes
    Piers Plowman in terms of Carlyle's Peasant Saint. Sees
    Langland, whose best poetry sprung from "the struggles and
    failures of his life," possessed of as violent an inferiority
    complex as was Carlyle. Unlike Chaucer, Langland was

interested in crowds (rather than the individual) and committed to reform, rather than merely comic acceptance, of the
world as he found it. Despite Langland's obvious differences
from Dante, the two poets are similar in their deep earnestness; and over and over again Langland emphasizes the three
points of the dignity of poverty, the importance of Truth,
and the everlasting significance of Christ's sacrifice.
Quarrels with Dawson's pessimistic assessment (1933.2) of the
end of the poem, as well as with his specifically Roman
Catholic reading of the significance of the poem. Sees,
instead, Langland as representing the Englishman whose ties
to Rome were becoming undone, "the man who was already beginning to feel it equally difficult to do without organized
religion or to do with it, and who was . . . in serious doubt
about Indulgences."

*3   DUNNING, THOMAS P. "Piers Plowman, an Interpretation of the A-
     Text." Dissertation, National University of Ireland.
          Source: Bilboul, vol. 1, p. 135. See Dunning, 1937.3.

*4   ELIASON, MARY H. "A Study of Some Relations between Literature
     and History in the Third Estate of the Fourteenth Century:
     Chaucer, Piers the Plowman, and the English Mystery Cycles."
     Dissertation, North Carolina, Chapel Hill.
          Source: Comprehensive Dissertation Index 1861-1972,
     vol. 30, p. 245.

5   HORT, GRETA. Piers Plowman and Contemporary Religious Thought.
     Church Historical Society, n.s. 29. London: Society for
     Promoting Christian Knowledge; New York: Macmillan Co.,
     170 pp.
          Langland regarded his poem as a theological work in-
     tended to define the salus animarum and its relation to the
     Church through mankind's need of forgiveness and the power to
     become good. The poem shows Langland's knowledge of the
     Breviary, the Missal, and the contents of theological works,
     and perhaps his direct knowledge of the Bible itself. He is
     extraordinary in his use of authorities in support of con-
     flicting opinions and in attempting to synthesize differing
     interpretations, as is done in theological works. Langland's
     psychology is scholastic and, in particular, is indebted to
     Aquinas who, as opposed to Augustine, considered the faculties
     as different but inseparable from the soul. Langland also
     accepts Aquinas's position on the morally neutral status of
     the senses, which likewise opposes the teaching of Augustine.
     Langland's kynde witte, which instructs conscience to follow
     reason, and so on, is Aquinas's lex natura, the intellectual
     light implanted by God that tells us what to do and what to

1938

avoid, and which issues in laws given by rulers for the
ordered life of society. Aquinas's synderesis, the force that
moves us to desire absolute good, is manifested in Langland's
notion of truth as a natural knowledge within man that teaches
him to love God more than himself.

Inwit, the guardian of the soul, is not conscience, but
Aquinas's sensus communis, or "the common source of everything
related to the senses." Augustine had stressed the superior
spiritual attributes of the soul over the body; Aquinas thought
that the soul was not only the spirit, but the form of the human being. Langland emphasizes the transcendence of the soul
over the body, but considers the soul as existing in some
parts of the body (e.g., the heart) more than in others.

With regard to the topic of predestination, Langland
cites authorities on both sides of the question, but concludes
by affirming the goodness and love of God which makes a "double predestination" unnecessary for pagans as well as for
Christians. Arguing in true scholastic fashion, Langland is
here able to expand the meaning of one of the terms at issue,
baptism, in such a way that synthesizes the apparently conflicting sources. With regard to the question of salvation
by unmerited grace or by mankind's will to do good, Langland
sees the apparently conflicting concepts in reality as but two
aspects of the same thing: the Holy Spirit as the free will
of the Father and the Son, and the free will in man. That
within mankind, aided by that external to him, leads mankind
to salvation. Langland's treatment of these related questions
is more optimistic than the prevailing rigid opinions of
Bradwardine and Wyclif; yet Langland does not avail himself
of the Augustinian and Boethian distinctions of foreknowledge
and predestination, necessary and contingent, and so on.

Langland believes that those under the old dispensation
can be saved by Law, and the remainder can be saved through
the righteousness of Christ. His notion of salvation is
essentially that of Anselm, in its emphasis on the debt due to
God from man, a debt that can be paid only through Christ's
free gift. With regard to penance, Langland sides with Ockham
(as opposed to Scotus) in stressing the ethical nature of the
sacrament--an insistence on contrition, an emphasis on love--
rather than on its forensic aspects. But Langland does not
treat the question of whether oral confession is a sine qua
non of foregiveness. Hort's definition of truth is rejected
by Vasta (1965.20). Her conclusions regarding Langland's use
of the Breviary are criticized by Adams (1976.1); her suggestion of parallels with Anselm is questioned by Erzgräber
(1957.3).

1938

6   MARCETT, MILDRED ELIZABETH. <u>Uhtred de Boldon Friar William</u>
     <u>Jordan and Piers Plowman</u>. Dissertation, New York University.
     New York: published by the author, vii + 75 pp.
            The Doctor of Divine in the dining scene at the house of
     Conscience (B XIII 21 ff.) is identified as the Dominican
     William Jordan, since the personality of the character--his
     pomposity, argumentativeness, mendacity, and disposition to
     ecclesiastical subtleties--matches Bale's characterization of
     Jordan, and B XIII 83 seems to contain a pun on his name.
     Langland would have sided with Uhtred de Boldon, the author
     of <u>Contra querelas fratrum</u>, which had been attacked by Jordan.
     Indeed, the text used by Jordan to begin his castigation of
     Uhtred's treatise is quoted in B XIII 69. The B-text is thus
     to be dated between 1366 (the time of the quarrel of Uhtred
     and Jordan) and 1378, when Jordan apparently left England.
     Reviewed by A.B., <u>Archiv</u> 174 (1938):260; J.A.W. Bennett,
     <u>Medium Ævum</u> 8 (1939):169-71; E. Blackman, <u>MLR</u> 34 (1939):
     255-56; C.O. Chapman, <u>MLN</u> 54 (1939):472-73; H. Koziol,
     <u>Englische Studien</u> 74 (1940):114-16; and Fr. Krog, <u>Anglia</u>
     <u>Beiblatt</u> 50 (1939):195-97.

7   MERES, FRANCIS. <u>Palladis Tamia (1598) by Francis Meres</u>. Intro-
     duction by Don Cameron Allen. New York: Scholars' Facsimiles
     & Reprints.
            See Meres, 1598.1.

8   STONE, GEORGE WINCHESTER, Jr. "An Interpretation of the A-Text
     of <u>Piers Plowman</u>." <u>PMLA</u> 53, no. 3 (September):656-77.
            An interpretive reading of the A-text, stressing that
     the main theme of the poem is "What must I do to be saved?"
     In answer to this question, Truth is first defined as it ap-
     plies to the individual qua individual, then to the individual
     as part of the social structure. Then, Truth is defined
     through the elaborate object lessons that serve to define
     Truth's opposite. In this fashion, the poem leads to the
     conclusion that doing well in this world leads to salvation
     in the next; the Dreamer, at first passive, gradually becomes
     an active questioner in search of what it means to do well and
     its relation to Truth.
            The poem differs from a morality play in that it does
     not conclude with a definite system that answers all ques-
     tions. <u>Piers Plowman</u> is in the long line of social satire,
     yet the poem is more eloquent and interesting than other
     English poems of social complaint. Almost all the criticism
     in the poem is directed against the vice of worldliness, al-
     though there is incidental personal satire. The poem may be
     less orthodox than is usually thought, as its conclusions
     point more and more to the insufficiency of man unaided by

1938

higher power; and the poet often questions the authority of
Scripture and the Church Fathers. Many questions--of the
value of faith versus works, predestination versus free will,
the authority of the Church, and so on--are aired without the
poet reaching a conclusion.

In a note to this article, Stone mentions the fact that
his essay was accepted for publication in spring 1937, but
that publication was held up until after the appearance of
Dunning, 1937.3. He also makes clear what he considers to be
differences in his and Dunning's approaches to the poem, that
is, what he sees as the main theme of the poem (salvation
rather than the proper use of temporal goods); his assumption
that the Visio and the Vita are artistically unified; and his
doubts of the poet's orthodoxy.

9   WELLS, HENRY W. "The Philosophy of Piers Plowman." PMLA 53,
    no. 2 (June):339-49.
        Cautions against too literal an explanation of the Three
    Lives, which are expressed most fully by the poet in the gen-
    eral conduct of the poem itself, rather than by aphorisms or,
    as Wells himself (1929.1) suggested, by citations of ulterior
    sources. Suggests that Coghill (1933.1) has qualified the
    distinctions between the Three Lives nicely, in insisting on
    the two phases of Dowel, that of honesty and that of the
    moral/intellectual life; yet Coghill may insist on too literal
    interpretations of Dobet as the life of the priesthood and
    Dobest as that of the episcopacy. Dunning (1937.3) sees the
    Three Lives as the Purgative, Illuminative, and Unitive,
    respectively, without, perhaps, realizing how close these are
    to the Active, Contemplative, and Mixed states that Wells
    (1929.1) has described. The Three Lives are not vocational
    states as much as mental states. Although they rise in an
    ascending scale of importance, it is possible for some to be
    saved through compliance with the first of the Three Lives
    alone, although the "fully developed" soul on earth, whether
    he is a bishop or not, would be "richly endowed" with all
    states.

1939

1   BLOOMFIELD, MORTON W. "Present State of Piers Plowman Studies."
    Speculum 14, no. 2 (April):215-32.
        Reviews the scholarship on problems of authorship, the
    identity of the author, and the intellectual influences on him.
    With regard to authorship, disagrees with Moore (1913.3) in that
    Bloomfield believes that there is a presumption of single
    authorship in common sense, if not in tradition. Finds that

as organization has been detected in what was once thought
disorganized, we tend to incline toward the idea of a single
author, but that the possibility of multiple authors must be
left open until new texts of the three versions appear.
Argues that the proper attitutde toward the "autobiographical"
elements in the poem lies between the view that everything the
poet says about the Dreamer is autobiographical and the view
that most of the seemingly autobiographical details are worthless. Suggests that the question of the poet's name cannot be
solved until further evidence is discovered, but that there is
some slight justification for the name William Langland in
B XV 148. The poet was probably brought up near Malvern Hills
and probably entered minor orders, though it is unlikely he
was a monk. His date of birth is unknown, though he may have
died in 1387.

The poet knew the Breviary well, and probably the Bible,
though there is little likelihood of his direct knowledge of
the classics. Notes the similarities of the poem to various
French allegories (see Owen, 1912.5), though there is no evidence of these poems reaching England during the poet's lifetime. The poet could not have known Dante's works, but he may
have been influenced by the Parlement of the Thre Ages and
Wynnere and Wastoure. His use of proverbs and the similarities of his poem to pulpit literature are part of Langland's
general indebtedness to medieval culture. Calls for work on
the meaning of Langland's words and lines, as well as on the
historical, social, and literary backgrounds of the poem.
Reprinted: Blanch, 1969.4.

2   BROWN, MARY. "'Piers Plowman': Illustrations." N&Q, c.s. 177,
(23 December):461.
Seeks illustrated MSS or editions of the poem, as well
as tapestries with scenes from the poem.

3   CHAMBERS, R.W. Man's Unconquerable Mind. London and Toronto:
Jonathan Cape, pp. 81-171.
A reading of the poem in light of the Three Lives, here
defined as the life of active labor in the world; the clerkly
or monastic life of contemplation, renunciation, charity, and
poverty; and the episcopal life in the world under the rule of
the Church. Notes the similarities of the Three Lives to
Walter Hilton's treatise on the "Mixed Life," but asserts that
Langland, unlike Hilton, puts Dobest, the mixed life of the
prelate, above the contemplative life, even if he does not
limit the life of Dobest to the religious.
Defends single authorship of the poem by William
Langland, son of Stacy de Rokayle, largely on the strength of
Chambers's own earlier arguments. Asserts that the C-text was

not meant to supersede the author's earlier work and that the
last two passūs of the C-text were not revised by Langland.
      The poem is seen as almost completely orthodox, and
manifesting very little "Wyclifism," even in its condemnation
of clerkly abuses. The poem seeks to justify the "ways of
God to man" and, like The Faerie Queen, Paradise Lost, and
the Prelude, ends with the individual soul refusing to accept
defeat. The B-text takes up questions of predestination,
salvation of the righteous heathen, and the importance of
learning--questions that were left unanswered in the A-version.
Langland's treatment of the Trajan legend is untraditional inasmuch as he has Trajan saved solely on the basis of his virtues and without his being baptized by Gregory.

4   DEVLIN, Sister Mary Aquinas. "Bishop Thomas Brunton and His
       Sermons." Speculum 14, no. 3 (July):324-44.
          Reviews the life and work of Brunton. Accepts with
       Owst (1925.6) the similarity of Brunton's social philosophy
       to that of the poem, but thinks the degree of Brunton's in-
       fluence on the poem is yet to be decided. Brings forward a
       record of a John Butt bearing a message from John, Duke of
       Lancaster, to an embassy including Brunton negotiating peace
       with France in 1380, and queries whether this Butt is the same
       person identified by Rickert (1913.4).

5   DURKIN, J.T. "Kingship in the Vision of Piers Plowman." Thought
       14, no. 54 (September):413-21.
          In the poem, the king is made such, democratically, by
       the power of the people; he rules with their advice and that
       of the nobles for the people's good. The king must rule with
       love, reason, and conscience; he must oppose bribery and re-
       ward-seeking, the great threats to the realm. Once installed
       by the people, the king must be obeyed unquestioningly; for
       his power, though given by his subjects, is confirmed by
       Christ. The poem steers between the "Scylla of kingly abso-
       lutism" and the "Charybdis of anarchy and nineteenth-century
       Liberalism-License."

6   HUPPÉ, BERNARD F. "The A-Text of Piers Plowman and the Norman
       Wars." PMLA 54, no. 1 (March):37-64.
          Argues that the A-text should be dated 1370-76. Skeat's
       explanation (1886.1) of A III 182-201 with reference to the
       period 1359-60 is insufficient, for the lines seem to imply a
       protracted winter campaign, starvation, and retreat to
       England--all of which conditions are met in the campaign in
       France of 1373 led by John of Gaunt. In this passage,
       Langland voices the popular discontent at the resumption of
       hostilities leading to reversals. Asserts that Skeat was

also wrong in identifying Conscience in this passage with
Edward himself, for the lines clearly distinguish between two
characters in Lady Mede's suggestion that had she been in control of the king's forces, victory would have been certain.
Lady Mede stands for Alice Perrers, who is criticized here in
ways reminiscent of her treatment in Gower's Mirour de l'Omme
and the political prophecies of John of Bridlington. Both
ascribe the English failures to Edward's staying home in the
power of Alice, rather than taking active command of his
forces. Moreover, the depiction of an irresolute and wavering
monarch fits better with what we know of Edward after the
death of Phillipa (1369) than with a time earlier in the
decade. The passage also alludes to Black Monday and the
treaty of Bretigny, in Langland's characteristic fashion of
disguising the exactness of contemporary reference by alluding
on the surface to past events while making it clear that the
present is intended.

*7 KILEY, Sister Reginald. "A Comparison of Pagan and Christian
    Satire: A Study of Horace and Langland." Dissertation,
    Boston College.
        Source: Comprehensive Dissertation Index 1861-1972,
    vol. 29, p. 773.

 8 KLETT, WERNER. Wörter im Sinnbereich der Gemeinschaft bei
    William Langland. Dissertation, Bonn. Bonn: Anton Brand,
    123 pp.
        Investigates words in the poem having to do with com-
    munity and social relations (kith, kin, kynde, blod, lynage,
    fere, make, companye, folk, peple, comune, kyng, and
    so on).
        Concludes that Langland emphasizes familial relation-
    ships as a form of community, and regrets that marriages are
    made on the basis of material considerations. Langland be-
    lieves that the natural condition of man is improved by
    Christianity; he stresses charity as an ethical norm and sees
    the Church's role as necessary only when relatives cannot help
    one another. His picture of the commons reflects contemporary
    conditions, especially its growing power. Langland believes
    in a king-comune relationship founded upon mutual trust, and
    exhibiting a Germanic element in the notion of the subjection
    of the king to law. The poet distinguishes between the
    Church's earthly and spiritual duties, and rejects any claim
    of the Church to worldly power.

1939

*9 MITCHELL, A.G. "A Critical Edition of Piers Plowman, Context,
     Prologue, and Passus I-IV." Dissertation, London, University
     College.
          Source: Bilboul, vol. 1, p. 135.

10 MITCHELL, A.G. "The Text of Piers Plowman C Prologue 1. 215."
     Medium Ævum 8 (June):118-20.
          Argues for "For hadde ȝe ratones ȝoure [reik] ȝe couthe
     nat reule ȝow suluen." Emending reed by reik, Mitchell feels
     the line more properly means "If, as you planned, you were
     able to have your own way, you could not keep yourselves in
     order." Finds MS support for reik in both subgroups of the i
     family of C-text MSS.

11 RICHARDSON, M.E. "Piers Plowman." TLS, 11 March, pp. 149-50.
          "Rose the Regratour" of A V 129 ff. is identified from
     Pleas and Memoranda Rolls of the City of London at the Guild-
     hall, vol. 1 (1323-84), p. 232, as Rose la Hokestere, tried
     17 March 1350 for the crime of forestalling.

                              1940

1 [CHAUCER, GEOFFREY.] The Text of the Canterbury Tales. Vol. 1.
     Edited by J.M. Manly and E. Rickert. Chicago: University of
     Chicago Press.
          See Stotevyle, 1459-60.1.

2 EVANS, B. IFOR. Tradition and Romanticism. Studies in English
     Poetry from Chaucer to W.B. Yeats. London: Methuen & Co.,
     pp. 28-29, 190.
          Langland's achievement was minimized by Chaucer's suc-
     cess, and although Langland was read at all periods from the
     time of Spenser to the nineteenth century, no great poet sub-
     jected himself to Langland's influence. Yet he succeeded in
     ways later poets strove for: the major Christian poem sought
     by the seventeenth century; the portrait of contemporary so-
     ciety that Coleridge urged on Wordsworth. Sees Piers Plowman
     as the closest version in English literature to Dante's
     Purgatorio, and concludes "had Langland come through, with
     whatever modification, as a great Christian and mystical poet
     into the sixteenth century, the tradition of our poetry would
     have been enriched." Hopkins may seem to reach back to
     Langland, but their verse is dissimilar: Langland uses a
     vocabulary and measure his audience would recognize as a
     medium of poetry; Hopkins's is so individual it seems "almost
     a private language."

3 GWYNN, AUBREY. The English Austin Friars in the Time of Wyclif.
   London: Oxford University Press, pp. 209-10, 221-24.
   Langland's denunciations of the mendicant orders are
   compared to those of William Flete: their criticisms are
   similar, but Langland sees no solution other than the destruction of the friars, whereas Flete's faith in the mendicants is
   "still unshaken, though sorely tried." Several passages in
   the B-text (XI 60-82; XII 151-65; XIV 213-14, and so on) recall the antimendicant preaching of Fitzralph's London sermons
   of 1356-57. The famous prophecy of B X 317 ff., in which
   friars are included along with possessionati, is understood as
   Langland's suspicion of the attempt by friars in the early
   1370s to expropriate the possessionati; Langland apparently
   feels this campaign derived from selfish motives. Elsewhere
   (B XV 501-29) Langland's thought parallels Wyclif's De civili
   dominio in suggesting that the clergy should be forced to live
   from the alms of the faithful.

*4 HUPPÉ, BERNARD FELIX. "The Dates of the A and B Texts of Piers
   Plowman." Dissertation, New York University, 195 pp.
   Source: Comprehensive Dissertation Index 1861-1972,
   vol. 30, p. 245.

5 RICHARDSON, M.E. "Characters in Piers Plowman." TLS,
   13 January, p. 24.
   Suggests that the portrait of Coveytise (B V 189 ff.) is
   modeled on one William Hervy, a weigher of wool, who was a
   Norfolk man connected with the Despensers and Malvern Chase.

6 SLEDD, JAMES. "Three Textual Notes on Fourteenth-Century
   Poetry." MLN 55, no. 5 (May):379-82.
   Note no. 1 (pp. 379-80) concerns Piers Plowman: Sledd
   punctuates C VI 66-67 as follows: "Thuse belongeþ to labour;
   and lordes children sholde seruen/Bothe God and good men, as
   here degree askeþ." Suggests that the sense of the lines,
   thus punctuated, is consistent with Langland's views of the
   duties of the various estates.

1941

1 BAYLEY, A.R. "Langland at Great Malvern." N&Q, c.s. 181
   (27 September):181.
   A reply to "Peregrinus" (1941.7), citing James Nott,
   Church and Monastery of Moche Malvern (1885), with regard to
   the tradition that the author of Piers Plowman composed the
   poem in a room over the gateway of the Priory.

1941

2   CHAMBERS, R.W. "Poets and Their Critics: Langland and Milton."
     The Warton Lecture on English Poetry, read 26 February 1941.
     Proceedings of the British Academy 27:109-54. Published
     separately, under the same title, by Humphrey Milford (London,
     1941).
          Langland and Milton are considered in the context of a
     tradition of fortitude and endurance in English literature,
     from Old English up to nineteenth-century literature. Lang-
     land is defended against "Higher Criticism" that would split
     his poem into parts produced by different authors; Milton is
     defended against biographical criticism that concentrates on
     real or alleged regrettable facts of his life. Piers Plowman,
     like other Christian epics, is concerned with the pilgrimage
     of the human soul on earth; seen in this light, the progres-
     sion of the Three Lives and the autobiographical aspects of
     the three versions confirm once again the single authorship
     of the poem. Both Langland's and Milton's poems offer out-
     lines of universal history from the fall of the Angels up to
     prophecies of the coming of the Antichrist; both see the
     Resurrection as the "vital moment" of that history; and both
     end with the beginning of a world-pilgrimage in which man's
     sin is shown as leading to a great good. Reviewed by Anon.,
     TLS, 22 August 1942, p. 419; and by William R. Parker, MLN 59
     (1944):205-6.

3   CHAMBERS, R.W. "A Piers Plowman Manuscript." Cylchgrawn
     Llyfrgell Genedlaethol Cymru The National Library of Wales
     Journal 2, no. 1 (Summer):42-43 (plus plate).
          MS. N (unknown to Skeat) is one of five composite texts
     that supplement the A-text with lines from B- or C-texts
     (others are MSS. T, K, H^2, and W). MS. N shows affinities
     with MS. W which, like MS. N, supplements A-text with C-text.
     After C XI, MS. N is mainly a C-text, though the end of XXII
     and all of XXIII are missing.

4   HOMANS, GEORGE CASPAR. English Villagers of the Thirteenth Cen-
     tury. Cambridge, Mass.: Harvard University Press, passim.
          The poem is used to illustrate the social and economic
     realities of village life, for example, abuses related to
     plowing another's land (C IX 112 ff.), conditions under which
     marriages are contracted (C VII 267-71), reciprocal relations
     of gentlemen and husbandmen (B IX 113-16), duties of the hay-
     ward (C XIV 43-50), duties of the steward or seneschal (C I
     93), and so on.

1941

5 HUPPÉ, BERNARD F. "The Date of the B-Text of Piers Plowman." SP
       38, no. 1 (January):34-44.
            Accepts the reference to the Good Parliament of 1376 in
       the Fable of the Rats (B Prol), but sees its particular ironic
       significance at a point when the acts of this Parliament were
       largely nullified by the "Bad" Parliament beginning February
       1377, influenced by John of Gaunt. Gaunt is the "cat" whose
       murder is proposed in the fable, just as during this period a
       riotous band of Londoners marched on the Savoy with murderous
       intentions. If the poem was begun shortly after February
       1377, it was most probably before July of that year, when
       Edward died; for the reference to the "kitoun," Richard II,
       implies his accession has not yet taken place. The terminus
       ad quem is supplied by B XIX 426-27 and 439-42, which are to
       be best understood as referring to the anti-Pope Clement VII,
       who claimed the papacy in summer 1378. The poem was probably
       finished before 1381, for it contains no reference to the
       Peasants' Revolt.

6 MITCHELL, A.G. "A Newly-Discovered Manuscript of the C-Text of
       'Piers Plowman.'" MLR 36, no. 2 (April):243-44.
            Description of MS. A (C-text), in which Piers Plowman
       breaks off at C XXIII 87 (fol. 97ᵛ). The text is closely
       related to MS. V, with which it may even have a common parent.
       The handwriting of both MSS is from the first quarter of the
       fifteenth century. Includes a short list of common errors
       found in these two MSS.

7 "Peregrinus." "Langland at Great Malvern." N&Q, c.s. 181
       (30 August):121.
            Queries information regarding the tradition, noted by
       Bright (1928.5), that Langland wrote in a room over what is
       now the Abbey Gateway of Great Malvern. Answered by Bayley,
       1941.1.

8 RICHARDSON, M.E. "The Characters in 'Piers Plowman': The Bishop
       of Bethlehem." N&Q, c.s. 180, no. 7 (15 February):116-17.
            The "Bishop of Surrye" (i.e., Bethlehem) of B IV 365 ff.
       and C XVIII 277 ff. is identified from Rymer's Foedera as
       William Bromfelde, appointed to the See of Llandaff in 1386,
       and empowered to grant indulgences and to preach in prepara-
       tion for John of Gaunt's expedition to Spain.

9 SANDERLIN, GEORGE. "The Character 'Librum Arbitrium' in the C-
       Text of Piers Plowman." MLN 46, no. 6 (June):449-53.
            Liberum Arbitrium's self-definition (C XVIII 183-98)
       which puzzled Skeat is understandable in light of medieval
       psychology which, following John Damascene and Hugh of St.

1941

Cher, identified free choice with all other powers of the
soul. Answers the criticism of Day (1928.4) by suggesting
that the Tree of Charity in the C-text stands for the natural
human soul turned toward God through the influence of grace,
which cooperates with free choice when evil threatens.

1942

1   KENT, MURIEL. "A Fourteenth-Century Poet Surveys the English
    Scene." Hibbert Journal 40 (July):381-85.
        Notes the relevance of Piers Plowman to our own times,
    by calling attention to Langland's indignation, humor, irony,
    compassion, and lack of cynicism.

1943

1   BENNETT, J.A.W. "The Date of the A-text of Piers Plowman."
    PMLA 58, no. 2 (June):566-72.
        Accepts Huppé's identification (1941.5) of Lady Mede
    with Alice Perrers, but establishes the terminus a quo at
    August 1369 on the basis of an allusion to the death of Queen
    Philippa in A III 190-91. Fixes the terminus ad quem at
    September 1370, the date at which Urban V returned from Rome
    to Avignon, since the papal court at Rome is alluded to in
    IV 109-16. Interprets III 184 ff. as referring to the cam-
    paign of 1359-60, rather than that of 1373. Rejects the dat-
    ing of 1376 put forward by Cargill (1932.3), because of the
    latter's reliance on the Chronicon Angliæ, which is biased in
    its references to John of Gaunt.

2   BENNETT, J.A.W. "The Date of the B-Text of Piers Plowman."
    Medium Ævum 12:55-64.
        References to Richard's induction into the Order of the
    Garter (B Prol 112-13), to Thomas Brunton in the Fable of the
    Rats (B Prol 145 ff.), and to the papal court at Rome (B IV
    128 ff.) suggest a terminus a quo of 1377. References to the
    Great Schism (B XIII 173-76; XIX 426 ff.) point to a date of
    1379 or even later. Bennett notes that this essay was written
    before Gwynn, 1943.6, and takes no account of Gwynn's re-
    searches.

3   BLOOMFIELD, MORTON W. "Was William Langland a Benedictine Monk?"
    MLQ 4, no. 1 (March):57-61.
        Accepts Bright's contention (1928.2) that Langland was
    Willelmus de Colewell, ordained an acolyte in 1348, and seeks
    to identify this person with William Colvill of the

Benedictine monastery at Whitby. That Langland was a Benedictine would help explain the comparative mildness of his
satire on monks, his siding with Uhtred de Boldon against
William Jordan (see Marcett, 1938.6), and his Augstinianism.

*4 DONALDSON, ETHELBERT T. "The C-Text of Piers Plowman in Its
     Relation to the B-text." Dissertation, Yale.
          Source: Comprehensive Dissertation Index 1861-1972,
     vol. 30, p. 245.

5   DUNNING, T.P. "Langland and the Salvation of the Heathen."
     Medium Ævum 12:45-54.
          Langland's references to predestination and to the sal-
     vation of the heathen in the A-text Vita, elaborated upon in
     B XI and XII, are completely consistent with medieval theol-
     ogy. Theologians were unanimous in requiring an act of faith
     in God and the remission of Original Sin in order to be saved;
     but they likewise insisted that God wills the salvation of
     all mankind and that no adult can be damned except through his
     own fault. By the thirteenth century, it was believed that an
     immediate divine inspiration was accorded to the righteous
     heathen, as seen in Aquinas's discussion of the twenty-fifth
     distinctio of the Third Book of the Sentences. Such divine
     revelations were thought possible both before and after the
     Incarnation; although baptism is necessary after Christ,
     Aquinas developed the notion of three kinds of baptism: of
     water, of blood, and of the Holy Spirit. These three types of
     baptism are described in Imaginatif in B XII. Langland's ver-
     sion of the story of Trajan closely follows that of the
     Legenda aurea where, as in Piers Plowman, he is not restored
     to life in order to be baptized.

6   GWYNN, A. "The Date of the B-Text of Piers Plowman." RES 19,
     no. 73 (January):1-24.
          Accepts Marcett's ascription (1938.6) of B XIII 83-84 as
     a reference to William Jordan and would date B XIII-XX as
     1370-72, for Jordan was last heard of in 1368 and was appar-
     ently inactive or dead by 1374. Moreover, other references in
     B XIII-XX conform with this earlier dating: XIII 172-76 re-
     fers to popular disappointment at the resumption of hostili-
     ties between England and France; XIII 247-49 may refer to the
     plague of 1369, rather than that of 1376; XIII 265-71 clearly
     refers to Chichester and suggests the date 1370; B XV 539 ff.,
     a satire of absentee missionary prelates, makes more sense if
     it refers to a date not later than 1370, since before then the
     practice was very common. Accepts the thesis that the Visio
     was revised 1376-77, but sees in the increased antimendicant
     bias of the B-Vita (especially X 314-31) echoes of the 1371

1943

attack on the <u>possessionati</u> by Austin friars taking the side of the laity; Langland in general adopts the argument, but suggests at the same time the intrigues of the friars. Brings forward documentary evidence of William Jordan's career, and corrects the error of Marcett (1938.6) in assuming Jordan was active in France in 1388. Gwynn's thesis is rebutted by Huppé, 1949.5.

7   HEATHER, P.J. "The Seven Planets." <u>Folk-lore</u> 44 (September): 338-61, esp. 351.
In a collection of scientific and pseudoscientific references to the planets and stars in Middle English literature, <u>Piers Plowman</u> is mentioned with reference to the fact that omens from the stars no longer can be considered trustworthy (C XVIII 94 ff.), that there is a connection between lunacy and the phases of the moon (C X 107-8), and that the darkness at the time of the Crucifixion was a solar eclipse (C XXI 139-40).

8   RAUCH, RUFUS WILLIAM. "Langland and Mediaeval Functionalism." <u>Review of Politics</u> 5, no. 4 (October):441-61.
Medieval society was founded in theory on ordered differences of being and function, stemming ultimately from Wisdom 11:21. To Langland and Chaucer, degree means functional order, based on the contributions to the common good, rather than on ownership, profits, or earning power. Langland believes evil is at first personal, then by effect becomes social and institutional. The hierarchic and functional structure of society is stressed in the scene of Piers, as leader of the Field of Folk, entering into a social contract with the representative of knighthood (B VI 25 ff.), as well as in the scene depicting the dependence of the king on the power of the comune and the law of God (Prol. 133 ff.).

9   SPENCER, HAZELTON. "Worth Both His Ears." <u>MLN</u> 58, no. 1 (January):48.
B Prol 78, "worth bothe his eres," is best to be glossed "fit to keep both his ears," rather than Skeat's interpretation as referring to one whose ears are of some use.

1944

1   COGHILL, NEVILL K. "The Pardon of Piers Plowman." The Sir Israel Gollancz Memorial Lecture, delivered on 28 February 1944. <u>Proceedings of the British Academy</u> 30:303-57.

The Pardon has been purchased by Truth, so its efficacy is unquestioned. The priest is a "sophist" and an "ignoramus," but A VIII ends with the problematic notion that perhaps no one can do well. The Pardon is concerned with the active life; Langland's thought branches out in A IX, however, to include the clergy and the episcopate, or the contemplative-returned-to-action. Langland becomes involved in the question of the place of learning in the scheme of salvation, and the search for Dowel (and with it the A-text) is abandoned. In his revision and expansion of the A-text into the B-version, Langland completes and transcends the picture of English society and reinforces the moral teaching of the poem. In particular, the B Prol anticipates a number of themes--such as the power of the Church to forgive sins, the cardinal virtues, the natural gifts of the Spirit--that in B XIX 177-84 illuminate the question of the Pardon and a vision of the redemption.

The treatment of the Three Lives in B X 230 ff. shows Dowel to be a life based on faith, rather than merely "simple plowmanship"; and Dobet is redefined in terms of suffering and practicing what one preaches. The introduction of Imaginatif allows the author to review his former, now discredited opinions. Christ, Who lived the Three Lives in His own person, appoints them advisers in the rule of His kingdom after His Crucifixion. The argument of faith versus works is resolved in the episode of the Good Samaritan, in a new unity of faith, hope, and charity leading to a final anagogic identification of the Three Lives with the Father, Son, and Holy Spirit. The language of the Pardon in the context of the A-text yields justice but no mercy; but in the B-text, with the power of the Incarnation, Atonement, and Pentecost made manifest in the life of Christ, mercy and justice are reconciled. Reviewed by George Kane, <u>MLR</u> 41 (1946):424-26; and reprinted, revised and abridged, in Blanch, 1969.4.

2   COULTON, G.G. <u>Fourscore Years. An Autobiography</u>. New York: Macmillan Co.; Cambridge: Cambridge University Press, p. 133.
        Identifies Bronsil Castle, under the Hereford Beacon, as Langland's "Dungeon in a Dale," and locates the "Castle on a Toft" on Eastnor. Thinks it quite possible, with Bright (1928.2), that Langland was the <u>clericus</u> William of Colwall.

3   FISHER, A.S.T. "Sheeps Milk." <u>N&Q</u>, c.s. 187 (26 August):95-98.
        In a survey of notices of the use of sheeps' milk, cites a variant of C XVIII 21 (MS. T, C-text): "Marie Magdalen by meris mylk lyvede & Ewis."

1944

4 MITCHELL, A.G. "Worth Both His Ears." <u>MLN</u> 59, no. 3 (March):
   222.
           Translates B Prol 78 as "worthy to have both his ears
   because he made proper use of them." If he did so, the bishop
   would learn the abuses of pardoners and not issue them li-
   censes. Explains <u>by Þe bishop</u> in B Prol 80 as indicating that
   the pardoner is allowed to preach by the parish priest, who
   shares in the pardoner's winnings. Finds corroboration by
   Johnston, 1959.7.

5 WHITE, HELEN C. <u>Social Criticism in Popular Religious Literature</u>
   <u>of the Sixteenth Century</u>. New York: Macmillan Co., pp. 1-40.
           The central issues of the poem are the problem of pov-
   erty (seen as a failure of justice and charity) and the meaning of the social aspects of the Christian life. The root of
   suffering is the love of personal, material gain, which betrays all to Mede, or bribery. The rich are indicted on the
   basis of their oppression of the poor and their waste, but
   Langland's satiric vision encompasses small sinners, too. The
   poor are neither a cause nor merely an object of social abuses;
   but in general they have better prospects of salvation than
   the rich. Langland, a loyal member of the Church, makes no
   call for revolt; instead, he enjoins patience and patient poverty. His avowal of poverty is somewhat similar to Wyclif's.
   The sixteenth century, however, saw Langland as a coworker
   with Wyclif in the struggle for reform, as witnessed by
   Crowley's preface and marginal notes (1550.1); the <u>Praier and</u>
   <u>complaynte of the Ploweman unto Christe</u> (1553), which chal-
   lenged the basic economic relations of society; <u>Pierce the</u>
   <u>Plowman's Crede</u>, which criticized the friars from the perspective of the working class; <u>Pyers Plowman's Exhortation, . . .</u>
   an exposé of the merchant class; <u>News from the North</u> (1579),
   an attack on rich magistrates; <u>I Playne Piers, . . .</u> a call
   for free circulation of Scriptures; and <u>A Godly Dyalogue and</u>
   <u>Dysputasyon betwene Pyers Plowman and a Popish Preeset, . . .</u>
   which aims to rouse the simple man to protest against the pre-
   tensions of the learned in the field of religion. All of
   these tracts present a view closer to Wyclif than to Langland
   in their attack on friars; on the pope and the power of the
   Keys; on images, while the image of God in the poor is desti-
   tute; on the Real Presence and confession. A second branch of
   the <u>Piers Plowman</u> tradition, exemplified by the <u>Plowman's Tale</u>
   and <u>Jack Upland</u>, links the poem with the apocryphal Chaucerian
   tradition.

1945

1   BENNETT, J.A.W. "Lombards' Letters ('Piers Plowman'), B. v,
    251." MLR 40, no. 4 (October):309-10.
        Langland's reference is to the use made by the papacy of
    Italian bankers as agents for the transfer of papal dues from
    collectors to the camera. The bills of exchange employed in
    these transactions were known as "letters of exchange"; and it
    is this practice, often corrupted, to which Langland refers.

2   COFFMAN, GEORGE R. "The Present State of a Critical Edition of
    Piers Plowman." Speculum 20, no. 4 (October):482-83.
        A report from J.H.G. Grattan on the status of a critical
    edition of all three texts projected for the Early English
    Text Society by R.W. Chambers and J.H.G. Grattan as general
    editors. Expresses the hope that C.T. Onions, director of the
    Early English Text Society, will bring together coeditors of
    this work, which was interrupted by the war.

3   LANIER, SIDNEY. The Science of English Verse. Vol. 2 of the
    Centennial Edition. Edited by Paull Franklin Baum. Baltimore:
    Johns Hopkins Press.
        Reprint of Lanier, 1880.2.

1946

1   BURTON, DOROTHY JEAN. "The Compact with the Devil in the Middle-
    English Vision of Piers the Plowman, B.II." California Folk-
    lore Quarterly 5 (April):179-84.
        The wedding compact of Mede and Falsehood is considered
    in the light of the folklore motif of the compact with the
    devil: Langland's version is unique in equating the wedding
    agreement with the compact, and it is extraordinary both in
    introducing more than two characters and in completely omit-
    ting the attempt by the human party to evade the compact.
    Notes that the C-text almost obliterates the overtones of the
    devil motif.

*2 KANE, G.J. "The B-text of Piers Plowman, Passus XVII-XX." Dis-
    sertation, London, University College.
        Source: Bilboul, vol. 1, p. 135.

1946

3 PERCY, THOMAS. The Percy Letters. Edited by David Nichol Smith
   and Cleanth Brooks. Vol. 2, The Correspondence of Thomas
   Percy and Richard Farmer, edited by Cleanth Brooks. [Baton
   Rouge]: Louisiana State University Press.
       See Percy, 1763.1.

1947

1 GRATTAN, J.H.G. "The Text of 'Piers Plowman': A Newly Discovered Manuscript and its Affinities." MLR 42, no. 1 (January):
   1-8.
       A description of MS. Ch, newly acquired by the Library
   of Liverpool University: it is a "conjunct" A-C-text (C-text
   joined to A-text, not mixed or contaminated) which is closely
   related to MS. T (likewise a MS of the A- and C-text) in errors involving omission of lines, wrong division of lines,
   telescoping of lines, changes of words that destroy meter,
   and so on. MS. Ch is more valuable in tracing the ancestry of
   MS. T than is the closely related MS. H^2.

2 GRATTAN, J.H.G. "The Text of Piers Plowman: Critical Lucubra-
   tions with Special Reference to the Independent Substitution
   of Similars." SP 44, no. 4 (October):593-604.
       When a MS deserts its own family and agrees with another
   family, the first step ought to be to test all such suspicious
   readings for the possibility of independent, fortuitous alteration rather than to label the phenomenon contamination. In
   general, agreement in a sufficiently large number of instances
   discounts the possibility of mere chance agreement, but what
   constitutes "a sufficiently large number" depends on the type
   of substitution and on the editor's estimate of the probable
   immediate cause of the scribe's error. The most valuable
   readings in this sense are "inexplicable nonsense-readings
   and substitutions of dissimilars."

3 HUPPÉ, BERNARD F. "The Authorship of the A and B Texts of Piers
   Plowman." Speculum 22, no. 4 (October):578-620.
       Argues for single authorship on the basis that the B-
   text revisions of A I-VIII show no lack of understanding of
   the original and no differences in thought or style; that the
   A-Vita is a necessary continuation of the A-Visio; and that
   the B-Vita carries out the same intention. Concerning the B-
   text revisions of the A-Vita, answers various objections and
   questions raised by Manly (1908.6) and Dunning (1937.3):
   B Prol 87-209 develops the argument of the A-text in condemn-
   ing worldly clergy and the corrupt civitas terrena; the
   changes in the confessions of Wrath and Sloth show the care

and understanding of the B-text reviser, as does the change in
Mede's parentage, which corrects an oversight in A IV 55-63;
the introduction of the Pardoner and the Whore in B V 648-51
makes an ironic contrast with the simple humility of the Cut-
purse, Waferer, and Apeward, and adds realistic humor; and the
apparent inconsistency of the views of the A- and B-texts on
charity is resolved in the understanding that the Bible "guar-
entees the effect of cautious liberality," and that charity
ought not to be overselective.

The Visio and Vita are not separate poems, but are
linked by the figure of Will who, at the end of the Visio, has
learned the importance of Dowel, but has yet to put Dowel into
practice. The Prologues of the A- and B-texts are essentially
unchanged; B I clarifies the thought of A I and develops the
important point of the necessity of Good Works. A II and the
Vita de Dowel of the B-text show how the B-poet has clearly
set off Will's wrongheadedness and removed Clergy's false
deduction that knights and earls "are Dobest of all." B XI
shows that the reviser understands the abortive beginning of
A XII, and develops the solution in a way consistent with the
representation of the Dreamer in A Prol-II. The world of the
Visio is objectively viewed by Will; that of the Vita is seen
subjectively, "as something he desires." Lady Mede is paralleled by Dame Fortune; and Loyalty, who appears at Will's
side, represents obedience, which is just what Will's earlier
teachers had tried to emphasize to him. At the dinner with
Clergy, Will shows that he truly understands Dowel.

The figure of Activa Vita, at the end of the Vita de
Dowel, parallels Piers in the Visio in understanding the lim-
itations of too much attention to making a living. Will, who
has been prefigured by Activa Vita, is now ready for Dobet.
At the end of the Vita de Dobest, Will sets forth to find
Piers, who has left the world for the Tower of Truth, or
Heaven.

*4   PEPLER, CONRAD. "The Beginning of the Way." Life of the Spirit
      1 (1946-47):101-5.
           Source: Colaianne, 1978.4, p. 124, no. 507. See
      Pepler, 1958.7.

*5   PEPLER, CONRAD. "Conversion in Langland." Life of the Spirit 1
      (1946-47):136-41.
           Source: Colaianne, 1978.4, p. 124, no. 508. See
      Pepler, 1958.7.

1947

*6   PEPLER, CONRAD. "The Way Opens." Life of the Spirit 1
     (1946-47):169-72.
          Source: Colaianne, 1978.4, p. 125, no. 511. See
     Pepler, 1958.7.

*7   PEPLER, CONRAD. "Langland's Way to Unity." Life of the Spirit
     1 (1946-47):198-204.
          Source: Colaianne, 1978.4, p. 124, no. 510. See
     Pepler, 1958.7.

1948

1   BAUGH, ALBERT C. "Piers Plowman and Other Alliterative Poems."
    In A Literary History of England. Edited by Albert C. Baugh.
    New York: Appleton-Century-Crofts, pp. 240-49.
         Analyzes the contents of the three versions, and accepts
    the dates of 1362, not long after 1377, and before 1387 (see
    Devlin, 1928.5) for their respective composition. Briefly re-
    views the authorship question and concludes that although
    Manly's belief in the differences in language and versifica-
    tion among the versions has not been proven, it appears that
    the A- and B-texts were by the same author. However, the at-
    titude toward the poor, the treatment of ecclesiastical fig-
    ures, the preoccupation with theological questions, and numer-
    ous changes for the worse in the C-text "raise serious doubts
    about the authorship of this version." Concludes that until
    Manly's theory of the "lost leaf" has been satisfactorily dis-
    posed of, multiple authorship cannot be ruled out. Finds the
    greatness of the poem in the powerful imagination, realistic
    depiction, trenchant satire, and moral earnestness of the A-
    and B-texts.

2   BENNETT, J.A.W. "A New Collation of a Piers Plowman Manuscript
    (HM 137)." Medium Ævum 17:21-31.
         Collation of MS. X (C-text) with Skeat's printed text
    shows that errors in the printed text are more numerous than
    Chambers (1935.2) believed.

3   CASSIDY, FREDERIC G. "The Merit of Malkyn." MLN 63, no. 1
    (January):52-53.
         Contrary to the interpretation of Skeat (1886.1),
    Malkyn is used in B I 182 ff. not necessarily as "a wanton,"
    but rather as someone not desired by anyone, hence, as an
    example of negative virtue.

4   CHAMBERS, R.W. "Robert or William Longland?" <u>London Mediaeval</u>
    <u>Studies</u> 1, part 3 (for 1939):430-62.
          The ascription to "Robert, or William Longland" in MS Hm
    (B-text) cannot be dated earlier than 1540, when the MS was
    rebound; hence, the tradition of Robert as the poet's name is
    only that old, and from this MS derives the information fur-
    nished by Bale. The name Robert probably arose as Skeat sug-
    gested, as is confirmed by the readings of two MSS. Allegori-
    cal vision poems almost invariably identify the dreamer with
    the author and use the author's name. All three versions of
    the poem, and even the two parts of the A-text (Manly's A₁ and
    A₂) identify the author as Will. The external evidence af-
    forded by MS. V and the record (from 1718) of a farm named
    Longlands five miles from the Malvern Hills make it possible
    that the son of Eustace de Rokayle took his name from this
    place. (This article was published posthumously.)

5   DOBSON, E.J. "Some Notes on Middle English Texts." <u>English and</u>
    <u>Germanic Studies</u> 1 (1947-48):56-62, esp. 60-61.
          Relates <u>aliri</u> (B VI 124) to OE <u>lyre</u>, "loss, damage," and
    cites the expression <u>limes lyre</u> used of a paralyzed person.
    From the noun, assumes an adjective *<u>lyrig</u> and related forms
    *<u>a-lyrig</u> or *<u>on-lyrig</u>, whence ME <u>aliri</u>.

6   DONNA, Sister Rose Bernard. <u>Despair and Hope: A Study in</u>
    <u>Langland and Augustine</u>. Dissertation, Catholic University of
    America. Washington: Catholic University of America Press,
    ix + 192 pp.
          Despair (ME <u>wanhope</u>) signifies the loss of hope of sal-
    vation, and is opposed by the virtue of hope. Despair is an
    act of the will deliberately turning from God and deciding
    that salvation is impossible; as such, it involves heresy in
    assuming that God will refuse anyone the grace necessary for
    salvation. Specifically, despair is a sin against the Holy
    Spirit and is unforgivable if persevered in until death.
    David is the Old Testament example of a sinner who is not
    drawn to despair; Paul, in Ephesians 4:17-19 and Romans 8:24-
    25, warns of its evil effects. The New Testament presents
    examples of repentant sinners such as Peter, Paul, and Mary
    Magdalene.
          Langland follows Augustine in the conventional descrip-
    tion of despair as a sin against the Holy Spirit in the de-
    scription of Liberum Arbitrium (B XVI 46 ff.) and in the words
    of the Good Samaritan (B XVII 195 ff.), where despair is shown
    to nullify Christ's sacrifice for man's redemption. Langland
    shows the relation of presumption to despair in the conversa-
    tion of Will and Scripture and its aftermath (C XII 186 ff.)
    where Recklessness (presumption) leads to <u>wanhope</u>; but at the

same time the necessary mean, good hope, is asserted. Augustine also associates presumption and despair. Langland similarly agrees with Augustine's teachings in making despair more heinous than other sins and in seeing despair as the cause of other sins (Haukyn's confession, B XIII 332 ff.), as well as in viewing the sin in primarily ethical terms. Both Augustine and Langland agree that despair derives from other sins and from the devil. Langland associates despair with Avarice, Gluttony, Sloth, and Envy, of which Sloth is the most important. Both authors stress the antidote to this sin must come from God, though Langland differs from Augustine in believing that the ignorant man is more prone to the temptation of despair because learning enables one to understand the power of perfect sorrow for sin. (Cf. B XII 145 ff. and C XV 86 ff. with Augustine's position that the higher dignity and moral responsibility of clerics make them more likely to despair.)

Both Langland and Augustine see hope as a moral force to uplift man, draw him away from evil, sustain him in trouble, and encourage him to do good. In B XVII, Langland follows Augustine in relating hope to other virtues. Langland believes that man hopes for heaven because he believes his soul is immortal. He trusts in God if he really believes, and he proves his faith in works. Faith and charity show man willing to cooperate with God and thus justify hope.

The motives that enable a man to hope are supernatural and are based on the promises made by God. The promise of the Pardon is a cause for hope; its fulfillment is dependent on the work performed and is echoed in the meeting of Haukyn and Conscience and Patience. Augustine shows that man's labor will never be in vain; because God is just, He will never requite good with evil. For Langland, too, God's mercy is associated with hope as the root of charity. For both authors, Christ's Incarnation and Crucifixion are a source of hope.

The fruits of the Incarnation--the miracles of Christ, the institution of the sacraments as channels of grace, the conversion of sinners by Christ, and the bestowal of His mother on all men--enable man to hope, prove God's mercy, and in the case of Mary, put forward an intercessor as a motive to hope. Langland makes mercy the mother of hope, the Mother of God, and an intercessor on our behalf; Augustine stresses Mary's importance, chiefly in terms of her as Mother of God and as perpetual virgin.

Such similarities of thought suggest that Augustine's teachings on hope and despair were passed on whole through the centuries, rather than that Langland used him as a direct source. Brink (1877.1), Green (1875.1), and Courthope (1895.2) have unduly emphasized the gloom and hopelessness

of the ending of the poem. The battle can only end with
death; and Langland continually insists on the necessity and
availability of hope. Other writers, such as Wells, Troyer,
and Dawson, may be said to use despair in an imprecise, non-
theological sense. Reviewed by E. Talbot Donaldson, MLN 68,
(1953):141-42; J.B. Dwyer, Speculum 26 (1951):498-99; and
S. Neuijen, English Studies 32 (1951):169-71.

7   FOWLER, D.C. Letter to the editor. TLS, 13 March, p. 149.
        Queries location of MS. J (A-text). (This is now
    Pierpont Morgan Library MS. M 818.)

8   MATHEW, GERVASE. "Justice and Charity in The Vision of Piers
        Plowman." Dominican Studies 1 (October):360-66.
        Piers Plowman is closer to Sir Gawain and the Green
    Knight than to Chaucer's works, in that its purpose is didac-
    tic and its moral values simple; in both poems, horror alter-
    nates with beauty. Yet the virtues extolled in Piers Plowman
    are social and public, those in Sir Gawain and the Green
    Knight personal. The world depicted in Piers Plowman is one
    in which justice, considered in the sense of Ambrose as "the
    unswerving determination to give each man that which is his
    due," is threatened. Only charity is shown to be strong
    enough to preserve justice; it is the "motive force" of jus-
    tice, in the same way as injustice is motivated by covetous-
    ness. And since charity is the cause of justice, what each
    man is due is determined by need, not by merits. The Three
    Lives represent the common scholastic division of caritas
    incipiens, proficiens, and perfecta, as seen in action. Sub-
    stantially incorporated in Mathew, 1968.8.

*9 FRANK, ROBERT WORTH, Jr. "Piers Plowman and the Scheme of Salva-
        tion." Dissertation, Yale, 407 pp.
        Source: Comprehensive Dissertation Index 1861-1972,
    vol. 30, p. 245.

10 GEROULD, GORDON HALL. "The Structural Integrity of Piers Plowman
        B." SP 45, no. 1 (January):60-75.
        The B-text is unified around the nine visions that be-
    fall the Dreamer, each of which begins a new stage in his
    spiritual development. The poem is a pilgrimage in time,
    which alternates dream and reality in order to emphasize the
    complexities that "beset all men of good will in the world."
    Dream I (Prol) establishes the theme of the necessity that man
    find Truth; Dream II introduces the problem of sin; Dream III
    (passus VIII-X) points out the insufficiency of a purely in-
    tellectual approach and then, in the dream-within-the-dream
    (XI-XII), shows the value of grace and love; Dream IV

(XIII-XIV) merges the search for the meaning of the Three
Lives with the search for Piers; Dream V (XV-XVI) prepares
for the re-emergence of Piers in the poem through Anima's
discussion of the Tree of Charity; Dream VI (not specified as
a dream, strictly speaking) shows the power of love for sinful
humanity in the figure of the Samaritan; Dream VII (XVIII)
elaborates upon this in the recounting of the Crucifixion;
Dreams VIII and IX (XIX and XX) answer the questions posed
earlier concerning the life of man on earth.

11 HULBERT, J.R. "Piers the Plowman after Forty Years." MP 45,
no. 4 (May):215-25.
Contends it is undeniable that the A-text and the B-text
differ markedly, that the B-text at points spoils the A-text,
and that the C-text occasionally spoils the B-text. Feels it
is impossible definitively to argue concerning authorship until proper psychological criteria are devised. Attacks the
various arguments of Chambers on the grounds of the under-
emphasis of disorganization of the B-text, the degree to which
the A-text is incomplete, and the conclusions to be drawn from
the fact that the B-text takes up questions introduced in A$_2$.
Sees the tendency to ascribe single authorship to the poem a
result of the influence of Skeat's editions (and the continuing
lack of critical editions); the disposition to associate the
name of an author with a text; and the conditions of modern
publication, where revision and enlargement of a work is cus-
tomarily done by the original author.

12 KANE, GEORGE. "'Piers Plowman': Problems and Methods of Editing
the B-Text." MLR 43, no. 1 (January):1-25.
The author of the C-text had a MS of the B-text closer
to the autograph than the archetype of all extant B-text MSS,
if in fact he did not actually use the autograph. The C-text
represents three degrees of revision of the B-text: B Prol-
XVI was most thoroughly revised; B XVII-XVIII was subjected to
a diminishing degree of revision; B XIX-XX shows little or no
revision. With regard to B-text readings in the C-text, when
the reading of the B-text archetype is meaningless and the C-
text reading is good, there is a strong likelihood that the
B-text reading needs to be emended from the C-text reading.
When the B-text reading is inferior to that of the C-text, but
not intrinsically bad, the C-text reading is likely to be correct, though the error in the B-text archetype should be accounted for. When the B- and C-text readings differ but are
equally good, it is necessary to show how one could have descended in error from the other, or that one is required by
the sense of the passage in both texts. When the reading of
the B-archetype is uncertain, but finds some support in the

C-text, then that supported reading is likely to be correct.
The editor of the B-text must remember that errors were introduced between the C-text autograph and the C-text archetype;
he cannot expect to rely on the C-text MSS to produce con-
sistently better readings than that of the B-text archetype.

13 MITCHELL, A.G. "Notes on the C-text of Piers Plowman." London
    Mediaeval Studies 1, part 3 (for 1939):483-92.
         Divides the C-text MSS into two families, the i-group
    (the better of the two, composed of MSS. XIP2OLBUD) and the
    p-group (made up of MSS. PERMQSFGN). Offers textual notes on
    C II 95; III 16-18; IV 140-42; and IV 77-120. In particular,
    the changes wrought by the C-poet in C IV 77-120 show an im-
    provement over the corresponding passage in the B-text and
    make explicit what is probably implicit in the A- and B-texts;
    as such, it is an argument for single authorship.

1949

1   DONALDSON, E. TALBOT. Piers Plowman: The C-Text and Its Poet.
    Yale Studies in English, vol. 113. New Haven: Yale Univer-
    sity Press, xiv + 255 pp.
         Argues that the exaggerated inferiority of the C-text to
    the B-text has become a large impediment to accepting the
    theory of single authorship, for the more inferior a poet the
    author of the C-text is assumed to be, the more likely the
    critic will believe in multiple authorship. Finds it impos-
    sible to judge which was the most popular version to the
    poet's contemporaries, though it is undeniable that Crowley's
    editions ensured the popularity of the B-text. Tyrwhitt, in
    Chaucer, 1775.1, called attention to MS readings different
    from Crowley's, and Ritson (1802.1) distinguished two versions,
    in reality the B- and C-texts. Wright, in [Langland], 1842.3,
    felt that the B-text was the original, the C-text by another
    hand. Skeat never doubted single authorship. Jusserand ac-
    cepted the inferiority of the C-text, whereas Chambers was
    ambiguous on the matter, in declaring the C-text to be the
    work of the now aged author of the A- and B-texts, but much
    interpolated. Burdach (1932.2) and Traversi (1936.6) are
    clear exceptions in not assuming the inferiority of the C-
    text. Does not argue the superiority of the C-text to the
    B-version, but seeks to show that the C-text in its own right
    is "a magnificent poem, intellectually profound, artistically
    effective," and to adduce evidence for the unity of authorship
    of Piers Plowman.
         Finds the C-poet's revision of the B-text more extensive
    than the B-poet's revision of the A-version, but constituting

an increase of only 1.5 percent of the length of the B-text.
The revision by the C-poet of the B-Visio is discussed under
four categories: line-by-line or passage-by-passage revision
(as in C I-V; IX-X); passages greatly altered (C VI-VIII);
simple omission without compensation; and addition of passages
that do not change the framework of the poem (I; VI). Finds
the basic form of the Visio in the B- and C-texts similar.
Some revisions suggest two stages of authorial work: line-by-
line revision of seven passūs and a thorough rewriting of
three, then a later insertion of passages that do not alter
the framework of the original. The C-poet's revision of the
Vita, beginning in B IX, are found to be motivated by a desire
to improve the structure of the narrative, though the poet may
have died before completing this revision. The divisions of
the text in the C-version appear to be a compromise between
the A-text's conformity to the requirements of sense and the
B-text's longer divisions that accord with natural pauses in
the action. Regarding alliteration, the C-text is only
slightly more regular than the B-version and shows no individual alliterative patterns that might distinguish the poet
from the author of the A- and B-texts. Compared with other
alliterative poems of the fourteenth century, the alliterative
patterns of the three texts of Piers Plowman "resemble closely
nothing but each other."

The C-text's revisions of the B-version are explained as
reflecting the poet's desire to clarify and emphasize the
moral and theological implications of the poem, a desire to
free the C-version from naiveté, and the reluctance of the C-
poet to overstate a case. Repetitions and borrowings from one
part of the poem to another indicate his sense of accuracy and
consistency of detail; yet his failure to rectify the apparent inconsistency of identification of False and Favel, and
Warren Wisdom and Wilyman, seems to argue for the identity of
the B- and C-poets.

Finds scholarly opinion deeply divided over the author's
political sentiments, but sees no discrepancy between the
political sentiments expressed in the B- and C-versions; for
the political thought of these two versions is distinctly
middle-of-the-road, displaying great conformity with corona-
tion oaths of the fourteenth century. Differences in the
structure of the kingdom (cf. B Prol 112-22 and C I 139-46)
are explained through the author's general use of comune
either as "commonwealth" or "common people" considered in a
nonpolitical sense, and without political bias in either version of the poem. The C-text removes from the entire community the power to make a king and gives it to the knights,
perhaps as a result of misuses of the B-version by the 1381
revolutionaries. The Rat Parliament in both the B- and

1949

C-versions expresses the author's disapproval of Parliament's usurpation of the king's functions of government and in neither version is the fable told ironically. The attitudes of the A-, B-, and C-texts regarding the occupations of human beings are largely identical and can be grouped under three headings: those considered generally reputable and wholesome (though capable of being abused); those seen to entail "occupational hazard," such as trade, law, and medicine; and those whose hazards are so great that honest practitioners are seldom found (pilgrims, pardoners, beggars, and so on). The C-text seems opposed to the B-text on the question of social responsibility to beggars, but the B-text is at variance with itself on this same question, perhaps for autobiographical reasons. The C-poet's uniform criticism of minstrels is seen as a development of the B-text's austere evaluation of them.

The C-text Visio deals with moral and social questions, the Vita with spiritual questions, and can itself be seen as a triad of Active, Contemplative, and Mixed Lives, though not in a vocational sense. The Tearing of the Pardon (signaling the renunciation of the Active Life) is omitted in the C-text because Piers's angry response is potentially confusing. Dowel is defined through Recklessness as patient poverty, the first step in the soul's journey to perfection; this virtue is also emphasized in the C-text's diminution of Haukyn's life and character. Dobet in the C-version, as in the B-text, is described as charity, though the C-version eliminates Piers from the Tree of Charity scene, since the depiction in the corresponding section of the B-text came dangerously close to the heretical doctrine of deification. Dowel as patience/humility and Dobet as charity correspond to the Bernardine steps of perfection that culminate in Unity; but Dobest, "which contains elements suggestive of the unitive condition of soul," is unrevised from the B-text.

The C-poet was a clerk in minor orders, either an acolyte or a tonsuratus, who would be allowed to marry. He probably made his living saying prayers in private houses, for both the living and the dead. The C-text's remarks about mendicants and hermits are perhaps colored by the similarities of those professions to the author's own. Appendices treat the MSS of the poem; the geneology and class of C-text MSS; and the authenticity of the C-text. It is argued that a critical edition of the C-text based on the best MSS will be more authentic than a critical edition of the B-version.

Reviewed by Anon., TLS, 10 February 1950, p. 87; J.A.W. Bennett, Medium Ævum 21 (1951):51-53; George R. Coffman, Speculum 24 (1949):422-27; Nevill Coghill, RES, n.s. 2 (1951): 268-69; J.R. Hulbert, MP 47 (1952):207-8; Bogislav von

1949

Lindheim, Anglia 71 (1952-53):352-55; A.G. Mitchell, MLR 45
(1950):368-69; and S. Neuijen, English Studies 33 (1952):
24-28.

*2   FOWLER, DAVID C. "A Critical Text of Piers Plowman A 2." Dis-
sertation, Chicago.
      Source: Comprehensive Dissertation Index 1861-1972,
vol. 30, p. 245, where the date is given as 1950; but cf.
Knott and Fowler, in [Langland], 1952.6, p. 22. The MS relations proposed in this dissertation are summarized in [Lang-
land], 1952.6, and by Kane, in [Langland], 1960.10.

3   GARDNER, HELEN. The Art of T.S. Eliot. London: Cresset Press,
pp. 4-5.
      Chaucer is less profoundly serious than Langland, whose
imaginative vision surpasses Chaucer's in scope. Chaucer's
creation of the English heroic line and his adaptation of
Italian verse forms to rhythms of English speech is compared
favorably with Langland's lack of what Eliot called an "auditory imagination."

4   GRAVES, ROBERT. "Poetry and Politics." In The Common Asphodel:
Collected Essays on Poetry 1922-49. London: Hamish Hamilton,
pp. 273-84.
      Reprints of Graves, 1937.5 (rev. title).

5   HUPPÉ, BERNARD F. "Piers Plowman: the Date of the B-Text Reconsidered." SP 46, no. 1 (January):6-13.
      Responds to Gwynn (1943.6): what Gwynn takes to be a
"new complaint" against the friars (B X 71-77) is based on
lines that do not represent changes made in the A-text itself;
this "new complaint" is in reality an expansion of A XI 58-60.
Gwynn's dating of Friar Jordan's activity supplies merely a
terminus a quo of c. 1370 for the B-text. The reference in
B XIII 172-76 is to unsuccessful attempts to make peace,
rather than to the breaking of the peace. Argues that the
discussion of vagabond bishops (XV 484-90) is taken out of
context. Concludes that no single piece of evidence compels
a date of before 1376 for any part of the B-text; and that the
MS tradition gives no indication that the latter part of the
poem was written years before the earlier sections with their
references to the Good Parliament.

6   KELLOGG, ALFRED L. "Satan, Langland, and the North." Speculum
24, no. 3 (July):413-14.
      Satan's preference of the north over the south in C II
109-15 is traced to Augustine's Enarratio in psalmum XLVII and
his De gratia Novi Testamenti liber, where choosing the north

is suggestive of depriving oneself of God's grace by an act of
the will. Reprinted: Kellogg, 1972.8.

*7   MAGUIRE, CATHERINE E. "Franciscan Thought in Piers Plowman."
      Dissertation, Fordham, 169 pp.
          Source: Comprehensive Dissertation Index 1861-1972,
      vol. 30, p. 245.

8   MAGUIRE, STELLA. "The Significance of Haukyn, Activa Vita, in
     Piers Plowman." RES 25, no. 98 (April):97-109.
          Haukyn appears in the poem at a time when the Dreamer
     has turned from speculative faculties to practical morality.
     Haukyn embodies the world of the Visio, with clear affinities
     to Piers; but Haukyn represents the active life only in its
     practical aspects, without the moral obligations of the active
     life which Piers represents. He is similar to the "good ele-
     ment" of the folk in the Prologue; yet as his coat suggests,
     the patient, self-satisfied performance of hard work is not
     sufficient for salvation. The pardon which Haukyn seeks, un-
     like Piers's, is a merely practical one. Haukyn's confession
     makes him a personification of a whole manner of life, not
     merely a typical human being. As in the Visio, repentance is
     not an end in itself, but a preliminary to the search for God,
     defined in the Visio as Truth, but in this episode as charity.
          Reprinted, with modernizations of Middle English quota-
     tions and translations from the Latin: Blanch, 1969.4.

9   OSBORN, JAMES M. "The First History of English Poetry." In Pope
     and His Contemporaries: Essays Presented to George Sherburn.
     Edited by James L. Clifford and Louis Landa. New York:
     Oxford University Press.
          See Spence, 1732-33[?].1.

10   STROUD, THEODORE A. "Manly's Marginal Notes on the Piers
     Plowman Controversy." MLN 64, no. 1 (January):9-12.
          Manly's handwritten annotations to his copy of Bright,
     1928.5, indicate he had not been convinced by Chambers's re-
     buttal of the multiple-authorship argument. In particular,
     Manly questioned whether all three versions were equally de-
     pendent on the Psalter and whether the B-continuator's orga-
     nized thinking could not (as Chambers [1937.2] contended) be
     stated in detail. Manly also suggested what might have been
     a new line in the argument--the fact that the C-text seemed
     to him much interpolated.

1950

1950

1 BENNETT, J.A.W. "William Langland's World of Visions." Listener
43 (2 March):381-82.
Though Langland may never have read Roger Bacon, William
of Ockham, Duns Scotus, or even Thomas Aquinas, he is philosophical in that, like Anselm and Augustine, he is occupied
with questions of order and purpose. Like the thirteenth-
century encyclopedists, he presents a picture of the visible
world through allegory. His recurrent symbols of the field,
the Plowman, and the wayfaring Dreamer clarify the meaning of
his allegory; yet Langland is in no way provincial in his
thought. He is unique in his power to relate the inner spiritual world to the larger natural or societal world. Like
Aquinas and Dante, Langland values love, which he sees as
capable of making man like God; but he joins his concept of
love to one of truth, and he applies the teaching of the
ascetics to the life of man in the world.

2 DAWSON, CHRISTOPHER. Religion and the Rise of Western Culture.
Gifford Lectures Delivered on the University of Edinburgh
1948-49. New York: Sheed & Ward, pp. 265-74.
Piers Plowman shows that the fundamental principles of
Christianity in the early Middle Ages had been more completely
assimilated by the new vernacular culture of the common people
than by the higher culture of the ruling elements of church
and state. The poem shows how the dualism of earthly/other-
worldly ideals and that of state/church might have been sur-
mounted; for in the poem the "otherworld" is immediately
present in every human relationship; every man's life is bound
up with that of the Church; and members of society differen-
tiated by rank are nevertheless all children of God. The
relevance of Dawson's remarks to the twentieth century is a
subject of Rutledge, 1954.6.

3 FRANK, ROBERT W., Jr. "The Conculsion of Piers Plowman." JEGP
49 (July):309-16.
The key to the conclusion of the poem is in B XX 378-84,
where Conscience describes the practices of the friars on the
basis of their theoretical poverty. Need's speech (B XX 1-49)
shows how the friars' poverty is different from the life of
patient poverty with its disregard for bodily wants and its
trust in God. Langland criticizes the friars for their assumption that need puts them beyond morality; he looks forward
to a regular provision of necessities, a fyndyng, for them.
In the last scene, Piers is not, as Glunz (1937.4) said,
the Christ of the Second Coming, but rather an ideal pope who
would reform the friars. The Antichrist here is not a prelude

to Doomsday; rather, he merely suggests an enemy within the Church--a bad pope or those Christians, especially churchmen, who lead men to sin. The end of the poem is "agonized," but not one of despair.

4   HULBERT, J.R. "Quatrains in Middle English Alliterative Poems." MP 48, no. 2 (November):73-81.
        Tests the theory of Kaluza of composition in alliterative poems in quatrains on A Prol 1-109. Allowing for the possibility of unoriginal lines inserted by the scribes, sees a reasonable regularity of quatrains up to Prol 44. Of twenty-nine "stanzas," fourteen appear to be self-contained quatrains; and there are three pairs of quatrains where a topic begun in one quatrain is concluded in the last line of the following. Suggests that the pauses gained by quatrains were intended to have an auditory effect and to guarantee the audience the opportunity to grasp "one by one the elements of the narrative."

5   HUPPÉ, BERNARD F. "Petrus id est Christus: Word Play in Piers Plowman, the B-Text." ELH 17, no. 3 (September):163-90.
        Examines word-play as a "factor in the structural coherence" of the poem, with word-play considered under such headings as consonance, assonance, vowel harmony, homonymity. Sees it used to emphasize meaning in individual lines and brief passages. Notes frequent puns on leaf; good; pure/poor; cardinal; kin/kind; mean/men; like/licam/likerous; savour/saviour; and suggests that word-play achieves a "large consistency of design and pattern" in such passages as B XV 342-55; XII 59-94; XVIII 134-60; XVIII 331-401. Word-play also gives coherence to the whole poem in echoes and re-echoes of the triple theme of truth, tower, and treasure first sounded in the Prologue. Will himself is a play on words, and the central character of his vision created from the play on the word Peter in XV 203-206.

6   KANE, GEORGE. "Textual Criticism of Piers Plowman." TLS, 17 March, p. 176.
        Criticizes a review of Donaldson, 1949.1, in TLS (10 February 1950, p. 87) on the basis of the reviewer's doubts of the sincerity of autobiographical material in the poem and his questioning of the existence of three and only three versions since many MSS do not conform with either the A-, B-, or C-texts. Kane shows how "mixed-text" MSS are probably scribal in origin and suggests that there is only one MS that might represent the author's own intermediate version. He also doubts the importance of oral transmission in the preservation of versions of the poem. The anonymous reviewer

1950

responds with some examples of self-deprecating authors of the
Middle Ages, whose statements cannot be taken as autobiograph-
ically factual: the author of the Roman de toute chevalrie
says he is illiterate; the author of Dafydd ab Gwilym admits
to cowardice and effeminacy, and Gower calls attention to his
"inadequate" French.

*7   KASKE, ROBERT E. "The Nature and Use of Figurative Expression
      in Piers Plowman." Dissertation, North Carolina, Chapel Hill,
      199 pp.
              Source: Comprehensive Dissertation Index, 1861-1972,
      vol. 30, p. 245.

8   LAWLOR, JOHN. "'Piers Plowman': the Pardon Reconsidered." MLR
      45, no. 4 (October):449-58.
              The Pardon scene completes the satire of the Visio and
      serves as a transition from the active life to the higher
      forms of spiritual perfection. Piers is the best man in the
      world of the poem; yet the Pardon scene forces us to inquire
      how really good he is, for Christian perfection is enjoined
      upon all, and Piers himself repents of his past life and
      throws himself upon Divine Mercy. As the priest says, the
      Pardon is no pardon, but a statement of perfection. Piers
      understands it as representing the entry into the higher
      Christian life that can only be gained through the recognition
      of man's helplessness. The Pardon proclaims the "final in-
      adequacy of doing," whereas the Visio had implied the neces-
      sity of good works in a wicked world. Only God, as Incarnate
      Deity, has fulfilled the Law as expressed in the Pardon; Piers
      tears it asunder when he realizes what he should have known
      already, and what any virtuous Jew or pagan could have told
      him. As with the tearing of the curtain in the Temple, the
      reign of grace here begins for Piers, and the Law is tran-
      scended.

9   MERONEY, HOWARD. "The Life and Death of Long Willie." ELH 17,
      no. 1 (March):1-35.
              Comparison of B XV 152 ff. with its source in I
      Corinthians 13:4, 5, 12 weakens the argument for the author's
      signature in acrostic, in favor of considering him as
      Longanima or Long Suffering or Great Desire. Precedents of
      such authors as Christine de Pisan and Rutebeuf signing in
      acrostic are discounted as only "remotely material"; and
      Chambers's reliance on a convention of introducing the
      author's name into the poem is based on reasoning that is
      "probable only."
              Mistaking Will's silence in the face of Lewte's repri-
      mand (B XI 97-98) underestimates the comedy of the poem, which

is intended not to spread the news of Dowel, but as a "songe
of solas," abounding in puns, sophisms, "stunts of diction,"
and vulgarity.
The poem imitates the threefold scheme of Christian
spirituality: the purgative (that of beginners or incipien-
tes); the illuminative (for proficientes who have grown in
charity); and the unitive (in which the perfecti of enlightened
faith are joined with the will of God). The purgative ends at
B XV 189; the illuminative at B XX 212a; and the unitive begins at B XX 212b and ends with the Dreamer's final awakening.
The progression is not from laity to clergy to episcopate; and
Unity is intended to bear its mystical sense as the perfect
contemplative life, not to suggest the mixed life.
Suggests that of the three versions, the B-text was the
original, containing the entirety of its design, and that
the A-text is an abridgement for a nonclerical audience by a
redactor of the B-text, who gave up when the poem became too
esoteric to be abridged under his criteria. Asserts not only
that the A-text often fails to comprehend the B-text, but that
the A-text systematically drops untranslated Latin quotations
as well as those lines in English dependent upon the Latin.
The A-text often avoids strange words of Romance origin and
adds English turns of expression. Contends that the A-text
author has "mismanaged" his source in B I 141; II 50; II 173;
II 283; IV 20; IV 26; V 17; V 196; V 228; V 370; VII 28; VII
52-55; and X 178.

1951

1   BROOKS, E. St. JOHN. "The Piers Plowman Manuscripts in Trinity
    College, Dublin." Library 5th ser., 6 (December):141-53.
         MS. E (A-text) probably can be traced to Archbishop
    James Ussher. MS. V (C-text) may once have belonged to the
    priory of Abergavenny; the annals that precede the note of
    authorship in this MS exhibit a knowledge of the South Wales
    border and point to Abergavenny in particular. These annota-
    tions may well derive from the monastic annals (related to
    those used by the scribe of the Peniarth MS. of the Brut) be-
    longing to the priory of Abergavenny. Doubts the attribution
    of Cargill (1935.1) of this MS as that belonging to Walter
    de Brug[g]e.

2   ELIASON, MARY. "The Peasant and the Lawyer." SP 48, no. 3
    (July):506-26.
         Brings forward facts presented in the poem regarding the
    condition of poor laborers and villeins, their legal responsi-
    bilities to large landowners, and their rights before the law.

1951

Comparison with Chaucer shows that Langland viewed lawyers as
a class, whereas Chaucer idealized the poor and saw the Man of
Law as an individual.

3   FOWLER, D.C.   "Contamination in Manuscripts of the A-Text of
    Piers the Plowman."   PMLA 66, no. 2 (June):495-504.
         Attempts to determine between contamination and genetic
    relationship of MSS of the A-text. MS. U, a member of the
    large group TH^{2}ChDURAWMH^3 and the subgroup TH^{2}ChDUR also
    agrees significantly with MS. J, which by itself comprises a
    separate branch of the y family of A-text MSS. But the nature
    of the agreements of UJ--minor insertions, the substitution of
    individual words--suggests contamination rather than a genetic
    relationship, whereas the agreement of MSS. UR is genetic.
    With regard to MS. D, Fowler sides with Knott (1915.1) against
    Chambers and Grattan (1916.1) by showing the agreement of MS.
    D with MSS. TH^{2}Ch is genetic, and its relation to MSS. UR(TAM)
    through contamination with the ancestor of that subgroup.

4   FRANK, ROBERT WORTH, Jr.   "The Pardon Scene in Piers Plowman."
    Speculum 26, no. 2 (April):317-31.
         Critical comment regarding the Pardon scene may be said
    to attack the validity of the Pardon; to declare that the
    Visio ends inconclusively; to suggest that the visions that
    follow the Pardon scene continue the lines of thought of the
    Visio; and to argue that the Tearing of the Pardon represents
    a rejection of the active life and a recommendation of the
    life of contemplation. Argues instead that Langland presents
    the Pardon in a context that proves it is valid, since
    Holicherch's advice to lead a good life amounts to almost a
    translation of the Latin text of the Pardon. Moreover, as
    opposed to Wells (1929.1), the Dreamer's acceptance of the
    Pardon proves that it is valid for all mankind, as is the
    authority from which the Pardon comes (Truth) and on which it
    is based (the Athanasian Creed). The Tearing of the Pardon
    must be interpreted on the basis of such evidence, rather than
    on Piers's dramatic, but ultimately inessential words and
    actions. Langland's main purpose is an attack on papal indul-
    gences. Just as Piers's Testament (B VI 88-106) is not really
    a will but instead "a device for communicating an ethical mes-
    sage dramatically because of the contrast between the conven-
    tional form and the novel content," the Pardon is a device
    designed to state in dramatic fashion an ethical principle.
    The content of the Pardon is an attack on pardons, which in
    fact prompts the Dreamer to make just such an attack. Hence,
    in accepting its message, Piers is "rejecting bulls and
    seals," spurning indulgences, and accepting the command to do

well, but unfortunately doing so through what was (and was later apparently perceived by the poet to be) a confusing sign.

The gloss on Piers's quotation from Psalm 22, to which Langland later (B XII 289) refers, suggests that in the Pardon scene Piers must either trust the Priest or the Pardon; and it is clear he does not trust the Priest. As opposed to Chambers (1937.2), Piers's anger is directed not at himself, but at the Priest. Since the Pardon is valid and is accepted, the Visio is complete as it stands, and the Vita develops new, though related themes--no longer what leads to the Dungeon of Care and what to the Tower of Truth, but what man must do in order to be saved.

That Piers resolves not to do so much manual labor does not mean he has turned from Dowel to Dobet, for he never identifies bodily labor with Dowel; likewise, his resolve to take up prayers and penance does not mean that he is embarking upon the contemplative life, for such spiritual activities are not confined to contemplatives nor do they distinguish the contemplative life from the active. The material of this essay is largely incorporated in Frank, 1957.4.

5   FRANK, ROBERT W., Jr. "The Number of Visions in Piers Plowman."
     MLN 66, no. 5 (May):309-12.
          Corrects the count of visions in the three texts, as
     follows: A-text, three visions: Prol 11-V 3; V 8-VIII 128;
     IX 58-XII 99-105; B-text, ten visions: Prol 11-V 3; V 8-
     VII 139; VIII 67-XII 293; XI 5-396 (within preceding vision);
     XIII 21-XIV 332; XV 11-XVII 350; XVI 20-166 (within preceding
     vision); XVIII 4-431; XIX 5-478; XX 50-384; C-text, nine
     visions: I 8-V 196; VI 109-X 292; XI 66-XV 217; XII 167-
     XIV 216 (within preceding vision); XVI 25-XIX 180; XIX 180-
     XX 332; XXI 6-479; XXII 5-483; XXIII 51-386.

6   KANE, GEORGE. "The Vision of Piers Plowman." In Middle English
     Literature: A Critical Study of the Romances, the Religious
     Lyrics, Piers Plowman. London: Methuen & Co., pp. 182-248.
          The plan of the poem and the development of its symbol-
     ism must be studied in the context of the whole poem and the
     highly original art of its author. The A-text is clearly not
     the work of a beginner; the B-text follows the plan of the A-
     version, and then "works out its course in opportunist fashion
     as it goes along"; the C-text makes changes that clarify, in-
     crease explicitness of satiric elements, treat new topical
     circumstances, and change emphasis.
          The poem was written for a larger audience than most
     alliterative poems and does not exhibit such faults of allit-
     erative poetry as artificiality, obscurity, and monotony.

1951

Much of the personality of the author can be inferred from his
work: he was apparently quick to anger; possessed no sense of
compromise; was stern, outspoken, and yet tender. His religion, that "condemns the sin while it tries to raise the sinner," served to balance his sternness and tenderness.
    The poet's irony is based on an implied contrast between
the ideal and the real, and an assumption he is addressing two
audiences, one more sophisticated than the other. The poem
expresses moral, intellectual, and emotional impulses, each
characterized by his religion, as well as an artistic impulse,
potentially at odds with religion and expressed in the poet's
anxieties over the use and value of poetic composition. His
intellectual impulse is manifest in his entertaining two sides
of a question, although his religion insists that "fides non
habet meritum"; the interplay of the emotional and religious
impulses enlivens the allegory and makes poetry out of di-
dacticism; the combination of the religious and moral shows
him to be a Christian moralist, rather than a satirist. The
poetry suffers when these three religious impulses are not
accompanied by "appreciable fulfillment of the author's
artistic impulse," especially when religious emotion replaces
the creative impulse. The poet is not interested in the
minutiae of his craft or in formal rhetoric; the poem is
characterized instead by fluency of idea and expression,
visual imagination, and striking metaphor. The symbolism
develops through the multiplication and accumulation of associations; the plan of the poem is explicable on the basis of
a set of imaginative associations, yet is marred by frequent
digressions. Reprinted: Kane, 1970.9.

7   KASKE, R.E. "The Use of Simple Figures of Speech in Piers
    Plowman B: A Study in the Figurative Expression of Ideas and
    Opinions." SP 48, no. 3 (July):571-600.
        Examines and classifies figures of speech that "contrib-
    ute directly to the presentation of ideas or opinions." Sur-
    veys figures that present sense-impressions; aim to stimulate
    the reader's imagination; or contribute to structural signifi-
    cance, narrative action, or atmosphere. Of those figures pre-
    senting ideas or opinions, subdivides as follows: those that
    present intellectual attitudes of either the poet or the
    characters (usually expressed in metaphors); those that il-
    lustrate or support statements by means of similitudes (usu-
    ally similes and exempla); those that state ideas that, by
    themselves, are abstract or otherwise difficult to express,
    such as psychological material, material of cosmic scope,
    didactic material, Church doctrine and spiritual material.

8   PERCY, THOMAS. <u>The Percy Letters</u>. Edited by David Nichol Smith
    and Cleanth Brooks. Vol. 3, <u>The Correspondence of Thomas</u>
    <u>Percy and Thomas Warton</u>, edited by M.G. Robinson and Leah
    Dennis. [Baton Rouge]: Louisiana State University Press.
    See Percy, 1761.1.

9   ROBERTSON, D.W., Jr., and HUPPÉ, BERNARD F. <u>Piers Plowman and</u>
    <u>Scriptural Tradition</u>. Princeton: Princeton University Press,
    xii + 259 pp.
         The poem is interpreted in light of its <u>sententia</u>,
    examined through its Scriptural quotations and their glosses
    in the exegetical tradition exemplified by Augustine, Gregory,
    Jerome, Bede, Rabanus Maurus, Bruno Astensis, the <u>Glossa</u>
    <u>ordinaria</u>, Peter Lombard, Hugh of St. Victor, Bernard, and
    Rupert. Piers is seen as representing God's ministry on earth
    in the <u>status prælatorum</u>; a central theme of the poem is the
    usurpation of the functions of the <u>status prælatorum</u> by the
    <u>status religiosum</u>, chiefly the friars, and its danger to the
    Church. The ideals and evils described in the poem are seen
    against the fundamental doctrine of the value of <u>caritas</u>,
    toward which virtue the will, aided by faith, hope, conscience,
    intellect, and grace, should strive; and against which stands
    <u>cupiditas</u>, or Augustinian <u>amor sui</u>.
         The Prologue shows the world in confusion, most of its
    inhabitants in a state of spiritual slumber. Holicherch's
    "preliminary lesson" is that the <u>temporalia</u> are given by God
    for His worship, and thus their use must be directed by char-
    ity. Passūs II-IV show the corruption of society caused by a
    vicious concern for <u>temporalia</u>, as well as a remedy for this
    situation in the victory of the king over Mede. But just as
    the king needs a confessor to interpret Reason's law, the
    Christian needs Piers to direct him to Truth. Piers serves as
    the intermediary between man and that divine grace made avail-
    able through the Redemption. The Priest's failure to recog-
    nize and appreciate the Pardon illustrates the corruption of
    the Church Militant, in which Will and all Christians must
    live while they are alive. The Vitae are concerned with the
    practical problems of the Christian life, not general princi-
    ples of perfection. At the end of VIII Will, who is without
    intellectual direction, submits to Intellect and the insuf-
    ficient definitions of the Three Lives put forward by Thought;
    at this point Will is shown to be seeking salvation without
    putting forward the necessary inner effort on his own part.
    He is corrected by Wit, the speculative intellect; and Dame
    Study's fears concerning Will's unwise speculations are justi-
    fied in Will's literal interpretations of Scripture and his
    acceptance of predestination. But Will learns fear of the
    Lord through Scripture's theme, "many are called but few are

1951

chosen." He learns humility, but lapses into an "unreasoning
preoccupation with the problem of evil" until, rebuked by
Reason and aided by Imagination, he comes to respect clerical
learning.
    The Haukyn episode shows the effects of the friars re-
placing Piers in the Church. The sequence of Anima's instruction, the vision of the Tree of Charity, and the Samaritan
episodes show Will no longer isolated, but instead directed
in charity toward God. The Dobest sections (XIX-XX) show how
Will's state of grace is tested in "leading a just life in
faithful loyalty to the Church," here defined as the true
succession of Christ embodied in Piers. Yet at the end of the
poem, Piers is absent from the earthly Church, and man's only
hope is "the collective force of the Christian Conscience insisting that in its priests the image of Piers be found."
    Reviewed by Anon., TLS, 25 July 1952, pp. 477-78; Morton
W. Bloomfield, Speculum 27 (1952):245-49; Stella Brook, RES,
n.s. 4 (1953):150-51; T.P. Dunning, Medium Ævum 24 (1955):
23-29; Robert Worth Frank, Jr., MLN 68 (1953):194-96; F.
Mossé, EA 6 (1953):57-58; S. Neuijen, English Studies 34
(1953):79-83; Randolph Quirk, JEGP 52 (1953):253-55; and
Meredith Thompson, Personalist 33 (1952):433-34. Reprinted:
Robertson and Huppé, 1969.30.

10 SMITH, A.H. Piers Plowman and the Pursuit of Poetry. Inaugural
    Lecture, University College, London, 23 February 1950.
    London: H.K. Lewis & Co., for the College, 24 pp.
        Calls for consideration of the poem as poetry, in light
    of Langland's perception of moral values, social principles,
    and preoccupation with human material, instead of an expres-
    sion of early reforming zeal or as the work of more than one
    author. Draws on unpublished papers of R.W. Chambers for
    sidelights on the history of the authorship debate. Reviewed
    by Anon., TLS, 8 February 1952, p. 106; and Howard Patch, MLN
    68 (1953):581.

1952

1   FOWLER, D.C. "The Relationship of the Three Texts of Piers the
    Ploughman." MP 50, no. 1 (August):5-22.
        Illustrates how scribes omit passages because of simi-
    larities in diction in the original, and how individual
    scribes of the A-text MSS attempted to remedy the situation
    once they realized their omissions. Argues that in numerous
    passages the archetypes of the B- and C-text MSS were scrib-
    ally corrupt and do not correct the scribally corrupt original
    reading of the A-text. The C-reviser had a MS of the B-text

that contained typical scribal errors; and the B-reviser based
his recension on a MS of the A-text that also contained
scribal errors. Doubts the contention of Day (1928.4) that
the C-reviser collated his B-text with the A-text, for lines
erroneously omitted in the B-text are not restored in the C-
text; but sees merit in Day's suggestion that the type of the
A-text MS used by the C-reviser was different from the one on
which the B-text was based. Agrees with Chambers and Grattan
(1931.2) that the archetype of the C-text MSS is often superior to that of the B-text MSS; but warns against drawing conclusions from this concerning the state of the original B- and
C-texts, since the archetypes do not represent the author's
originals. Suggests that if there are typical scribal errors
in the B-text preserved in the C-text, then the author's original C-text is founded on an impure copy. See Donaldson,
1953.1, and Mitchell and Russell, 1953.5.

2   FOWLER, DAVID C. "The 'Forgotten' Pilgrimage in Piers the
    Plowman." MLN 67, no. 12 (December):524-26.
        The pilgrimage to Truth announced in A VII is not "for-
    gotten"; rather, A VIII 1 refers to the warning of an impend-
    ing famine made in the preceding lines, and thus Piers is
    explicitly told to give up the plan for a pilgrimage and stay
    at home.

*3 GRACE, T.J. "A Study of the Ascetical Elements in Piers Plowman
    and Their Bearing on the Structure and Meaning of the Poem;
    with Special Reference to the B-Text." D.Phil. thesis,
    Oxford, Campion Hall.
        Source: Index to Theses, vol. 2, p. 8.

*4 HUSSEY, S.S. "Eighty Years of Piers Plowman Scholarship: A
    Study of Critical Methods." M.A. thesis, London, University
    College.
        Source: Index to Theses, vol. 2, p. 7.

5   KASKE, R.E. "A Note on Bras in Piers Plowman, A, III, 189; B,
    III, 195." PQ 31, no. 4 (October):427-30.
        Would gloss bras in these lines as "household utensils
    of copper or bronze," not "money" as do Skeat (1886.1) and
    Huppé (1939.6), who see in these lines a reference to a time
    after Edward III retired from active leadership in the
    Normandy campaigns. Although unattested in the OED, this use
    of bras is found in three wills from the first half of the
    fifteenth century.

1952

6   [LANGLAND, WILLIAM.] Piers the Plowman: A Critical Edition of
    the A-Version. Edited by Thomas A. Knott and David C. Fowler.
    Baltimore: Johns Hopkins Press, xiv + 302 pp.
         Draws upon Knott (1915.1), unpublished materials by
    Knott, and Fowler (1949.2), the last of whom continued Knott's
    researches by presenting a critical text from the point at
    which Knott stopped (VIII 126, or the end of A_1) to the end of
    the poem. Dates the three versions of the poem as 1369-70,
    after 1370, and 1377-87, respectively. Recapitulates the
    publication history of the poem and the recognition of the
    three texts by Ritson, Whitaker, Price (Warton, 1824.1), and
    Skeat.
         Accepts the division of the A-text into two poems, a
    prologue and eight passūs of the Visio, and a prologue and two
    passūs of the Vita. Admits there is no evidence the two parts
    ever circulated independently, but asserts that "there is in
    A_1 no sign that A_2 is to follow, though within A_1 there is
    preliminary motivation and preparation for every important
    event, and considerable skillful use of suspense." Sees,
    moreover, the topics dealt with in the second poem following
    logically from the prefatory material at the end of passus
    VIII (VIII 127-81).
         Asserts that as long as it was not recognized that Piers
    Plowman existed in more than one version, the assumption of
    single authorship was natural. Cites incidents in literature
    produced before printing of scribe-editors or poets rewriting
    the entire work or adding extensions. Reviews Manly's theory
    of multiple authorship, and leaves the question to the reader,
    suggesting a careful and unprejudiced reading of A_1, A_2, and
    the B-text continuation with an eye for similarities and dif-
    ferences.
         Regarding the establishment of the text, criticizes
    Skeat's choice (1867.3) of MS. V as the base text, for this
    MS clearly represents an inferior tradition in the transmis-
    sion of the A-version. For A_1, divides the MSS into three
    families: x (comprised of VH); y (comprised of the remaining
    extant MSS); and z (represented by the readings of the A-text
    preserved in the B-text). The y family is further divided
    into four subfamilies, comprised of L, J, WNK, and
    TH^{2}ChDUREAMH^3, although it is clear that MSS. UR have dif-
    ferent affiliations in different parts of the text. For A_2,
    likewise finds three families, though here the x family is
    comprised solely by MS. V (MS. H ends at VIII 139); and, in
    the y family, MS. W joins the minor group AMH^3 instead of the
    minor group NK. Uses MS. T as the basis of the critical text
    because of its early date, its good spelling, and its compara-
    tively small number of errors. With regard to dialect,

concludes that the author (or authors) of the A-text knew more than one dialect, or perhaps used varying dialect forms in his own speech.

Includes an historical introduction, an appendix presenting the work of John But (XII 1-117), explanatory notes, a table of lines omitted by MSS of the A-text, textual notes (a selection of variants admitted wherever the critical text is not readily apparent, or wherever the critical text deviates from the reading of the base MS), a glossary, and an index.

Reviewed by Anon., TLS, 11 September 1953), p. 576; J.A.W. Bennett, MLR 50 (1955):193-94; Stella Brook, RES, n.s. 5 (1954):179-81; Norman E. Eliason, MLN 69 (1954):191-92, Robert Worth Frank, Jr., MLQ 16 (1955):85; Thomas A. Kirby, English Studies 35 (1954):129-32; Bogislav von Lindheim, Anglia 71 (1952-53):495-97; F. Mossé, EA 6 (1953):56-57; Tauno F. Mustanoja, NM 55 (1954):225-28; and J.F. Vanderheyden, Leuvense Bijdragen 45 (1956):25-26. Knott and Fowler's proposed genealogies of the A-text MSS are criticized by Kane, in [Langland], 1960.10. Reprinted: [Langland], 1969.21.

7   SMITH, HALLETT. Elizabethan Poetry: A Study in Conventions, Meaning, and Expression. Cambridge, Mass.: Harvard University Press, pp. 208-16.
    The influential place of Piers Plowman (and Pierce the Plowman's Crede, thought in the Renaissance to be by the same author) in the tradition of English satire is described with reference to the poem's emphasis of the unity of religious and social concerns, its preservation of the medieval "estates" view of society, and its bestowal of prestige on plain or "uncouth" style. This tradition is seen as continuing in such works as Churchyard's Dauy Dicars Dreame, Gascoigne's Steel Glass, Spenser's Prosopopoia or Mother Hubberds Tale, and Hake's Newes out of Powles Churchyarde. Contends that the influence of Piers Plowman did not allow formal satire on classical models to appear until the last decade of the sixteenth century.

8   TILLYARD, E.M.W. The English Renaissance: Fact or Fiction? London: Hogarth Press, pp. 90-96.
    Considers the poem the only work of English medieval literature that has serious epic proportions. Sees Langland's faults as primarily of organization: "Langland is extremely prone to venial sins of construction; at one point he is near the mortal sin of letting go the rudder altogether; but in the end he steers a straight and magnificent course." His flexible alliterative line is used for sententious effects, sustained thought and exalted feeling. He surveys with the "eyes of his age" the entire social scale.

1952

9   WILSON, R.M. <u>The Lost Literature of Medieval England</u>. London:
      Methuen & Co., pp. 62-63, 128-29, 156-57.
          The poem is briefly discussed in relation to stories of
      Emma and the Ploughshares, Robin Hood, and Randolph, Earl of
      Chester. Lists wills and inventories that mention the poem.
      For the second edition of this work, revised, see Wilson,
      1970.20.

                              1953

1   DONALDSON, E.T. "The Texts of <u>Piers Plowman</u>: Scribes and
      Poets." <u>MP</u> 50, no. 4 (May):269-73.
          Criticizes Fowler (1952.1) for the assumption that the
      reconstructed A-text will reproduce the poet's autograph bet-
      ter than the reconstructed B- or C-text, and hence that we can
      know for any given passage exactly what the A-poet wrote; for
      the B-text (supported by the C-text) might in fact reproduce
      the order of lines of the A-text autograph, whereas the scribe
      of the A-text archetype might have introduced errors into his
      copy. Also criticizes Fowler for claiming not to rely on lit-
      erary judgments, when in fact to decide between a scribal er-
      ror and a conscious revision entails literary judgment, and
      the entire hypothesis of multiple authorship (of which Fowler
      is a proponent) rests on the criteria of literary evaluation.
      Explains some of Fowler's examples of the presence of an in-
      tervenient scribe (e.g., A VII 164-70/B VI 181-82) as con-
      sistent with the B-text's omission of concrete detail rather
      than the product of scribal eyeskip; and others (e.g., B II
      147 ff./C II 167) in terms of the C-text poet's pervasive
      knowledge of the poem he was copying and revising. Takes
      Fowler to task for distinguishing the habits of scribes from
      those of poets, since it is clear that poets copying their own
      work act very much <u>like</u> scribes.

2   FRANK, ROBERT WORTH, Jr. "The Art of Reading Medieval
      Personification-Allegory." <u>ELH</u> 20, no. 4 (December):237-50.
          Distinguishes personification allegory (exemplified in
      <u>Piers Plowman</u>), in which abstractions are used as if they were
      concrete substances, from symbol allegory (as exemplified in
      the <u>Divina Commedia</u>), in which "characters and significant
      details are presented in concrete form"; admits, however, that
      Langland's and Dante's works include both kinds of allegory.
      Symbol allegory requires the reader to discover the meaning of
      the symbols and to interpret the relation of meaning between
      them; personification allegory requires merely the interpreta-
      tion of the pattern or relationship of meaning or activity,
      for the characters are "literal" in that they mean what their

                              194

names designate. In personification allegory, the names of
characters are thus important and must be understood in their
contemporary context (e.g., Imaginatif). Not all the characters in a personification allegory need be abstractions, and
there is usually a relationship between the writer's meaning
and the physical form and activity of his personifications.
Contends that the fourfold method of allegorical interpretation developed independently of personification allegory and,
for that reason, is "impossible for the form."

3   MAISACK, HELMUT. William Langlands Verhältnis zum zisterzien-
    sischen Mönchtum: Eine Untersuchung der Vita im Piers Plowman.
    Dissertation, Tübingen. Balingen: Herman Daniel, 142 pp.
         Dowel is the path of the soul; Dobet, the path of
    Christ; Dobest, the history of Holicherch Unite. The basic
    idea of the Dowel section is the education of the monastic
    perfection of love and the appearance of the mystic Christ in
    the soul (B XVI). Piers is a symbol of the mystical, rather
    than the historical Christ; the literary source of the plowman
    symbol is the mystical interpretation by the Cistercians of
    the Hohen Lied. Langland was probably a Cistercian lay
    brother; the poem shows monastic ideas outgrowing their orig-
    inal milieu and becoming common knowledge at the time before
    the Peasants' Revolt, as lay brothers left their cloistered
    communities and spread their ideas among the populace, giving
    farmers a class consciousness in their struggles against
    property owners. Assumes a common Latin tradition accessible
    to Langland, from which theological questions could be trans-
    ferred into allegorical poetic productions. Reviewed by T.P.
    Dunning, RES, n.s. 8 (1957):456-57.

4   MILTON, JOHN. Complete Prose Works of John Milton. Vol. 1.
    Edited by Don M. Wolfe. New Haven and London: Yale Univer-
    sity Press.
         See [Milton], 1642.1.

5   MITCHELL, A.G., and RUSSELL, G.H. "The Three Texts of 'Piers the
    Plowman.'" JEGP 52 (October):445-56.
         Fowler (1952.1) is criticized for not establishing
    scribal corruption clearly and unmistakably (i.e., by not
    ruling out other explanations); for assuming that the rela-
    tionship of the archetypes is the relationship of the auto-
    graphs; for not taking fully into account the possibility of
    error introduced between the original and the archetype of all
    extant MSS; and for not confining his researches to passages
    in which no considerable revision is apparent. Fowler's ex-
    amples are reconsidered to show that often supposed error in
    fact shows a change in the author's intention.

1953

6   QUIRK, RANDOLPH. "Langland's Use of Kind Wit and Inwit." JEGP
     52 (April):182-88.
          Langland uses wit with various, though conventional
     meanings as referring to any mental or sensual faculty, to the
     "outer" senses, and to acumen. Kind wit to Langland is wit in
     only one of its senses, that of "wisdom by nature"; it is
     natural and inborn in creatures, connected with the bodily
     senses, and thought of as the companion and teacher of con-
     science. In Middle English, inwit is used most often to sig-
     nify the human faculties of comprehension and, far less fre-
     quently, conscience, the more narrowly it was applied to the
     scholastic concept of intellectus. Langland does not use the
     word for conscience; instead, he sees it as intellect, the
     agens aspect of intellectus which, according to Aquinas,
     functions to apprehend the truth and for that reason is con-
     cerned with distinguishing right from wrong. Conscience is
     thus one aspect of inwit, its "awareness of right and wrong
     brought to bear upon one's actions." Reprinted: Quirk,
     1968.11.

7   YUNCK, JOHN A. "Nummus, Munera, and Lady Mede: The Development
     of a Medieval Satirical Theme." Dissertation, New York Uni-
     versity.
          Source: McNamee, vol. 1, p. 138.

                              1954

1   CEJP, LADISLAV. "Zum Problem der Anagramme in Langland's Piers
     the Plowman." Zeitschrift für Anglistik und Amerikanistik, 2
     (November):444-53.
          Discovers anagrams in the poem for John Wyclif (vyc- +
     leue, lyf, leve) and Wat Tyler (what, water + tyler, tylier,
     helyere, and so on). Identifies Wat Tyler with Piers Plowman.
     Asserts that the poet is cloaking his interest in social ques-
     tions in allegory.

2   DAWSON, CHRISTOPHER. "The Vision of Piers Plowman." In Medieval
     Essays. New York: Sheed & Ward, pp. 212-40.
          Reprint of Dawson, 1934.5.

3   HUIZINGA, J. The Waning of the Middle Ages. A Study of the
     Forms of Life, Thought and Art in France and the Netherlands
     in the Dawn of the Renaissance. Garden City, N.Y.: Doubleday
     & Co.
          Reprint of Huizinga, 1924.2.

                              196

*4   KNIGHT, DAVID JAMES. "The Relation between Symbolic and Dramatic
      Characterization in <u>Piers Plowman</u> (Considered from the B
      Text." Dissertation, Yale, 288 pp.
          Abstracted: <u>DA</u> 31:1763A.

5   QUIRK, RANDOLPH. "Vis Imaginativa." <u>JEGP</u> 53 (January):81-83.
          Accepts the analysis of Imaginatif by Jones (1914.2) and
      notes the rarity of Langland's use of the term in Middle En-
      glish in a deliberate, rather than reproductive function.
      Traces this concept to Aristotle, which was passed to the
      Middle Ages by Boethius (<u>Philosophiæ consolationis</u>, V,
      pr. 4). Besides Langland, Lydgate (<u>Troy Book</u>, I, line 3577)
      is the only writer in Middle English to use the term in its
      deliberative aspect. Reprinted: Quirk, 1968.11.

6   RUTLEDGE, Dom DENYS. "Langland and the Liturgical Tradition."
      <u>Dublin Review</u> 228, no. 466 (4th quarter):405-16.
          Enlarges upon Dawson (1950.2) in noting that the litur-
      gical tradition of monastic communities, which harmonizes ma-
      terial and spiritual life in the poem, is now in evidence in
      a wider diffusion of religion among the laity and in the rise
      of lay Christian communities.

7   TILLYARD, E.M.W. <u>The English Epic and Its Background</u>. New York:
      Oxford University Press, pp. 151-71.
          None of the three versions is satisfactory without the
      others, but it is impossible to devise a satisfactory confla-
      tion of the texts. The C-text sometimes "does violence to the
      B-text," yet often improves upon it. Langland is gifted in
      the power of enriching sense through sound; his writing has a
      prophetic terseness about it that in its sententiousness is
      reminiscent of Milton. Like an epic, the poem speaks for a
      great number of people, with a capaciousness and variety of
      substance. The overall effectiveness of the poem is somewhat
      diminished by Langland's repetitions of homiletic material and
      irrelevant moralizing, though a much more serious structural
      flaw lies in the repetition of Dowel, the active life, in both
      parts of the poem. <u>Piers Plowman</u> is similar to later English
      epics in its combination of a public theme of political or
      religious significance with the individual and tragic theme
      of personal salvation.

8   TRAVERSI, DEREK. "Langland's <u>Piers Plowman</u>." In <u>The Pelican
      Guide to English Literature</u>. Vol. 1, <u>The Age of Chaucer</u>,
      edited by Boris Ford. Harmondsworth, Middlesex: Penguin
      Books; Baltimore: Penguin Books, pp. 129-47.
          Recasts Traversi, 1936.6. Retains a discussion of the
      affinities of the poem with sermon techniques. Defines Dowel

1954

as "the acceptance of the conditions of daily life, lived truly in the sight of God and in accordance with the precepts of the Church"; Dobet as a "life of positive dedication to spiritual realities and to the practice of the supreme virtue of Charity"; and Dobest as "the state of active spiritual dedication" and the life of spiritual authority. Sees in Langland's habit of revealing the human figure under a dominating aspect a foreshadowing of the later English comedy of humours. Does not retain the comparison with Spenser drawn in Traversi, 1936.6.

1955

1   CEJP, LADISLAV. "An Interpretation of Piers the Plowman." Phililogica, supplement to Časopis pro Moderní Filologii 7, no. 2:17-30.
        The B-text possesses formal unity: the four great visions in terms of lines stand in the relation of 3:3:2:1; the eleven "partial" visions stand in the same relation to the larger visions. Many of the passūs manifest a formal unity in beginning with an introductory paragraph, followed by groups of four paragraphs. This formal unity is considered as an image of the allegorical unity of the poem, reflecting the social conditions and situation of Langland's time. The allegorical significance can be approached through study of the use of anagrams, direct and inverted; allusive homonyms and synonyms; and symbols for names. Many of these veiled allusions were revised out of the poem after the Peasants' Revolt, though the C-text does introduce some new ones.

2   DONALDSON, E. TALBOT. "MSS R and F in the B-Tradition of Piers Plowman." Transactions of the Connecticut Academy of Arts and Sciences 39 (September):177-212.
        Attempts to place MSS. R and F (B-text) in the manuscript tradition. These two MSS are unique in containing about 175 lines found in no other B-text MSS (many of which lines have equivalents in the C-text); in omitting about 170 lines that appear in other B-text MSS (some of these lines are also missing from the A-text); in showing similarities to the A-text in a passage that is given a more extended treatment in the B-text; in containing a distinctive number of uniquely shared readings, some superior, some clearly erroneous; and in sharing a distinctive number of readings with MSS. L and M.
        Rejects the opinion of Skeat (1886.1), that MSS. R and F represent a stage between the B- and C-texts, that is, that their common ancestor was copied from the C-poet's autograph after he had begun his revision. Rejects also the hypothesis

198

of Blackman (1918.1) that MSS. RFLM form a genetic group descended from a single subarchetype not in the same line as that of the other MSS. Hypothesizes instead that all extant B-text MSS are derived from a single, inaccurate copy of the poet's original; that this archetype (Copy 1) was twice copied: as Copy 2, the ancestor of all B-text MSS except MSS. R and F, and as Copy 3, the ancestor of MSS. R and F. Posits also that Copy 2 was transcribed in a form (Copy 4) that became the ancestor of all B-text MSS except MSS. RFLM. Copy 1 omitted an indeterminate number of lines from the author's original; Copy 2 accidentally omitted about 175 lines from its original; Copy 3 accidentally omitted about 55 lines; and Copy 4 omitted only 3 lines from its original, Copy 2. The uniquely shared errors of MSS. RFLM need not mean a common subarchetype, for an error in Copy 1 might have been transmitted to Copy 2 and Copy 3, but might have been corrected in Copy 4, and hence not appear in the B-text MSS other than RFLM. Suggests that many of the "additions" of MSS. R and F necessary to the sense of the B-text were omitted from Copy 2 by accident. Concludes that RF represent a stage in the B-text slightly older than that of the rest of the B-text MSS, that is, that Copy 2 received some changes that the poet made later which were not reflected in Copy 1 when it was transcribed into Copy 3 (and hence MSS. R and F). MSS. R and F represent in their unique readings and lines a genuine B-text tradition.

3   ERZGRÄBER, WILLI. "William Langlands 'Piers Plowman' im Lichte der mittelalterlichen Philosophie und Theologie." Anglia 73: 127-48.
       Summarizes Erzgräber, 1957.3 (completed in 1954).

4   JEFFERSON, THOMAS. Catalogue of the Library of Thomas Jefferson. Vol. 4. Compiled with annotations by E. Millicent Sowerby. Washington: Library of Congress.
       See Jefferson, 1798.1.

5   PANTIN, W.A. The English Church in the Fourteenth Century. Cambridge: Cambridge University Press, passim.
       The poem is referred to in the context of the social structure of the Church (unbeneficed clergy); papal provisions; Church endowment (the Donation of Constantine); stoic and early medieval views of private property as an arrangement imposed upon the natural condition of common ownership; the doctrine of grace and the salvation of the unbaptized; Uhtred of Boldon; Thomas Brunton; and manuals for parish priests and treatises in the vernacular.

1955

6 SUDDABY, ELIZABETH. "The Poem Piers Plowman." JEGP 54 (January):
   91-103.
        An appreciation of the poem for its "poetic" qualities
   of style and angle of vision. B I 177 ff. in particular is
   analyzed as representative of Langland's effective use of
   alliteration for emphasis, his narrowing of focus from a general conception to selected details, and his use of the concrete and specific. Sees the effect of Langland's style as
   imparting a vigor and freshness to the treatment of the central incidents of Christianity. The poem's "sound sense of
   values" is illustrated in Langland's emphasis on mercy and
   love in the Harrowing of Hell scene. Likewise, his stressing
   human kindness and neighborly love is seen in opposition to
   the medieval ideal of exaggerated asceticism.

                              1956

1 BLOOMFIELD, MORTON W. "The Pardons of Pamplona and the Pardoner
   of Rounceval: Piers Plowman B XVII 252 (C XX 218)." PQ 35,
   no. 1 (January):60-68.
        Sees in this line an allusion to the Hospital of St Mary
   Rounceval, Charing Cross, whose excesses in the selling of
   indulgences Langland here satirizes through comparison with
   those of the pope in Rome. Finds evidence that the hospital
   was under the control of the bishop of Pamplona, under whose
   name it distributed indulgences that were apparently valid
   outside his immediate diocese. Also finds evidence in the
   Chronicon Johannis de Reading of a scandal in England in 1366
   regarding the hospital's forging a bull of excessive indul-
   gence.

2 CEJP, LADISLAV. An Introduction to the Study of Langland's Piers
   the Plowman B Text. Acta Universitatis Palackianæ Olomucen-
   sis, no. 9. V Olomouci: Palackého Universita, 83 pp.
        In English, with a Czech summary. Langland is a master
   of the maximum use of lexical, acoustic, and semantic associations of words to develop the allegory on the basis of hom-
   onymity, synonymity, and the manipulation of polysemantic
   words. The syntactic ambiguity of English word order, the
   lack of punctuation in medieval manuscripts, the vague use of
   pronouns, and the tone of the poetry are all used to develop
   allegorical identifications. The poem has three meanings:
   the literal, symbolic, and allegorical. The literal is obscure and full of contradictions; the symbolic level does not
   help to explain the unity of meaning in the poem. The allegorical aspect yields the chief meaning of the text.

1956

Anagrams, either direct or inverted, or those that invert sounds rather than syllables, are an important allegorical method: from anagrams in B V 542-45; B XX 383-84; B XIII 235-40; C XXIII 385-86, and so on, it becomes clear that Piers is to be identified with Wat Tyler. Chaucer is allegorically introduced in the poem through use of the words calcare/cauken, allusions to the Latin form of his name, Calcearius. He is connected with peacocks in the poem and found in the company of the rich men of the realm. Chaucer is also the unknown tale-teller of B XX 118-19. References to Wat Tyler in the B-text are founded upon tilier, tilie, til combined with what wot, water (see A VII 244-51). Wat Tyler is linked with Reason, Peace, and Christ's human nature.

The text contains allusions to Will Langland, but the poet's real name is Robert de Rokayle; this name was stripped from him by the king (C IV 369-70). The poet identifies himself with Recchelesness (recche/roghte alternation, perhaps associating on Rokele); and he admits to having led a precarious life. Other characters identified through these methods include Edward III, John of Gaunt, William Walworth. The emphasis on Unity in B XIX-XX is meant to allude to the Great Society, not the Church. The Samaritan of B XVII 48-51 resembles John Ball, who rode to the south. Analysis of structural units--visions, passūs, paragraphs, and so on-- yields numerous correlations between passūs and visions, as well as numerical harmony in recurring proportions and recurring triadic structure.

3   DUNNING, T.P. "The Structure of the B-Text of Piers Plowman." RES, n.s. 7, no. 27 (July):225-37.
       Gregory, following Cassian, defines the contemplative life as an act of the mind raised above itself to the simple intuition of God by a close union of love, and founded on a disengagement of the things of the world by the exercise of works of the active life. Hence, the active and contemplative lives are not meant to be lived by two different categories of people. The active life is not mere manual labor, but the active practice of virtue. The Visio defines the proper regard for the needs of the body; then the Vita shows the individual, spiritual journey through growth in charity, often represented in the active life, the religious life, and the life of prelates. Reprinted in Blanch, 1969.4.

*4   GRANT, CLYDE MURRELL. "A Vocabulary Study of Skeat's Edition of the A Text of Piers Plowman." Dissertation, Oklahoma, 645 pp. Abstracted: DA 17:850.

1956

*5   HAZELTON, RICHARD MARQUARD. "Two Texts of the Disticha Catonis
      and Its Commentary with Special Reference to Chaucer, Langland
      and Gower." Dissertation, Rutgers, 310 pp.
          Abstracted: DA 16:1899.

6   HUSSEY, S.S. "Langland, Hilton and the Three Lives." RES,
      n.s. 7, no. 26 (April):132-50.
          Hilton's views of the Three Lives are significantly dif-
      ferent from Langland's. Hilton does not place the mixed life,
      which appears to have become popular in the late fourteenth
      century, above the contemplative. The resemblance of Hilton's
      idea of the active life to Langland's Dowel is probably co-
      incidental: Hilton's notion is not limited to manual labor
      and encompasses much that corresponds with Dobet. Although
      Hilton views the contemplative life somewhat differently in
      the Scale of Perfection and his treatise on the Mixed Life, he
      seems to insist on enclosure of the mind (if not the body) to
      a degree Langland does not; moreover, whereas Langland's Dobet
      stresses the practice of beliefs, Hilton's notion of contem-
      plation stresses a growing awareness of grace in the soul.
      The Bernardine triad of purgative, illuminative, and unitive
      states offers no close correlation with Langland's Three
      Lives, for Dobet is not closely similar to the illuminative
      state. Langland has simple, nontechnical notions of the Three
      Lives: Dowel is "living a good life in whatever state you are
      called"; Dobet and Dobest follow from this as degrees, rather
      than different lives or states. Reprinted with minor changes:
      Vasta, 1968.18.

7   MITCHELL, A.G. Lady Meed and the Art of Piers Plowman. The
      Third Chambers Memorial Lecture, delivered 27 February 1956,
      University College, London. London: H.K. Lewis & Co., 27 pp.
          Mede is almost morally neutral: no moral principles
      dictate her antipathies; she is incapable of faithfulness and
      is readily compliant. She speaks sincerely in the belief she
      is indispensable to man and advocates that the king should
      ensure loyalty through reward. But conscience distinguishes
      more closely between measureless mede and measurable mercede;
      and it becomes clear that under the rule of Reason most of
      what Mede claims to control would apply to mercede. Because
      she makes the good man suffer and rewards the wicked, she is
      discredited by A IV 126-27, nullum malum impunitum, nullum
      bonum irremuneratum (from De contemptu mundi of Innocent III).

8   ORRICK, ALLAN H.   "Declynede, Passus IV, L. 133, Piers the Plow-
    man, A-Text."   PQ 35, no. 2 (April):213-15.
        Takes declynede here as an adjective meaning "narrated,"
    rather than a verb, which would require emendation.

9   PETER, JOHN.   Complaint and Satire in Early English Literature.
    Oxford: Clarendon Press, esp. pp. 1-103.
        Piers Plowman is considered a complaint, rather than a
    satire as exemplified in the portraits of Chaucer's General
    Prologue: complaint is impersonal, satire develops the per-
    sonality of the satirist; complaint is of narrower range, be-
    cause it aims to be sober and reasonable; complaint is easily
    applied by the reader to himself, whereas satire addresses a
    "third party."   Sees complaint emerging from Christian Latin
    literature of the early Middle Ages, out of the conflict of
    the Roman principle of sanative castigation and the Christian
    principle of sufferance and restraint.   Considers Langland as
    sharing such common concerns of medieval complaint as the
    servile fear of death; calamities as representing divine
    vengeance for sins; and a retributive view of immoral eccle-
    siastics.   But Langland's is a minority view concerning Dooms-
    day, which he considers with "something like equanimity" be-
    cause he thought of it in terms of the Second Coming, rather
    than of punishment.   Peter's designation of the poem as a
    complaint is denied by Martin, 1979.10.

*10 RÓNA, ÉVA.   "Piers the Plowman és az 1381-es paraszt-forradalom"
    [Piers the Plowman and the 1381 Peasant Revolt].   Dissertation,
    Budapest.   Budapest: Library of the Hungarian Academy of
    Sciences.
        Source: MHRA Annual Bibliography, vol. 37 (1962),
    p. 121, no. 2190.

11 SCHLAUCH, MARGARET.   English Medieval Literature and Its Social
    Foundations.   Warsaw: Państwowe Wydawnictwo Naukowe,
    pp. 213-17.
        Finds the author conservative in sociopolitical theories,
    and democratic in spiritual matters and in his broad human
    sympathies regarding the equality of all men before God and
    the equal responsibilities of all to their neighbors.   The
    poem is seen as one of hope and triumph, yet its positive con-
    clusion is one arrived at through increasing mysticism, which
    becomes "more obscure as it becomes more rapturous."
        Compares the genre-realism of the Visio with the work of
    Wit Stwosz of Poland.

1957

1957

1   BURROW, J.A.   "The Audience of Piers Plowman."   Anglia 75:373-84.
    From bequests of manuscripts of the poem and allusions
    to it in the letter of John Ball, the wide distribution and
    influence of the poem can be inferred among the clerical
    class. The style and condition of the MSS suggest the poem
    did not circulate among rich patrons. Nor was Langland a
    popular poet; rather, he wrote for a class that cut across
    local lines and was composed of prosperous, apparently con-
    servative literate bourgeoisie. This newly emerging audience,
    the ancestor of the modern reading public, modifies the tradi-
    tionally close relationship of author and public in the allit-
    erative tradition and accounts for the extreme economy with
    which Langland uses the alliterative poetic diction.

2   CRAWFORD, WILLIAM R.   "Robert Crowley's Editions of Piers Plowman:
    A Bibliographical and Textual Study." Dissertation, Yale,
    227 pp.
    Argues the correctness of Skeat's chronology of Crowley's
    editions and impressions of the poem: of the second edition,
    STC 19907a (Crawford BB) is the first impression and STC 19907
    (Crawford D) is the second impression. BB and D agree in
    readings, additions, and omissions from STC 19906, Crowley's
    first edition (Crawford B); but of the differences between BB
    and D, the largest number is shared by B and D against BB; BB
    omits three lines shared by D and B; and correction of errors
    of D restores the B-reading in BB. Crowley's first edition
    was based on a MS closely resembling MS. W, but possessing
    lines MS. W lacked; this first edition also shows the influ-
    ence of a C-text MS. The two impressions of the second edi-
    tion are based on a copy of the first edition "corrected" by
    an A-text MS and a B-text MS related to MSS YOCC^{2}BoBmCot.
    Discovers an anomalous quire ("I") in 550c Yale, resembling
    that of the first edition; and suggests the possibility of a
    second impression of the first edition (Crawford C). De-
    scribes the five copies of Crowley's editions/impressions in
    the Yale libraries; and collates MS. L (that MS used by
    Skeat) with these editions.

3   ERZGRÄBER, WILLI.   William Langlands "Piers Plowman" (Eine
    Interpretation des C-Textes). Frankfurter Arbeiten aus dem
    Gebiete der Anglistik und der Amerika-Studien, no. 3.
    Heidelberg: Carl Winter, 248 pp.
    In the Visio, Langland's theological and philosophical
    position is close to that of Thomas Aquinas, especially in the
    evaluation of the natural condition of mankind where both au-
    thors seek to justify mankind's natural tendencies in light of

1957

a natural moral law which man, on the basis of kynde witte, can recognize. Thomas Aquinas affirms the desire for posses- sions as necessary and potentially beneficial for both those in the active and those in the contemplative life; so too for Langland, in C II-V, who insists at the same time that man is continually in danger of exploiting earthly goods and falling into sin. Langland therefore demands that man's use of tem- poral goods be dictated by reason and natural morality; he also insists that man has conscience to guide him. By con- science Langland understands the scholastic concepts of both synderesis and conscientia; Thomas understood conscientia solely as the application of the moral function to individual cases, whereas synderesis is awareness of general moral values. Langland parallels Thomas likewise in the belief that man has a natural tendency toward the good, and the task for him is to develop and perfect the virtues implanted by God. If he does this, he perfects not only himself but society.

Both Langland and Thomas see the king as the necessary head to direct man's actions toward the highest good in so- ciety. Langland's king will reinstitute the life of a healthy social order and best decide the use of earthly goods. When Langland points to the Decalogue as a norm of human action, he parallels Thomas's notion that the Decalogue was just a form of the natural law. Yet both Thomas and Langland (in Dobest, but anticipated in the Visio) were aware of the limitations of earthly power: man must obey the law of the state in matters of civilian welfare, but the king is subject to the pope in questions of spiritual health. Langland, like Thomas, be- lieves that man can achieve good out of his own powers; yet man needs grace as an aid to perfect and accomplish what God has bidden him to do. This conception of human nature and its powers, uncongenial to that of Augustine, is figured for both Thomas and Langland in the context of human labor--for Lang- land, exactly at the point where Piers is introduced.

At the same time, Langland is shown to lay different emphases than does Aquinas. In the Pardon scene Piers as- sumes an almost Pelagian position in trusting man's moral strength to the extent that he does not accept sin as inherent to human nature and instead believes that man will be rewarded for his good deeds--in effect, placing himself in opposition to a false trust in God's grace, as represented in the mer- chandising of pardons. The Priest's position is reminiscent of Augustine's notion that grace precedes man's virtuous acts, is active when he acts virtuously, and brings his action to perfection. The antithesis here is resolved in Dowel, which transcends Thomas's position by questioning (through Dame Study) the knowledge to which man is capable, and by suggest- ing that although man can see the moral demands made upon him,

such knowledge does not make him do well. Dowel shows Langland's affinities with Augustinian thought in its denial of
ancient philosophy, criticism of Pelagianism, and emphasis on
divine grace and the notion of predestination which renders
all natural morality and knowledge useless and superficial.

Langland's use of predestination suggests he contended
more with Augustine as taught in the fourteenth century (e.g.,
Bradwardine) than with Augustine's works directly. Duns
Scotus, who had stressed the limits of human reason, nevertheless did not deny philosophy and affirmed metaphysics as a
pure science. Like Duns Scotus, Langland feels that theology
has the practical task of leading man to salvation and spread-
ing the knowledge and teaching of God. The Trajan episode is
intended by Langland to show that faithful fulfillment of the
natural moral law will find recognition before God, that the
moral striving of man will find its completion in God's mercy.
Superficially this seems a return by Langland to his original
position; but Langland's idea of natural morality has changed
from the Visio to Dowel, in which Langland has recognized the
danger of superbia in man's moral achievements, and in which
the poet presents a new ideal of patient poverty, grounded
upon humility. This ideal shows the influence on Langland of
the thought of Francis of Assisi, for to both authors poverty
is understood in both its material and spiritual senses where
to be poor is to be free from the world and free for God. At
the end of Dowel patient poverty becomes a remocia curarum,
indicating that the individual who lives in patient poverty is
relieved of the obligation to judge others.

Langland also parallels Duns Scotus in the special value
placed on the will, as a faculty higher than reason and one
which is fulfilled in love, the greatest of all virtues. Duns
Scotus insists on the involvement of the creature's will for
the operation of caritas in a way that is sympathetic to
Langland's thought in the Visio of man's responsibility for
his own salvation. The Samaritan scene likewise shows that
man can love God and his fellowman from his own being; and in
C XV 14 Langland substitutes kynde love for caritas. The resulting idea of God is the same for both Langland and Duns
Scotus: founded on John 4:8, 16, "Deus caritas est." Just as
Duns Scotus stresses the freedom of the divine will but asserts that God is always bound to the order of His reason, so
Langland, in the Harrowing of Hell, has Christ declare that in
so doing He does not act against order founded upon reason
(C XIX 119). Langland also parallels Duns Scotus in repre-
senting the Trinity as a "divisible unity."

The claim of Hort (1938.5) of the influence of Anselm on
Langland is undercut by the absence in Piers Plowman of the
basic Anselmic teaching that Christ took death upon Him to

restore the injured honor of God (in Langland, Christ's death is, as it is for Duns Scotus, the expression of God's unending love for man). Moreover, Langland's (traditional) treatment of the Harrowing of Hell expressed through a legal argument contrasts with Anselm's notion that God could punish any of His servants whenever He felt the need.

The similarity which Donaldson (1949.1) finds between Langland's and Bernard of Clairvaux's ideas of the divine similitude of free will and the love that has risen out of man's free will is just as much in evidence in the works of Duns Scotus. Langland does not see the fulfillment of human destiny through caritas in terms of a mystical lifting up of the individual into God. He recognizes that man must assume responsibility in the temporal sphere; and although Piers in the B-text seems to have his origin in mystical ideas, his figure is drawn more carefully in the C-text, where his equation with Christ (B XV 206) is removed, and where instead Piers largely, if not exclusively, represents human nature.

Wells's connection (1938.9) of the Three Lives with the thought of Hilton ignores the fact that the patient poverty defined in Dowel manifests the unity of the active and contemplative lives. Meroney's theory (1950.9) misinterprets Langland's Unite, which is less the unio mistica than the wholeness of the baptized Christ.

Langland and Wyclif can be compared for their criticism of contemporary religious abuses and their representation of the bonus pastor as the ideal religious. But Wyclif attacked the entire medieval Church and its foundations; Langland never wanted a revolutionary change in the exterior forms of the religious life and always felt himself bound to the religious and political forms he had inherited. Langland distances himself from predestinarian thought in Dowel and affirms the power of the pope to lead and teach. Whereas Wyclif emphasized only contritio of the three aspects of Penance, Langland, at least in the C-text, asserts that all three conditons are necessary. Reviewed by Morton W. Bloomfield, Anglia 76 (1958): 550-54; David C. Fowler, MLQ 20 (159):285-87; and George Kane, MLR 55 (1960):264-65.

4   FRANK, ROBERT WORTH, Jr. Piers Plowman and the Scheme of Salvation: An Interpretation of Dowel, Dobet and Dobest. Yale Studies in English, vol. 136. New Haven: Yale University Press, xiv + 123 pp.

Reads Piers Plowman as a literal poem filled with personification allegory (see Frank, 1953.2), and organized according to dreams and interludes in the real world that ground the visions in real experience. Follows Mensendieck (1900.3) in rejecting the Three Lives in favor of one way of life,

described in Dowel and further elaborated upon in Dobet and
Dobest. Sees the active life as other than a life of physical
labor without spiritual activity, and similarly rejects the notion that the contemplative life does not consist in doing
deeds of charity for others. Considers the poems a response
to the Dreamer's question regarding salvation. The Visio
presents the principles that define damnation and salvation,
the way of Falseness (Mede) and the law of love. The Vita
considers the question--answered affirmatively in a variety of
ways--of whether sinful man can do well; in particular, Piers
represents the poet's belief that man can be saved "because
of, as well as in spite of, his human nature." The Trinity is
the organizing principle of the second part of the poem.
Dowel is concerned with the moral power of man, as guaranteed
by God's gift to him of a rational soul; Dobet puts forward
God the Son as an example of how better to know and obey the
law; and Dobest teaches how to know and obey perfectly through
the gifts of the Holy Spirit.

In particular, the two visions of the Visio present
problems in the poet's world and imbue these issues with
spiritual significance. The message of the Pardon (which is
valid) is Dowel. The Dreamer accepts the Pardon; Piers accepts its message; and by tearing it he "rejects bulls with
seals." His anger is directed toward the Priest; and he does
not as a result abandon bodily labor, but merely adopts the
principle of ne solliciti sitis (see Frank, 1951.4).

In the Dowel section, the first vision shows man's power
to know the good, and the dream-within-the-dream exposes the
delusions of a life without learning and morality. The
Dreamer's doubts concerning learning and morality are resolved
by Imaginatif's solution to the problem of the righteous
heathen. The second dream of this section shows man how to
do good; the advice of the Doctor at Patience's Feast ought to
be heeded, even though the Doctor himself is a lost soul.
Patience teaches love; and Haukyn shows that life in the world
necessarily involves one in sin, but that penance and patient
poverty put one back on the road to salvation.

The life of Dobet is involved with greater moral
strength and knowledge, founded upon Christ, and is not a
new life. Knowledge of the Trinity, the Crucifixion, Harrowing of Hell, and the Redemption of man from the devil's power
are shown to be examples of Christ's charitable gifts. In the
Dobet section, Langland insists on the importance of faith and
good works of charity in gaining salvation.

Dobest is based on the Gifts of the Holy Spirit in their
relation to man and his salvation. The poet believes that
contrition, confession, and satisfaction are all necessary to
penance, but especially values contrition. The transformation

of the gift of grace into the gifts of labor have the effect
of declaring labor to be God-given. Redde quod debes is more
than the mere restitution of stolen goods: it involves the
forgiveness of others' sins against one; and love of one's
neighbor becomes the theme of the second vision in this section. The last vision is not apocalyptic in any literal
sense; Antichrist is there used as merely a term of abuse.
The purpose of the vision is to show the external danger to
the plan of salvation, that is, the friars' corruption of the
sacrament of penance. This is opposed by the internal threat,
as described in the abuse of redde quod debes.
    Reviewed by Guy Bourquin, EA 11 (1958):245-46; T.P.
Dunning, RES, n.s. 11 (1960):67-69; Willi Erzgräber, Anglia
77 (1959):83-86; David C. Fowler, MLQ 20 (1959):285-87; S.S.
Hussey, MLR 54 (1959):84-85; R.E. Kaske, MLN 74 (1959):730-33;
John Lawlor, Medium Ævum 28 (1959):215-16; D.W. Robertson,
Speculum 33 (1958):395-97; and Theodore Silverstein, MP 56
(1961):204-5. Reprinted: Frank, 1969.12.

5   KASKE, R.E. "Gigas the Giant in Piers Plowman." JEGP 56:177-85.
        Gigas the geaunt of B XVIII 250-51 is considered an
    allusion to Psalm 18:6, the standard commentaries on which
    interpret the giant as Christ and stress both His indomita-
    bility and His double nature, which is also the central point
    of Book's entire speech. Sees the gynne of line 250 as the
    "trick" of the Incarnation. Psalm 18 was often interpreted as
    a prophecy of the life of Christ, which may be roughly paral-
    leled in B XVIII 228-39; 243-44; 253; 256-57. Briefly alluded
    to in Kaske, 1960.7. A further treatment of Psalm 18 is found
    in Kaske, 1959.9.

6   KASKE, R.E. "Langland and the Paradisus Claustralis." MLN 72,
    no. 11 (November):481-83.
        B X 300-5 is traced through Benvenuto da Imola's Com-
    mentary on the Divina Commedia, Par. XI, 12, to the Sermo in
    Festo S. Nicolai Myrensis Episcopi of Nicholas of Clairvaux.
    The image is a conventional one, but is given a more human-
    istic treatment by Langland.

7   LAWLOR, JOHN. "The Imaginative Unity of Piers Plowman." RES,
    n.s. 8, no. 30 (May):113-26.
        The imaginative appeal of the poem is the Dreamer's
    failure of inquiry in attempting to search out the problem
    without realizing the necessity of his own practice of the
    life he seeks to learn about. The theme of the poem is the
    spiritual regeneration of man; the poet's dominant faculty is
    a satiric intelligence used to expose the difference between
    what we believe and what we in fact are. The poem begins by

1957

describing the misdeeds of others, and then, by humbling the
best man the world can produce, moves beyond Justice to Mercy.
But the progress of the poem is in showing how the Dreamer is
brought with difficulty to realize the truths that Piers is
able to grasp more readily. Reprinted: Blanch, 1969.4.

*8   PALMER, WILLIAM PACKARD. "The Intellectual Background of The
     Vision of Piers Plowman with Particular Reference to the
     English and Latin Writings of John Wyclif." 2 vols. Dis-
     sertation, Kansas, 479 pp.
          Abstracted: DA 20:1769.

*9   PATCH, GERTRUDE KEILEY. "The Allegorical Characters in Piers
     Plowman." Dissertation, Stanford, 257 pp.
          Abstracted: DA 17:2598.

10   PERCY, THOMAS. The Percy Letters. Edited by David Nichol Smith
     and Cleanth Brooks. Vol. 4, The Correspondence of Thomas
     Percy and Evan Evans, edited by Aneirin Lewis. [Baton Rouge]:
     Louisiana State University Press.
          See Evans, 1764.1.

                                1958

1   BLOOMFIELD, MORTON W. "Piers Plowman and the Three Grades of
     Chastity." Anglia 76, no. 2:227-53.
          Sees as the central issue of the poem the quest for
     Christian perfection, perhaps as influenced by the philosophy
     of monasticism and expressed in the poem in the traditional
     formulation of ascending grades or degrees, figured in the
     conventional triad of marriage, widowhood, and virginity.
     Explores two obscure passages, B XII 31-52 and B XVI (C XIX),
     in light of the chastity theme. In the first, Langland has
     Imaginatif refer to the three grades of perfection symbolized
     by the three grades of chastity through the use of various
     exempla that illustrate the evils of lechery, the opposite of
     the virtue of chastity. Documents Solomon, Samson, Job,
     Aristotle, Hippocrates, Vergil, Alexander, Felice, Rosamund,
     and even Lucifer (on the basis of the semantic association of
     pride in some of its meanings with sex and lechery) as victims
     of lechery, or Minnesklaven. Interprets the three of B XVI in
     light of iconography of tree illustrations in MS. Troyes 252
     and a Joachistic figure that develop its meaning as Heilsge-
     schichte. The lower boughs are filled with the matrimonial
     fruit of the Old Law and the middle boughs with the vidual
     fruit of the New Testament; the highest boughs by implication
     suggest the Holy Spirit and a future age. Compares the

treatment of the tree in the B- and C-texts and promises a
further study of these ideas in the context of the whole poem.
These ideas are developed in Bloomfield, 1961.2; 1961.3.

2   COLLEDGE, ERIC. "Aliri." Medium Ævum 27:111-13.
        Agrees with Dobson (1948.5) on the etymology of aliri
    from OE (lima) lyre, "made their legs lame," and sees the
    practice illustrated in Bosch's Temptation of St. Anthony.
    Suggests the word may be preserved in the children's game in
    which a leg is swung in a loop over a bouncing ball with the
    cry of "alairy."

3   HAMILTON, A.C. "Spenser and Langland." SP 55, no. 4 (October):
    533-48.
        The Epilogue to the Shepheardes Calendar proves
    Spenser's close knowledge of Piers Plowman, in that Spenser
    refers to the climactic stages of the poem in which the pil-
    grim Piers plays the role of the plowman. The "Piers Plowman
    tradition" of satire was the only continuous tradition of
    satire available to Spenser, who appreciated the poem as a
    "Protestant" satire against the Roman Church and as a reli-
    gious epic-allegory that emphasized the imitation of Christ.
    Piers Plowman and Book I of The Faerie Queene can be com-
    pared as analogues: In both passūs I-V and cantos I-V the
    protagonist is guided by a lovely lady (Holicherch/Una);
    which scene is followed by the appearance of evil (Mede/
    Duessa) witnessed, respectively, by Will and the knight
    whose "Will was his guide." Passūs VI-VII parallel
    cantos VI-VII in presenting a vision of man's fallen state
    ameliorated by the appearance of God's grace (Piers/Arthur);
    in each case, Christ's Descent into Hell is the reason
    for the availability of this grace (cf. VII 502 ff. with
    Arthur's victorious entry into Orgoglio's castle). Both
    the rending of Arthur's veil and Piers's Tearing of the Pardon
    "mark the violent irruption of divine grace into the world."
        Both poems see man sub specie æternitatis; both are
    structured in two parallel parts, featuring a translation from
    an external to an inner pilgrimage that passes from degrada-
    tion to regeneration, with both the Vitae and the episodes of
    the House of Penance, the slaying of the dragon, and the mar-
    riage of Red Cross with Una seen as combining the purgative,
    illuminative, and unitive states. In the differences of the
    ends of the respective poems (Langland's vision of chaos and
    the reign of the Antichrist; Spenser's vision of divine
    order), Spenser may be said to have begun where Langland left
    off; for the defeat of Unite corresponds to the wanderings of
    Una before the Reformation. See also Hamilton, 1961.10.

1958

*4   HAVENS, ANNE ELIZABETH. "The Function of Scripture in Piers
     Plowman." Dissertation, Yale.
          Source: Comprehensive Dissertation Index, 1861-1972,
     Vol. 30. See Fuller, 1961.9.

5   KELLOGG, ALFRED L. "Langland and Two Scriptural Texts."
     Traditio 14:385-98.
          In the Latin quotation following C II 108-11, Langland's
     apparently original substitution of pedem for sedem increases
     the force and allusiveness of the paraphrase of Isaiah 14:13-
     14 by suggesting that Satan's boasted equality with God is
     linked to self-love, defined by Augustine as pes. With regard
     to the horses, carts, and riders of B II 161-65; 179-82,
     Langland heightens the satire by synthesizing the Bernardine
     tradition of the sins as horses with that of Origen's repre-
     sentation of the sinner as a human horse ridden by a demon or
     vice. Reprinted: Kellogg, 1972.8.

6   MOE, HENRY ALLEN. "'The Vision of Piers the Plowman' and the Law
     of Foundations." PAPS 102, no. 4 (August):371-75.
          See B VII 26-32 as significant in the history of the
     concept of "gifts to pious uses" by taking the purposes of
     gifts made pro anima mea, pro salute animæ meæ out of the
     class of those made for the repose of the donor's soul and
     putting them into the class of gifts for the general public
     good. Considers the wording of Act of 43 Elizabeth, Chapter 4
     (which serves to determine the form and function of founda-
     tions) as extremely close to that of the B-text. A slightly
     revised version of this paper was published as Moe, 1959.11.

7   PEPLER, CONRAD. "The First Step--Sin: Conversion: The Way
     Opens." In The English Religious Heritage. London: Aquin
     Press, pp. 40-66.
          The poem presents a world of sin from which it is pos-
     sible to be raised by grace to a life based on truth and love.
     Although Langland was probably himself a sinner in youth, the
     object of the poem is to escape from the sins of society, not
     merely one's personal sins; thus, reform in the poem is that
     not of isolated "morals" but of economic reform founded upon
     justice and charity. "Conversion" is a matter of putting into
     action the inoperative ideas of the spiritual and synthesizing
     them with the sinner's ideas of practical reality. Faith,
     even faith as yet without charity, is a necessary first step;
     and a belief in truth turns the sinner from the things of the
     earth toward conversion to God. With conversion come the
     gifts of the Holy Spirit and a view of the general life of the
     Church, signaled in the poem by the liturgical references.
     Langland emphasizes participation in the Mystical Body, rather

than merely physical membership in the Church. His depiction
of Christ is the quiet, restrained, hierarchic figure of early
Christian art, with little of the late medieval realistic devotion to His humanity. The Three Lives are based on Hilton's
Scale of Perfection and find their model in the Trinity.
Dowel is to some extent identical with the better form of the
active life, but all of the Three Lives are best regarded as
contemplative "in so far as they are supernatural and devoted
ultimately to God."

*8 ŚWIECZKOWSKI, WALERIAN. "Word Order Patterning in Middle English
     (A Quantitative Study Based on Piers Plowman and the Middle
     English Sermons)." Dissertation, Harvard.
          Source: Comprehensive Dissertation Index, 1861-1972,
     vol. 30, p. 245. Published as Świeczkowski, 1962.15.

9 ZEEMAN, ELIZABETH. "Piers Plowman and the Pilgrimage to Truth."
     Essays and Studies, n.s. 11:1-16.
          Compares the journey to Truth in Piers Plowman with that
     described by Hilton, Julian of Norwich, and the Cloud of Un-
     knowing with respect to the seeking of a guide; the authority
     with which this guide speaks; the emphasis on obedience, meek-
     ness, prayer, and repentance; and the necessary discovery of
     the divine within oneself through grace. Sees Piers enlarged
     in the poem to become a symbol of the operation of the divine
     upon the human, in a fashion similar to the treatment of
     Christ by the mystics. The weakening of the symbol of Piers
     in B XVI-XVIII is accounted for by Langland's reluctance to
     represent the potentially heretical equation of Piers and
     Christ, the pilgrim traveling toward truth and truth itself.

1959

1 BOWERS, R.H. "Piers Plowman and the Literary Historians." CE
     21, no. 1 (October):1-4.
          Argues that traditional literary historians err in de-
     scribing Piers Plowman as a satire or poem of social protest
     which is flawed in structure and design. The poem contains
     satire, though it is more properly an example of the consolatio
     genre, in which a bewildered, disconsolate human receives con-
     solation, instruction, and education in a long platonic dia-
     logue with an allegorical character. Perhaps under the influ-
     ence of the tradition of the Roman de la Rose, there is more
     than one teacher in Piers Plowman; and Langland's poem is
     likewise extraordinary in the large number of allusions to
     contemporary life. But to see the poem as one of "education"
     explains the nature of its design.

1959

2   BURROW, J.A. "An Approach to the Dream of the Rood."
    Neophilologus 43, no. 2 (April):123-33.
        Piers Plowman is compared to the Dream of the Rood in
    the representation of the Crucifixion with little pathos or
    passivity. In Langland's poem, the allegorical image of
    Christ jousting in Piers's arms stresses the distinction be-
    tween the natural and the supernatural Christ; and in both
    poems deitas patris is held in mind. Both poems show the
    development of the narrator's emotional state as a result of
    the Crucifixion.

3   CEJP, LADISLAV. "Some General Meanings of Langland's Fundamental
    Concepts." Philologica Pragensia 2:2-22.
        Supplements Cejp, 1956.2, by documenting the identifica-
    tion of mice/commons in the work of Henryson, and that of
    plowing/preaching by Alanus de Insulis. Glosses Petrus id est
    Christus (B XV 206) on the basis of Alanus's interpretations:
    (1) Petrus Ecclesiam figurat: sicut enim a petra Christo,
    Petrus dicitur, sic Ecclesia ab angulari lapide Christo nomen
    interius mutuatur; and (2) Tu es Petrus et super hanc petram
    ædificabo. Hence, both Christ and Peter are identified with
    petra, and Peter (Piers) is thus identified with Christ.

4   GOODRIDGE, J.F., trans. Introduction to Piers the Ploughman.
    Harmondsworth, Middlesex: Penguin Books; Baltimore: Penguin
    Books, pp. 7-58.
        Sees the subject of the Visio as the reform of society,
    that of the Vita as the spiritual life. Considers that to
    Langland allegory is a way of thinking, not merely a poetic
    device, and admits that Langland is not interested, as was
    Spenser in The Faerie Queene, in sustaining an illusory dream
    world. Denies the relevance of a fourfold allegorical ap-
    proach to the poem, as well as that of the realistic view
    that sees allegory as a mere convention.
        Sees the poem's development organized around the
    Dreamer's growth in knowledge and spiritual understanding.
    Accepts the character Will as somehow representative of the
    human will, "seeking to find its proper course, and guided on
    its way by Conscience and Reason." Piers is an honest plowman
    who knows Truth and how to reach it, yet who also stands for
    the ministry of God, the source of the Church's physical and
    spiritual nourishment, and Christ's real presence on earth in
    the Mystical Body, His Church. The Pardon scene presents
    three alternatives: the Law (which would damn most of man-
    kind), the abuses connected with the Church's policy of
    indulgences-for-cash, and the idea of Dowel, which the indi-
    vidual soul can follow even if the reform of society and the
    Church has failed. The Dreamer's progress is seen in the

extent that things once shocking to him are at a later point
turned into comedy, as in Patience's Feast. B XIV suggests
that a complete denunciation of worldly vanity in favor of a
positive love of poverty can bring the Active Man of the world
to repentance. The Samaritan scene manifests the nature of
Dowel and Dobet and the meaning and source of Charity. The
end of the poem does not mean that Conscience has abandoned
the Church to its fate, for Langland believes that the Christian life is a perpetual battle against Antichrist. Revised
as Goodridge, 1966.6.

5   HALL, G.D.G. "The Abbot of Abingdon and the Tenants of Wink-
    field." Medium Ævum 28, no. 2:91-95.
        Extends the findings of Coghill (1935.3) concerning B
    X 326-27, with researches in the Chancery Miscellanea.
    Langland may well have known of the imprisonment of the
    Winkfield men (1393-94), but Coghill is wrong in contending
    that the abbot of Abingdon had ordered their incarceration,
    for in fact it was the king. The manor of Winkfield belonged
    to the abbot from before the Domesday Book; but the merits of
    this case are difficult to determine, since there were also
    tenants of the crown in Winkfield since 1359, and jurisdic-
    tional prerogatives are hard to decide.

6   HIRSCH-REICH, B. "Eine neue 'oeuvre de synthese' über Joachim von
    Fiora." Recherches de Théologie ancienne et médiévale 26:
    128-37, esp. 135-36.
        Comments that Bloomfield (1958.1) is correct in seeing
    no direct parallel in the Figurenbuch to Langland's tree
    symbol, though Bloomfield is probably incorrect in citing a
    parallel to Tafel XVI of Joachim based on the three props of
    the tree. On the other hand, the correspondence of the ordo
    coniugatorum with God the Father, the ordo clericorum with the
    Son, and the ordo monachorum with the Holy Spirit, which
    Bloomfield develops from a (1360) treatise of the monk of Bury
    St. Edmunds, most probably goes back to Joachim himself. But
    it is doubtful that Abraham as a foot of God's faith is an
    echo of Joachim.

7   JOHNSTON, G.K.W. "Piers Plowman B-Text, Prolouge, 78-9." N&Q,
    c.s. 204, no. 7 (July-August):243-44.
        Defends the explanation of the lines by Mitchell
    (1944.4) on the basis of Herod's remarks to his servant in
    the Towneley Plays, ed. George England and Alfred W. Pollard
    (Early English Text Society, e.s. 71 [London, New York, and
    Toronto: Oxford University Press, 1897], pp. 171-72).

1959

8   KASKE, R.E.   "Langland's Walnut-Simile."   JEGP 58 (October):
     650-54.
          The walnut-simile of B XI 247-57 (C XIII 140-49) is
     shown to be paralleled in exegetical writings on Canticles
     6:10 and Numbers 17:8.   Langland's distinction of material
     hardship and spiritual consolation is illustrated in the
     Aurora of Peter Riga; his allusions to mercy and devotion are
     seen also in the fifteenth-century Ennarratio of Denis the
     Carthusian; and his reference to Christ as a kirnelle can be
     found both in Adam of St. Victor's Splendor Patris et figura
     and in the work of Alanus de Insulis.   Langland's treatment of
     this conventional image shows his attention both to realism
     and to the "metaphysical firmness" underlying the figure.
     Briefly alluded to in Kaske, 1960.7.

9   KASKE, R.E.   "The Speech of 'Book' in Piers Plowman."   Anglia 77:
     117-44.
          B XVIII 228-57 is analyzed in terms of the traditional
     commentary on the theme of the witness of the elements to
     Christ's divinity, Psalm 18:1-8, as a prophecy of the career
     of Christ, and the Joachistic prophecy of the Evangelium
     æternum and world-age of the Holy Ghost.   The witness of the
     elements forms part of the standard exegesis of Matthew 2:1-2
     and is present in the liturgy of the Epiphany.   A fourteenth-
     century English metrical homily, In Epiphania Domini, features
     a semipersonification of the Bible in a way that might have
     influenced the creation of the "character," Book.   Book pri-
     marily represents the littera of the New Testament; and ref-
     erences to the context of the Epiphany and the Crucifixion
     emphasize the break of the Old and New Law.   Echoes of the
     prophetic Psalm 18 (used in the liturgy of the Epiphany sea-
     son) stress Christ's indomitability and twofold nature.   In
     combining the witness-theme with echoes of the psalm, Langland
     emphasizes the transition from the Old Law to the New; for
     Book's speech is delivered between the Crucifixion and the
     Harrowing of Hell, and images such as the eyes of Book, the
     sons of Simeon, and the Joys of Mary present the antitheses
     of the two dispensations.
          Notes the grammatical difficulties of lines 252-57, and
     suggests the rendering "I, Book, will be burned, but Jesus
     (will) rise to life" for line 252, taking rise as a second
     infinitive governed by an understood wil, and taking the verbs
     of the following lines as a series of infinitives parallel to
     rise.   Suggests the lines contain an allusion to Joachim of
     Flora's prophecy of the evangelium æternum, a spiritual under-
     standing of both the Old and New Testaments which would re-
     place the letter of both and initiate a reign of Love and
     Peace.   Based on III Kings 18:30-38, the Joachite notion of

216

1960

the intellectus spiritualis of this time will consume the letter of both Testaments like the fire of Elias's sacrifice.
Just as Book's echoes of the eighteenth psalm show the foreshadowing of the New Testament in the Old, and the witnessing
elements emphasize the littera of the New Testament, the
Joachistic allusion points to a time of deeper spiritualiza-
tion of the Christian Testament after the Resurrection.
Briefly alluded to in Kaske, 1960.7. For a different interpretation of Book's speech, see Hoffman, 1964.5; but cf.
Donaldson, 1966.1.

10 McKISACK, MAY. The Oxford History of England. Edited by Sir
George Clark. Vol. 5, The Fourteenth Century 1307-1399.
Oxford: Clarendon Press, 526-27.
    Describes Piers Plowman as the greatest of the English
alliterative poems, and its author as a learned, austere
seeker after truth and a bitter critic "of the whole top-
heavy ecclesiastical system . . . and of the rich and proud."
Admits the importance of the poem for its social history, but
suggests that its value as poetry has been less recognized.
Finds, nonetheless, that Langland's figures are presented two-
dimensionally; and "whereas Gower presents us with the conventions of a polite society, and Chaucer with human nature
as we know it, Langland speaks to us from a forgotten world,
drowned, mysterious, irrecoverable."

11 MOE, HENRY ALLEN. "The Power of Poetic Vision." PMLA 74, no. 2
(May):37-41.
    A slightly revised version of Moe, 1958.6.

12 RYAN, WILLIAM M. "Modern Idioms in 'Piers Plowman.'" American
Speech 34, no. 1 (February):67-69.
    The earliest attestation of overdo used in the active
voice is noted in C XIV 191; the earliest usage of why's and
the earliest usage of the article with either the singular or
plural form of the noun is noted in B XII 217-18; plenty and
peace, a variant of peace and plenty, is noted in C XVIII
91-93; the earliest attestation of life and limb is to be
found in B XIX 100-101; and the earliest attestation of first
and foremost seen in B XIX 115-17.

1960

*1 ADAMS, JOHN FESTUS. "The Dreamer's Quest for Salvation in Piers
Plowman." Dissertation, Washington, 252 pp.
    Abstracted: DA 21:1553.

1960

2   BENNETT, J.A.W. "Sum Rex, Sum Princeps, etc. (Piers Plowman B,
    Prologue 132-38)." N&Q, c.s. 225 (n.s. 7), no. 10 (October):
    364.
        The lines are discovered to be included on fol. 147^v of
    MS. Lambeth 61, in a form closely corresponding to the C-text;
    they follow a sermon in the MS which was preached by Henry
    Harclay in 1315. See Strang, 1960.14.

3   DAICHES, DAVID. A Critical History of English Literature.
    Vol. 1. New York: Ronald Press Co., pp. 122-27.
        An interpretive summary of the poem, showing that
    Daiches is not committed to single authorship of the three
    versions. The author of the B- and C-versions is not able to
    "subdue his material to an adequate literary form," but the
    main design of the poem--the search for the good life, salva-
    tion, truth, and God--is visible nonetheless. Sees the strug-
    gle against evil in the poem carried out on several different
    planes, for example, against the "dead letter," corruption in
    the Church, and false religion. Suggests that the poem shows
    none of Chaucer's enjoyment of the human scene for its own
    sake.

4   DONALDSON, E. TALBOT. "Patristic Exegesis in the Criticism of
    Medieval Literature: The Opposition." In Critical Approaches
    to Medieval Literature: Selected Papers from the English
    Institute, 1958-59. Edited by Dorothy Bethurum. New York and
    London: Columbia University Press, pp. 1-26, esp. pp. 5-16.
        Criticizes Robertson and Huppé (1951.9) for substituting
    meanings drawn from the exegetical tradition for the meanings
    suggested by the poem itself. In particular, criticizes
    Robertson and Huppé for their identification of the patristic
    Babylon symbol in the opening lines of the poem; their de-
    scription of the folk of the field as being occupied in the
    world; the spiritual meaning they attach to the occupation of
    plowman in the Prologue; and their misreading of the Rat
    Parliament scene as a less than idealized picture of the
    political community. For an opposing view of the value of
    exegetical criticism of vernacular texts, see Kaske, 1960.7.

5   FERGUSON, ARTHUR B. The Indian Summer of English Chivalry:
    Studies in the Decline and Transformation of Chivalric
    Idealism. Durham, N.C.: Duke University Press, pp. 130-39.
        Piers Plowman illustrates the late medieval depiction of
    the ideal of knighthood embracing the entire governing class.
    The relatively few references to knighthood in the poem tend
    to treat the knight as a member of the landed governing class,
    rather than primarily of a military class. He is the enforcer
    of the king's justice and, in the scene with Hunger and the

wastours, he acts as the local "justicier." "That [in this scene] he appealed in vain is a commentary on the effectiveness of the system, not on its structure, which Langland accepts." Gower reflects the changing status of knighthood less vividly, though both Langland and Gower accept the connection of chivalry with practical affairs and neither was preoccupied with courtly idealism over Christian ethics.

*6   HARRINGTON, DAVID Van. "Techniques of Characterization in Piers the Plowman." Dissertation, Wisconsin, 203 pp.
            Abstracted: DA 21:1554.

7   KASKE, R.E. "Patristic Exegesis in the Criticism of Medieval Literature: The Defense." In Critical Approaches to Medieval Literature: Selected Papers from the English Institute, 1958-59. Edited by Dorothy Bethurum. New York and London: Columbia University Press, pp. 27-60, esp. pp. 32-48.
            Argues that the value of exegetical interpretation lies in "specific, documented examples of its importance" and that exegetical imagery and allusion are used with poetic subtlety, as illustrated with recourse to the researches of Kaske, 1957.6; 1959.8; 1959.9. Finds the rationale of Petrus id est Christus (B XV 206) in a commentary on Exodus 17:6 and I Corinthians 10:4, among other passages in which Christ is identified with a rock. Piers's teaching leechcraft to Christ is found in the common medieval tradition of interpretation of John the Baptist as God's grace, and his Piers-like status as a representative of the virtuous precursors of Christ.

8   KELLOGG, ALFRED L. "Langland's 'Canes Muti': The Paradox of Reform." In Essays in Literary History (in honor of J. Milton French). Edited by Rudolf Kirk and C.F. Main. New Brunswick, N.J.: Rutgers University Press, pp. 25-35.
            Traces the "doumbe houndes" of B X 256 ff., an allusion to Isaiah 56:10, back from the Glossa ordinaria and Gregory's Cura pastoralis, 2, 4, as a reference to prelates who do not correct evil when they see it. The passage from Isaiah was well known in the British Isles from the time of Gildas; to Bromyard and the Wyclifite Nicholas Hereford it was to refer specifically to the secular clergy who did not preach when they should have. Langland shares this indictment of negligent pastors, but unlike Bromyard and Hereford, he fears the effect on the unity of the Church if such criticism became popular. Instead, he hopes for reform of the secular clergy from within. Reprinted: Kellogg, 1972.8.

1960

9   LANGENFELT, GÖSTA. "The Attitude to Villeins and Labourers in
    English Literature until c. 1600." Zeitschrift für Anglistik
    und Amerikanistik 8, no. 4:333-80, esp. pp. 347-54.
        Langland realized that the well-being of the laborers
    depended on the fluctuations of the market, and his descrip-
    tion of their comfort in economically favorable conditions is
    not criticism of them. His portrayal of the permanent servi-
    tude of the laborers is sensitive, despite his religious pur-
    pose, and he clearly convinced the lower classes he was on
    their side. His pity for the poor allows the poem to be com-
    pared with Hali Meidenhad and the Cursor Mundi.

10 [LANGLAND, WILLIAM.] Piers Plowman: The Three Versions. Edited
    by George Kane. Vol. 1, Piers Plowman: The A Version.
    Will's Vision of Piers Plowman and Do-Well. An edition in
    the form of Trinity College Cambridge MS R.3.14 corrected from
    other manuscripts, with variant readings. London: University
    of London, Athlone Press, xii + 458 pp.
        Describes the seventeen MSS and one fragment that con-
    tain the A-text of the poem. Establishes the existence of the
    A-text as a distinct version of the poem on the basis of lines
    or passages (amounting to approximately four hundred lines) in
    Prol-XI that are either not found in the B- and C-text or are
    "echoed" in the B- and C-texts but with major changes in
    sense, or are "substantially altered" in the B- and C-texts
    but still recognizably equivalent. Such distinctive A-text
    material is found in the MSS irrespective of their shapes: in
    DVAM, which contain Prol-XI; in RUJ, which contain some or all
    of XII; in EHL, which lack VIII-IX or IX-XI; in TChH^2, which
    follow XI with material from the C-text, but present the A-
    text with great fidelity up to that point; in H^3, which begins
    as a MS of the B-text but becomes a distinctive A-text MS from
    between V 100-150 until it ends with XI; and in WNK, which
    conform to the A-text thus identified through the possession
    of distinctive lines and passages but contain additional mat-
    ter from the B- and C-texts. The shape of the "mixed text"
    MSS. TChH^{2}H^{3}WNK is shown to be the product of scribal compila-
    tion and is not authorial.
        Inspection of the variant readings of the A-text MSS
    convinces Kane that the genealogies put forward by Knott and
    by Fowler (see [Langland], 1952.6) are inadequate for recen-
    sion, since they do not take into account the many random
    groups that signify conflation or coincidence of error or
    conflicting agreements of as much weight as those on which the
    classification was founded; they present some well-attested
    groups that may in fact be the products of correction, rather
    than of a genetic relationship; and they produce as readings
    of the critical text some that are easier, repugnant to

1960

context, or incapable of producing the rejected variants.
Because of abundant conflation and extensive coincidence of
variation, Kane decides against the possibility of any recoverable genealogy of the extant MSS that might allow recension as a means of establishing the A-text. Working from
smaller to larger variational groups, suggests that a genetic
relationship of MSS. TH^{2}ChDRU may exist, but that a great number of variants in these MSS originate not as a result of any
such presumptive genetic relationship. Likewise, although it
appears likely that EAMH^3 in Prol-VII and AWMH^3 in IX-XI are
genetically related, "the evidence fails to authorize a more
precise description of this." MSS. VH may comprise a genetic
pair, but the relation of this pair to the other MSS is un-
clear. Finds not a single instance of agreement "in the same,
clearly unoriginal variant, or in unoriginal variants demon-
strably related" among Knott's group TRUDH^{2}EAH^3 (see Knott,
1915.1) or Fowler's group TRUDChH^{2}AWMH^3 (see [Langland],
1952.2). Likewise denies the existence of Knott and Fowler's
y family, comprising all extant A-text MSS except VH.
    Chooses as a base-text MS. T, which sets the linguistic
form of the edited text, although it is assumed that this
linguistic form is not necessarily that of the original, and
the readings of this base MS are not taken to be of greater
authority than other readings. Selects among the variant
readings and corrects the base MS on the basis of characteristic scribal tendencies of substitution--both the mechanical,
such as derive from fatigue, distraction, verbal association,
copying from auditory memory, forming an incorrect verbal impression of the exemplar, confusion of letter-forms, anticipa-
tion of copy, homoteleuton, and so on; and the deliberate,
arising from a desire to make the text more explicit, intelligible, emphatic, or metrically smooth. In the absence of
all other considerations, the agreement of a considerable
majority of MSS is taken to be presumptive of originality,
though what constitutes a majority is affected by what evidence the genetic relations of the MSS can furnish. But
"knowledge of typical scribal substitutions becomes more
reliable than considerations of manuscript representation,
for, although a variant may be well attested, if it appears
to originate in a scribal tendency of substitution this may
explain the frequency of its occurrence."
    The text with variants is followed by an appendix that
presents passus XII (which Kane, agreeing with Knott and
Fowler, believes was probably not in the archetype of the extant MSS), and critical notes.
    Reviewed by Anon., TLS, 13 May 1960, p. 304; J.B.
Bessinger, JEGP 60 (1961):571-76; Morton W. Bloomfield,
Speculum 36 (1961):133-37; Guy Bourquin, EA 14 (1961):141;

1960

Norman Davis, N&Q, n.s. 8 (1961):115-16; A.I. Doyle, English
Studies 43 (1962):55-59; David C. Fowler, MP 58 (1963):212-14;
P.M. Kean, Library 5th ser. 16 (1962):218-24; John Lawlor, MLR
56 (1961):243-45; Tauno Mustanoja, Anglia 80 (1962):172-76;
Herbert Pilch, Archiv 201 (1964):132-34; J. Swart, Neophilo-
logus 45, (1961):249-50; and C.L. Wrenn, MLN 76 (1961):856-63.

*11 OIJI, TAKERO. "Why Did Piers Rend His Pardon Asunder--A Personal
Approach to the Pardon Scene." Liberal Arts Review (Tohuku
University):5, 1-15.
    Source: MHRA Annual Bibliography, 1960, p. 102,
no. 1812.

12 OLIPHANT, R. "Langland's 'Sire Piers of Pridie.'" N&Q, c.s. 205
(n.s.7), no. 5 (May):167-68.
    Derives Pridie from L. qui pridie, from the liturgy of
the Mass, referred to by Myrc's Institutions for Parish
Priests as the phrase to use if the priest finds he has forgotten either the bread or wine. Suggests, therefore, Sire
Piers's carelessness in the performance of his duties.

13 SPEARING, A.C. "The Development of a Theme in Piers Plowman."
RES, n.s. 11, no. 43 (August):241-53.
    Verbal repetition and recurrence is considered a method
to develop the poem's ideas, especially in the C-text, where
thematic recurrence of the words and motifs associated with
hunger and bread illuminate the "autobiographical" passage
(C VI); the episode of the Half-acre (C IX); and the episode
of Haukyn (C XVI).
    In the Hunger episode, verbal repetition and recurrence
establish the thematic opposition of the advice of the mate-
rialist Hunger to deprive the lazy of bread to Piers's notion
that "the root of the trouble on the half-acre is a lack of
love; the people must be led to love as well as to labour."
The Haukyn episode reiterates this conflict, but goes further
to suggest in Patience's speech (C XVI 249-51) a solution in
the "food" of patient poverty. Earlier in the "autobiographical" passage, the Dreamer (C VI 82-88) has defended his way of
life on the basis of the same principle of fiat voluntas tua,
but in a spur-of-the-moment fashion, applied only to his own
case.

14 STRANG, BARBARA M. "Piers Plowman B Prologue 132-8." N&Q,
c.s. 205 (n.s. 7), no. 11 (November):436.
    Notes in lines from MS. Lambeth 61 quoted by Bennett
(1960.2) the error Nudum vis for Nudem ius, suggesting "at
least one written record between Lambeth copy and author."

15 WENZEL, SIEGFRIED. The Sin of Sloth: Acedia in Medieval Thought
and Literature. Chapel Hill: University of North Carolina
Press, pp. 135-47.
        Langland's conception of sloth is a popular one in its
presentation by the poet as a stain on the coat of grace; in
a confessional formula; in connection with branches; in its
emphasis on external faults of neglect, rather than insufficient love or lack of spiritual courage; and in its connection
with gluttony. But his emphasis on the social aspects of the
sin is unique. Argues against the lost-leaf theory of Manly
(1906.3) on the basis that restitution is an aspect of acedia
in confessional literature, though it is not tied directly to
stolen goods. Moreover, Langland often does not distinguish
between restitution as satisfactio operis (the third part of
the sacrament of penance) and the restitution of ill-gotten
gains. The episode of Robert the Robber is included by
Langland to suggest that despair, which is a form of sloth
Langland sees derived from the inability to make amends, can
be warded off by a reminder of restitution. Reprinted:
Wenzel, 1967.10.

                              1961

*1 BIGGAR, RAYMOND GEORGE. "Langland's and Chaucer's Treatment of
Monks, Friars, and Priests." Dissertation, Wisconsin, 380 pp.
        Abstracted: DA 22:1992.

2   BLOOMFIELD, MORTON W. "Piers Plowman as a Fourteenth-Century
Apocalypse." Centennial Review 5, no. 3 (Summer):281-95.
        The apocalypticism of the poem is considered with regard
to such themes as the poem's social orientation viewed under
Christian perfection; the figure of Piers and his attendant
agricultural imagery; the poet's predilection for prophecy;
and the eschatological significance of the culmination of the
poem (i.e., the Harrowing of Hell foreshadowing the Last
Judgment, and the coming of the Antichrist as a mirror of the
present time). Like all millenarians, Langland is an opti-
mist; he looks forward to the reform of the friars' erroneous
conception of poverty as crucial to the salvation of society.
Sees the poem sharing with many apocalypses such characteristics as the vision form, revelation, and criticism of contemporary society, but admits there is no literary genre of
the apocalypse, strictly speaking. Reprinted: Vasta, 1968.18;
Bloomfield, 1970.4. See also the fuller treatment of this
subject in Bloomfield, 1961.3.

1961

3 BLOOMFIELD, MORTON W. Piers Plowman as a Fourteenth-Century
   Apocalypse. New Brunswick, N.J.: Rutgers University Press,
   ix + 259 pp.
          The poem is concerned with Christian perfection, rather
   than the more narrow subtopic of salvation; this accounts for
   the division of the poem between different grades or levels.
   The artistic form employed by Langland is a reflection of his
   own personal dilemmas and those of contemporary history.
   Though probably not a literary genre of its own, the apocalypse, employing dreams, revelation, and eschatologically
   oriented criticism of society, best describes the poem in its
   search for perfection. The apocalypse depends on three literary genres: the allegorical dream narrative, the dialogue/
   consolatio/debate, and the encyclopediac (or Menippean)
   satire. The poem also shows the influence of such medieval
   forms as the complaint, commentary, and sermon, most particularly the sermo ad diversos status. The poem is written in
   the Middle Style, apparently for an audience of clerics and
   educated laymen. Various aspects of this style--the use of
   personifications, word play, the mixture of representational
   and nonrepresentational elements--suggest the perplexity and
   uncertainty of the Dreamer and poet.
          Monastic philosophy describes monasticism as the model
   for mankind in its attempt at perfection, in relying on a
   repudiation of this world in favor of the next and an antici-
   pation of the future through the figure of the cloister as an
   image of Paradise and the image of the communal life as a
   reflection of the peace of man. Monasticism in the West is
   always linked to the process and stages of perfection, though
   the Augustinian social orientation of this process is closer
   to Langland's views than the more personal relationship of
   man and God discussed through Bernard's psychological emphases. Langland accepts the notion that monks are an image of
   the Age of the Holy Spirit, and that they will take over the
   world when the Age of the Holy Spirit is instituted. In general, Langland spares the monks scathing satire and takes
   their side in the monk-friar dispute regarding virtue and
   place in the Church Militant.
          Dates the A-text 1362-65 on the basis of the allusion
   in A V 140-41, the B-text about 1377, and the C-text about
   1385 on the basis of Thomas Usk's apparent use of this version. Asserts that 1365 was a popular date among millenarians
   for the coming of the Antichrist and the dawn of a new age.
          Langland believes that man must reform the world to re-
   turn to Paradise; in particular he believes that the friars
   must be reformed. He sees society as comprised of various
   status, and each must perform his proper role and function--
   hence the value of restitution and measure. Piers brings the

224

social, extrapersonal dimension into the poem, for Will himself is fallen and impotent. The figure of the plowman points
to Paradise, salvation, and the perfectibility of all men.
Likewise, the Fable of the Rats, though it has an undeniable
contemporary significance, represents the rex justus of a new,
reformed age. The Prologue shows social decay with the promise of renewal. The Three Lives do not conform with the
active, contemplative, and mixed lives so much as they designate grades of increasing perfection, culminating in vast
social transformation; they may perhaps be correlated with the
Ages of the Father, Son, and Holy Spirit.

Will is historical and normative, standing for all
men. His decay and his condition at the end of the poem
stand for that of the world; but both his death and Antichrist
can be defeated. The poem emphasizes social controls, the
social order, and the cardinal virtues, chiefly humility (as
in monkish philosophy), for the cardinal virtues are essentially social. The poem is basically "dialogic and dialectic,"
reflecting the struggle toward perfection through opposites in
order to transcend them. The theme of the whole poem is explicit in the scene with Holy Church: moderation in self and
society, a return to the ideal, especially by the clergy, and
the need for love and justice.

Four appendices treat Joachim of Flora in fourteenth-
century England, Langland and scholasticism, the problem of
Imaginatif, and the place of the apocalyptic view of history
in the later Middle Ages. Reviewed by Guy Bourquin, EA 16
(1963):70-71; T.P. Dunning, RES, n.s. 16 (1965):188-90; David
C. Fowler, MLQ 24 (1963):410-13; S.S. Hussey, N&Q, n.s. 10
(1963):232-33; R.E. Kaske, JEGP 62 (1963):202-8; John Lawlor,
MLR 58 (1963):89-90; and Gervase Mathew, Medium Ævum 32
(1963):72-74.

4   BOWERS, R.H. "'Foleuyles lawes' ('Piers Plowman,' C.XXII.247)."
    N&Q, c.s. 206 (n.s. 8), no. 9 (September):327-28.
        Sees in the line a reference to the Folville brothers of
    Ashby-Folville, Leicestershire, and Teigh, Rutland; these were
    notorious criminals who were thought of as performing a "rough
    kind of justice." Hence, they were included in the poem in a
    eulogistic context.

5   BROOKE-ROSE, CHRISTINE. "Ezra Pound: Piers Plowman in the
    Modern Waste Land." REL 2 (April):74-88.
        Piers Plowman and the Cantos are compared on the basis
    of concern for the proper use of wealth, satire of the corrup-
    tions of government, allusiveness, "echoing orchestration,"
    movement among different levels of meaning and interpretation,
    and concern with metamorphoses of figures and identities.

1961

6   CEJP, LADISLAV. <u>Metody Středověké Alegorie a Langlandův Petr</u>
    <u>Orač</u> (The Methods of Medieval Allegory and Langland's Piers
    <u>the Plowman</u>). Edited by Jiri Levy. Acta Universitatis
    Palckianae Olomucensis. Facultas Philosophia 8 Philologica 5
    (Státní Pedagogické Nakladalelství v Praze), 208 pp.
        In Czech, with an English summary. Analyzes medieval
    allegorical technical devices and draws upon Cejp, 1956.2,
    for quantitative analyses of structural units, and so on.
    Translates the Prologue into Czech alliterative verse, and
    summarizes the entire poem. Cejp believes that the tradi-
    tional view of Langland as a conservative social reformer is
    somewhat incorrect, that Langland, instead, is more radical
    in his idea of <u>necessitas</u> <u>non</u> <u>habet</u> <u>legem</u> and in the idea of
    a conqueror who is entitled to abolish privilege and promote
    the downtrodden. Dates the A-text c. 1370, the B-text 1376-81,
    and the C-text post 1381. Sees as important C-text additions
    the sermon on <u>nisi</u> <u>granum</u> <u>frumenti</u> (C XIII), which declares
    that death for a good cause is not useless; C XI 196-99, which
    asserts that the preacher must not fear persecution; and C XVI
    149-52, which, in the disappearance of Piers, likens that
    character to Wat Tyler (as does the allegory of John Ball's
    Letter). Sees Piers not as a representative of well-to-do
    farmers, but as a spokesman for many of the peasants' com-
    plaints. Piers stands for <u>humana</u> <u>natura</u> <u>Christi</u> on a symbolic
    level, but as a savior who is entitled to liberate bondsmen
    and live the life of an outlaw, and as a conqueror who may
    assume a higher position than the king. Asserts that veiled
    allusions in the poem are reliable only in those cases "where
    they are accompanied by, and form a system with, the corre-
    sponding circumstances." Sees Wyclif alluded to in B XIX
    406-7, 477-78, and so on; Alice Perrers in A II 8-12; William
    Walworth in C XIV 1-2, Prol 117, XIII 190-91, and IV 121-23.

7   FISHER, JOHN H. "Wyclif, Langland, Gower, and the Pearl Poet on
    the Subject of Aristocracy." In <u>Studies in Medieval Litera-</u>
    <u>ture in Honor of Professor Albert Croll Baugh</u>. Edited by
    Macedward Leach. Philadelphia: University of Pennsylvania
    Press; London: Oxford University Press, pp. 139-58.
        Langland does not seek to justify the wealth of the
    knighthood or to find any political function in society for
    knights. Whereas Wyclif identifies the aristocracy with
    political power, Langland identifies it with wealth; and
    whereas Wyclif for the most part confines his praise of pov-
    erty and denunciation of riches to the clergy, Langland fol-
    lows the homiletic tradition in extending this praise and
    condemnation from the ecclesiastical to the secular sphere.
    Langland seems to support the notion of a hereditary aris-
    tocracy more specifically than does Wyclif, but in reality

his system of government leaves no place for the class. Instead, he thinks of the king as all-important, and the knights
as simply part of the comune, which is regulated by elected
mayors and "men that kepen lawes."

8   FOWLER, DAVID C. Piers the Plowman: Literary Relations of the
    A and B Texts. Seattle: University of Washington Press,
    xiii + 260 pp.
        The Vita of the A-text originates in the Pardon scene,
    in which Piers offers a model of true repentance in contrast
    to the "learned" priest, and which is intended to prove that
    learning is not the way to salvation. The Vita takes the form
    of an internal debate or meditation; the Three Lives are con-
    sistently defined in the context of the commons, clergy, and
    episcopate, with the sharpest criticism directed toward
    Clergy's learning which lacks charity.
        The B-text continuation is based on the Bible and its
    tradition of commentary and popular treatment in the Cursor
    Mundi, the cycle plays, the Cornish Ordinalia, and so on, as
    well as on the traditions and conventions of romance literature
    (e.g., the treatment of Christ as a knight, and the Dreamer as
    a fool). B XI-XV describes the Creation, and modifies the A-
    text in teaching the Dreamer the value of learning and sub-
    ordinating both Clergy and Kynde Wit to Patience-Humility-
    Charity. Anima's discourse on Charity is developed in relation
    to patient poverty and serves as a prelude to the Redemption
    drama, begun with the Fall of Man (XVI 1-166) and developed
    through the patriarchs and prophets (XVI 167-XVII 350) and the
    actual Redemption (XVIII). These events are correlated with
    the Dreamer's movement through Lent to Easter, or from re-
    pentance to regeneration. The Fall itself is interpreted by
    the B-text poet on the traditional four levels of exposition,
    and romance elements are apparent in the Longinus scene. The
    Samaritan's exposition of the Trinity remedies a deficiency of
    the A-text, as well as continues the B-text poet's emphasis on
    the necessity of grace. The Ascension is treated in B XIX
    1-193, Pentecost in XIX 194-256, the history of the early
    Church in XIX 257-330, and the Last Judgment in XIX 331-478.
        In contrast to the A-text, the Visio and the Vita of the
    B-text are treated by the poet as one poem. References to
    violence (e.g., B XVII 203-92) may indicate a date of composi-
    tion post 1381. Satire in the B-text against lawyers is some-
    what softened, although satire against friars and the episco-
    pate is intensified in this version. Changes like these
    suggest the author of the B-text may have been a ranking
    member of the secular clergy, sympathetic toward the wealthy,
    but a fearless opponent of secular and ecclesiastical corrup-
    tion. The author may even have been John Trevisa, whose

1961

comments in his translation of Higden's Polychronicon offer
similarities to ideas and expressions in the B-text. Reviewed
by Morton W. Bloomfield, Speculum 37 (1962):120-23; Guy
Bourquin, EA 15 (1962):277-78; S.S. Hussey, RES, n.s. 14
(1963):177-79; George Kane, Medium Ævum 33 (1964):230-31;
R.E. Kaske, JEGP 62 (1963):208-13; D.W. Robertson, MLQ 23
(1962):84-85; and R.M. Wilson, MLR 57 (1962):627.

9   FULLER, ANNE HAVENS. "Scripture in 'Piers Plowman' B." MS 23:
    352-63.
        A list of passages from Scripture in the B-text that
    supersedes that of Skeat (1869.2); and a list that corrects
    Skeat's specific errors in citations from Deuteronomy, Psalms,
    Proverbs, Isaiah, Matthew, Luke, John, and I Corinthians.

10 HAMILTON, A.C. "The Visions of Piers Plowman and The Faerie
    Queene." In Form and Convention in the Poetry of Edmund
    Spenser: Selected Papers from the English Institute. Edited
    by William Nelson. New York and London: Columbia University
    Press, pp. 1-34.
        Restates and develops the material of Hamilton (1958.3).
    Contrasts the rhetorical development of Book II of The Faerie
    Queene, in which the content is viewed within a structure and
    form, with Piers Plowman, where the "structure seems to emerge
    out of its content as though the poem were shaped as the poet
    was writing." Finds that the literal level in both poems must
    be understood and retained by the reader as metaphor, rather
    than merely being translated, though Spenser more deliberately
    than Langland asserts the value of fiction over that of moral-
    ity or belief.

11 JUSSERAND, J.J. English Wayfaring Life in the Middle Ages.
    Translated by Lucy Toulmin Smith. London: Methuen; New York:
    Barnes & Noble.
        Reprint of Jusserand, 1889.2.

12 ORSTEN, ELISABETH M. "The Ambiguities in Langland's Rat Parlia-
    ment." MS 23:216-39.
        Langland may have known the fable from Nicholas Bozon's
    treatment, contained in a MS that circulated in the Worcester
    area, or from John of Bromyard's Summa prædicatum, which
    stresses the "uselessness of laws without providing for their
    execution, but suggests the laws are good in themselves."
    Even more probable is Langland's knowledge of Brunton's Sermo
    69, Domenica Quinta post Pascham, preached in London 18 May
    1376 during the deliberation of the Good Parliament. Con-
    cludes that although Langland is most probably referring to
    the Good Parliament in his fable, the mouse is not his

spokesman. Although we can approve of his attempt to work for the common profit, his appeal is to slothful ease and compromise with evil; and his technique one of skillful exaggeration. Superficially, the fable seems to attack the Good Parliament; in reality, it is an attack on John of Gaunt and the Parliament of 1377.

13 SCHOECK, R.J. "The Use of St. John Chrysostom in Sixteenth-Century Controversy: Christopher St. German and Sir Thomas More in 1533." Harvard Theological Review 54, no. 1 (January):21-27.
    The maxim on the effects of a healthy and of a corrupt priesthood (B XV 115 ff.; C XVII 271 ff.) is compared with its source, the Opus imperfectum, long attributed to Chrysostom. Though not a verbatim copy, there is nothing to indicate that Langland's citation shows the influence of the Catena aurea of Thomas Aquinas, used by Gerson in his Declaratio by Taft (in the Apologye of Syr Thomas More, Knyght).

14 SMITH, BEN H., Jr. "Patience's Riddle, Piers Plowman B, XIII." MLN 76, no. 12 (December):675-82.
    Interprets ex vi transicionis as "by the power, or by the principle, of grammatical transitivity," a reference to the notion that the components of a grammatical construction are interpreted either to pertain to the same thing (intransitivity) or to different things (transitivity). Hugh of St. Cher, in his comment on Psalm 4:7, interprets countenance (vultus) as reason, light (lumen) as grace; Smith sees this very line in "half a laumpe lyne in latyn" (B XIII 151), and would render lines 150-51 as "God the Father desired to become manifest . . . by the fiats of the creation, which he stamped with reason; and by (with) the Word of the new Creation, which he stamped with grace." Saturday of line 153 is taken to be the seventh day of creation, often correlated with charity; Wednesday, the fourth day of the nexte wyke after, is the fourth day of the Re-creation, or the Passion. The myddel of the mone is Easter, which supplies the might of both Saturday and Wednesday because neither the Creation nor the Passion has significance from a human point of view without the Resurrection. See Smith, 1966.19.

15 TILLYARD, E.M.W. Some Mythical Elements in English Literature. Being the Clark Lectures 1959-60. London: Chatto & Windus, pp. 41-43.
    Langland's version of the Harrowing of Hell, combined with the Four Daughters of God, is so free and peculiar that the Harrowing almost loses its identity. It is impossible to determine whether Langland's refashioning of the story became

1961

"valid beyond himself, whether for his audience it became a
classic and operative version of the myth, alternative to the
more conventional versions."

1962

1   ADAMS, JOHN F.   "Piers Plowman and the Three Ages of Man."   JEGP
    61, no. 1 (January):23-41.
        The poem is seen as a description of the progress of the
    Dreamer in his chronological maturity and increasing moral
    understanding from the time of his youth to that of his im-
    minent death. The Dreamer is confronted successively with the
    temptations and moral problems of youth, middle age, and
    death; and the mental faculties characteristic of each period
    are introduced. The Visio presents a "panoramic view of life
    as it is lived" and introduces the question of the possibility
    of salvation and the way to achieve it. The Three Lives
    roughly correspond to the three ages. The life of Christ in
    the poem recapitulates the life of man; and the temptations
    of the world, the flesh, and the devil are made to correlate,
    in the Tree of Life episode (B XVI 26 ff.), with the three
    ages, where each is opposed by a specific Person of the
    Trinity and appropriate mental faculties. The Vita de Dobest
    accomplishes a transition from explication of the rational to
    explication of the concept of grade; it demonstrates the
    abuses of the natural faculties, and it places the Dreamer in
    a contemporary milieu where he participates in the quest for
    salvation. Piers is best to be understood as an intermediary
    between man and the proper understanding of grace. Since
    Christ began to "do best" after the Harrowing of Hell, Dobest
    corresponds to no condition of life, but rather encompasses
    salvation and perfection that can only be approached, but not
    attained, before death.

2   COGHILL, NEVILL.   "God's Wenches and the Light that Spoke (Some
    Notes on Langland's Kind of Poetry)." In English and Medieval
    Studies Presented to J.R.R. Tolkien on the occasion of his
    Seventieth Birthday. Edited by Norman Davis and C.L. Wrenn.
    London: George Allen & Unwin, pp. 200-218.
        Langland's poetic gifts express themselves in a fluidity
    of time and space and a fusion of allegory (expressing the
    immaterial in material fashion) and symbol (viewing the mate-
    rial in transcendental fashion). Langland's personifications
    often seem derived from his own real experience; and the
    range of Piers's associations shows a coalescence of allegory,
    symbol, and parable. Comparison of the allegory of the Castle
    and the Debate of the Four Daughters of God in Piers Plowman

and Grossteste's <u>Castel d'amour</u> shows Langland's imaginative blending of elementary allegory, down-to-earth comic collo- quialism, and the transcendent portrayal of Christ. Re- printed: Newstead, 1968.10.

3   JOHNSTON, G.K.W. "A Reading in <u>Piers Plowman</u>." <u>AN&Q</u> 1, no. 3 (November):35-36.

Agrees with Kane (in [Langland], 1960.10) that the per- sonal pronoun in A III 151 ought to be masculine, referring to Law rather than Mede. Renders the sense of lines 150-51 as "Law is so arrogant and procrastinating, and, as he does not give bribes, pleases very few."

4   LAWLOR, JOHN. <u>Piers Plowman: An Essay in Criticism</u>. London: Edward Arnold (Publishers), 340 pp.

Offers a passus-by-passus interpretation of the B-text, largely developed from Lawlor (1950.8 and 1957.7), in which the poem is seen as the record of the experience of a dreamer whose initial impetuous theorizing and inability (or unwill- ingness) to see the relevance to himself of that for which he censures others gradually gives way to a recognition of applicability and personal responsibility. The Visio, in depicting the pervasive ill-effects of the mercenary motive, emphasizes man's universal blameworthiness and the theme of the law. But the one just man called forth to remedy this situation--the Plowman--is shown in the Pardon scene to be wanting. This movement is paralleled in the second part of the poem, the Vita, by the Dreamer, who must gradually and with great effort come to learn that which Piers saw in a moment, when he realized that God's righteousness, were it not for His mercy, would lead but to despair.

Describes the verve and directness of Langland's lan- guage, which often draws its poetic effects from the principle of contrast of native and Romance vocabularies, suggesting the poles of present and real versus an imagined future, or the authentic versus the ideal, and so on. Describes Langland's meter as based on the phrasal unit. Hence it is particularly suited for reading aloud and especially appropriate for the turnings of thought and the varying pace and intensity of his thematic development. Sees the poem as concerned with the familiar medieval topos of <u>auctoritee</u> and <u>experience</u>; it di- rects the attention of the reader not merely to the sum of its arguments "but to their varying force and distinctive quality in the Dreamer's experience."

Defines <u>allegory</u> as "a work of imagination employing narrative elements which are coherent and interesting in their own right but from which transferred meanings naturally arise"; and warns against both the predilection to see

231

1962

allegory as but a stage on the road toward naturalistic representation, and the disposition to paraphrase rather than allow
the "pressure and movement of the poet's imagination" its distinctive effect. Agrees with Frank's critique of the applicability of the fourfold method of exegesis to Piers Plowman
(1953.2) and, while admitting that the poem is at points literal and moral, literal and anagogical, sees that it is so in
unsystematic fashion, as guided by the turns of the poet's
thought and the shift from an emphasis on intellectual facul-
ties to moral virtues. Sees the fundamental objection to a
resolutely allegorical approach based on multiple reference in
the actual meaning and effect of an image or metaphor in a
particular context. Concludes that, as an allegorist,
Langland shows a great power of graphic description that has
the effect of making his truths incarnate; a desire to explain
and clarify his allegories; and a disposition to foreshorten
his design in order to accommodate established significances,
even at the cost of consistency of representation.

Langland's persona, like those those of Chaucer and
Gower, depends for its effectiveness on a tradition of humorous self-deprecation, through which the reader is gradually
brought to the truths the poem affirms. Though these personae
all show both an eagerness to learn and an undeniable stub-
bornness, Piers Plowman is distinctive among the dream-visions
in ending on a note of continued search rather than one of
disclosure and acceptance. Sees the Three Lives neither as
strictly progressive nor as stages in an order of experience.
Dowel and Dobest have the world of man as their central points
of reference, but Dobet shows in Christ's life the perfect
fulfillment of the law insisted upon in Dowel.

Reviewed by Anon., TLS, 1 November 1963, p. 888; Morton
W. Bloomfield, Speculum 38 (1963):369-70; Guy Bourquin, EA 17
(1964):289-90; D.S. Brewer, Listener 68 (1963):1061; J.A.
Burrow, Critical Quarterly 5 (1963):380-81; S.S. Hussey, N&Q,
n.s. 10 (1963):351-52; P.M. Kean, RES, n.s. 14 (1963):395-97;
Kevin Margery, Southern Review 1 (1964-65):106-9; and Bohumil
Trinka, Philologica Pragensia 6 (1963):316-17.

5   MARTIN, JAY. "Wil as Fool and Wanderer in Piers Plowman." TSLL
     3:535-48.
          Although Langland used the satiric forms of the hori-
     zontal dialogue--the diatribe, memorabilia, and chreia--he
     also chose forms that do not univocally sustain the satiric
     thrust of the poem. His use of the Fool ties together the
     series of dreams that make up the A-text; suggests that all
     mankind, like the Dreamer, can become foolish concerning sal-
     vation; and sustains the satire by relying on the traditional
     audience acceptance of that which a fool says to be true. But

Langland's use of the figure of the Wanderer (often a vehicle of encyclopedic satire) works in Piers Plowman against the satire, since the poem satirizes without exception the wandering life, while at the same time it includes Will as a wanderer.

6   MOHL, RUTH. The Three Estates in Medieval and Renaissance Literature. New York: Frederick Ungar Publishing Co.
Reprint of Mohl, 1933.6.

*7 O'GRADY, GERALD LEO. "Piers Plowman and the Medieval Tradition of Penance." Dissertation, Wisconsin, 713 pp.
Abstracted: DA 23:2117-18.

8   PEACHAM, HENRY. The Complete Gentleman, the Truth of Our Times, and the Art of Living in London. Edited by Virgil B. Heltzel. Ithaca, N.Y.: Cornell University Press, for the Folger Shakespeare Library.
See Peacham, 1622.1.

9   RUSSELL, G.H. "The Evolution of a Poem: Some Reflections on the Textual Tradition of Piers Plowman." Arts (University of Sydney, Faculty of Arts) 2:33-46.
Hypothesizes that the close relations of the extant B-text MSS and the high degree of corruption in the B-archetype mean that the B-text is a chance survivor of a revision of the A-text which for whatever reason was recalled or suppressed; and that the existing MSS are descendants of a single copy which survived this recall, but was later subjected to thoroughgoing and unintelligent editorial interference. Sees the C-version as a result of the failure, for extraliterary reasons, of the B-text to hold its ground. Notes the comparatively restricted area of the language of the C-text MSS (the valley of the Severn). Finds three families of MSS witnesses of the C-archetype and pronounces Skeat's text, MS. Hm, a representative of the worst of the three. Announces that his edition will be based on MS. X and will be closer to the B-text than was Skeat's C-text. Accepts the theory of single authorship, though admits that the fact of the C-text reviser's retention of scribal errors in the B-text weakens the case. Suggests that the poet's own revision of the B-text was interrupted by his death or incapacitation, and that an editor, probably using the same B-text MS as did the poet, incorporated revisions into it left by the poet, but did not attempt to put these revisions into final, polished form.

1962

*10 SAITO, ISAMU. "Piers' Half Acre--Passus VI of Piers Plowman--."
    In Essays Presented to Naozo Ueno in Honour of His Sixtieth
    Birthday. Tokyo: Nan'undo.
        Source: Saito, 1964.11, p. 2.

11 SALTER, ELIZABETH. Piers Plowman: An Introduction. Oxford:
    Basil Blackwell, v + 111 pp.
        Piers Plowman is not merely or primarily a satirical
    commentary on medieval realities, a subtle exercise in reli-
    gious allegory, or an analysis of sin; it is essentially a
    work of art which depends on the inseparability of its reli-
    gious and artistic factors. The poem blends beauty with use-
    fulness; its "realism" cannot be divorced from allegorical
    significance. Like other alliterative poems, Piers Plowman
    shows a wide range of rhythmical variation, a digressive
    nature, and an abrupt, episodic quality. Yet the poem shows
    no interest in the more elaborate forms of alliterative poetry
    and features a simpler diction and more frequent interruptions
    of closely reasoned writing. In its relatively unsophisti-
    cated alliterative style, the poem may be characteristic of
    the writing of the southwest country related to popular oral
    tradition. The artes prædicandi, like Piers Plowman, offer a
    justification of artistic "makynges" based on their larger
    usefulness, and encourage out of a religious purpose poetic
    adornment to emphasize sense and increase emotional appeal.
    As opposed to medieval drama and Biblical narratives such as
    Cursor Mundi, the unity of Piers Plowman cannot be argued on
    narrative grounds; instead, it develops its central themes
    through sermonlike techniques such as echo, association, cor-
    respondence, and cross-references. This unity is demonstrated
    in four sections of the poem which are linked by the presence
    of the Dreamer and appearances or references to Piers. It is
    seen likewise in Langland's linkage and cross-reference of
    sound and idea, as well as in his personal and universal use
    of dream-experience by which the Dreamer is "gradually made
    subject to a higher power." It is unnecessary to expect
    Langland's consistent use of the fourfold allegorical method,
    as long as we realize that the journey of the poem should be
    understood in its fullest allegorical implications. Langland
    often does not preserve continuity in his allegorical pattern;
    he often varies the depth and texture of the allegory, as in
    the Ancrene Riwle, in order to achieve greater spiritual sug-
    gestiveness. Much like the writings of the mystics, the poem
    teaches "the process of discovery how, through love, man is
    able to reach the Truth, which is God."
        Reviewed by Morton W. Bloomfield, MP 62 (1964-65):62-64;
    D.S. Brewer, Listener 67 (1963):567-68; A.C. Cawley, MLR 58
    (1963):458; Basil Cottle, JEGP 62 (1963):213-14; T.P. Dunning,

Medium Ævum 33 (1964):147-49; S.S. Hussey, RES, n.s. 14
(1963):279-80; and Bohumil Trinka, Philologica Pragensia 6
(1963):314-17.

*12 SMITH, BEN HUDDLESTON, Jr. "Traditional Christian Love Imagery
in Piers Plowman." Dissertation, North Carolina, Chapel Hill,
142 pp.
Abstracted: DA 23:4690.

*13 SPITZBART, GÜNTER. Das Gewissen in der mittelenglischen Litera-
tur mit besonderer Berücksichtigung von Piers Plowman. Dissertation, Cologne. Cologne: Photostelle der Universität zu
Köln, 232 pp.
Source: McNamee, vol. 1, p. 158, where it is listed
under 1963.

 14 STROUD, PARRY. Stephen Vincent Benét. New York: Twayne
Publishers, p. 85.
Briefly discusses Benét's use of Piers Plowman in his
novel, The Beginning of Wisdom (1922): the protagonist,
Philip, resolves to imitate Langland and seek Piers, the
people's Christ; but Philip, unlike Langland, "chooses to
seek arrogance as well as love."

 15 ŚWIECZKOWSKI, WALERIAN. Word Order Patterning in Middle English:
A Quantitative Study Based on Piers Plowman and Middle English
Sermons. Janua Linguarum, vol. 19, Studia Memoriæ Nicolai
Wijk Dedicata, edited by Cornelius H. van Schooneveld. The
Hague: Mouton & Co., 114 pp.
Analyzes subject-predicate relations, relation of predi-
cate to other elements of the clause, and position of the ob-
ject in Piers Plowman as compared to Middle English sermons
(Woodburn O. Ross, ed., Middle English Sermons [London:
Oxford University Press, 1940]). The ratio of the subject-
predicate order to the predicate-subject order in Piers
Plowman (the average of all three texts) is 77.6 percent to
22.4 percent; in the Middle English sermons it is 89.0 percent
to 11.0 percent. Finds that preposition influences word-order
patterns inasmuch as the percentage of predicate-subject order
depends on the relationship of prepositional and predicate,
and the semantic load of the prepositional often influences
the semantic-load pattern of subject and predicate. The
typical place for the predicate is the first position after
the subject, though it is found more often in the rarer medial
and final positions in Piers Plowman than in the sermons.
Notes a tendency to end the clause with "heavy words" in both
Piers Plowman and the sermons, but finds the use of "light
predicates" to be more frequent in the sermons. In both

1962

comparison texts, the subject-predicate-object order is typical, but especially in Piers Plowman the object often precedes both the subject and predicate in predicate-subject
order.

16 WOOLF, ROSEMARY. "Some Non-Medieval Qualities of Piers Plowman."
     Essays in Criticism 12, no. 2 (April):111-25.
          The literal level is unimportant in Piers Plowman,
     whereas medieval allegory, guided by the typological inter-
     pretation of the Old Testament, accepts the literal level and
     sees it comprising a whole with the allegorical meaning. The
     character of Piers is surprising in that his meaning is not
     indisputably clear; the combination in him of uncertain sig-
     nificance and deep emotional power is the reverse of what is
     found in characteristic medieval allegory. The poem lacks the
     visual quality characteristic of medieval literature, and the
     use of the dream form shows a real dreamlike indifference to
     time and place. Also uncharacteristic of medieval literature
     up to the end of the fourteenth century is the use of a
     dreamer figure to convey the personal truth of the author of
     the work; in this regard, the lack of poetic resolution to the
     various conflicting arguments presented in the poem suggests
     that the author did not himself know where these arguments
     were leading him. Lacking the characteristic clarity of
     medieval literature, Langland's style relies instead on a
     subtle and complex texture in which ideas are "interwoven" and
     compressed, rather than set out "one by one" or "side by side."
     Woolf's remarks on the "uncertainty" of the poem are extended
     by Kratins, 1963.6.

1963

1 BRUNEDER, HANS. Personifikation und Symbol in William Langlands
     Piers Plowman. Herrn Universitätsprofessor Dr. Herbert Koziol
     zum 60. Geburtstag gewidmet. Vienna: n.p., 12 pp.
          For both Langland and Chaucer, gender relationships
     generally follow from natural gender or from imagined gender
     of the personifications as traditionally conceived. To
     Langland in particular, however, gender of personification is
     decided on the basis of individual situations, rather than on
     Latin or Romance traditions. Such topics as world, heaven,
     heavenly goodness, countries, and cities are masculine or
     feminine; rivers, seas, and mountains are masculine. Although
     we have been led to expect that only in such concepts as
     sunne, moon, and sterre, can we expect the congruence of Old
     and Middle English, and that otherwise the gender will be de-
     termined from the French or Latin translations of these words,

236

Langland shows that such terms as feith, hunger, shifte, and licam are masculine, despite their Romance translation parallels.

2 GLUNZ, H.H. Das Abendland: Forschungen zur Geschichte euro-
    päischen Geisteslebens. Edited by Herbert Schöffler. Vol. 2,
    Die Literarästhetik des europäischen Mittelalters: Wolfram--
    Rosenroman--Chaucer--Dante. Frankfort on the Main: V.
    Klostermann.
        Reprint of Glunz, 1937.4.

*3 IKEGAMI, TADAHIRO. "Piers Plowman and Monastic Tradition."
    Rising Generation 109:217-18.
        Source: Saito, 1966.17, p. 11.

4 KASKE, R.E. "'Ex vi transicionis' and Its Passage in Piers
    Plowman." JEGP 62 (January):32-60.
        B XIII 135-56 is interpreted in light of Scriptural
    exegesis. Kynde loue coueiteth nouȝte no catel but speche
    (line 150) is explained through the commentary on I Corinthians
    13-14 as implying that the Christian ruled by caritas will
    covet only the further gifts of that virtue, such as the gift
    of speech; this concept is linked to that of love of neighbors,
    as described in lines 142-49. Ex vi transicionis (line 151)
    refers in late medieval grammatical theory to the power of
    transitivity by which a verb governs the accusative case of
    its object; laumpe of the same line probably alludes to the
    command "tene hanc lampadem" in Priscian's Institutiones, and
    is here associated by Langland with charity on the basis of
    the familiar exegesis of Canticles 8:6. Patience thus sug-
    gests through this grammatical metaphor that the possession of
    Dowel is inevitably governed by patientia, and more directly
    by caritas. Saterday of line 153 and wednesday of line 154
    refer to the Creation and the Passion, respectively; these
    days are customarily linked both with caritas and prudentia/
    sapientia/scientia, all of which draw their power from the
    Resurrection. Bouste of line 152 (a reading Kaske substitutes
    for Skeat's aboute) is either patientia itself or the heart of
    a Christian fortified by patientia. Reprinted with revisions
    by the author: Blanch, 1969.4.

5 KRAPP, GEORGE PHILIP. The Rise of English Literary Prose. New
    York: Frederick Ungar Publishing Co.
        Reprint of Krapp, 1915.2.

1963

6   KRATINS, OJARS. "Piers Plowman and Arthurian Romance." Essays
     in Criticism 13, no. 3 (July):304.
            The tone of "romantic uncertainty" which Woolf (1962.16)
     finds in the poem is noted as a chief characteristic of
     Arthurian literature. Piers's role in the poem is considered
     more symbolic than allegorical; as in much Arthurian litera-
     ture, he is a symbolic figure who raises the atmosphere of the
     work to a "mysterious significance."

7   MUSCATINE, CHARLES. "Locus of Action in Medieval Narrative."
     Romance Philology 17, no. 1 (August):115-22.
            Argues that Langland's use of locus and space is almost
     "surrealistic" in that while sometimes employing flat, "Roman-
     esque" space in which a patterned setting expresses immutable
     moral relationships, and sometimes using naturalistic space to
     represent psychological and emotional experience, neither "be-
     comes a controlling locus of his narrative." Rather, the
     locus of Langland's actions and characters is continually
     shifting; different spatial concepts are invoked for tempo-
     rary, limited effects without the poet's concern for the
     relationship between them. Sees in this formal trait
     Langland's problematic sense of the structure of the moral
     world, an insecurity that belies the orthodoxy of the poem's
     message. Some of the material of this essay is developed in
     Muscatine, 1972.18. Salter (1971.25) puts a different con-
     struction on the changeable locus of action in the poem.

*8   PANČENKO, A.M. "Srednevekovyj allegorizm i istoričesky smysl
     'Petra Paxarja.'" Izvestija Akademii nauk S.S.S.R., Otdelenie
     literatury i. jazyka (Moscow) 22:151-52.
            Source: M.H.R.A. Annual Bibliography, 1963, p. 94,
     no. 1675.

9   RUSSELL, G.H., and NATHAN, VENETIA. "A Piers Plowman Manuscript
     in the Huntington Library." HLQ 26 (February):119-30.
            MS. [Ht], dating from the first quarter of the fifteenth
     century, is a carefully edited version made by a scribe with
     access to all three texts of the poem. It is basically a MS
     of the B-text, as Chambers (1935.2) thought, but one that is
     altered into a form widely differing from all other B-text MSS
     and one that has substantial borrowings from the A- and C-
     texts, as the scribe apparently desired to present what he
     thought was the best reading. There is little editorial
     activity evidenced in the early and late portions of the text,
     and no A- or C-readings in the Prologue. Lists MS borrowings
     from A- and C-texts, as well as unique, spurious additions.

1963

*10 SAITO, ISAMU. "On the Three Biblical Quotations in the Pardon
     Scene of Piers the Plowman." Jinbungaku (Doshisha Univer-
     sity), 67, 1-22.
          Source: Saito, 1964.11, p. 1.

11 SAMUELS, M.L. "Some Applications of Middle English Dialectology."
     ES 44, no. 2:81-94, esp. p. 94.
          At least thirty-six MSS of Piers Plowman can be local-
     ized. C-text MSS circulated in the Malvern Hills; B-text MSS
     had a more cosmopolitan circulation, especially in the
     Worcester and London areas; and there are no extant MSS of the
     A-text in the more central areas where the B- and C-MSS were
     produced. Rather, A-text MSS can be assigned to S. Sussex,
     Essex, Norfolk, Durham, N. Warwickshire, N. Worcestershire,
     S. Shropshire, and Ireland.

12 SEN GUPTA, JASODHARA. "Piers Plowman." Essays in Criticism 13,
     no. 2 (April):201-2.
          The shifting layers of allegory in Piers Plowman are
     compared with Durrell's "sliding panel" technique. Such nar-
     rative aspects as the suddenness with which a character ap-
     pears or disappears, and the fading of one episode into another
     are noted as akin to the techniques of cinematography.

13 SPEARING, A.C. "Verbal Repetition in Piers Plowman B and C."
     JEGP 62, no. 4:722-37.
          Sees verbal repetition, used for rhetorical purposes,
     intensified in the C-version, as in the repetition of trewe/
     trewth in C II 93-97 (cf. B I 97-100), rich in C III 8-16,
     and the more complex interlocking repetition of C XI 187-202
     and C XVIII 126-40. Suggests as perhaps the most effective
     use of verbal repetition that of various verbal clusters asso-
     ciated with the motifs of liȝte, drynke, and gyle in the
     Harrowing of Hell scene (C XXI). Whereas repetitions in
     devotional prose are used to produce a decorative effect,
     Langland uses the device more in the fashion of the ars
     prædicandi to make his argument clearer. But the central
     effort of the poem seems directed against the making of fine
     scholastic distinctions in favor of constructing intellectual
     concepts that partake, through verbal repetitions, of "sig-
     nificant vagueness." Revised and developed as Spearing,
     1964.12.

14 STRANG, BARBARA M.H. "Piers Plowman, B-Text, Passus V, 491-92."
     N&Q, c.s. 208 (n.s. 10), no. 8 (August):286.
          The inverted syntax of B V 492 (C VIII 127) suggests
     Langland's familiarity with a lyric on the theme of the felix
     culpa as represented in a fifteenth-century copy of a lyric

239

1963

printed by Carleton Brown, ed., Religious Lyrics of the Fifteenth Century (Oxford: Clarendon Press, 1939), no. 83.

15 TANNER, THOMAS. Bibliotheca Britannico-Hibernica: sive, de
Scriptoribus, qui in Anglia, Scotia, et Hibernia ad sæculi
XVII initium floruerunt, literarum ordine juxta familiarum
nomine dispositis Commentarius . . . London: Societas ad
literas promovendas, 1748. Reprint. Tucson, Ariz.: Audax
Press.
See Tanner, 1748.1.

*16 THIMMESH, HILARY DONALD. "A Synoptic Reading of Central Themes
in Piers Plowman." Dissertation, Cornell, 295 pp.
Abstracted: DA 24:3733-34.

*17 VASTA, EDWARD. "The Spiritual Basis of Piers Plowman." Disser-
tation, Stanford, 189 pp.
Abstracted: DA 24:1165. See Vasta, 1965.20.

18 YUNCK, JOHN A. The Lineage of Lady Meed: The Development of
Mediaeval Venality Satire. Notre Dame, Ind.: University of
Notre Dame Press, 1963, passim.
The history of the venality theme is traced through the
Roman satiric tradition (Vergil, Georgics II; Ovid, Metamorphoses I; Juvenal, Saturæ I); Scriptural sources (Ezekiel
22:12; Michah 3, 11; IV Kings; Acts of the Apostles 7:18-24);
the exegetical tradition (Jerome, Augustine, Gregory); Latin
verse satire of the early Christian era; the rebirth of the
theme in the period of ecclesiastical reform and the transition to a money economy; and its flowering in medieval Latin
and vernacular literature.
Langland's Lady Mede is seen as a vivid allegorical
demonstration of the power of money, all the more important
because the poet sees human venality as a major obstacle on
the road to salvation. The satire of the poem is not an isolated phenomenon: the cross on the coin of B XV 500-509 is
paralleled in the works of Walter of Castillon, among others;
the Romans de carité (first quarter of the thirteenth century) employs a pilgrimage to charity; the argument of Mede
and Conscience before the king is paralleled by a thirteenth-
century debate between Master Denier and a sheep; the
attempted marriage of an evil figure to one who is double in
nature is seen in the Roman de Fauvel (as pointed out by
Cornelius, 1932.6), as is the complaint that man thinks only
of getting ahead.
Langland's Mede is the Munera of the earlier moralists
and, like her, Mede is ambivalent in nature. The debate over
her marriage shows Langland's concern that the goods of the

1964

world, even in their most innocent form, can distract the conscience; the question Langland asks is how can the Christian
"in public life escape the taint of the World"? The amorality
of Mede reflects the economic amorality of the money economy
which Langland detested. Mede shows herself more than a match
for scientia (which is a donum Dei), and her followers show
her pervasiveness. Yet Langland is more interested in the
influence of venality on the lower levels of society than in
the more conventional attack on papal venality and sacerdotal
simony. Langland's success with the theme is largely due to
his secularization of the concept and his ability to natural-
ize his abstractions.

1964

1   COGHILL, NEVILL. Langland: Piers Plowman. Bibliographical
     Series of Supplements to "British Book News" on Writers and
     Their Work, no. 174. London: Longmans Green & Co., for the
     British Council and the National Book League, 48 pp.
          Accepts for the date of the A-text a time after January
     1362 (on the basis of A V 14); 1377 for the B-text (on the
     basis of an allusion to the coronation of Richard II in B Prol
     112-209); and before 1388 for the C-text (on the basis of
     Usk's quotation from the C-text, as demonstrated by Devlin,
     1928.5). Also accepts the connection of the poet with the
     Rokayle family, the poet's unbeneficed clerical status, and
     Bright's location of Longland in Colwell (1928.2).
          The Visio shows the world in need of salvation, the
     entire poem being a search for the true nature of love ex-
     plained in B Prol 25-27. The Pardon scene is to be explained
     by Jesus's jousting in Piers's armor: Truth has bought a
     pardon on Calvary, which is available to all who pay their
     debt of confession and whatever else they owe to the Church;
     "that done, they would be doing well, however many times a day
     they, like the just man, had fallen."
          Chaucer is interested in the personality, Langland in
     the soul; Chaucer features romantic love, Langland the love of
     God. Both authors are ironists, though Chaucer's irony is
     urbane and Langland's is better described as "blazing like the
     Hebrew prophet's." Piers in the B- and C-texts is the image
     of man in God's image and God in man's image, a vision that
     Bunyan, otherwise similar to Langland, does not offer. Our
     own age recognizes the need for an image of man "raised to the
     power of Christ" in a way that earlier times did not.

1964

2   COLLEDGE, E., and EVANS, W.O. "Piers Plowman." Month, n.s. 32,
     no. 12 (December):304-13.
          The poem in its perplexing and enigmatic qualities is
     seen as unique among medieval English religious works. It is
     probably the work of one author, who might well have composed
     a "D-text," had there been time. Piers Plowman is neither a
     mystical theological treatise nor a key to the Scriptures, but
     instead a poetic account of the intellectual struggles of one
     concerned with the question of salvation. The poem is seen as
     manifesting the expanding horizons of Christian charity during
     the medieval period and emphasizing the brotherhood of man.
     Searching for Dobest comes to equal searching for Christ,
     tantamount to the sacrament of baptism that Langland felt
     could be received in spirit by those denied active knowledge
     of Christ. The descriptions of the Crucifixion and the
     Harrowing of Hell stress God's mercy, available to all men,
     rather than His justice.

3   d'ARDENNE, S.T.R.O. "'Me bi-fel a ferly, A Feyrie me Þouhte'
     (PPL.A.Prol.6)." In English Studies Presented to R.W.
     Zandvoort on the Occasion of His Seventieth Birthday [a
     supplement to English Studies 45]. Amsterdam: Swets &
     Zeitlinger, pp. 143-45.
          Readings of the better A-text MSS indicate that
     Langland wrote not A Feyrie, but of fairie. The line is to
     be translated, then, not "a marvel befell me, a magic thing
     it seemed to me," but "a marvel befell me, from Faërie it
     seemed to me."

*4   DAVLIN, Sister Mary Clemente. "Treuthe in Piers Plowman: A
     Study in Style and Sensibility." Dissertation, California,
     Berkeley, 298 pp.
          Abstracted: DA 25:1905.

5   HOFFMAN, RICHARD L. "The Burning of 'Boke' in Piers Plowman."
     MLQ 25, no. 1 (March):57-65.
          In contrast to Kaske (1959.9), translates B XVIII 252-57
     as "And I, Book, will be burned unless Jesus rise to live/ In
     all mights of man, and (to) gladden His mother,/ And (to)
     comfort all His kin and (to) bring them out of care,/ And (to)
     unjoin and (to) unlock all the Jews' joy;/ And unless they
     (the Jews) reverence His Rood and His Resurrection,/ And
     believe on a New Law, (I, Book, will) be lost life and soul."
     Sees "Book" as suggestive of the New Testament in its entirety,
     in both letter and spirit. Sees the testimony of Book pre-
     sented here in chronological order, with B XVIII providing the
     context for Book's speech in fulfilling the conditions alluded
     to in lines 252-55. Denies any Joachistic interpretation, and

sees in the last lines quoted the traditional orthodox belief in the ultimate conversion of the Jews by Enoch and Elias. Cf. the different interpretation of Donaldson, 1966.1.

6   JEREMY, Sister Mary. "'Leggis A-lery,' Piers Plowman A VII, 114." ELN 1, no. 4 (June):250-51.
        Suggests aliri survives in a children's ball game popular in England and America.

7   JOCHUMS, MILFORD C. "The Legend of the Voice from Heaven." N&Q, c.s. 209 (n.s. 11), no. 2 (February):44-47.
        Adds to Skeat's notes (1886.1) on the Voice from Heaven (C XVIII 220-28).

8   KEAN, P.M. "Love, Law, and Lewte in Piers Plowman." RES, n.s. 15, no. 59 (August):241-61.
        B Prol and I associate the Law with love and mercy, and compare divine and earthly law through leadership of the king, all of which topics are part of accepted and traditional legal and political theory of the Middle Ages. Mede, "the reward of a life directed to the wrong end," is opposed by the just use of temporal goods and the idea of true reward; lewte, considered as virtue and Aristotelian justice, controls the administration of justice and is paired with love in opposition to Mede. The Pardon scene turns the attention of the poem from strictly political concerns in suggesting that even when the state is properly constituted, the individual must choose how he will live. Reprinted: Blanch, 1969.4. Kean, 1969.19, is a continuation of this essay.

9   KIRK, ELIZABETH DOAN. "The Method of Piers Plowman: A Critical Study of the A-Text." Dissertation, Yale.
        Source: Comprehensive Dissertation Index 1861-1972, vol. 30, p. 244

10 LONGO, JOSEPH. "Piers Plowman and the Tropological Matrix: Passus XI and XII." Anglia 82:291-308.
        Sees B XI and XII as complementary sections which together serve as a spiritual and intellectual climax in which Scripture and Imaginatif refute the various objections raised by Will in his denunciation of Christian principles at the end of B X. Scripture attacks the root of Will's problem by castigating his lack of self-knowledge. The resulting dream of the Land of Longing teaches Will humility and a sense of the inadequacies of trusting to fortune. Trajan illustrates the necessity of love in the process of salvation. Kynde reveals a true image of the world, in order to correct that of fortune. Reason shows Will that God controls evil, the

1964

purpose of which is to test man. Imaginatif, the specific
duty of which is to reproduce in the mind an image of God,
shows Will that grace is a divine gift, that God's love is
dynamic in the world, that action in life determines position
in heaven, that predestination is not an active, potent force,
and that virtuous pagans can be saved.

11 SAITO, ISAMU. "Piers' Destruction of the Pardon--A Critical
Comparison of the B and C-Text of Piers the Plowman--."
Doshisha Literature 23 (May):1-7.
    Accepts the validity of the Pardon, and sees Piers's
destruction of it as his acceptance of Dowel (see Frank,
1957.4). Sees the omission of the Tearing of the Pardon in
the C-text as prompted by a desire for logical clarity, since
the latest version of the poem explicitly argues the priority
of Dowel over indulgences (C X 323 ff.). But the Tearing of
the Pardon in the B-text is psychologically consistent with
the state of vexation and irritation in which Piers finds
himself once the folk lapse into idleness as soon as Hunger
falls asleep (B VI 186 ff.). In the Pardon scene, the irony
of the Priest's quoting Psalm 13 is unwittingly to identify
him as one of the corrupt who do abominable works.

12 SPEARING, A.C. "The Art of Preaching and Piers Plowman." In
Criticism and Medieval Poetry. New York: Barnes & Noble,
pp. 68-95.
    Recasts and elaborates upon Spearing, 1963.13. Sees the
problem of the poem's organization (dispositio) to some extent
answered by the poem's affinities to the methods of the ars
prædicandi, as described, for example, by Thomas Waleys's De
modo componendi sermones and Robert de Basevorn's Forma
prædicandi. The poem as a whole resembles a sermon in its
return in its conclusion to the point at which it began (the
life of the "felde ful of folke") now seen in a significantly
different fashion, in its numerous examples of homiletic discourse, and in its threefold divisio (in a fashion similar to
that of the "university sermon") of the Three Lives, whose
main topic or theme is drawn from Matthew 19:16, "What good
thing shall I do, that I may have eternal life?"
    Sees a sermonlike "circling or spiralling" development
of the theme of punishment and penance in C VI and a use of
digression, as in C XXI, that is reminiscent of sermon techniques in its effort to clarify and edify the matter at hand.
The use of verbal repetition in the poem to emphasize and
clarify ideas also parallels employment of the device in
sermons. Reprinted: Newstead, 1968.10; Spearing, 1972.21.

13 TILLYARD, E.M.W. <u>The English Epic and Its Background</u>. New York:
    Barnes & Noble.
        Reprint of Tillyard, 1954.7.

                                    1965

*1 ANDERSON, JUDITH H. "Aspects of Allegory in <u>Piers Plowman</u> and
    the <u>Faerie Queene</u>." Dissertation, Yale, 240 pp.
        Abstracted: <u>DA</u> 26:4622. See Anderson, 1976.2.

2   BURROW, JOHN. "The Action of Langland's Second Vision." <u>Essays
    in Criticism</u> 15, no. 3 (July):247-68.
        The plot of the second vision is composed of a sermon,
    confession, pilgrimage, and pardon, and thus offers the co-
    herence of the penitential process, here adapted to the con-
    version of the community to the rule of Reason. Langland's
    distrust of the efficacy of pilgrimages is reflected in his
    substitution of St. Truth for St. James and the saints of
    Rome (B V 57-58). His later substitution of a "pilgrimage at
    the plough" of the Half-acre scene for the pilgrimage to
    Truth implies that the life of the Half-acre is to be identi-
    fied with that of truth, and for this reason it is unsurpris-
    ing that the Pardon is offered. Agrees with Frank (1951.4)
    that in Tearing the Pardon, Piers rejects paper pardons from
    Rome, not this (valid) Pardon itself. Considers this a con-
    fusing scene, for unlike the substitution of one pilgrimage
    for another, Langland here found no objective correlative for
    what was to be substituted in place of such invalid pardons.
    Reprinted: Blanch, 1969.4.

*3 CARRUTHERS, MARY JEAN. "The Mind of Will: A Preface to <u>Piers
    Plowman</u>." Dissertation, Yale, 260 pp.
        Abstracted: <u>DA</u> 26:4625. See Carruthers, 1973.2.

4   CAZAMIAN, LOUIS. <u>The Development of English Humour Parts I and
    II</u>. New York: AMS Press, Inc.
        See Cazamian, 1930.3.

*5 DiPASQUALE, PASQUALE, Jr. "The Form of <u>Piers Plowman</u> and the
    Liturgy." Dissertation, Pittsburgh, 217 pp.
        Abstracted: <u>DA</u> 26:4626.

6   FERGUSON, ARTHUR B. <u>The Articulate Citizen and the English
    Renaissance</u>. Durham, N.C.: Duke University Press, pp. 42-69.
        Gower and Langland are compared as representative of
    medieval social critics and political thinkers. Neither poet
    goes beyond registering popular complaint in the hope that the

                                    245

1965

king and his advisers will adopt needed regulatory measures;
neither proceeds far beyond an analysis of the individual's
moral responsibility in a society of hierarchical status.
Neither explores the relationship of church and state seriously; both see the cause of agrarian unrest as the failure
of all concerned to discharge appropriate duties and, although
Langland is more sympathetic to the plight of the poor, both
see commercial values as essentially moral values. Both poets
share the traditional criticism of the legal profession for
its venality, though Gower goes beyond Langland in recognizing
a connection between private discontent and public disorder.
Government to both is essentially a protective agency, ensuring stability and order if its leaders are virtuous, rather
than a creative agency designed for constructive policy making.

7   FULLER, THOMAS. The History of the Worthies of England. Edited
    by P. Austin Nuttall. Reprint. New York: AMS Press Inc.
        See Fuller, 1662.1.

8   GORDON, JOHN D. "An Anniversary Exhibition: The Henry W. and
    Albert A. Berg Collection 1940-65 (Part I)." Bulletin of the
    New York Public Library 69, no. 8 (October):537-54, esp.
    p. 539.
        Describes a copy in the collection of [Langland], 1550.1,
    printed on vellum, "one of four known copies thus." See Anon.,
    1922.1.

*9 HIGGS, ELTON DALE. "The Dream as a Literary Framework in the
    Works of Chaucer, Langland and the Pearl Poet." Dissertation,
    Pittsburgh, 182 pp.
        Abstracted: DA 27:1030A.

10 HUSSEY, S.S. "Langland's Reading of Alliterative Poetry." MLR
    60, no. 2 (April):163-70.
        Of the various alliterative poems written before Piers
    Plowman, sees the possible influence of only Wynnere and
    Wastoure, Parlement of the Thre Ages, Somer Soneday, and
    William of Palerne, with the strongest case to be made for
    Wynnere and Wastoure, in the arguments of Wastoure (lines
    246 ff.; 295 ff.), similar to those of Mede, regarding the
    virtues of large expenditure, and the notion in both poems
    that the diet of the poor keeps them in their place. De-
    scribes Langland's genius, however, in four stylistic features
    uncharacteristic of alliterative poetry: couplets that
    graphically represent the lessons of the preceding lines,
    contrast between the ideal and its opposite, interest in ex-
    plaining a difficult concept in familiar terms, and sudden
    lyrical outbursts.

11 JUSSERAND, J.J. Piers Plowman: A Contribution to the History of
      English Mysticism. Translated by M[arion and] E[lise]
      R[ichards]. New York: Russell & Russell.
         See Jusserand, 1894.6.

12 KANE, GEORGE. The Autobiographical Fallacy in Chaucer and
      Langland Studies. The Chambers Memorial Lecture Delivered at
      University College, London, 2 March 1965. London: H.K.
      Lewis, 20 pp.
         All "biographies" of Langland are constructed through
      the process of free biographical inference and are thus essen-
      tially "imaginative, affective, subjective, pure speculation."
      Bright (1928.5) is the worst offender in this regard. The
      medieval practice of recitation by an author in public induces
      the writer to identify himself with his narrator, and dream
      visions in particular are authenticated by the identification
      of dreamer and poet; yet poet and dreamer are distinct enti-
      ties that are not meant to be fully identified by the audience.
      Reviewed by Anon., TLS, 20 January 1966, p. 49; S.T. Knight,
      Medium Ævum 36 (1967):282-85; and Barbara Raw, N&Q, n.s. 13
      (1966):194.

13 KANE, GEORGE. Piers Plowman: The Evidence for Authorship.
      [London]: University of London, Athlone Press, 72 pp.
         The differences among the versions in language, dialect,
      versification, sentence structure, and even figures of speech
      cannot be used as evidence in support of single or multiple
      authorship because such differences are not determinable given
      the textual situation of the poem. The breadth of moral, so-
      cial, and theological topics introduced in the poem is not
      such as to constitute radical inconsistencies and oppositions
      among versions; and claims based on such supposed differences
      in thought do not adequately deal with challenges made on the
      basis of the intellectual development of a single poet. Spe-
      cifically literary differences fail to recognize different
      aims and intentions of a single poet. The supposed evidence
      of the B-poet's incomprehension of the A-text rests on the
      unproved assumption that the texts cannot be better explained
      as a result of revision or change of intention by a single
      author, as well as on the dubious assumption that authors
      always achieve through revision the complete eradication of
      all errors, discrepancies, and inconsistencies. The notion of
      "antecedent probability," invoked by Moore (1913.3), has been
      grossly overstated and, moreover, may be said to deny the
      recognizable, distinctive style of the author.
         The ascription of MS. V (C-text) is most probably
      authoritative, written within living memory of the poet by a
      person knowledgeable regarding the South Wales area. Contrary

1965

to earlier denials, there is evidence of the name Langlands in
Shropshire. And what is most probably the poet's baptismal
name receives contemporary support in the testimony of John
But, who was capable of knowing the truth, as well as in the
explicit of MS. Ch (A-C-text), dated c. 1425. The ascriptions
of Willielmi .W. in five C-text MSS all go back to one reading, probably a scribal error. Ascriptions of Robert are in
extant form from only the sixteenth century and testify to a
concerted search to discover the name of the author. Skeat's
contention regarding the origin of Robert is further substantiated by the reading of the first line of the Vita in MS. M
(A-text), formerly Bright's MS. Sixteenth-century antiquaries
may have chosen Robert over Will because they sensed a distinction between the Dreamer and the author. The designation
in the MSS ascriptions Piers Plowman is always applied to the
whole poem, not merely to the Visio. A convention in the
fourteenth century is that of the poet signing a dream poem
and giving to the dreamer his own name. In all three versions
of Piers Plowman, the passages revealing Will's name reflect a
plan of disclosing his identity. B XV 148 offers a nickname
and, if read as a cryptogram and supported by the ascription
of MS. V (C-text), is distinguished by its failure to "mesh"
in context; its main function may thus perhaps be to identify
the author. Concludes that neither external nor internal evidence contains any reason for believing in the multiple authorship of the poem.
    Reviewed by Anon., TLS, 12 August 1965, p. 698; Guy
Bourquin, EA 19 (1966):439-40; Donald F. Chapin, Humanities
Association Bulletin 17 (1966):71-72; David C. Fowler, ELN 3
(1966-67):295-300; R.E. Kaske, JEGP 65 (1966):583-86; P.M.
Kean, RES, n.s. 17 (1966):439-40; John Lawlor, MLR 61 (1966):
268-69; Barbara C. Raw, N&Q, n.s. 12 (1965):470-71; T.A.
Stroud, MP 65 (1967-68):366-67; P.J. Verhoeff, Neophilologus
51 (1967):312-13; and R.M. Wilson, English 16 (1967):17-18.

14 KEAN, P.M. "Langland and the Incarnation." RES, n.s. 16, no. 64
    (November):349-63.
        The traditional basis of the imagery of the Church's
    definition of Truth or Love (B I 146-56) is explored. The
    image of the triacle as an antidote against spiritual poison
    is shown to be fairly common in the Middle Ages (exemplified
    in Lydgate's works); and the conventionality of the image
    argues for reading spise of I 147 to mean "spice," rather than
    "species." The imagery of the medical ointment depends on
    Exodus 30:22-25 (Moses' unction), Song of Songs 1:2, and the
    ointments of the Gospels. It is appropriate that Moses is
    introduced in this context, for the secret of the "oil of holy
    ointment" was first entrusted to him. The variant reading

plente, "plentitude" (line 150), accords well with the variant
ʒoten of line 152 on the basis of Canticles 1:2 and Phil-
lipians 2:7, which are brought together by Origen in his
Commentary on the Song of Songs and carried over by Bernard in
his Sermons on the Song of Songs. It appears, however, that
the variant represents the poet's own exploration of traditional possibilities of the material. The plante of peace
image is partly classical in origin (Ovid, Metamorphoses XIV,
291-92) and partly Biblical (the notion of Incarnation as a
flower of the Root of Jesse). The images of heaviness and
weight recall the Aristotelian notion of pondus, linked by
Augustine to the idea of will; implicit in the passage is the
idea of balance, ultimately stemming from Job 6:2-3. The comparison of love to a piercing needle is drawn from Wisdom
7:22 ff., and perhaps Hebrews 4:12.

*15 LATTIN, LINDA L. "Medieval Number Symbolism in Langland's Piers
Plowman." M.A. thesis, Kansas State Teachers College.
        Source: Patsy C. Howard, Theses in English Literature
1894-1970 (Ann Arbor, Mich.: Perian Press, 1973), p. 167.
See Lattin, 1965.16.

16 LATTIN, LINDA. "Some Aspects of Medieval Number Symbolism in
Langland's Piers Plowman, A-Text." Emporia State Research
Studies 14 (September):5-13.
        Considers the poem in light of accepted and conventional
medieval number symbolism. Finds the "subjects" of the twelve
passūs are revealed by their number in order: I: God; II:
the diversity of matter and spirit (Mede and Falsehood versus
Truth); III: the Trinity; IV: the physical world and the
spiritual state of creation by the Trinity (the justice that
would result from the marriage of Conscience and Mede); V:
incompletion and imperfection (the sins of mankind); and so
on. The poem can be said to be divided into two parts concerned with physical acts and the spiritual life; and the
Three Lives draw on the notion of three as symbolic of completion and the Trinity.

17 MAUNSELL, ANDREW. The First Part of the Catalogue of English
printed Bookes: Which concerneth such matters of Diuinitie,
as have bin either written in our owne Tongue, or translated
out of anie other language. London: Iohn Vvindet for Andrew
Maunsell. Reprint. London: Gregg Press.
        See Maunsell, 1595.1.

*18 MROCZKOWSKI, PRZEMSLAW. "Piers Plowman: The Allegory in Motion."
Prace historycznoliterackie 8:7-45.
        Source: Colaianne, 1978.4, p. 119, no. 478. See
Mroczkowski, 1966.11.

1965

19 REIDY, JOHN. "Piers the Ploughman, Whiche a Pardoun He Hadde."
    <u>PMASAL</u> 50:535-44.
            Analyzes the Pardon scene of the A-text. In contrast to
    Coghill (1944.1) and Chambers (1939.3), accepts the validity
    of the Pardon; similarly, denies Dunning's de-emphasis of the
    importance of plowing the Half-acre (1937.3) on the basis of
    Hilton's <u>Epistle on the Mixed Life</u>, which supports "bodily
    works." Criticizes Frank's interpretation of the Pardon scene
    (1957.4), in noting that Piers, the Priest, and the poet all
    agree that indulgences are not better than a good life. Can-
    not fully explain the Tearing of the Pardon, but sees Piers's
    new resolution as completing the active life in conformity
    with the <u>Cloud of Unknowing</u> and Hilton's <u>Scale of Perfection</u>:
    the <u>Cloud of Unknowing</u> equates the higher active life and the
    lower contemplative life in bodily works of mercy, contrition,
    and penance; the <u>Scale of Perfection</u> combines fasting, watch-
    ing, and penance to control the flesh--just what Piers does
    after Tearing the Pardon--with the more familiar bodily works
    of the active life.

20 VASTA, EDWARD. <u>The Spiritual Basis of Piers Plowman</u>. London,
    The Hague, and Paris: Mouton & Co., 143 pp.
            Aims to define the nature of salvation according to
    Langland, and sees the goal as that of the mystic quest for
    union in this life of the soul and God. The unity of the poem
    depends on the character of the Dreamer, who represents the
    individual soul. The subject of both parts of the poem is
    growth in the spiritual life, with falling asleep representing
    the reception of grace that makes growth possible. As in the
    writings of St. Bernard, conversion comes about through self-
    knowledge--what the Dreamer experiences in the first two
    passūs. Self-confrontation begins in the episode of Lady
    Mede, for here Will sees that which concerns him personally.
    Langland describes the way to perfection, rather than to
    "simple salvation": the poem is not concerned with the
    ordinary state of grace achieved through common means, but
    instead the state of spiritual sanctity achieved through dif-
    ficult means that merit higher degrees of grace. Will is of
    superior moral sensibility, although his questions to
    Holicherch indicate that he has never experienced the truth
    she speaks of, a <u>kynde knowyng</u> or knowledge known immediately
    rather than mediately. Will is "contemplative man" who is
    imperfect but still has the capacity for perfection. Holi-
    cherch offers guiding ideas, many of which Langland presumes
    knowledge of on the part of his audience.
            In the poem, salvation is seen in terms of truth and its
    concomitant psychological change in the Dreamer's makeup, and
    in terms of love and the virtues by which the soul is saved.

1965

Truth is moreover viewed as a conformity of man's will with
God's and is synonymous with rectitude, righteousness, and
justice; it is interchangeable with love, the act, rather than
the fact of such conformance. The background of this concept
lies in the mystics' notion of deification, as expressed in
Bernard's De diligendo deo. The possibility of man becoming
like God is based on the doctrine of the Creation and the
Redemption, whereby the divine image, obscured by the Fall,
can be restored to man by Christ. The mystics placed the
divine image in man's free will; the episode of Lady Mede
allegorically dramatizes the soul's rejection of self-will and
the re-establishment of free will, as well as the progression
of the soul from a state of unlikeness with God to a quest to
re-establish divine similitude. By the end of Dowel, self-
love is overthrown and Liberum Arbitrium is defined (C XVII
69-72) as the point of contact between the soul and God.
Progress toward likeness with God requires charity; to know
love kyndely is a process that presumes a mutual response of
the soul's love for God and God's love for the soul. Union
with God is complete when the Holy Spirit (love) is sent into
the soul "that has made a free response to God's love." This
is the act of contemplation according to the mystics, achieved
through the practice of humility and active charity. The Deus
Caritas text (I John 4), of great importance to the mystics,
recapitulates the themes of truth as a conformity of wills,
deification, growth in truth through growth in love, and the
kynde knowyng of God in one's heart. Piers's Highway to
Truth is more detailed than Holicherch's directions, with
respect to the particular moral steps toward perfection, as
seen in light of the medieval division of the Beatitudes (1-3,
4-5, 6-7, 8).
     Finds the key to the poem in medieval works that de-
velop the psychology of the mystics' ways, for example,
Bernard's On Conversion and Steps of Humility and Pride. The
Visio and the Vita are two successive parts of the same poem
in all three versions: the scheme of salvation is not fulfilled until perfection is reached. The experience sought by
Will is achieved in the Vision of Christ; the Debate of the
Four Daughters of God allegorizes the change in Will's spiritual condition as a result of meditation on the Passion. The
appearance of Piers like Christ is best to be understood in
light of Bernard's interpretation of the Bride of Christ in
his sermons on the Song of Songs, as symbol of both the individual soul and the Mystical Body.
     Reviewed by Guy Bourquin, EA 19 (1966):440-41; Morton W.
Bloomf:eld, Speculum 42 (1967):205-9; and P.M. Kean, RES,
n.s. 18 (1967):188-90.

1965

21 VASTA, EDWARD. "Truth, the Best Treasure, in Piers Plowman."
    PQ 44, no. 1 (January):17-29.
        Contrary to Hort ([1938].5), truth as it applies to man
    is not innate knowledge placed in the soul, but a spiritual
    state in which all the faculties are governed by a will put
    into conformity with that of God. In this state, the indi-
    vidual achieves the unitive life, and his soul is made recep-
    tive to the grace of contemplation. Suggests the poem should
    be studied more closely in regard to the Bernardine theology
    of perfection and doctrine of deification.

22 WALKER, MARSHALL. "Piers Plowman's Pardon: A Note." English
    Studies in Africa 8 (March):64-70.
        Criticizes as "sociological" the view of Lawlor (1962.4)
    and others that the Tearing of the Pardon is intended as a re-
    jection of the active life in favor of the contemplative.
    Piers moves from animale to spirituale in the poem, but with-
    out canceling all that has gone before. The Pardon is condi-
    tional, in that it makes eternal felicity dependent on con-
    tinuing to do good. The Priest, however, apparently expects
    no such conditions. In Tearing the Pardon, Piers thus offers
    a comment on the relative values of papal pardons and good
    works. He rejects the "outward show" in favor of the "inner
    experience." The Priest's response serves as the stimulus for
    Piers to go beyond the minimal requirements of a life of
    honest labor.

23 WILKES, GERALD L. "The Castle of Vnite in Piers Plowman." MS
    27:334-36.
        Suggests Ancrene Riwle (edited by Mabel Day, Early
    English Text Society, o.s. 225 [London: Oxford University
    Press, 1946], pp. 109-10) as the source of Langland's Castle
    of Unity. Notes that the surrounding context in both poems is
    identical in describing resistance to the Devil founded on the
    unity of true belief.

1966

1 DONALDSON, E. TALBOT. "The Grammar of Book's Speech in Piers
   Plowman." In Studies in Language and Literature in Honour of
   Margaret Schlauch. Edited by Mieczyslaw Brahmer, Stanislaw
   Helsztyński, and Julian Krzyżanowski. Warsaw: Państwowe
   Wydawnictwo Naukowe [Polish Scientific Publishers], pp. 103-9.
       Replies to Kaske (1959.9) and Hoffman (1964.5), dealing
   with B XVIII 252-57. In line 252, but is a subordinating con-
   junction governing the subjunctive ("unless Jesus rise"); to
   lyue in line 252 is a prepositional phrase with a "petrified"

inflection of the noun ("to life"); gladye, conforte, and
brynge in lines 253-54 are examples of the Middle English use
of the infinitive to express "either a future action strongly
hypothesized by the speaker or a present action strongly
visualized by him" with the effect of inevitability.

2 DONALDSON, E. TALBOT. Piers Plowman: The C-Text and Its Poet.
   With a new preface by the author. [Hamden, Conn.]: Archon
   Books; London: Cass, xiv + 255 pp.
           See Donaldson, 1949.1.

3 ERDMAN, DAVID V., and FOGEL, EPHIM, eds. Evidence for Author-
   ship: Essays on Problems of Attribution with an Annotated
   Bibliography of Selected Readings. Ithaca, N.Y.: Cornell
   University Press.
           Contains (pp. 415-19) a discussion and summary of Kane,
   1965.13, added by the editors to Farris, 1966.4. See also
   Chambers, 1919.2.

4 FARRIS, SUMNER J. "Piers Plowman." In Evidence for Authorship:
   Essays on Problems of Attribution with an Annotated Bibliography of Selected Readings. Edited by David V. Erdman and
   Ephim G. Fogel. Ithaca, N.Y.: Cornell University Press,
   pp. 408-15.
           Reviews scholarship on the authorship question, concen-
   trating on the progress of the argument since the time of
   Manly (1906.3). Considers Manly's various points to have been
   answered over the years; in particular, values the contribution of Chambers (1948.4). Sees Fowler (1952.1) as having
   "inaugurated the only real controversy about the authorship
   of PP in recent years," but declares in light of Donaldson
   (1953.1), and Mitchell and Russell (1953.5), that "Fowler's
   case must be considered disproved." Concludes that the recent
   advocates of single authorship have been "more numerous, more
   convincing, and more resourceful" than the advocates of multiple authorship. Sees the possibility of a contribution to
   the question to be made through the field of stylstatistics,
   but agrees with Donaldson that the issue must finally be de-
   cided through literary judgment, "and to date most of the best
   literary judges of PP have thought all three versions to be by
   the same author." See Erdman and Fogel, 1966.3.

*5 GALLEMORE, MELVIN ALVIN. "The Sermons of Bishop Thomas Brinton
    and the B-text of Piers Plowman." Dissertation, Washington,
    254 pp.
            Abstracted: DA 27:3008A.

1966

6   GOODRIDGE, J.F., trans. Introduction to Piers the Ploughman.
       Rev. ed. Harmondsworth, Middlesex: Penguin Books; Baltimore:
       Penguin Books, pp. 9-22.
            Accepts as dates of composition of the three texts
       c. 1370, 1377-79, and post 1390. Sees the theme of the poem,
       in common with that of the Divina Commedia and Paradise Lost,
       as "the meaning of man's life on earth in relation to his
       ultimate destiny"; yet unlike those epics, Langland's poem
       both begins and ends in the world as the author knows it, and
       Langland's visions are consistently translated into an im-
       mediate application to practical reality. Unlike Blake or
       Milton, Langland was a master of comic effects, and one effect
       of his self-mockery is to associate the Dreamer and the
       audience with the action, "so that we are directly involved,
       and made to feel the difference between knowledge and full
       participation, which is one of the poem's main themes." His
       imagination is visual and dramatic; his allegories do not
       depend on any fixed scheme of symbolic reference. The various
       allegorical characters Will encounters reflect his own limita-
       tions; Piers himself represents "the human ideal which is the
       ultimate object of the search." The irregularity of the
       poem's construction may account for its appeal to modern
       readers, for instead of offering a "finished picture of the
       Christian view of life," it reflects doubts, uncertainties,
       and an organic process of thought. But Langland's art is
       functional in that his language is always directed to a
       didactic or religious purpose.

7   HOLLERAN, J.V. "The Role of the Dreamer in Piers Plowman." AM
       7:33-50.
            Sees the Dreamer as a center of consciousness in the
       poem for Langland's audience. The narrative structure of the
       poem is simple and is composed of three quests: I-VII repre-
       sents the search of a young idealist for truth; VIII-XI por-
       trays his disillusionment with the hope of ever finding it;
       and XII-XX presents a return to the quest toward the end of
       his life. The first two divisions are progressive steps in
       the Dreamer's spiritual awareness and move from political to
       ecclesiastical concerns. The Dreamer is for the most part an
       observer in Part One but becomes an actor in Part Two. From
       VIII-IX 83 the Dreamer moves in the wrong direction of seeking
       truth through intellectual abstractions. The appearance of
       Fortune is a turning point, for when the Dreamer abandons in-
       tellectual abstractions in favor of action, he rejects those
       qualities that would aid him in his search for salvation.
       During Part III the Dreamer becomes again an observer, for the
       progress of the poem is to show him discovering the way to
       salvation, only to realize he must act on that discovery. Of

the eight dreams in this section of the poem, the Dreamer is
an actor in four, an observer in four. The dramatic movement
of Part III is organized around the Dreamer's setbacks due to
his impetuosity; he is finally led to realize that his redemption lies in Christ's activity and that the search for truth
is a lifelong task.

8   HOWARD, DONALD R.   "The Body Politic and the Lust of the Eyes:
    Piers Plowman."   In The Three Temptations: Medieval Man in
    Search of the World.   Princeton, N.J.: Princeton University
    Press, pp. 161-214.
         The poem is concerned with what man does, and should do,
    in the world, where the needs of the temporal body must be
    provided for, but where the world, the flesh, and the devil
    tempt man to misuse his earthly goods. Examines the A- and
    B-texts (ignoring the changes the B-poet makes of lines in the
    A-text), and determines that the critical turning points in
    the A-text involve the king's determination to dwell with
    Reason and the Pardon scene. The episode involving the king
    presents the ideal course of action; the rest of the poem
    explains the reasons why this ideal is not followed. The
    Pardon scene contrasts the idealism of Piers with the practi-
    cality of the Priest, in pointing out the insufficiencies of
    the "perfect" Pardon to make things work in the world. The
    search for Dowel takes up the question of our relation to a
    world which "by its very nature prohibits perfection." The
    scene involving Haukyn and the end of the poem show temper-
    ance, along with love and mercy, as the ideal solution to the
    problem of temporal goods; both scenes likewise suggest such
    a solution will prove impossible. The Dreamer's waking
    moments dramatize the movement from unconsciousness to con-
    sciousness of dream-experience, bringing into focus the
    "diffuse, chaotic content that precedes them." The poem is
    unlike Chaucer's Troilus and Criseyde in that in Piers
    Plowman, the evanescence of the world is experienced within
    the work.

9   LOWELL, JAMES RUSSELL. My Study Windows. Boston: J.R. Osgood
    & Co. Reprint. New York: AMS Press.
         See Lowell, 1871.2.

10 MOULTON, CHARLES WELLS. Moulton's Library of Literary Criticism
    of English and American Authors through the Beginning of the
    Twentieth Century. Abr., rev., and with additions by Martin
    Tucker. Vol. 1, The Beginnings to the Seventeenth Century.
    New York: Frederick Ungar Publishing Co., pp. 20-24.
         Quotations from [Langland], 1550.1; Webbe, 1586.1;
    [Percy], 1765.1; Warton, 1774.2; Campbell, 1819.2; [Langland],
    1842.3; Langland, 1867.3; and Scudder, 1898.4.

1966

11 MROCZKOWSKI, PRZEMYSLAW. "Piers and His Pardon: A Dynamic
    Analysis." In Studies in Language and Literature in Honour
    of Margaret Schlauch. Edited by Mieczyslaw Brahmer, Stanislaw
    Helsztyński, and Julian Krzyźanowski. Warsaw: Państwowe
    Wydawnictwo Naukowe [Polish Scientific Publishers], pp. 273-92.
        A commentary on B VI-VII, forming a continuation of
    Mroczkowski, 1965.18, which sees Will's Testament as defining
    the Mystical Body of Christ; the Half-acre scene as insisting
    that salvation depends on the performance of one's duty; and
    the episode of Hunger as revelatory of a sternness of the
    poet's temperament difficult to reconcile with his sense of
    charity. With regard to the problem of the just and sturdy
    beggars, "the poem shows the conflict between the traditional
    teaching of the Church and the principles of a capitalist
    economy; the author shows himself between a point of view that
    would rigorously chastize cheating beggars in order to channel
    their wasted labor for useful purposes, and the feeling that
    such a solution cannot be perfectly applied." The conflict
    of Piers with the Priest of the Pardon scene is one of medie-
    val humanism with the traditional contemptus mundi. Much of
    Piers's address appears improvised; and Piers's readiness for
    penitence dramatizes the conflict of the poet caught between
    a program for the material and spiritual development of hu-
    manity and a fear "of the slightest disparagement of the union
    with God."

*12 ORSTEN, ELISABETH MARIA. "The Treatment of Caritas, Iustitia,
    and Related Theological Themes in the B Text of Piers
    Plowman." Dissertation, Toronto.
            Abstracted: DA 28:2218A-19A.

13 PREVITÉ-ORTON, C.W. Political Satire in English Poetry. Being
    the Members' Prize Essay for 1908. New York: Haskell House.
            See Previté-Orton, 1910.11.

14 RISSE, ROBERT G., Jr. "The Augustinian Paraphrase of Isaiah
    14.13-14 in Piers Plowman and the Commentary on the Fables of
    Avianus." PQ 45, no. 4 (October):712-17.
        Suggests that the commentary on the Fables of Avianus
    (specifically, Fables II and IV) is as probable a source of
    Langland's paraphrase of Isaiah 14:13-14 in B I 116 and C II
    117 as is Augustine's Ennarrationes, suggested by Kellogg
    (1958.5). The absence of any scribal variant pedem for sedem
    in MSS of the commentary is seen as added proof that
    Langland's substitution is original.

1966

*15 ROUSCH, GEORGE JONATHAN. "The Political Plowman: The Expression
of Political Ideals in Piers Plowman and Its Successors."
Dissertation, California, Berkeley, 216 pp.
Abstracted: DA 27:752A.

16 RUSSELL, G.H. "The Salvation of the Heathen: The Exploration
of a Theme in Piers Plowman." Journal of the Warburg and
Courtauld Institutes 29:101-16.
Explains the absence in Langland's account of the necessity of sacramental baptism by the author's adopting the radical (and censured) opinion of Uhtred de Boldon, that every
human being at the moment before death enjoys a clara visio
of God, and must choose or reject Him then, with baptism
apparently irrelevant. Accepts for C XVIII 124 the reading
In the lettynge [rather than lengthynge] of hir lyf, as the
original.

17 SAITO, ISAMU. A Study of Piers the Plowman with Special Reference to the Pardon Scene of the Visio. Tokyo: Nan'undo,
262 pp.
B V-VI are based on the medieval idea of penance. In
the first half of the second vision of the Visio, the notions
of contrition and penance are presented in Reasons's exposition of contemporary sins and the Dreamer's tears over them,
and then by the confession of the Deadly Sins themselves.
Will's tears are suggestive of the will of the people moved to
contrition. Piers is more than an agricultural laborer: he
is a spiritual guide, to be likened to the "laborer" of
Matthew 9:36-38 in its usual exegesis of the laborer as
savior. Piers's speech on Truth, stressing the Ten Commandments, is the "exhortation of doing charitable works before
attaining Truth." Salvation is possible, but requires a
struggle which is evidenced in good works of charity. The
idea is allegorically developed in VI, where eryen and sowen
in the Half-acre scene should be interpreted in light of its
exegesis as to realize and practice charity in earthly life.
(See in this regard Isaiah 2:4; Hosea 10:12-13; II Corinthians
9:6-8.)
The suspension of the pilgrimage in VII suggests that
the poet believes that man may gain his pardon at home through
honest work alone. The actual work required of all Christians
is described with regard to the duties of the nobility, clergy,
and commons in a repetition and development of the duties
enumerated in Prol-VI. The message of the Pardon is an echo
of Holicherch's sermon of I 126 ff. Piers's Pardon a culpa et
poena was not considered another aspect of punishment. The
cupidity of the Priest is exposed in his criticism of the
Pardon, for he cannot imagine a pardon freely given. Piers's

decision in Tearing the Pardon is not that he will give over
worldly concerns in favor of contemplation, but that he will
cease to work merely for bread.

The Three Lives do not have individual meanings, but
rather express the single teaching of Dowel. Similarly,
Piers's Biblical quotations--Psalm 22:4; 41:4; Matthew 6:25--
are not evidence of any emphasis on contemplation as much as
they are of doing well. Piers tears the Pardon not to reject
it but to accept it as a sign of his zeal and in a fashion
emotionally consistent with his mounting frustration in the
Half-acre scene. Contains appendices on the Prologue and
Passus I, Lady Mede and her character.

18 SCHOLES, ROBERT, and KELLOGG, ROBERT. The Nature of Narrative.
    New York: Oxford University Press, pp. 143-46.
        Langland is compared with Dante in representing the
    late medieval tendency to illustrate the truths of authority
    through the particular facts of experience. The allegory of
    the Divina Commedia infuses representational images with high
    seriousness, whereas Piers Plowman illustrates "an urgently
    apocalyptic theology" through the representation of social
    and political types. The satire of both poets is directed to
    the lack of conformity of the Cities of Man they see around
    them to the City of God.

19 SMITH, BEN H., Jr. Traditional Imagery of Charity in Piers
    Plowman. The Hague and Paris: Mouton & Co., 106 pp.
        Discusses four passages of the B-text relating to
    Charity--Holicherch's description of the virtue (I 146-62),
    Patience's riddle (XIII 135-56), the Tree of Charity (XVI),
    and the parable of the Good Samaritan (XVII)--in light of
    commentary on Scriptures, chiefly that of Hugh of St. Cher.
    Langland is found to invoke traditional associations of
    Scriptural imagery, though often to recast such associations;
    to transpose images directly from the exegetical tradition to
    the poem, when such an image is not found in Scripture; and to
    imbue an image not found explicitly in Scripture or commentary
    with exegetical overtones.
        Holy Church's description of charity is in two parts:
    lines 146-68 describe the abstract quality of the virtue
    through traditional images of the healing salve, the summation
    of all law, the source of peace, and the mediator between God
    and man; lines 173-201 assert the individual's obligation to
    lead the life of charity and is expressed through the tradi-
    tional interpretation of the parable of the Wise and Foolish
    Virgins.
        The progression of disce, doce, dilige in Patience's
    speech shows the traditional interrelationship of wisdom and

charity, as well as the traditional distencio charitatis of
love of self, to love of all mankind (including enemies), to
love of God. The cryptic XIII 150-51, glossed as "Latin half-
line containing reference to a lamp," is related to Psalm 4:7,
traditionally interpreted in the context of the Creation and
Redemption (see Smith, 1961.14). Kynde love is here to be
understood as charity characteristic of God, seeking self-
expression in the Incarnation.

The Tree of Charity reflects the traditional conflation
of various "trees": the Tree of Jesse, the lignum vitæ, the
tree of virtues, the tree of descent from Adam. The apparent
contradiction of meaning of the fruit of the Tree of Charity
is resolved in the traditional image of the three grades of
charity as "fruits" of charity and that of Old Testament figures as representatives of these three grades.

Langland's conception of the Good Samaritan is influenced by the traditional interpretation of the parable. The
priest is often construed as a type of patriarch, and Moses is
traditionally considered a priest--thus can be explained the
presence of Abraham and Moses in Langland's version, where
Abraham/Faith and Moses/Hope are both fulfilled in the New Law
of caritas.

20 SPENCE, JOSEPH. Observations, Anecdotes, and Characters of Books
and Men. Vol. 1. Edited by James M. Osborn. Oxford:
Clarendon Press.
See Pope, ante 1744.1.

*1 CALÍ, P. "Dante and Langland as Visionaries." M.A. thesis,
National University of Ireland.
Source: Index to Theses, vol. 17, p. 26. See Calí,
1971.6.

*2 HAMMOND, DONALD FREDERICK. "The Narrative Art of Piers Plowman."
Dissertation, Florida, 162 pp.
Abstracted: DA 29:870A-71A.

3 HEYWORTH, P.L. "Jack Upland's Rejoinder, a Lollard Interpolator
and Piers Plowman B.X. 249f." Medium Ævum 36:242-48.
A fifteenth-century interpolation in the holograph of
Jack Upland's Rejoinder in Bodley MS. Digby 41 enlarges upon
the general similarity of a section of the Rejoinder to B X
249 ff. by adding a development of Langland's remarks concerning the partial reading of Biblical texts. This is perhaps to
make a point against Friar Daw's Reply's misuses of

1967

authorities in defense of begging. Suggests close familiarity
with Piers Plowman by fifteenth-century readers.

4 HIEATT, CONSTANCE B. The Realism of Dream Visions: The Poetic
    Exploration of the Dream-Experience in Chaucer and His Con-
    temporaries. The Hague and Paris: Mouton, pp. 89-97.
        The dreamlike qualities of Piers Plowman perhaps include
    punning and ambiguity of diction, but may certainly be said to
    extend to loose syntax and an associative logical development.
    The Dreamer is concerned with the world; his dreams are
    psychologically motivated, with his confused, bemused state-
    of-being consistent with dream psychology. The poem is com-
    posed of a series of dreams, and it is often difficult to
    decide between waking and sleeping, for the waking sequences
    are often allegorical. The dream-within-the-dream of B XI
    5-396 and XVI 20-166 is consistent with our sense in dreams
    that we have "woken up" when in fact we have passed into
    another phase of the dream. The division of the C-text be-
    tween waking and sleeping is even more ambiguous. The Dream-
    er's meeting in waking life with Need (B- and C-texts) and
    with Conscience and Reason (C-text) provide personal motiva-
    tion for the visions that follow. The confusion, discon-
    tinuity, and illogic of the poem is understandable in terms
    of condensation, transference, and fusion experienced in
    dreams; so too is the lack of final solutions to the problems
    raised. Dreams are "the glorious excuse" the poet uses to
    "spread out the products of his vast imagination."

*5 MURTAUGH, DANIEL MAHER. "Piers Plowman and the Image of God."
    Dissertation, Yale, 213 pp.
        Abstracted: DA 29:876A. See Murtaugh, 1978.15.

6 St-JACQUES, RAYMOND. "Langland's Christ-Knight and the Liturgy."
    Revue de l'Université d'Ottawa 37:146-58.
        Seeks to correct the inadequacies of Gaffney (1931.4)
    and Le May (1932.12) by focusing on the liturgy as a source of
    Langland's conception of the Christ-knight. Finds the old
    tradition of God tricking Satan reflected in the Good Friday
    hymn Pangue lingua, a more likely influence on Langland than
    the poem of Nicholas Bozon (Gaffney, 1931.4). Finds the
    important Scriptural influences on the tradition, Ephesians
    6:10-17, I Thessalonians 5:8, and II Timothy 2:3, incorporated
    in the liturgy. Suggests that Isaiah 63:1-7, a lesson for the
    Mass of Wednesday of Holy Week, is a probable source for B XIX
    5-14; and notes various liturgical occurrences of the motifs
    connected with the battle of Christ and Satan and the descrip-
    tion of Christ's weapons and armor. Finds the Warrior-Christ
    in a Middle English sermon for the twenty-second Sunday after

Trinity. Suggests that Christ's "borrowed armor" in Piers
Plowman may have been influenced by a tradition of commentary
that viewed priestly vestments as symbols of the Incarnation,
the Passion, and pieces of a warrior's armor.

7   SALTER, ELIZABETH. "Piers Plowman and 'The Simonie.'" Archiv
    203:241-54.
        Suggests that the fourteenth-century semialliterative
    Simonie, found in the Auchinleck MS. and two others, may have
    been available to Langland in London and may have influenced
    Piers Plowman. Notes such relevant aspects of the Simonie as
    the variable nature of its verse-line, its range of alliter-
    ative patterns, its attack on secular and spiritual malprac-
    tices, its mingling of abstract concepts in realistic settings,
    and its depiction of truth. Suggests that other popular semi-
    alliterative poems, such as the "Song of the Husbandman" and
    Thomas of Erceldoune's Prophecy (both found in BM MS. Harley
    2253), may perhaps have influenced Langland.

8   SALTER, ELIZABETH, and PEARSALL, DEREK, eds. Introduction to
    Piers Plowman. York Medieval Texts. London: Edward Arnold
    (Publishers); Evanston, Ill.: Northwestern University Press,
    pp. 1-58.
        Sees Langland's concern as the exposure and clarifica-
    tion of the social issues raised by his conscience, and his
    use of various allegorical techniques dictated by the inten-
    tion "to illustrate and elucidate the great themes of the
    poem." Sees the designation of "personification allegory"
    insufficient to distinguish Langland's use of this device from
    the more static or ceremonial treatment found in the Roman de
    la Rose and Wynnere and Wastoure. Notes the mixture in Piers
    Plowman of real and allegorical characters, and the poet's
    habit of stopping at the very brink of an allegorical sequence.
    Langland occasionally offers precise and formalized diagram-
    matic allegory, but at times steers us away from an allegori-
    cal visualization. The most distinctive feature of his
    illustrative material, lying somewhere between full-scale
    allegorical sequence and formal allegorical design, is in its
    positioning as reported allegory, experienced by the Dreamer
    at one remove. The symbolic import of Langland's realism and
    of much of the realism of the late Middle Ages lends itself to
    consideration through the figural method (see Salter, 1968.13).
        Denies the Three Lives and the figure of Piers are orga-
    nizing principles of the poem's structure, and defends Lang-
    land's "loose-woven fabric of procedures" as a method designed
    to capture "something of a kaleidoscopic vision of truth."
    Langland is shown not to be committed to a narrative structure
    in any continuous fashion, in a way uncharacteristic of

1967

medieval allegorical works; he is often willing to abandon
narrative continuity for spiritual implication and richness of
significance. Finds the formal cohesive elements of the poem
in the figure of the Dreamer and the device of the dream vision. Sees the influence of the sermon in the poet's digres-
sive style and his use of repetitions, correspondences, and
cross-references. Finds Langland's poetry at its best when
"his religion and his imagination are in perfect accord, and
direct, jointly, his verbal skills." Prints selections from
the C-text, based on MS. X.

9 SCHMIDT, A.V.C. "A Note on the A Text of 'Piers Plowman,'
   Passus X.91-4." N&Q, c.s. 212 (n.s. 14), no. 10 (October):
   365-66.
        In these lines, Goddis worde probably refers to Romans
   14:23, holi writ to Richard of St. Victor's gloss upon it in
   his commentary on the Song of Songs. Langland here stresses
   the importance of conscience, but requires that its counsel be
   "acordyng with holy chirche."

10 WENZEL, SIEGFRIED. The Sin of Sloth: Acedia in Medieval Thought
   and Literature. Chapel Hill: University of North Carolina
   Press, 1967.
        A reprint of Wenzel, 1960.15.

                           1968

*1 CASE, ANNE MERRITT. "Pursuit of Wisdom: A Study of the Knowl-
    edge of Good and Evil in Piers Plowman." Dissertation, Yale,
    344 pp.
         Abstracted: DA 29:562A-63A.

2   DONALDSON, E. TALBOT. "'Piers Plowman' Textual Comparison and
    the Question of Authorship." In Chaucer und seine Zeit.
    Symposion für Walter F. Schirmer. Edited by Arno Esch.
    Buchreihe der Anglia Zeitschrift für Englische Philologie,
    vol. 14. Tübingen: Max Niemeyer Verlag, pp. 241-47.
         Defends the assumption of Kane and Donaldson of single
    authorship underlying editions of the poem, although admits
    that decisive textual proof is lacking. Sees multiple-
    authorship theory as resting on a separation of the poet from
    the text and the reconstruction of a hypothetical poet inde-
    pendent of surviving textual testimony of his existence.
    Notes that belief in single authorship allows one to use the
    A- and C-texts as glosses in the editing of the B-text, which
    cannot be done if the versions are by different hands.

*3   ENGELS, HERBERT. <u>Piers Plowman: Eine Untersuchung der Text-</u><u>struktur mit einer Einleitung zur mittelalterlichen Allegorie</u>. Dissertation, Cologne, 265 pp.
   Abstracted: Werner Habicht, ed., <u>English and American Studies in German</u>. <u>Summaries of Theses and Monographs</u>, (Supp. to <u>Anglia</u>), vol. 1 (Tübingen: Max Niemeyer Verlag), pp. 26-28, no. 11.

4   JONES, FLORENCE. "Dickens and Langland in Adjudication upon Meed." <u>VNL</u> 33 (Spring):53-56.
   Compares <u>Hard Times</u> and <u>Piers Plowman</u> as products of conservative-minded authors who share both a sense of society as a commonwealth in which the use of property is governed by the welfare of all, and a deep distrust of the profit motive which "substitutes aggrandizement for stewardship and violates the collective responsibility of men in society." Views Mr. Bounderby as a Mede-figure, and Stephen Blackpool as similar to Piers in function. Casts the events and characters of <u>Hard Times</u> in terms of Langland's setting and metaphors.

5   KASKE, R.E. "<u>Piers Plowman</u> and Local Iconography." <u>Journal of the Warburg and Courtauld Institute</u> 31:159-69 (with plates).
   The detail of the "two gredy sowes" of B V 347 is mirrored in the elbow of a choir stall (apparently fourteenth century) in the priory church of St Giles in Little Malvern where, unmatched elsewhere in medieval decoration, two sows are shown eating from the same pot. Either the poet had seen this carving, or both the detail in the poem and the carving reproduce some popular local expression. The spanking of Wrath in B V 174-76 is noticed in the Norman fonts at Southrop, Glos., in which "Paciencia belabours the bared posterior of <u>Ira</u> with a scourge." Other, less conclusive examples include: a mirror held by Youth in the Wheel of Life iconography, perhaps in evidence in the priory church of Sts Peter and Paul at Leominster, Herfordshire (a representation of the "Myroure that hiȝt Mydlerd" of B XI 8); the iconography of Abraham with the souls of the just in his bosom, perhaps to be seen in the outer wall of the church of St Mary in Cleobury Mortimer, Salop.; and other common iconographical details of the Tree of Jesse (B XVIII 59), and the wheel of virtues (C XVI 162) seen in the counties surrounding the Malvern area.

6   LANGLAND, WILLIAM. <u>The Vision of William concerning Piers Plowman, together with Vita de Dowel, Dobet, et Dobest, Secundum Wit et Resoun, by William Langland (about 1362-1380 A.D.) Edited from Numerous Manuscripts, with Prefaces, Notes and a Glossary, by the Rev. Walter W. Skeat, M.A.</u> Vol. 1,

1968

The "Vernon" Text; or Text A. Early English Text Society,
o.s. 28. London: Oxford University Press.
    Reprint of Langland, 1867.3.

*7   McNAMARA, JOHN F. "Responses to Ockhamist Theology in the Poetry
of the Pearl-poet, Langland, and Chaucer." Dissertation,
Louisiana State, 198 pp.
    Abstracted: DA 29:3148A-49A.

8   MATHEW, GERVASE. The Court of Richard II. London: John Murray,
pp. 83-91.
    Sees the astonishing degree of textual corruption of the
poem in manuscript transmission as suggestive of Langland's
slight prestige and as due not only to scribal alterations but
to adaptations by minstrels. The variant readings suggest two
audiences of the poem--the devout middle class of London and
the towns to the south and west, and "the occasional religious
house, serious-minded parish priest and devout landowner."
Although the poem clearly appealed to Lollards, its inclusion
in MSS containing treatises and manuals of orthodox religious
instruction and spirituality shows its currency in a right-
wing conservative milieu. The plan of the poem becomes clear
in light of Langland's ideas on justice and its motive force,
charity (see Mathew, 1948.8).

*9   MILOWICKI, EDWARD JOHN. "Piers Plowman and the Ways of Provi-
dence: A Study of Structure in Relation to Content." Dissertation, Oregon, 221 pp.
    Abstracted: DA 29:3582A.

10   NEWSTEAD, HELAINE, ed. Chaucer and His Contemporaries. Essays
on Medieval Literature and Thought. Literature and Ideas
Series, edited by Irving Howe. New York: Fawcett World
Library.
    Contains reprints of Coghill, 1962.2, and Spearing,
1964.12.

11   QUIRK, RANDOLPH. Essays on the English Language Medieval and
Modern. Bloomington and London: Indiana University Press,
pp. 20-26, 27-29.
    Reprint of Quirk, 1953.6 and 1954.5.

12   RYAN, WILLIAM F. William Langland. New York: Twayne Publishers,
166 pp.
    Notes the peculiar features of style of each of the
versions, and calls for new scholarly editions of the B- and
C-texts; but in the meantime, feels it important to compare
the three versions, for the published scholarship and criticism

1968

show a neglect of the three texts taken together. Accepts single authorship on the basis of diction, rhetorical figures, and the fact the author of the C-text used <u>both</u> the previous texts for his revision (though in different proportions in different parts of the poem). Sees Langland in the course of the three versions "easily perceived in the process of growth, of aging"; in particular, sees Langland as writing more mildly as he grew older without sacrificing his conviction. His decreased use of <u>heuene</u> suggests his thoughts were more concerned with earth in the C-version; and his use of fewer oaths suggests his increased sense of the dignity of God.

Surveys the use of poetic devices in the development of such "characters" as Mede and the Deadly Sins. Surveys the social satire in the poem and finds it directed against all levels of the Church, trades, and the laboring classes, though Langland never appears to have an ill word for <u>hewes</u>, "workmen." Of all the secular professions, Langland is hardest on doctors; he is careful regarding lawyers and concerned about minstrels. He differs from many satirists in that he exposes faults but aims to reform and improve.

Considers the frequent use of puns and alliterated matched pairs of words in the poem in the context of the late Old English homiletic tradition, and notes that in <u>Piers Plowman</u> these devices are instruments of meaning that show the poet's verbal skill, humor, and delight in language. Suggests that the poetry of <u>Piers Plowman</u> should not seem alien to a contemporary audience in a time of absurdism, obscurantism, and nihilism.

13 SALTER, ELIZABETH. "Medieval Poetry and the Figural View of Reality." Sir Israel Gollancz Memorial Lecture, read 24 January 1968. <u>Proceedings of the British Academy</u> 44:73-92.
    Argues that the figural approach, with its acceptance of the historicity of an act and its understanding of the fuller significance of that act in the scheme of salvation, is a better alternative to the criticism of the poem that emphasizes either literal meanings at the expense of spiritual significance or systematic allegorical approaches. <u>Piers Plowman</u> and <u>Pearl</u> are considered poems of a "secondary" type of figural composition, in that the historical reality of these works is not susceptible of total proof, yet is presented in the poem as if real and seen as completed by divine reality. Thus Piers and the Good Samaritan are presented as if they were as historical as Moses, Trajan, and so on, but they function to expose the spiritual mysteries that find their meaning and completion in Christ's life on earth. Considers the various techniques of anticipation noted by Coghill (1944.1) as reflections of the figural view of reality; and

265

1968

sees the continuous pattern of search and fulfillment as being
rather than a formal defect, a technique of typological allu-
siveness which looks forward to the attainment of salvation
through Christ.

14 SCHMIDT, A.V.C. "A Note on the Phrase 'Free Wit' in the C-Text
     of 'Piers Plowman' (Passus XI.51)." N&Q, c.s. 213 (n.s. 15),
     no. 5 (May):168-69.
          Suggests that free wil and free wit represents
     Langland's attempt to translate liberum arbitrium, which ought
     to signify both a cognitive and an affective element.

15 SCHMIDT, A.V.C. "A Note on Langland's Conception of 'Anima' and
     'Inwit.'" N&Q, c.s. 213 (n.s. 15), no. 10 (October):363-64.
          Probable sources of A X 43-45 and 49-54 are the De anima
     of Cassiodorus and the De spiritu et anima attributed to
     Alcher of Clairvaux, which deal with the wandering location
     of the soul throughout the body and its more intense presence
     in one part. Langland's inwit refers to the rational powers
     rather than specifically to conscience.

16 STRANGE, WILLIAM C. "The Willful Trope: Some Notes on Personi-
     fication with Illustrations from Piers (A)." AM 9:26-39.
          Much of what the modern reader calls personification
     (e.g., the description of Piers's family in A VII 71-74) would
     not have been so considered according to medieval rhetoric,
     which insisted that true personification was a figura
     sentiarum, not merely a figura verborum. Piers's description
     of the way to Truth (VI 50-58) is a particular kind of per-
     sonification, topothesia. Character and personification are
     indistinguishable "whenever a moment of psychological reality
     is captured in a web of words, though they approach this
     moment of discovery from opposite directions, as it were."
     Langland's personification is capable of exploring the depths
     of the psyche, as can be seen in a Jungian analysis of Mede as
     an anima-figure. In general, metaphor, which is "condensed,
     investigative and tolerant," is the opposite of personifica-
     tion, which is often not concise, but presentational, and
     "asserts that analogy is a metaphysical fact and not just a
     rhetorical strategy."

*17 TROWER, KATHERINE BACHE. "The Plowman as Preacher: The Alle-
     gorical and Structural Significance of Piers the Plowman in
     Piers Plowman." Dissertation, Illinois, 294 pp.
          Abstracted: DA 30:712A.

18 VASTA, EDWARD, ed. Interpretations of Piers Plowman. Notre
    Dame, Ind., and London: University of Notre Dame Press,
    xix + 378 pp.
        Anthologizes Owst, 1933.8 (selections); Coghill, 1933.1;
    Dunning, 1937.3 (selections); Wells, 1938.9; Donaldson,
    1949.1, rev. ed. 1966.2 (selections); Robertson and Huppé,
    1951.9 (selections); Frank, 1953.2; Hussey, 1956.6; Dunning,
    1956.3; Lawlor, 1957.7; Frank, 1957.4 (selections); Kaske,
    1960.7; and Bloomfield, 1961.2. These works are reprinted
    with quotations of the poem normalized to Langland, 1886.1,
    and with consistency of spelling and documentation and minor
    stylistic preferences introduced by the editor. The reprint-
    ing of Donaldson, 1949.1, rev. ed., 1966.2, has a few minor
    excisions from the original; that of Dunning, 1956.3, and
    Donaldson have short translations supplied by the editor. An
    introduction places the included works in a historical context
    of commentary on the poem. Includes a bibliography arranged
    according to editions, translations, text, date and author-
    ship, criticism, and notes.

19 WEDEL, THEODORE OTTO. The Mediaeval Attitude toward Astrology
    particularly in England. Yale Studies in English, vol. 60.
    New Haven: Yale University Press. Reprint. [Hamden, Conn.]:
    Archon Books.
        See Wedel, 1920.4.

20 WESLING, DONALD. "Eschatology and the Language of Satire in
    'Piers Plowman.'" Criticism 10, no. 4 (Fall):277-89.
        Describes three types of satire in the poem: dialectic,
    invective, and apocalyptic. Notes the concentration of satire
    at the beginning, middle, and end of the work, at B I, III
    (Mede); VI (Hunger); XIII (Doctor of Divinity); XIX-XX (Dobest
    section). B III is an extended example of dialectic satire;
    B VI is an example of invective which, though it applies to a
    wide variety of satiric effects, is distinguishable from
    dialectic by its lack of continuity; B XIII is the best ex-
    ample of invective satire. B XIX-XX is apocalyptic satire in
    the sense that Langland "uses the idea of disaster to make his
    readers feel on their pulses contemporary spiritual deficien-
    cies; his satire is ever at the service of his eschatology."
    Although satire is a disintegrative mode in its disposition
    to catalogue and digress, the poem achieves a unity of moral
    judgment because Langland's norms are consistent.

1968

21 WOOLF, ROSEMARY. The English Religious Lyric in the Middle Ages.
    Oxford: Clarendon Press, pp. 209-10, 212.
         B XI 195-96 is discussed in the context of the tradi-
    tional theme of Christ's noble birth and that of Christ as the
    true source of gentility; B II 74-113 (the Charter of Favel)
    is mentioned in the context of the tradition of medieval
    charter literature.

                              1969

1   ALPERS, PAUL J., ed. Edmund Spenser. Penguin Critical Antholo-
    gies, edited by Christopher Ricks. Harmondsworth, Middlesex:
    Penguin Books; Baltimore: Penguin Books.
         Contains an abridgment of Traversi, 1936.6.

*2 BARNEY, STEPHEN ALLEN. "Piers Plowman and the Bible: Agricul-
    tural and Food Imagery." Dissertation, Harvard.
         Source: Comprehensive Dissertation Index 1861-1972,
    vol. 30, p. 244. See Barney, 1973.1.

3   BENNETT, J.A.W. "Chaucer's Contemporary." In Piers Plowman:
    Critical Approaches. Edited by S.S. Hussey. London: Methuen
    & Co., pp. 310-24.
         Langland and Chaucer are compared on the basis of attri-
    butes and characteristics common to both: their variety of
    scenes of urban life and the countryside; their juxtaposition
    of tone and content; their attitude regarding the covetousness
    of merchants; their depiction of plowmen, parsons, religious
    and chivalric figures; even the idea of a company of pilgrims
    telling tales. Feels it to be probable that Chaucer knew
    Langland's poem, and perhaps even owned a copy, before he
    began the Tales of Canterbury.

4   BLANCH, ROBERT J., ed. Style and Symbolism in Piers Plowman.
    Knoxville: University of Tennessee Press, xi + 275 pp.
         Reprints, with a short preface, Bloomfield, 1939.1;
    Smith, 1951.10 (selections); Coghill, 1935.3 (selections);
    Dunning, 1956.3; Lawlor, 1957.7; Zeeman, 1958.9; Kean, 1964.8;
    Troyer, 1932.15; Mitchell, 1956.7; Maguire, 1949.8; Burrow,
    1965.2; Kaske, 1963.4; and Donaldson, 1966.1. The essays of
    Bloomfield, Kaske, and Donaldson have been revised by their
    authors. Reviewed by S.S. Hussey, YES 1 (1971):214-16;
    Michael Masi, Cithara 11 (1971):107-12; and Barbara C. Raw,
    N&Q, n.s. 17 (1971):357-58.

1969

*5   BRIAN, BEVERLY DIANNE. "Satire in Piers Plowman." Dissertation,
      Duke, 290 pp.
         Abstracted: DA 30:4936A.

6   BURROW, J.A. "Words, Works and Will: Theme and Structure in
      Piers Plowman." In Piers Plowman: Critical Approaches.
      Edited by S.S. Hussey. London: Methuen & Co., pp. 111-24.
         Langland is concerned with the problem of the difficulty
      of knowing another's will, as opposed to merely his words or
      his works which often hide the intentions of hypocrites, like
      the friars, or formalists, like the Palmer and the Priest of
      the Visio. Imaginatif's challenge to Will concerning his
      literary activity (B XII) shows that Langland is sensitive to
      the moral issues involved in writing words about the Good
      Life; the Tearing of the Pardon testifies to the poet's sense
      of the inadequacy of images to represent the inner realities
      of the will; and the third vision presents the problem of
      likewise finding a stable representation for what the Dreamer
      knows already through natural knowledge. Concerns such as
      these result in a poetic structure that relies on a "series
      of attempts, running in circles and epicycles, to embody ade-
      quately" the images of the inner world represented by Will.

7   CHADWICK, D. Social Life in the Days of Piers Plowman. New
      York: Russell & Russell.
         Reprint of Chadwick, 1922.3.

8   DUNNING, T.P. "Action and Contemplation in Piers Plowman." In
      Piers Plowman: Critical Approaches. Edited by S.S. Hussey.
      London: Methuen & Co., pp. 213-25.
         Langland is not very much interested in the contempla-
      tive life as a state or way of life; rather, he is one with
      theological treatises and popular manuals in using contempla-
      tive to denote the means by which the mind is led to the con-
      templation of God. Thus it is best to be seen as a set of
      activities, a part of the active spiritual life. The Three
      Lives likewise have no essential connection with actual states
      or ways of life; and Dowel in particular concerns the efforts
      of one to devote himself to the practice of the contemplative
      life. The Haukyn episode is the climax of the poet's examina-
      tion of penance and patient poverty; and the main object of
      Dobet and Dobest is to establish foundations of the Christian
      life within the Church.

1969

9   ELLIOTT, R.W.V. "The Langland Country." In Piers Plowman:
    Critical Approaches. Edited by S.S. Hussey. London: Methuen
    & Co., pp. 226-44.
        As opposed to other alliterative poems, the landscape
    and topography of Piers Plowman is most often vague and un-
    particularized, signaling Langland's interest in social and
    spiritual landscapes, rather than the physical landscape of
    his environment. The often-changing terrain of the poem re-
    flects the poem's circuitous argument; and the terrain tra-
    versed by the Dreamer expresses the confusion as well as the
    understanding of his quest.

10 EVANS, W.O. "Charity in Piers Plowman." Piers Plowman:
    Critical Approaches. Edited by S.S. Hussey. London: Methuen
    & Co., pp. 245-78.
        Langland believes that love can achieve anything; his
    complaint against the clergy is often that their lack of
    charity renders null their great spiritual power. Study with-
    out charity is shown to be false; and all the definitions of
    the Three Lives are based on the love of God and Man. Chris-
    tian charity is differentiated from other ethical systems in
    that it is universal and not limited to the close associations
    of kith or kin. Langland believes charity is natural; he
    stresses the need of practical generosity toward the poor, and
    sees this as primarily, though not exclusively, the responsi-
    bility of the Church. He opposes violence and killing, but
    seems to believe that some sins demand justice. His attitude
    toward the Jews, uncharacteristic of his time, suggests that
    God, as the source of charity, would not destine unbelievers
    to damnation; indeed, Langland may even accept the Origenist
    heresy that God's love and mercy would not allow eternal pun-
    ishment for sin.

11 FOWLER, DAVID COVINGTON. "Poetry and the Liberal Arts: The
    Oxford Background of Piers the Plowman." In Arts libéraux et
    philosophie au moyen âge. Actes du quatrième congrès inter-
    national de philosophie médiévale, Université de Montreal,
    27 April-2 September 1967. Montreal: Institut d'études
    médiévales; Paris: Libraire Philosophique J. Vrin,
    pp. 715-19.
        Sees Langland, like Chaucer, siding with the secular
    clergy against the regular clergy and, by extension, Piers
    Plowman deriving from the tradition of the liberal arts,
    rather than from the scholasticism of the friars. Examines
    the end of the B-text in light of the confrontation of secular
    and regular clergy at Oxford in 1382, centering around the
    condemnation of Wyclif led by Archbishop Courtenay and the
    resulting threat to academic freedom. Claims that the Barn of

1969

Unity represents not only the Church, but Oxford University
under attack by the Antichrist and his forces of friars. That
hypocrisy wounds many teachers in the Barn is perhaps an
allusion to the recantation by members of the faculty under
Courtenay's pressure of an inquisition in November 1382.

12 FRANK, ROBERT WORTH, Jr. Piers Plowman and the Scheme of Salva-
    tion: An Interpretation of Dowel, Dobet and Dobest. Yale
    Studies in English, vol. 136. New Haven: Yale University
    Press, 1957. Reprint. [Hamden, Conn.]: Archon Books.
        See Frank, 1957.4.

13 FRAUNCE, ABRAHAM. The Arcadian Rhetorike or the Praecepts of
    Rhetorike made plaine by examples. A Scolar Press Facsimile.
    Menton, England: Scolar Press.
        See Fraunce, 1588.1.

14 HONE, WILLIAM. Ancient Mysteries Described, especially the
    English Miracle Plays, Founded on Apocryphal New Testament
    Story, Extant among the Unpublished Manuscripts in the British
    Museum. . . . London: Printed for William Hone; Detroit:
    Reissued by Singing Tree Press, Book Tower.
        See Hone, 1823.1.

15 HUSSEY, S.S., ed. Introduction to Piers Plowman: Critical
    Approaches. London: Methuen & Co., pp. 1-26.
        Discusses the three texts and the various "shapes" of
    the poem as found in the extant MSS; questions of dating and
    authorship; and recent attempts to view the plan of the poem
    as coherent and unified. Sees the figures of Piers and the
    Dreamer as of greater assistance than the Three Lives in dis-
    covering the plan of the work. Considers the influence of
    sermon literature as mainly analogous rather than direct.
    The audience of the poem--probably composed of prosperous
    fifteenth-century laymen, parish priests, and clerics in
    minor orders--and the unesoteric style of the poem argue
    against the necessity of applying the fourfold method of
    scriptural interpretation to the work. For main entry, see
    Hussey, 1969.16.

16 HUSSEY, S.S., ed. Piers Plowman: Critical Approaches. London:
    Methuen & Co., ix + 366 pp.
        An anthology of original essays, including an introduc-
    tion (Hussey, 1969.15) and the following: Russell, 1969.31;
    Woolf, 1969.39; Kean, 1969.19; Burrow, 1969.6; Jenkins,
    1969.17; Raw, 1969.27; Mills, 1969.23; Dunning, 1969.8;
    Elliott, 1969.9; Evans, 1969.10; Knight, 1969.20; and Bennett,

1969

1969.3. Reviewed by John Lawlor, YES 2 (1972):237-41; and
Michael Masi, Cithara 11 (1971):107-12.

17 JENKINS, PRISCILLA. "Conscience: The Frustration of Allegory."
In Piers Plowman: Critical Approaches. Edited by S.S.
Hussey. London: Methuen & Co., pp. 125-42.
Whereas allegory in the poem deals with clear-cut moral
distinctions, the literal mode is concerned with "compromise,
confusion and frequent indifference to moral issues." The
juxtaposition of these two modes suggests that Langland considers allegory indispensable in the formulation of moral
concepts, but that it must be modified by actual situations
and conditions. The scenes involving Conscience's proposed
marriage with Mede, his decision at the end of the dinner
scene (B XIII) to accompany Patience on pilgrimage, and the
admission of Friar Flatterer to the Castle of Unity show
Langland's self-conscious questioning of the allegorical mode.
Much of the material of this essay was adapted and included in
Martin, 1979.10.

18 KANE, GEORGE. "Conjectural Emendation." In Medieval Literature
and Civilization: Studies in Memory of G.N. Garmonsway. Edited by D.A. Pearsall and R.A. Waldron. London: University
of London, Athlone Press, pp. 155-70.
The editing of Piers Plowman affords an ideal occasion
for re-examining the relation between the theory of conjectural emendation and its practice, for the archetypal text of
the three versions is generally recoverable, and the ideal
classification of typical error is possible.

19 KEAN, P.M. "Justice, Kingship and the Good Life in the Second
Part of Piers Plowman. In Piers Plowman: Critical Approaches.
Edited by S.S. Hussey. London: Methuen & Co., pp. 76-100.
The Pardon scene is a logical conclusion to the political concerns of the Visio and a prologue to the exploration
in the Vita of what constitutes the Good Life. When Langland
treats the Good Life in its most comprehensive sense, he
equates Dowel with Law, Dobet with Lewte, and Dobest with
Love, though Love as the basis of all moral action belongs to
all of the Three Lives. The king in Thought's Speech (B VIII
98-106) represents a principle of order of the "inner commonwealth," just as the king of the Visio stood for the source of
law and order in the "outer commonwealth." The kingship of
Christ is related by the poet to the acts of His life on
earth and is considered as the perfect embodiment of the good
life, only partially able to be imitated by mankind. This
essay is a continuation of Kean, 1964.8.

20   KNIGHT, S.T.   "Satire in Piers Plowman."   In Piers Plowman:
     Critical Approaches.   Edited by S.S. Hussey.   London: Methuen
     & Co., pp. 279-309.
        Satire in the poem is seen as "a literary mode in which,
     through a fiction of some sort, an author is critical of human
     affairs in relation to themselves."   In Piers Plowman
     Langland's conceptual point, that a divinely ordered world
     is being "appallingly run by men," is enforced through the
     poet's method of combining realistic and theological modes of
     representation.   The poem passes from the primarily satiric
     visions of the beginning to extended discussions of theologi-
     cal standards, grounded by the satire in reality, to a final
     satiric vision of the world seen in its spiritual as well as
     material aspects.

21   [LANGLAND, WILLIAM.]   Piers the Plowman: A Critical Edition of
     the A-Version.   Edited by Thomas Knott and David C. Fowler.
     Baltimore: Johns Hopkins Press, xiv + 302 pp.
        Reprint of [Langland], 1952.6.

22   LANGLAND, WILLIAM.   The Vision of William concerning Piers the
     Plowman in Three Parallel Texts together with Richard the
     Redeless.   Edited by Walter W. Skeat.   2 vols.   Oxford:
     Clarendon Press, vi + 628 pp., and cii + 484 pp.
        Reproduces verbatim Langland, 1886.1, and includes a
     select annotated bibliography (Vol. 2, pp. xcv-cii) assembled
     by J.A.W. Bennett.

23   MILLS, DAVID.   "The Rôle of the Dreamer in Piers Plowman."   In
     Piers Plowman: Critical Approaches.   Edited by S.S. Hussey.
     London: Methuen & Co., pp. 180-212.
        The Dreamer is established in the context of reality,
     yet in an ambiguous relationship to society and the contempo-
     rary world.   A similar ambiguity is evident in his situation
     as a visionary, and in the extent to which his dream is an
     objective and prophetic and/or a subjective, personal crea-
     tion.   The Dreamer's participation in the vision is bound by
     a "real" sense of time, space, language, and logical under-
     standing; even the abstractions he encounters are largely
     personal faculties, subjective as well as objective, whose
     arguments must be questioned by the reader.   The Dreamer's
     search for Dowel, an action treated as if it were an object,
     suggests the inherent difficulties of a verbal expression of
     ideas; the analogous inadequacy of imagery is seen in
     Holicherch's explanation of Love (B I 146 ff.) and the de-
     scription of the Tree of Charity.   Opposed to this stands
     Piers, representing the nominal and ideal, who "asserts the
     unifying principle of reality and of the poem against the

1969

Dreamer who at all levels disrupts the concept of order."
Between the two stands Haukyn, whose repentance signals a
progress towards the ideals of Piers.

24 ORSTEN, ELISABETH M. "Patientia in the B-Text of 'Piers
    Plowman.'" MS 31:317-33.
        Langland accepts the traditional Christian understanding
    of patience as neither negative nor passive, but instead as an
    active component of fortitude. He seems to echo Augustine's
    notion of man's dependence on the free gift of God's grace,
    which concept Augustine applies to patience. Patience is
    described in B XIII as humble, cheerful, authoritative,
    related to caritas, and possessing that which is necessary to
    the Three Lives. The second half of B XIII and the Haukyn
    episode (B XIV) define the poet's notions of patient poverty:
    when patient resignation is transformed into positve accep-
    tance, "then a burdensome economic condition suddenly becomes
    the road to sanctity." Langland is not interested in giving
    hope to the poor that they might improve their material con-
    dition; his patience is an active force, deliberately exer-
    cised by God (XI 370-73) and thus enjoined upon man. Will is
    shown to grow in patience through the course of the poem.

*25 PALMER, BARBARA DALLAS. "The Guide and the Leader: Studies in a
    Narrative Structural Motif (Langland, Spenser, Dante, Chaucer,
    Hemingway)." Dissertation, Michigan State, 212 pp.
        Abstracted: DA 31:1236A-37A. See Palmer, 1971.23.

*26 PRINCE, HELEN MORRIS. "Long Will: The First-Person Narrator in
    Piers Plowman." Dissertation, Northwestern, 157 pp.
        Abstracted: DA 30:4423A-24A.

27 RAW, BARBARA. "Piers and the Image of God in Man." In Piers
    Plowman: Critical Approaches. Edited by S.S. Hussey.
    London: Methuen & Co., pp. 143-79.
        The meaning of Piers and of Will is to be found in the
    doctrine of deification, whereby the resemblance of man to
    God, his memory, intelligence, and will, can be restored in
    spite of Adam's sin through the Incarnation. The restoration
    of the divine image in history and in the individual soul
    comes about in three stages: the Visio represents the Old
    Testament period, defined through man's natural aptitude for
    knowing God; Dobet, in the dramatization of Christ's life; and
    Dobest, in the image of the restored divine likeness, which is
    attainable only in heaven. The same progression is seen in
    the development of the character of Piers in the poem, from a
    just man living under Old Testament law in the Visio, to his
    increasing similarity with Christ from the point of announcing

1969

the Incarnation in defense of the Tree of Charity, to his dis-
appearance in the final two passūs after having become a "restored image." Will represents the imprint of the divine on
the individual man, whose psychological development parallels
the development of mankind: he progresses from arrogance and
worldliness through the proper exercise of memory and understanding (Reason and Imaginatif) toward the transformation of
will into love of God. Following Piers helps Will to regain
his resemblance to God, but for a human the true and complete
restoration of the divine image can occur only after death.

28 RAYMO, ROBERT. "Piers Plowman." In The Critical Temper: A
   Survey of Modern Criticism on English and American Literature
   from the Beginnings to the Twentieth Century. Vol. 1. Edited
   by Martin Tucker. New York: Frederick Ungar, pp. 182-93.
        Quotes selections from James, 1932.11; Coghill, 1935.3;
   Dawson, 1934.5; Lewis, 1936.4; Chambers, 1939.3; Graves,
   1949.4; Kane, 1951.6; Robertson and Huppé, 1951.9; Smith,
   1951.10; Tillyard, 1954.7; Dunning, 1956.3; Frank, 1957.4;
   McKisack, 1959.10; Lawlor, 1962.4; Salter, 1962.11; Krapp,
   1915.2; Wells, 1929.1; Bennett, 1950.1; Lucas, 1934.7; Lawlor,
   1957.7; Traversi, 1936.6; and Bloomfield, 1961.3.

29 RIACH, MARY. "Langland's Dreamer and the Transformation of the
   Third Vision." Essays in Criticism 19, no. 1 (January):6-18.
        Although all the experiences of the Dreamer cannot be
   taken as accounts of the poet's actual life, a few points encourage the autobiographical interpretation. The end of the
   A-text, in which the poem comes to a close in the Dreamer's
   confusion, in particular suggests a close correlation of the
   Dreamer and the poet. The A-text Dreamer is a personality
   only in the Vita, but becomes progressively more in the B- and
   C-texts. The quarrel with Scripture in the A-text appears to
   have halted the poem; in the B-text we find a new resolution
   of this dilemma in which the Dreamer is shown to be more inti-
   mately involved, and the material of the A-Vita is used ironically against him. This is accomplished in the B-text addition of the dream-within-the-dream in which Imaginatif defends
   learning and reproves the Dreamer's pride and presumption.

30 ROBERTSON, D.W. and HUPPÉ, BERNARD F. Piers Plowman and Scriptural Tradition. New York: Octagon Books.
        Reprint of Robertson and Huppé, 1951.9.

1969

31 RUSSELL, G.H. "Some Aspects of the Process of Revision in <u>Piers</u>
    <u>Plowman</u>." In <u>Piers Plowman: Critical Approaches</u>. Edited by
    S.S. Hussey. London: Methuen & Co., pp. 27-49.
        Defends the traditional notion of the three texts of the
    poem against charges that the differences between the versions
    are merely changes introduced by scribal tinkering and con-
    tamination. The revision of the B-text over the A-text is
    seen as twofold in nature: careful adaptation of the A-text
    material, and its augmentation in expansions, additions, and
    development. Revision of the B-text to the C-text is "not one
    of substantial accretion or of major rearrangement," but
    rather one of detail. The C-poet had as a working copy a MS
    of the B-text better than any extant B-text MS (and hence
    better than their common ancestor), but not a fair copy of the
    B-text. Nor did he have access to the A-text. The C-text
    poet's revision of the B-text is neither orderly nor system-
    atic. Often he will correct what he takes to be a corruption
    in his B-text MS, then subject the passage to close scrutiny
    and revision. Other revisions attest to his decision to mod-
    ify the poem's theme and meaning, but such revisions are
    selective, rather than systematic. The revision of the C-text
    is unfinished, and suggests that the archetypal text of the
    C-version may have been a conjoint text made up of twenty-one
    passūs in revised form and two unrevised B-text passūs to fill
    in what was lost or lacking.

32 RYAN, WILLIAM M. "Word-Play in Some Old English Homilies and a
    Late Middle English Poem." In <u>Studies in Language, Litera-</u>
    <u>ture, and Culture of the Middle Ages and Later</u>. Edited by
    E. Bagby Atwood and Archibald A. Hill. Austin: University
    of Texas at Austin, pp. 265-78.
        Considers the word-play of <u>Piers Plowman</u> in the context
    of pre-1100 Old English homilies, in light not only of
    <u>annominatio</u>, the two-word pun, but also the alliterating
    matched pair, or copulative alliterative phrase. Notes the
    high frequency of matched pairs in the A-text, B XI-XX, and
    C XII-XXI, though can offer no single conclusive reason for
    the phenomenon. Langland's use of alliterative pairs is
    greater than Wulfstan's, whose is greater in turn than that
    of the other homilists. Five formulaic matched pairs are
    found in both pre-1100 homilies and <u>Piers Plowman</u>. Langland
    occasionally shows his delight in word-play in his use of
    "inter-textual puns," or puns made in the C-text "by substi-
    tuting nearly homophonous words for key words in B." This
    essay was written in 1964 and hence precedes the treatment of
    the same topic in Ryan, 1968.12.

33 St-JACQUES, RAYMOND. "The Liturgical Associations of Langland's
    Samaritan." MS 25:217-30.
        The Samaritan episode in B XVII is related to the
    virtues of faith and hope, as well as to the Passion and
    Incarnation, in a way not suggested by the account of Luke
    10:30-35, but in a fashion that is manifest in the Mass of
    the Thirteenth Sunday after Pentecost, the Epistle of which is
    Galatians 3:16-22 (the Gospel of which relates the Samaritan
    episode), as well as in liturgical homilies and commentary for
    the same Sunday. Other details not in the Gospel narrative
    are likewise derived from the liturgy: Faith, Hope, and Will
    riding off after the Samaritan (B XVII 78-85) is suggested by
    the Collect of the Thirteenth Sunday after Pentecost; the
    habitual thievery practiced in the forest and the proper
    remedies for the wounded man (B XVII 98-99, 87-93, 119-21) are
    suggested in homilies for the day. Moreover, the liturgy for
    this day provides the overall pattern of Will's search that
    culminates in a vision of Christ as the true solution of the
    way to salvation.

*34 SAITO, ISAMU. "Haukyn and His Way of Life in Piers the Plowman."
    Studies in English Literature (English Literary Society of
    Japan, University of Tokyo), English Number, pp. 1-32.
        Source: MLA International Bibliography, 1969, p. 61,
    no. 2243.

35 SALTER, ELIZABETH. Piers Plowman: An Introduction. 2d ed.
    Oxford: Basil Blackwell, v + 111 pp.
        See Salter, 1962.11.

36 SCHMIDT, A.V.C. "Langland and Scholastic Philosophy." Medium
    Ævum 38, no. 2:134-56.
        Takes issue with Donaldson (1949.1) and Sanderlin
    (1941.9) over their use of the definition of liberum arbitrium
    by St. John Damascene to elucidate the nature of the faculty
    in Piers Plowman (C XVII 183-98). Langland does not accept
    liberum arbitrium as a "universal" power of the soul; in the
    C-text he shows that it is the most significant part of the
    soul, and hence the spokesman for the entire soul. Sees the
    background of this concept in Michael Ayguani's commentary on
    the Sentences of Peter Lombard. Langland's granting of some
    degree of free will to animals is seen as perhaps based on a
    notion in the Sentences of Gandulph of Bologna.

1969

37 SCHMIDT, A.V.C. "Two Notes on 'Piers Plowman.'" N&Q, c.s. 214
    (n.s. 16), no. 8 (August):285-86.
          Notes the general similarity of C IV 335-409, dealing
    with direct and indirect relation, to a passage in Wyclif's
    De compositione hominis. Suggests that the phrase "Donum
    Dei" (B XIV 275) may have been derived from Augustine's De
    patientia. Langland alludes to Augustine at the end of B XIV;
    and Augustine's coupling of patience and conscience seems to
    be echoed in B XIII 215.

*38 WITTIG, JOSEPH S. "Piers Plowman B. Passus IX-XII: Elements in
    the Design of the Inward Journey." Dissertation, Cornell,
    147 pp.
          Abstracted: DA 30:5425A. See Wittig, 1972.23.

39 WOOLF, ROSEMARY. "The Tearing of the Pardon." In Piers Plowman:
    Critical Approaches. Edited by S.S. Hussey. London: Methuen
    & Co., pp. 50-75.
          To a medieval literary audience, a pardon would carry
    associations of a legal document written in Christ's blood
    that signified the benefits of the Redemption. Yet the con-
    text of the form of the Pardon in Piers Plowman, verses 40-41
    of the Athanasian Creed, is that of the Last Judgment, where
    salvation depends solely on good works as determined by the
    justice of God. At this point in the poem, the pilgrims have
    confessed, but their perseverance in virtue is suspect.
    Piers's Tearing of the Pardon declares the supremacy of
    Christ's mercy over His justice up until the Last Judgment.
    The context of the Pardon may imply a condemnation, but the
    document "becomes" a pardon when Piers, representing Christ
    in His redemption of man, tears it asunder. In its depiction
    of the stimulus to action, Piers's emotional response, and the
    triviality of the symbolic actions on the literal level, the
    scene can be compared to that of the Tree of Charity (B XVI).

                              1970

1   ALDERSON, WILLIAM L., and HENDERSON, ARNOLD C. Chaucer and
    Augustan Scholarship. University of California English
    Studies, no. 35. Berkeley, Los Angeles, and London: Univer-
    sity of California Press.
          See Ruddiman[?], 1710.1.

*2 ALFORD, JOHN ALEXANDER. "Piers Plowman and the Tradition of the
    Biblical Imitatio." Dissertation, North Carolina, Chapel
    Hill, 226 pp.
          Abstracted: DA 31:3536A-37A.

1970

3   AMES, RUTH M. The Fulfillment of the Scriptures: Abraham,
     Moses, and Piers. Evanston, Ill.: Northwestern University
     Press, passim.
          The traditional teaching on the fulfillment of the
     Scriptures regarding the Trinity, Messias, and the Law is
     seen to inform Langland's Scriptural references, his choice of
     heroes, and his theology.
          Regarding the Trinity, Langland is traditional in his
     belief that the Trinity appeared to Abraham and was thus
     taught in both Testaments, and that the nature of the Triune
     God is Love, as manifested in the Creation and Incarnation.
     B IX 35-44 shows Langland's use of the conventional "faciamus
     text" (from Genesis 1:26) that modernizes the old exegesis in
     parable and to which Langland links his conception that all
     goodness is the image of God.
          Although Langland's knowledge of the Messianic prophe-
     cies is clear in the poem, he places particular emphasis on
     those Messianic prophecies of the kingship of Jesus and the
     related topic of the rejection of the Jews. Langland is in-
     consistent, if not contradictory, regarding the Jews: he
     argues on the one hand that those who live according to truth
     will be saved; yet in the context of the Messianic prophecies,
     he refers to Jews as deservedly rejected by both God and man.
     In Piers Plowman, unlike the Gospels, the Jews are responsible
     for the Centurion's act on Calvary; and in the C-text,
     Longinus himself is made a Jew. The rejection of the Jews in
     the poem is seen in the context of the iconography of Synogoga
     and Ecclesia; the Jews are rejected in the prophecy of faith
     after the Centurion's eyes are opened by Christ's blood.
          Langland is conventional in believing that the Moral Law
     was unchanged from the Old to the New Testament. The Fall of
     Man requires a New Law, begun by Jesus as a fulfillment,
     rather than as an abrogation, of the Old. Langland is much
     more interested in the spiritual meaning of the New Law than
     in its ceremonial aspects. In the Pardon scene, the Priest
     represents the Old Law and Piers the New Law; both are "true,"
     yet the Old needs fulfillment as revealed by Christ. Piers's
     Pardon is a prophecy of the New Law of Charity.
          The identification of Abraham as Faith and Moses as Hope
     likewise shows Langland's knowledge of the fulfillment doc-
     trine, but Langland transforms Abraham's circumcision from
     betokening a change in ceremonial law (baptism) to betokening
     the love and loyalty that unite humans in Christ.

4   BLOOMFIELD, MORTON W. Essays and Explorations: Studies in
     Ideas, Language, and Literature. Cambridge, Mass.: Harvard
     University Press.
          Reprint of Bloomfield, 1961.2.

279

1970

*5   COLEMAN, JANET. "Sublimes et Litterati: The Audience for the
     Themes of Grace, Justification, and Predestination, Traced
     from Disputes of 14th Century Moderni to the Vernacular Piers
     Plowman." Dissertation, Yale, 231 pp.
          Abstracted: DAI 32:382A.

*6   ELLIOTT, THOMAS JOSEPH. "Complaint as a Middle English Genre: A
     Survey of the Tradition Culminating in the School of Piers
     Plowman." Dissertation, Michigan, 211 pp.
          Abstracted: DAI 31:4116A. See Elliott, 1973.5.

7   HARWOOD, BRITTON J., and SMITH, RUTH F. "Inwit and the Castle of
     Caro in Piers Plowman." NM 71, no. 4 (December):648-54.
          Inwit functions in B IX 1-70 like synderesis as it was
     early conceived of by the Dominicans, that is, as a separate
     rational faculty, "intuitive not deliberative, perfected by
     its habitual knowledge of natural law."

*8   HARWOOD, BRITTON JAMES. "Piers Plowman and the Ways of Knowing."
     Dissertation, State University of New York, Buffalo, 571 pp.
          Abstracted: DAI 31:4772A.

9   KANE, GEORGE. Middle English Literature: A Critical Study of
     the Romances, the Religious Lyrics, Piers Plowman. London:
     Methuen.
          Reprint of Kane, 1951.6.

*10 KAULBACH, ERNEST NORMAN. "The Imagery and Theory of Synderesis
     in Piers Plowman B, Passus V, 544 f. and Passus XIX." Dis-
     sertation, Cornell, 328 pp.
          Abstracted: DAI 31:4720A.

11   MacQUEEN, JOHN. Allegory. The Critical Idiom, no. 14. London:
     Methuen & Co., pp. 59, 63.
          The poem is seen as illustrative of the medieval transi-
     tion from battle-allegory to the allegory of the individual
     quest or pilgrimage, in which, as in Deguilleville and Bunyan,
     the allegorical emphasis is placed on "common humanity."

12   ORSTEN, ELISABETH M. "'Heaven on Earth'--Langland's Vision of
     Life within the Cloister." ABR 21:526-34.
          Langland's idyllic picture of cloister life (B X 300-303)
     is paralleled by Bishop Thomas Brunton's in Sermo 98. Brunton,
     however, uses it to remind monks of their essential religious
     obligations, whereas Langland intends it as a reminder to
     monks to remain behind the convent walls. Langland's view of
     monastic life presents an idiosyncratic ideal, certainly not

what one would expect of a monk himself; yet the poet may well
have come under the influence of the Benedictines at Worcester.

13 POLAK, LUCIE. "A Note on the Pilgrim in 'Piers Plowman.'" N&Q
    205 (n.s. 17), no. 8 (August):282-85.
        The Pilgrim of A VI is considered in the historical con-
    text of the late medieval influx of pilgrims to Rome. Lang-
    land may mention India and Asia after "Babylon" (Cairo) in
    A VI 17-18 because Cairo was often confused with Babylon of
    Chaldea. Concludes that the Pilgrim is not necessarily a mere
    vagabond, for despite manifest abuses and criticisms, many
    medieval pilgrims were motivated by sincere piety.

14 PUTTENHAM, GEORGE. The Arte of English Poesie. Introduction by
    Baxter Hathaway. Kent English Reprints: The Renaissance.
    General Editor, Hilton Landry. [Kent, Ohio]: Kent State
    University Press.
        A facsimile reproduction of the 1906 reprint published
    by A. Constable and Co. and edited by Edward Arber. See
    Puttenham[?], 1589.1 and 1869.1.

15 St-JACQUES, RAYMOND C. "Conscience's Final Pilgrimage in Piers
    Plowman and the Cyclical Structure of the Liturgy." Revue de
    l'Université d'Ottawa 40 (April–June):210-23.
        The pilgrimage of Conscience is considered in relation
    to the liturgy of Pentecost and Advent: the construction of
    Unity is handled in the same metaphor of building as in the
    Sequence Laus jocunda; the attack on Church unity by the vices
    is common in sermons for Pentecost; the defense by penance and
    mortification is a central theme of the liturgy of Ember Days,
    as is the use of the farming metaphor to describe Church
    unity. Antichrist (as seen in B XX) is a theme of the Advent
    liturgy, for example, the Gospel for the Second Sunday of
    Advent. Moreover, the Advent liturgy refers to spiritual
    revitalization in terms suggestive of a pilgrimage. The
    cyclical structure of the liturgy mirrors both the progress
    of the poem's pilgrimages and the promise at the end of the
    poem that this pilgrimage will itself only lead to many more
    like it, "until, in death, the pilgrim finally reaches the
    home of the Father." On the topic of the circularity of the
    liturgy, see Adams, 1976.1.

16 SCHROEDER, MARY C. "Piers Plowman: The Tearing of the Pardon."
    PQ 49, no. 1 (January):8-18.
        The Pardon is genuine; and Piers's tearing of it is to
    be understood in the context of Exodus 32, Moses' breaking
    the Tables of the Law. There are four parallels between these
    scenes: the principals are angry; this anger is occasioned by

1970

the misguided counsel of a priest; this anger leads to the
destruction of a valuable document; and the destruction of
this document in no way negates its promises. The breaking of
the tablets is commonly interpreted as a change from the Old
Law to the New. The Visio represents the state of man under
the Old Law, the change from which into the New can be seen
recapitulated in a moral sense in the life of every Christian.
This change is one from an order based merely on law and justice (the Visio) to that of one based on grace (the Vita).
Largely incorporated in Carruthers, 1973.2.

17 SCHROEDER, MARY C. "The Character of Conscience in Piers
    Plowman." SP 57, no. 1 (January):13-30.
        Analyzes the development in the poem of the character of
    conscience, seen in the context of the various meanings of the
    term in patristic and medieval thought. In B III-IV, against
    Lady Mede, Conscience is seen primarily as a judge of right
    and wrong, though guided by natural comprehension and knowl-
    edge, and not yet a Christian conscience illuminated by grace.
    In B XIII, at the scene of his dinner party, he is shown to
    become more aware of the necessity of charity; he leaves
    Clergy behind and sets out on a pilgrimage with Patience, who
    has replaced Reason in his estimation of what is the king's
    best counselor. When Grace, who has installed him as defender
    of Unite, departs in XIX, he is defenseless and is betrayed by
    his own weakest part, his conscientiousness. "At the very
    end, having learned the bitter lessons of Passus XX, we see
    him starting out in search of the one figure that can save
    him, Piers the Plowman." Sees this development in the alle-
    gorical character as one of accretion and education, imparting
    a richness and vitality to the figure. Largely incorporated
    in Carruthers, 1973.2.

18 SHEPHERD, GEOFFREY. "The Nature of Alliterative Poetry in Late
    Medieval England." The Sir Israel Gollancz Memorial Lecture,
    read 21 January 1970. Proceedings of the British Academy, 56,
    57-76; and published separately, London: Oxford University
    Press.
        Piers Plowman in particular, and Middle English alliter-
    ative poetry in general, is considered mnemonic in that infor-
    mation thought valuable is presented by the poet in a fashion
    that allows it to be "accepted within the frame of the story
    and extracted from it without discomfiture." The alliterative
    poet is often a memorialist, commemorating past times; but the
    actual making of poetry is a function of memory, and the
    poetics of alliterative poetry in relation to form, matter,
    and art is a poetics of memory. The poet aims not for the
    impression of visible things but for the verbal scheme for

conceptualizing, for its usefulness in generating concepts in
the mind. Piers Plowman is seen as a series of illuminations
to which Langland must struggle to give meaning, much as does
Julian of Norwich in the Revelations. The revisions of the
Pardon scene of the B- and C-texts show Langland attempting to
make the meaning plainer to himself.

19 WILLIAMS, D.J. "Alliterative Poetry in the Fourteenth and Fif-
    teenth Centuries." In Sphere History of Literature in the
    English Language. Vol. 1, The Middle Ages, edited by W.F.
    Bolton. London: Sphere Books, pp. 107-59, esp. 135-41.
        The poem is atypical of alliterative poetry in its un-
    courtliness, social diversity of audience, and popularity in
    all parts of England. Langland is a disturbing combination of
    innovator and traditionalist. His poem can be considered as a
    multiplication of the allegorical dream form that is not gov-
    erned by chronological time or continuity of place. Rather
    than displaying an achieved solution, it concerns itself with
    the difficulty of seeing itself. The structure of the poem
    presents characteristic images and patterns as the reader
    experiences them; and the extent to which Langland combines
    various allegorical modes is unprecedented.

20 WILSON, R.M. The Lost Literature of Medieval England. 2d ed.
    rev. London: Methuen & Co.
        See Wilson, 1952.9.

21 WIMSATT, JAMES I. Allegory and Mirror: Tradition and Structure
    in Middle English Literature. New York: Pegasus, pp. 49-58,
    105-13, 128-30.
        Disagrees with Baugh (1948.1) that the poem lacks an
    orderly plan. Sees the Visio as furnishing a general view of
    society in its progress toward perfection, and the Vita as
    representing the individual's experience, without which there
    can be no social progress. Notes that the dreams have a se-
    quential relationship. The quest for Dowel shows the value
    and limitations of progressively higher faculties of the
    psyche; as in the Divina Commedia, the power of reason gives
    way to the revelation of spiritual truths. Anima can be com-
    pared to Virgil of Dante's poem; Beatrice (revelation), clad
    in the red of charity, can be likened to Piers in his presen-
    tation of the Tree of Charity.

*22 WOOD, ANN DOUGLAS. "Long Will and His Dreams: A Study in Piers
     Plowman and Related Mediaeval Visions." Dissertation,
     Harvard.
         Source: Comprehensive Dissertation Index 1861-1972,
     vol. 30, p. 244.

1971

1971

1   AMASSIAN, MARGARET, and SADOWSKI, JAMES. "Mede and Mercede: A
Study of the Grammatical Metaphor in 'Piers Plowman' C: IV:
335-409." NM, 72, no. 3 (September):457-76.
      Both mercede and mede are "reward," but mercede is
founded upon justice, and hence is probably not as valuable
as mede, which is founded upon love. Mercede is like an indirect grammatical relationship (where there is no agreement
in case between a relative and its antecedent) and like an
adjective which depends on a substantive for its meaning.
Mede is like the direct grammatical relationship (showing conformity of gender, case, and number) of a relative to its
antecedent, which gives meaning to the receiving relative.
Conscience defines a direct relationship as a "recorde of
treuthe," that is, as a record and recollection of faith or
of a previously known veracitas, probably referring to the
proper relationship of man to God, the Divine Substantive.
This direct grammatical relationship is similar to the agreement of an adjective with its antecedent. C IV 365 ff. describe the indirect relationship, seen in a pejorative context
in which "indirect man," lacking "case agreement" of faithfulness with his "antecedent" God, is thus unable to assume his
meaning. C IV 407-9 wittily reverse the metaphoric equiva-
lents of God as substantive, man as adjective: Christ's
Incarnation transforms accidental humanity into a divine
substantive.

2   BAIRD, JOSEPH L. "Secte and Suit Again: Chaucer and Langland."
ChR 6, no. 2 (Fall):117-19.
      B V 495-98 (cf. C VIII 130-31) is used as evidence that
secte in the Epilogue of the Clerk's Tale (E 1171) means
"petition, suit of law." Argues that Skeat (1886.1) has
misconstrued the passage in Piers Plowman, which properly
refers to Christ leading a secte, not the sorwe. In context,
this refers to "a bringing forward of a legal action in
court" and "a bringing forth, as a result of that action,
those clothed in our suit, i.e., mankind in the flesh."

*3   BLYTHE, JOAN HEIGES. "Images of Wrath: Lydgate and Langland."
Dissertation, North Carolina, Chapel Hill.
      Abstracted: DAI 32:908A.

4   BOWERS, R.H. "The Comic in Late Medieval Sensibility (Piers
Plowman B.v)." ABR 22 (September):353-63.
      Argues that medieval scholarship emphasizes the pessi-
mistic aspects of Catholicism--for example, the Deadly Sins,
the contemptus mundi tradition--rather than the optimistic

aspects, which are grounded in Genesis 1:26, 31 and Psalm
145:9. In B V, Repentance prays for mercy for the confined
sinners in the optimistic spirit of the Christian pastor who
realizes Christ's concern and mercy. Langland appreciates
that we are "all pretentious human beings, imperfect and un-
perfected creatures, struggling as best we can with contin-
gency and circumstance." This same spirit is seen in
Hrotsvitha's Abraham and Paphnutius.

5 BURROW, J.A. Ricardian Poetry. London: Routledge & Kegan
   Paul, passim.
        Compares Chaucer, Gower, Langland, and the Pearl Poet in
   an attempt to define a period style, a sense of narrative, and
   a common image of man. Langland, like Gower, avoids traditional poetic diction and phraseology, or uses such language
   ironically; his attributions of expository utterances to allegorical characters is a fictional form comparable to Chaucer's
   pilgrim-framing of his stories; his use of a dream-narrator of
   limited perceptions is common to all the authors under discussion.
        Piers Plowman shares its period's concern with narration
   and description; a new sense of form and structure in divisions of the text, enclosed forms, and circular structures;
   and the manner of signifying meaning based on the literal mode
   emphasizing exemplary characteristics. Langland is also
   characteristic of his period in his disinterest in the epic
   conventions of warfare and in "great moments" of beginnings
   and endings. The hero's confrontation with allegorical characters, the confessions of his faults, his humorous self-
   deprecation, and the self-deprecation of the author for which
   he stands are all to varying degrees characteristic of the
   four authors under discussion.

6 CALÍ, PIETRO. Allegory and Vision in Dante and Langland.
   University College, Cork: Cork University Press, 198 pp.
        Grants that the Divina Commedia and Piers Plowman are
   different in conception, execution, and style, that they were
   intended for different audiences, and that Langland did not
   know Dante's work directly or indirectly; nevertheless, compares the poems on the basis of their approach to the nature
   of evil, the theme of repentance and regeneration, the role of
   the central figure (Beatrice and Piers), and the ability of
   each poet to relate the allegorical method to human experience.
        As in Dante's poem, the opening vision of Piers Plowman
   stresses the spiritual crisis in man and society, made victim
   of cupidity, though Langland embodies the theme in scenes of
   "varied humanity" while Dante relies on bestiary symbolism.
   Intervention from above (Virgil, Holicherch) offers

1971

directions to moral renewal and prompts the desire of the
Dreamer to learn the nature of the false. Passūs II-IV are
compared with the Inferno as an examination of sin presented
to the Dreamer, though for Langland the emphasis is almost
wholly on cupidity, whereas Dante presents all manifestations
of the sinful life. Both the Visio and the Inferno affirm the
implementation of Divine Law and Justice.
    The first part of the Dowel section parallels Dante's
Antepurgatory in that in both, the Dreamer acquires a clearer
awareness of the duties and hardships of movement away from
sin, between a determination to do good and a definite orientation toward it. The second vision of Dowel (the lessons of
Conscience, Patience, and the appearance of Haukyn) parallels
the movement of the Pilgrim in the Purgatorio, after the confrontation with the Deadly Sins. The attainment of a higher
level of spirituality is seen in the vision of the Earthly
Paradise in Purgatorio XXVIII and the Dobet and Dobest sections of Piers Plowman.
    The appearances in the poem of both Beatrice and Piers
are "charged with a sense of emotional urgency and anxious
expectation"; both appear at an indeterminate stage of the
Dreamer's/Pilgrim's spiritual progress; both are "God-bearing
images" whose importance passes from merely an individual's
salvation to wider, sacramental significance. The end of
Piers Plowman and of the Purgatorio are similar in warning of
the Church's disintegration but promising at the same time the
incorruptibility of the eternal Church. Reviewed by S.S.
Hussey, N&Q, c.s. 207 (n.s. 19) (1972):388-89.

7   CAMPBELL, JOHN. The Polite Correspondence: or, Rational Amuse-
    ment, being a Series of Letters, Philosophical, Poetical, His-
    torical etc. New York: Garland Publishing.
        Facsimile reprint of [Campbell], [1741].1.

8   CHATTERTON, THOMAS. Miscellanies in Prose and Verse. London:
    Fielding & Walker. Westmead, Farnborough, Hants., England:
    Gregg International Publishers.
        Reprinted from the copy in the Brighton Public Library.
    See Chatterton, 1778.1.

9   CHESSELL, DEL. "The World Made Flesh: The Poetry of Langland."
    Critical Review (Melbourne) 14:109-25.
        Comments on numerous scenes of the poem--the fall of the
    Angels (B I), the confession of the Deadly Sins (B V), the
    Haukyn episode (B VI), the Tree of Charity (B XVI), the
    Harrowing of Hell (B XVIII), and so on--to emphasize the
    vivid, metaphysical qualities of Langland's poetry. Sees B
    XVIII as the center of the poem, after which Will, though

still dreaming, puts to work in the world his new knowledge of
the mystery of the Cross and understands the possibilities of
immortality for human nature.

10 DAVLIN, Sister Mary Clemente. "Kynde Knowyng as a Major Theme in
Piers Plowman B." RES, n.s. 22, no. 85:1-19.
    Rather than fading in importance after B XV, the theme
of kynde knowyng remains central to the poem. The Dowel section shows Will failing to gain kynde knowyng because he seeks
only a theoretical definition of Dowel. Anima's speech (XV
47 ff.) serves as the turning point. The Dobet section shows
Will's search has changed in its object and its mode of knowing, as manifested in direct, vigorous syntax and word-play.
In learning to love, Will begins to suffer--first from Anima's
rebuke, then in viewing Christ's passion, then later in long-
ing for Piers and his pursuit of the Samaritan. The debate of
the Four Daughters of God is seen to parallel the theoretical
knowledge of theology with experiential wisdom achieved
through love. The Incarnation is considered as God's desire
to achieve a kynde knowyng of man, hence the responsibility of
man to try to become like God. The Dobest section shows
Will's experiences in a larger social context and clarifies
the difference between the gift of wisdom and its living out
in life.

11 FOWLER, DAVID C. "Piers Plowman." In Recent Middle English
Scholarship and Criticism: Survey and Desiderata. Edited by
J. Burke Severs. Pittsburgh: Duquesne University Press;
Louvain: Editions E. Nauwelaerts, pp. 9-28.
    Reviews major scholarship on the poem since Bloomfield
(1939.1). Praises such scholars and critics as Robertson and
Huppé, Bloomfield, and Frank; forecasts the importance of the
studies of Woolf, Muscatine, and Burrow that suggest the poem
expresses a loss of faith in traditional medieval values.
Argues against a biographical reading of the poem and calls
for an historical study of the C-text (which Fowler believes
was written by the same man who wrote the B-version) in an
effort to reappraise social and religious reform.

*12 EBY, JAMES ARTHUR. "The Alliterative Meter of Piers Plowman A."
Dissertation, Michigan, 153 pp.
    Abstracted: DAI 32:3948A.

*13 GLOBE, ALEXANDER V. "Apocalyptic Themes in the Sibylline
Oracles, the Revelation, Langland, Spenser, and Marvell."
Dissertation, Toronto.
    Abstracted: DAI 32:918A-19A.

1971

14 GRADON, PAMELA. Form and Style in Early English Literature.
    London: Methuen & Co., pp. 60-62, 66-77, 84, 98-113.
        B XX 120-27, the attack of Coveityse, is seen as charac-
    teristic of Langland's nonmetaphoric allegory (comparable to
    Everyman, rather than to Prudentius), displaying a shift from
    allegorical to literal action.
        B V 188-208, Langland's description of Coveityse, is
    compared with that of Robert Holcot's Commentary on the
    Prophets; it is the difference between a portrait of a human
    being and one of a monster that functions as an emblem. Com-
    pared with Chaucer's treatment of the Physician in the "General
    Prologue," however, Langland's portrait disappoints as a result
    of the poet's insistence on intellectually appropriate and
    emotionally evocative images.
        Langland is seen as the English writer most like Dante
    in making concrete the physical details of the allegory, in
    his ability to fuse the sensuous with the symbolic.
        Piers functions in the poem as a figura--acting like a
    person while typifying some general idea--rather than as a
    personified abstraction. He is probably never to be identified
    with Christ. Instead, he functions as an idealized projection
    of the Dreamer, both the dominant theme of the poem and the
    center of the Dreamer's attention. "The structure is a func-
    tion of the dramatic interplay between the Dreamer and Piers,
    vitalised by Piers' figural nature."

15 HARWOOD, BRITTON J. "Piers Plowman: Fourteenth-Century Skepti-
    cism and the Theology of Suffering." Bucknell Review 19
    (Winter):119-36.
        Although the Dreamer believes in God's reality and His
    transcendence, he lacks knowledge of His immanence. This
    vision of an immanent God is impaired by sin, the nominalists'
    ideas of God's potentia absoluta, and their insistence on the
    importance of intuition as the basis of all genuine knowledge.
    Piers Plowman develops in an epistemological fashion, turning
    from one way of knowing to another; the Dreamer's search is
    metaphysical rather than moral. Man discovers in himself the
    image of God when Conscience supplies a sense of God's suffer-
    ing for our sins and our suffering remorse.

16 HICKES, GEORGE. Institutiones Grammaticæ Anglo-Saxonicæ et
    Mœso-Gothica. A Scolar Press Facsimile. English Linguistics
    1500-1800 [A Collection of Facsimile Reprints], selected and
    edited by R.C. Alston, no. 277. Menston, England: Scolar
    Press.
        See Hickes, 1689.1.

17 HOBSBAUM, PHILIP. "Piers Plowman through Modern Eyes." Poetry
   Review 61 (Winter):335-62.
       Piers Plowman is really two poems, the Visio and the
   Vita, as suggested in their different moral stances, lapse in
   continuity of the argument, alteration of tone (from sermon by
   example to sermon by precept), and great decline in the value
   of the poetry. The poem must be modernized for contemporary
   readers, and the B-text is best for both content and poetry.
   Langland parallels Ockham in his radical conscience, assuming
   a middle position between Marsilius of Padua and John of
   Jandum on the left and Bernard's De consideratione ad Eugenium
   Papam and Dante's De monarchia on the right. The Visio creates
   a view of life that is shared, communal property of preachers,
   theologians, and satirists. The characterizations of the
   Deadly Sins, drawn from sermon material, link Langland to the
   later Vice-figures of the drama. Sees Langland as representing the best of English poetry in pithy, proverbial, local,
   and alliterative qualities. Reprinted with minor revisions:
   Hobsbaum, 1979.5.

18 JOSIPOVICI, GABRIEL. The World and the Book: A Study of Modern
   Fiction. London and Basingstoke: Macmillan & Co., pp. 52-56.
       Piers Plowman and the Divina Commedia are compared as
   works in which the hero-narrator realizes he is lost, a figure
   of authority points the way to salvation through experience,
   and such experience comes to be appreciated as a reinforcement
   of the teachings of the Church, for the world is a book of
   God's meaning. These attitudes are contrasted with those of
   Chaucer, in which authority and experience are divorced, and
   the folly of making fictions by anyone seriously interested in
   the truth is emphasized.

19 LEE, B.S. "Antichrist and Allegory in Langland's Last Passus."
   University of Cape Town Studies in English 2 (February):1-12.
       The structure of B XX resembles that of the Prologue in
   a more complicated fashion: the satire is now dependent on
   the allegory; it is dynamic rather than static, primarily
   spiritual rather than secular. Langland's portrayal of the
   Antichrist is consistent with the down-to-earth picture of the
   world he presents in the poem: there are no miraculous witnesses such as Enoch and Elias; no overt acts of tyranny or
   miracles—just the representation of sinners indifferent to
   grace.

*20 MULLANEY, CAROL A. "Piers Plowman: A Study of Voice and Address
   Relationships in the Confessions of the Deadly Sins." Dissertation, Catholic University of America, 136 pp.
       Abstracted: DAI 32:2063A.

1971

*21 OIJI, TAKERO. "Four Figures of Piers the Plowman." Bulletin of
     the College of General Education of Tohoku University (Sendai,
     Japan) 12, no. 2:23-46.
          Source: MLA International Bibliography, 1971, p. 39,
     no. 2357.

22 OWEN, DOROTHY L. Piers Plowman: A Comparison with Some Earlier
    and Contemporary French Allegories. Folcroft, Pa.: Folcroft
    Press, xiii + 125 pp.
          Reprint of Owen, 1912.5.

23 PALMER, BARBARA. "The Guide Convention in Piers Plowman." LSE,
    n.s. 5:13-28.
          Sees the main problem of the poem as structural rather
    than thematic. Of the three main structural elements--dream
    vision, personification, and the quest motif--none is main-
    tained throughout the poem. Confusion between dream and wak-
    ing periods obscures the poem's geography; the personification
    shows a mixture of allegorical and representational, external
    and internal elements; and the expected linear order of the
    quest consequently suffers. The guide figures are insuffi-
    cient: Holicherch's behavior lapses into "jealousy" of Lady
    Mede, and Piers vacillates in his identity and is hence un-
    reliable. Will's roles as Dreamer and as commentator are not
    sufficiently distinguished; the tone is confused, and as a
    result, the audience is unable to gauge the questor's progress.

*24 RYAN, THOMAS ANTHONY. "The Poetry of Reform: Christian Socra-
     tism in the First Dream of Dowel." Dissertation, Brown,
     286 pp.
          Abstracted: DAI 32:5750A.

25 SALTER, ELIZABETH. "Piers Plowman and the Visual Arts." In
    Encounters: Essays on Literature and the Visual Arts. Edited
    by John Dixon Hunt. London: Studio Vista, pp. 11-27.
          Argues that the locus of action in the poem is change-
    able but, as opposed to Muscatine (1963.7), that this does not
    indicate insecurity of structure. Rather, as in the Cloud of
    Unknowing, such dislocations suggest a new stability in
    spiritual themes that inform history. Sees in the pictorial
    tradition of the Utrecht Psalter a similar juxtaposition of
    disparate subjects, guided by the spiritual meanings of the
    text that inspires them. Notes Langland's probable knowledge
    of schematic illustrations of works of spiritual instruction,
    but sees in the works of Hieronymus Bosch the best comparison
    with Langland's themes and methods: the movement of man
    toward damnation; the questioning of accepted boundaries of
    the ordinary and the extraordinary; the understanding of

1971

varied phenomena effected through the medium of a central
character--a saint or, in Piers Plowman, a dreamer.

26 SCHIPPER, JAKOB. A History of English Versification. New York:
AMS Press.
Reprint of Schipper, 1910.13.

*27 SZITTYA, PENN RODION. "'Caimes Kynde': The Friars and the Exe-
getical Origins of Medieval Antifraternalism." Dissertation,
Cornell, 293 pp.
Abstracted in DAI 33:287A-88A.

*28 TAITT, P.S. "A Comparison of the Treatment of Ecclesiastical
Figures in Chaucer's Canterbury Tales and Langland's Vision of
William concerning Piers the Plowman." M.A. thesis, Durham.
Source: Index to Theses, vol. 21, p. 14. See Taitt,
1975.20.

29 TAITT, PETER. "In Defence of Lot." N&Q, c.s. 216 (n.s. 18),
no. 8 (August):284-85.
Langland was not following the Vulgate account of Lot's
incest, in which Lot was exonerated. Rather, both Langland
and Chaucer (who likewise connects Lot with Herod) probably
derive their accounts from Peter Comestor's Historia scholastica, chapter 54.

*30 VAN'T HUL, BERNARD. "Didactic and Mimetic Ambivalence in the A-
Visio of Piers Plowman." Dissertation, Northwestern, 183 pp.
Abstracted: DAI 32:5205A-206A.

31 WHITE, BEATRICE. "Poet and Peasant." In The Reign of Richard II:
Essays in Honour of May McKisack. Edited by F.R.H. Du Boulay
and Caroline M. Barron. [London]: University of London,
Athlone Press, pp. 58-74.
Places Langland's sympathetic and realistic treatment of
peasants in the context of prevailing hostility directed toward
this class in medieval literature. Contrasts Langland's Piers
with Chaucer's Plowman as the difference between a spiritual
experience and a "correct rhetorical exercise." Sees Gower's
view of the peasant as one of distrust and suspicion, if not
actual dislike. Concludes that medieval poets were often un-
reliable and prejudiced witnesses of the peasant's life,
"tending to present him as a humble saint, surly, embittered
serf, carousing bumpkin, patient toiler, or menacing figure
of evil." Suggests that literary evidence on this topic must
be balanced by that supplied by the chroniclers.

1972

1972

*1   ADAMS, IRA ROBERT. "Narrative Techniques and the Apocalyptic
      Mode of Thought in Piers Plowman." Dissertation, Virginia,
      232 pp.
            Abstracted: DAI 33:3627A-28A.

*2   AERS, D. "Allegorical Modes: A Critical Study, with Special
      Reference to Piers Plowman." Dissertation, York.
            Source: Index to Theses, vol. 22, p. 16. See Aers,
      1975.1.

3   ALFORD, JOHN ALEXANDER. "A Note on Piers Plowman B.xviii.390:
      'Til Parce It Hote.'" MP 69, no. 4 (May):323-25.
            Considers the phrase an allusion to Job 7:16, rather
      than Psalm 15:1, as Fuller (1961.9) believed. The phrase was
      taken over into the beginning of the first lectio of the
      Office of the Dead for Matins, stressing penitence and mercy,
      and said for the souls in Purgatory. This lectio also seems
      to have given rise to penitential prayers in the fourteenth
      century in which parce appears to be a common formula.

4   CANTAROW, ELLEN. "A Wilderness of Opinions Confounded: Allegory
      and Ideology." CE 34, no. 2 (October):215-52, esp. pp. 215-27.
            Contends that allegory idealizes authoritarian, ahistori-
      cal, conservative ideology; and Piers Plowman in particular
      asserts the institutional inviolability of the Church.
      Langland, who probably had a "not inconsiderable" position as
      a clerk, was orthodox in religion, conservative in politics,
      and more interested in improving the administration of things
      than in changing their basic structure. The effect of the
      realism of his social pictures is to show the typical, change-
      less conditions that he feels reflect a timeless order, as-
      severating ideals so that social evils can be endured. In
      particular, C IX portrays the aristocratic life graciously,
      and the laborers, described in the "low" style, are seen at
      best as "poor dupes of circumstances, victims of an inevitable
      poverty and of their own ignorance." Piers is a mouthpiece
      for the clerical-autocratic establishment: the allegory makes
      him represent moral living while it makes the peasantry repre-
      sent moral deprivation. The effect of the poetry is "to
      apologize for the medieval power structure and its institu-
      tions, while thrusting the blame for social ills onto the very
      individuals who are most victimized by them."

1972

*5   COVELLA, Sister Francis Dolores.   "Formulaic Second Half-Lines in
     Skeat's A-text of Piers Plowman: Norms for a Comparative
     Analysis of the A-, B-, and C-texts."   Dissertation, New York
     University, 265 pp.
          Abstracted: DAI 33:2887A.

6   CREWE, J.V.   "Langland's Vision of Society in Piers Ploughman."
     Theoria (University of Natal, Pietermaritzburg) 39 (October):
     1-16.
          The Incarnation, in its joining of the earthly and the
     transcendent, is central to Langland's depiction of society
     seen "always and only" in relation to the ideal society of
     perfect human brotherhood.   Although Mede is necessary to the
     world in some form, Langland is able to suggest her true
     ultimate worth in comparison with Holicherch.   Similarly, the
     comic-realist depiction of Gluttony also suggests the beastli-
     ness at the expense of spirituality and true sociability.
     Though the temporal sphere is not finally renounced in the
     poem, Piers Plowman shows Langland's partial withdrawal into
     the realm of private conscience, in a movement away from the
     particulars of contemporary society toward a visionary state.

7   DAVLIN, Sister Mary Clemente.   "Petrus, Id Est, Christus: Piers
     Plowman as 'the Whole Christ.'"   ChR 6, no. 4 (Spring):280-92.
          Coherence of the figure of Piers is supplied through the
     doctrine of the Mystical Body of Christ, which connects and
     relates all the partial meanings of Piers--the good man,
     Christian, Peter, Christ, the Church--for the Church, the
     Christian man, and God are united in the mystical Christ.
     Piers is first established as the good man; then he is Christ
     and God while at the same time remaining a man; then he later
     becomes Peter--though he does not always represent these fig-
     ures equally.   He becomes God through the Incarnation, when
     man shares his nature with God; but he can later be referred
     to as distinct from God for men remain themselves as well as
     become part of the Mystical Body.

8   KELLOGG, ALFRED L.   Chaucer, Langland, Arthur: Essays in Middle
     English Literature.   New Brunswick, N.J.:   Rutgers University
     Press, pp. 29-31, 32-50, 51-58.
          Contains reprints of Kellogg, 1949.6, 1958.5, and
     1960.8.

9   KIRK, ELIZABETH D.   The Dream Thought of Piers Plowman.   Yale
     Studies in English, no. 178.   New Haven and London: Yale
     University Press, 214 pp.
          Progress in editorial treatment, resolution of the
     authorship controversy, and recent attempts to view the poem

in the context of late medieval art and thought allow study of
Piers Plowman in terms of the dramatic structure of the unfolding of the theme of God's interaction with men. Langland's
manipulation of the conventions of dream-allegories causes the
dream-world to become the "real life" of human society and thus
alters the audience's perspective on its own experience. The
additions of the B-text to the A-Prologue--the portrayal of
kingship and the Rat Parliament--add a more complex temporal
perspective and an emblematic quality to the A-text's literal
portrayal of society. The confrontation of the Dreamer and
Holicherch complements the Prologue's establishment of actual
human experience as the basis of the poetic world and formu-
lates the question of the resolution of authority and experiential knowledge in the idea of "kynde knowying." The Trial
of Lady Mede serves to reject the principle of the mere manipulation of socioeconomic forces that influence behavior, in
favor of that of the transformation of human motivation itself. The late medieval use of the first-person narrator
suggests that the Confession of the Deadly Sins involves the
Dreamer himself; the scene is designed to show the effect of
Reason and Conscience on problems of human action. The portrayal of the decay of the human spirit is shown to result
from man's refusal to accept subordination to God; but the
poem balances this refusal with a positive movement toward
repentance. The B-text adds the confession of Wrath in keep-
ing with the A-text's unusual attitude toward the sin as not
an unambiguously bad thing, and identifies it with the poet.
The B-text also forestalls possible objections by placing
restitution at the end of the sequence by introducing the
topic in the dialogue of Avarice and Repentance. Sinful man
is shown to be unable to save himself; and Piers, who embodies
pietas rather than caritas, is equally helpless to change the
motivation of the folk. The Pardon scene provides a new
rationale in paralleling Romans in the recognition of the
incommensurability of the order of law and the order of
Christ. Tearing the Pardon parallels the psychological event
described by Paul in which the resentment of the righteous man
at Christ's superseding man's view of his own responsibility,
resulting in violence and destruction, transforms man. The
scene resolves the conflict of the Nominalists and the
Augustinians over the value of works in salvation.
    The A-Vita is a movement from natural human faculties
toward authorities that complement human insight with revelation. Yet the A-Vita disintegrates, since it is focused
around the perceptions of the Dreamer who continues patterns
of thought that have been superseded in the Pardon scene. The
B-Vita recasts the characters Clergy and Learning in order to
emphasize the relationship of man to a transcendent God--a

problem at the basis of the Dreamer's resistance. The B-poet
adds the Trajan sequence and the Nature-Reason-Imagination
sequence in order to bring the poem back to the point reached
in the Pardon scene. The Banquet scene clarifies the meaning
of Patience and Conscience which, along with the Dreamer's
shame, can approach Dowel. Haukyn, an emblem of the Dreamer,
Piers of the Visio, the Priest at Mass and recipient of the
Pardon, suggest that Dowel is ultimately involved with a theo-
centric understanding by man of his own good and evil. B
XV ff. expand this emblem into the drama of salvation history
on the basis of the transitional figure Anima and the Tree of
Charity scene, the development of Piers, and the stages of
Christ's life.

The B-text centers on three confrontations of God's will
and man's: the Pardon scene, the Crucifixion, and the Pentecost. The poem's dramatic structure is based on a pattern of
echo, development, recapitulation, and resolution carried by
the liturgy, the events of human history, and typology. The
action of the poem is patterned by such metaphors of human
activity as farming, quest, war, and the portrayals of moments
"in which a consciousness grasps its finitude in the face of
reality and, in the very moment of its despair and rebellion,
breaks through to a new level of being." Reviewed by David C.
Fowler, MP 71 (1974):393-404 (see Fowler, 1974.9); Johan
Kerling, English Studies 56 (1975):256-57; Barbara Raw, N&Q,
c.s. 218 (n.s. 20) (1973):437-39; and Katherine B. Trower,
Costerus, n.s. 1 (1974):151-64 (see Trower, 1974.19).

10 LANGLAND, WILLIAM. The Vision of William concerning Piers the
Plowman, together with Vita de Dowel, Dobet, et Dobest,
Secundum Wit et Resoun, by William Langland (about 1362-1380
A.D.) Edited from Numerous Manuscripts, with Prefaces, Notes,
and a Glossary, by the Rev. Walter W. Skeat, M.A. Vol. 2,
The "Crowley" Text; or Text B. Early English Text Society,
o.s. 38. London: Oxford University Press.
Reprint of Langland, 1869.2.

*11 LICHSTEIN, DIANE PURDY. "Piers Plowman: An Image of Neo-
Platonic Christendom." Dissertation, Pennsylvania, 347 pp.
Abstracted: DAI 33:1690A.

*12 LINDEMANN, ERIKA CAROLINE DOROTHEA. "Translation Techniques in
William Langland's Piers Plowman." Dissertation, North
Carolina, Chapel Hill, 228 pp.
Abstracted: DAI 34:279A.

1972

13 LUNZ, ELISABETH. "The Valley of Jehosaphat in Piers Plowman."
       TSE 20:1-10.
             Langland's reference in C XXI 402-17 of the Valley of
       Jehosaphat (from Joel 3) in the context of the Harrowing of
       Hell and the universal salvation effected thereby shows the
       author's emphasis on Christ's love over His justice, as well
       as his independence from patristic interpretations that stress
       the pending judgment on unbelievers.

*14 MALARD, SANDRA GENE. "The Rhetorical Structure of Piers Plowman
       C." Dissertation, Michigan, 162 pp.
             Abstracted: DAI 33:2334A-35A.

*15 MATLOCK, CHARLES MICHAEL. "An Interpretation of Piers Plowman
       Based on the Medieval Dream Background." Dissertation,
       S.U.N.Y., Albany, 199 pp.
             Abstracted: DAI 33:2940A-41A.

16 MEANS, MICHAEL H. The Consolatio Genre in Medieval English Lit-
       erature. University of Florida Humanities Monograph, no. 36.
       Gainesville: University of Florida Press, pp. 66-90, passim.
             Piers Plowman is considered as a representative example
       of the consolatio genre, whose generic model is Boethius's
       Consolatio philosophiæ, in which "in an essentially philo-
       sophical or eschatological dialogue (or series of dialogues)
       with one or more allegorical instructors, the narrator is
       reconciled to his misfortunes, shown how to attain his goal,
       or enlightened and consoled in a similar way." As opposed to
       the Latin consolation genre (e.g., Cicero's Tusculan Disputa-
       tions), the medieval consolatio is addressed to a narrator or
       persona; the tone, therefore, is often impassioned, rather
       than calm or detached, and the arguments put forward are
       psychologically and pedagogically structured. The "purest"
       examples of the genre in Middle English are Pearl and Gower's
       Confessio Amantis, in both of which the narrator is consoled
       by a single instructor, though in the Confessio Amantis, as in
       Piers Plowman and the Roman de la Rose, the resolution of the
       narrator's problem requires more than one instructor. The
       consolatio in Piers Plowman, as in the Roman de la Rose and
       Hawes's Pastime of Pleasure, is modified by the quest motif.
       The subject of the poem is the narrator's education in the
       nature of perfection; the "authority and bias of each instruc-
       tor is limited by his nature, the mental faculty or the social
       or cosmological status he personifies." The Dowel section in
       particular shows the psychological drama of Will's encounters
       in learning the nature of perfection.

17 MIDDLETON, ANNE. "Two Infinites: Grammatical Metaphor in Piers
      Plowman." ELH 39, no. 2 (June):169-88.
           Argues that infinites in B XIII 127, referring to Dowel
      and Dobet, is to be taken in the sense of "lacking boundaries,
      formal limits," and hence imperfect, rather than in the sense
      of "all-inclusive, self-defining, perfect." Dowel and Dobet
      are thus properly seen as positive and comparative degrees of
      something (i.e., Dobest) intelligible only in its completed
      form. In grammatical theory, to which Langland was attracted
      for his metaphor because it was said to mirror natural law,
      the word "infinite" is used with reference to the uninflected
      verb or verbal substantive, and the interrogative pronoun.
      To define the Three Lives through the uninflected verb is to
      describe them as "occurrence without occasion, the essence of
      Christian action rather than exemplary instances of it"; and
      just as the interrogative pronoun seeks as answer a name or
      substance, Dowel and Dobet seek perfected charity, Dobest,
      which restores the divine similitude in man.
           The obscurities and inconsistencies in Langland's uses
      of the Three Lives and in allegorical "characters" such as
      Hunger, Peace, and Recklessness testify to the poet's moral
      doubts "about whether a narrative fiction can adequately em-
      body the truth--doubts inherited from the sermon tradition's
      distrust of the worth of its own medium of persuasion." The
      poet is obsessed with the need to speak the truth, yet is dis-
      trustful of the means at his disposal to communicate adequately
      the kind of reality he wishes to express. In this context,
      grammar, which reflects the relation of concepts in the mind
      which corresponds to the relationships of "real entities in
      the universe," offers one of the "least unreliable explanatory
      models" to overcome the distorting tendency of personification
      allegory.

18 MUSCATINE, CHARLES. Poetry and Crisis in the Age of Chaucer.
      University of Notre Dame Ward-Phillips Lectures in English
      Language and Literature, no. 4. Notre Dame, Ind., and London:
      University of Notre Dame Press, pp. 71-110.
           Argues that the form and style of Piers Plowman is
      symptomatic of the cultural crisis of the fourteenth century.
      The characteristic Gothic formal structures of scholarly dis-
      putation, the procession narrative, and the genres of dream-
      vision, allegory, romance, fabliau and sermon cannot be said
      to govern the poem; nor does the definitions of the Three
      Lives. The poem mixes the concrete and the abstract in an
      unstable allegory and creates a surrealistic sense of space.
      The rich poetic texture of the work, relying on a wide range
      of tone, arresting imagery, and continual susceptibility of

1972

its rhythms to irruptions, suggests a crisis of belief in orthodoxy and a "failure of hope."

19 PAULL, MICHAEL R. "Mahomet and the Conversion of the Heathen in Piers Plowman." ELN 10, no. 1 (September):1-8.
Mahomet is seen in Piers Plowman as the creator of medieval heathenism and as symptomatic of the chaos of the fourteenth-century Church; typologically he is a precursor of the Antichrist. A complete rendition of the story of Mahomet as originally a Christian who strove to be pope is found in the thirteenth-century Legende de Mahomet of Jean le Clerc; the story was also probably known to Dante (see Inferno XXVIII). The story of Mahomet's training the dove is from a more popular tradition linking him with Antichrist. To Langland, as to Wyclif, Mahomet is symbolic of the cupidity of the false clergy which weakens the Church.

20 PROPPE, KATHERINE. "Piers Plowman: An Annotated Bibliography for 1900-1968." Comitatus 3:33-90.
Lists 265 items, including 35 dissertations.

21 SPEARING, A.C. Criticism and Medieval Poetry. 2d ed. London: Edward Arnold (Publishers), pp. 107-34.
Reprint of Spearing 1964.12.

22 WHITWORTH, CHARLES W., Jr. "Changes in the Roles of Reason and Conscience in the Revisions of 'Piers Plowman.'" N&Q, c.s. 217 (n.s. 19), no. 1 (January):4-7.
In the changes from the B- to the C-text, Langland shows himself attentive to the distinction of synderesis, "the innate sense of moral propriety," and the practical reason as sources of moral action. At the end of the poem, Conscience does not have the aid of Reason, but only that of synderesis which has been shown inadequate in the Lady Mede episode.

23 WITTIG, JOSEPH S. "'Piers Plowman' B, Passus IX-XII: Elements in the Design of the Inward Journey." Traditio 28:211-80.
Reads B IX-XII in terms of a program of spiritual ascent, as found in the pseudo-Bernardine Meditationes piisimæ de cognitione humanæ conditionis. Will, the reluctant affectus, must supply what Wit, the spokesman for the soul's cognitive abilities cannot, in order for the affective and cognitive aspects of anima to conform to the image in which man was created. Inwit and the dispositions of the Three Lives must imitate the Creator to contribute both words and work. The Dreamer's reluctance to reform his affectus is shown in the application of his wit, which leads him to that which he will not accept. Scripture informs him that he is neither in conformance with the imago dei nor acting to

1973

discipline his _affectus_ through the exercise of charity. The
first inner dream mirrors his folly; in the second vision of
the world (passus XI), he sees himself viewing the world more
as he should. Langland's emphasis in the Trajan story is on
salvational, rather than intercessional aspects. The emphasis
on good works serves to expose the low regard for such that
Will has felt and leads to feelings of remorse and shame and
the need for personal affective reform. Imaginatif suggests
"vivid representation to oneself involving conceptual, sensory,
and emotive aspects"; by presenting to Will his last end,
Imaginatif makes Will receptive to understanding the relationship of _bona spiritualia_ to his personal situation.

24 WOOLF, ROSEMARY. The English Mystery Plays. Berkeley and Los
    Angeles: University of California Press, pp. 124, 165.
        B V 612 is briefly discussed as an example of the common
    medieval motif of the triviality of the action that precipi-
    tates the Fall of man. Contemplacio's Prologue in _Ludus
    Coventriæ_ is likened in style to _Piers Plowman_, rather than
    the "normal limpid style of the Mystery plays."

                            1973

1   BARNEY, STEPHEN A. "The Ploughshare of the Tongue: The Progress
    of a Symbol from the Bible to _Piers Plowman_." MS 35:261-93.
        Traces the symbolic use of agricultural imagery from its
    locus classicus in I Corinthians 9:8-10 (itself a comment on
    Deuteronomy 25:4) and its various aspects, such as God as the
    planter of Israel or of mankind, mankind's fruitfulness or
    barrenness, the world as seed, the soul as field, and penance
    as cultivation, through the Old and New Testaments and later
    commentary, including Augustine's _Sermo_ 213 and Gregory's
    Moralia in Job (the latter a key "source" text for the con-
    ception of Piers). The metaphor of plowing as preaching was
    first analyzed by St. Eucher in his _Liber formularum spiri-
    tualis intelligentiæ_ and was continued by such as Hrabanus
    Maurus, Alain de Lille, Pierre Bersuire, the _Glossa ordinaria_,
    and Thomas Brunton. The author of _Piers Plowman_ shows his
    knowledge of the tradition in such passages as B X 471-74,
    B XV 451 ff., C VI 42-48, C XI 196-99, and C XXII 252-336,
    where connections between the plowman and the cleric are re-
    inforced. Argues that Piers has symbolic status as a purveyor
    of grace from his first appearance in the poem in all three
    versions, and rejects the notion that Piers is ever the type
    of the honest laborer. Reads the Half-acre scene of the C-
    text in light of the allegorical meaning of Piers as spiritual
    laborer and purveyor of grace.

                            299

1973

2   CARRUTHERS, MARY. The Search for St. Truth: A Study of Meaning
    in Piers Plowman. Evanston, Ill.: Northwestern University
    Press, 173 pp.
        The baffling meaning of the poem is in part related to
    the fact that in Piers Plowman words are shown to be ambig-
    uous as both revealers of truth and corruptors of understand-
    ing. The multiple definitions of the Three Lives suggest that
    all of their definitions are inadequate to Will's understand-
    ing and that the verbal sign itself is under examination. The
    central problem of the poem is epistemological, rather than
    moral--"a problem of knowing truly." Langland uses allegory
    as an exploratory tool; he sees language, when used properly,
    as a truthful sign of divinity; and like Augustine, he insists
    on the necessity of a truly Christian rhetoric to lead man to
    truth, as manifested in the various methods he employs to
    "define" Dowel and the various types of allegory he presents.
        The confusion produced by the poem is a reflection of
    its constantly changing elements and Langland's disregard for
    naturalistic narrative structures. The search for St. Truth
    is a search "for the signs that reveal him"; the variety and
    confusion of the types of signs in the Prologue indicate its
    signs are inadequate. Passūs II-IV show language as corrupted
    and ambivalent as is society in the Prologue, but manifesting
    a displacement of earthly realities from the divinity "that
    should inform them." Personification is used by Langland to
    explore the nature and limitations of language, as in the pre-
    sentation of False, seen as formlessness without fixed mean-
    ings, and in the irreconcilable double identities of Mede.
    The Deadly Sins lack spiritual resonance in the language used
    to describe them, formal coherence, and distinction of one
    from another.
        In the Visio, the only successful guides are Conscience
    and Piers, though Conscience, guided by his own natural intel-
    lect rather than by divine grace, is not infallible. Piers,
    who signals the change in the poem from personification to
    figural allegory, conflates plowing and pilgrimage as actions
    directed toward the same spiritual end, the attainment of the
    Pardon. Tearing the Pardon indicates that Piers, in a fashion
    analogous to Moses' breaking the Tables of the Law, expresses
    the change from the Old to the New Law, from that of the let-
    ter to that of the spirit. Passūs VIII-X present Will, repre-
    senting the will (an appetitive faculty) misunderstanding the
    kynde of Dowel as a substantive quality; his reactions to the
    various figural mirrors presented to him--the Vision of Middle
    Earth, Trajan, and so on--suggest that he does not realize
    man's responsibility for his condition. Imaginatif, the
    source of visions and the keeper of images, sets him on the
    right track by providing the means whereby he may understand

himself. Patience at the Dinner Party of Clergy introduces a
figural mode of understanding to replace the more limited
personification allegory. The character of Will also changes
in XIII in concentrating completely on his visions. Haukyn,
a mirror image of Will, is "resignified" in figural terms,
bringing the Dowel section to a climax. Anima turns the poem
from Dowel to charity. The Vision of the Tree of Charity
demonstrates the union of eternal truth and the temporal
world, raised to the level of figura. The Harrowing of Hell
likewise views history as figure and effects a resignification
through the Word, though the debate of the Four Daughters of
God suggests that this redeemed language, founded on redefi-
nition through paradox, is inexpressible in human language.
The ruin of the world as depicted in the final passus is seen
as a parody of the very process of the poem's comprehension,
with language and verbal meaning turned toward the destruc-
tiveness of Antichrist. Reviewed by Margaret Williams, JEGP
74 (1975):108-11.

3   COLES, E[LISHA]. An English Dictionary. London: Samuel Crouch.
     Reprint. Hildesheim and New York: Georg Olms Verlag.
          Facsimile reprint of Coles, 1676.1.

*4   CURRAN, SONIA TERRIE. "The Dreamer and His Visions: Rhetorical
     Determinants of Structure in Piers Plowman, B." Dissertation,
     Wisconsin, 249 pp.
          Abstracted: DAI 34:3339A.

5   ELLIOTT, THOMAS J. "Middle English Complaints against the Times:
     To Contemn the World or to Reform It?" AM 14:22-34.
          Aims to correct the misconception that complaints in the
     Middle Ages were primarily expressions of the contemptus mundi
     tradition and that, as asserted by Peter (1956.9), complaint
     is little more than a "vast medieval literature of reproof
     that ranges from comprehensive works like Handling Synne down
     to lyrics and epigrams a few lines long." Notes that many
     complaints call for social reform in the present time. Con-
     cludes that Piers Plowman is too complex to be called merely
     a complaint, and agrees with Bloomfield (1961.3) in consider-
     ing the poem as partaking of the genres/modes of dream narra-
     tive, dialogue, consolatio, debate, and encyclopedic satire.

*6   FARIS, DAVID EARL. "Symbolic Geography in Middle English Litera-
     ture: Pearl, Piers Plowman, Yvain and Gawain." Dissertation,
     Yale, 303 pp.
          Abstracted: DAI 34:7228A.

1973

7   HARWOOD, BRITTON J.   "'Clergye' and the Action of the Third
      Vision in Piers Plowman."   MP 70, no. 4 (May):279-90.
          Clergye "personifies an object of knowledge identifying
      a power of the mind" closely related to Scripture, designating
      the proper construance of Scripture and perception of the law
      that is essential to all Scripture.   Clergye can no longer
      offer a vision of God (see C XII 149-58), perhaps because of
      an historical shift in the late Middle Ages from allegory to
      the literal meaning and the consequences of Ockhamist episte-
      mology.   Since grace acts independently of Clergye, Clergye
      does not convert Will by providing a knowledge of Christ.

8   HARWOOD, BRITTON J.   "Librum-Arbitrium in the C-Text of Piers
      Plowman."   PQ 52, no. 4 (October):680-95.
          Librum Arbitrium is a separate faculty, composed of
      reason and will, as described by Stephen Langton and Robert
      Kilwardby; it is not, as asserted by Sanderlin (1941.9), all
      the powers of the soul and ought not to be identified with the
      Bernardine concept of the will, as does Donaldson (1949.1).
      Librum Arbitrium personifies one of the possibilities of the
      Dreamer's mind; the "action" of the episode examines the
      utility of Librum Arbitrium in relation to the Dreamer's
      search.   Librum Arbitrium uses all three planks in the C-text
      to describe the Librum Arbitrium of an individual in the state
      of grace using all the powers of the mind to fight the tempta-
      tion to stray from charity.   The loss of fruit signifies the
      uselessness of Librum Arbitrium to unregenerate man; but that
      the Dreamer does not love does not affect the uncontingent
      nature of God's love from which Christ issues.

9   HILL, THOMAS D.   "The Light That Blew the Saints to Heaven:
      Piers Plowman B, V. 495-503."   RES, n.s. 24, no. 95:444-49.
          Christ is the "liȝte that lepe" out of God the Father;
      at the words fiat lux (Genesis 1:3) the light that will blind
      Lucifer was generated.   Langland chooses the word blew to re-
      fer to the action of this light in freeing the saints in order
      to suggest that the Holy Spirit participates in the Harrowing
      of Hell.

*10 HERTZIG, MARIE JACOBUS.   "The Early Recension and Continuity of
      Certain Middle English Texts in the Sixteenth Century."   Dis-
      sertation, Pennsylvania, 372 pp.
          Abstracted: DAI 34:1913A-14A.

1973

11 LANGLAND, WILLIAM. The Vision of William concerning Piers
   Plowman, together with Vita de Dowel, Dobet, et Dobest, and
   Richard the Redeles. Edited by Walter W. Skeat. Part 4,
   section 1: Notes to Texts A, B, and C. Early English Text
   Society, o.s. 67. Millwood, N.Y.: Kraus Reprint Co.
   Reprint of Langland, 1877.2.

12 [LANGLAND, WILLIAM.] The Vision of William concerning Piers
   Plowman, together with Vita de Dowel, Dobet, et Dobest, and
   Richard the Redeles. Edited by Walter W. Skeat. Part 4,
   section 2: General Preface, Notes and Indexes. Early English
   Text Society, o.s. 81. Millwood, N.Y.: Kraus Reprint Co.
   Reprint of [Langland], 1884.2.

13 McFARLANE, K.B. The Nobility of Later Medieval England (The Ford
   Lectures for 1953 and Related Studies). Oxford: Clarendon
   Press.
   See Charleton, 1465.1.

14 MEDCALF, STEPHEN. "Piers Plowman and the Ricardian Age in Literature." In Literature and Western Civilization: The Mediaeval
   World. Edited by David Daiches and Anthony Thorlby. London:
   Aldus, pp. 643-96, esp. pp. 643-54, 684-89.
        The poem is discussed in the context of Ricardian liter-
   ature (see Burrow, 1971.5) with reference to Langland's use of
   "drastic similies" that combine the rough and the delicate,
   the mixture of idiosyncratic and didactic modes, and the
   visionary landscape that is full of significance yet is often
   realized in actual physical details. The Prologue is seen as
   an examination of the "way in which men live carelessly while
   eternity . . . surrounds them" and the difficulty of making a
   "satisfactory society out of a crowd." Tearing the Pardon is
   suggestive of Moses breaking the Tables of the Law. The many
   meanings of Piers is compared to Usk's treatment of Margaret
   in the Testament of Love.

15 PEARSALL, DEREK, and SALTER, ELIZABETH. Landscapes and Seasons
   of the Medieval World. London: Elek Books, pp. 133-35, 139.
        Langland shares the conventional attitudes of summer as
   a spiritual state of ease, winter as suffering, seasonal
   change as mutability. The margin illustrations of the
   Luttrell Psalter are compared to Langland's depiction of the
   hard facts of sowing-to-harvesting, yet both the psalter and
   the poem present the landscape in only fragmentary fashion.
   With regard to the adversities of winter weather, Langland's
   treatment (C XVI 293-94) merely provides an analogy of man's
   condition in an argument for the virtues of patient poverty.

1973

*16 TAITT, PETER STEWART. "The Quest Theme in Representative Works
     of the Thirteenth and Fourteenth Centuries." Dissertation,
     British Columbia.
          Abstracted: DAI 35:3703A.

17 TROWER, KATHERINE BACHE. "Temporal Tensions in the Visio of
    Piers Plowman." MS 35:389-412.
         The Visio dramatizes the transition in salvation history
    from the pre- or near-Christian period to the Sixth World Age
    (the Age of the Church), which begins at Christ's birth.
    Piers is either representative of the Old Testament Just Man
    (e.g., Abraham or Moses), or a type of the Apostles or disci-
    ples, or any man in the Sixth Age who imitates Christ. Mean-
    ings such as these are conveyed through Langland's use of the
    plowman figure, as informed by Matthew 20:1-16 (the parable of
    the laborers called to the vineyard) and Luke 13:6-9 (the
    parable of the barren fig tree), in both of which the preacher/
    husbandman serves as a mediator between time and eternity, man-
    kind and divinity, who gains a respite for mankind to seek
    repentance before the final "harvest."
         Although Piers is a transitional figure overlapping the
    Old and New Laws, the B-text establishes him in the Pardon
    scene in a pre-Christian age as one who dramatically expe-
    riences that he will not be imminently delivered to eternal
    reward. The C-text, by changing fifty to forty years (B V
    549/C VIII 188) and its interpolation into the gloss on the
    Pardon, represents Piers in the present age, to which the
    Pardon will only apply in the future. Piers's anger in the
    Tearing of the Pardon is directed perhaps at himself for not
    realizing he lives in the last days; in the C-text, however,
    he knows there is much to be done before the end.

18 TROWER, KATHERINE B. "The Figure of Hunger in Piers Plowman."
    ABR 24:238-60.
         Hunger in B VI is seen as operating on three levels,
    namely, as famine which, unlike the other eschatological woes
    prophesied in the passus, can be dispelled; as "the lack of
    spiritual food in forgetfulness of the creator" (from Bede;
    see Robertson and Huppé, 1951.9); and as the folk's hunger for
    God/Christ and His hunger for souls, seen in the context of
    salvation history. This last and most important sense is in-
    formed by the parable of the cursed fig tree (Matthew 21) and
    that of the barren fig tree (Luke 13) which, taken in combina-
    tion, indicate the two courses possible for mankind who refuse
    to work with Piers toward salvation or who are saved by the
    efforts of the intermediary. That Hunger teaches Piers
    lechecraft, which is associated in the poem with love, Christ,
    and moderation, further links Hunger with Christ. Lechecraft

1974

is shown to involve charity and patient poverty, which must be implemented by the faithful servant of Christ to assuage His hunger. The incongruous action of Hunger turning glutton may be inspired by the Sixth Beatitude of the Sermon on the Mount, which describes a satisfaction that is traditionally construed as impossible in this life; the scene affords a contrast between Piers and the folk in their use of physical goods. And although Hunger is capable of destroying the folk, that he does not do so shows at the end of B VI that Christ's justice and judgment is informed and balanced by His mercy. Piers's acceptance of Hunger's teaching enables him to "express his resolution at the end of Passus VII and to become the clearly defined figure of Christ later in the poem."

*19 VAUGHAN, MICEAL FRANCIS. "The Tropological Context of the Easter Awakening: Piers Plowman B, Passus 16-20." Dissertation, Cornell, 239 pp.
       Abstracted: DAI 34:7205A-206A.

1974

1   ALFORD, JOHN A. "Haukyn's Coat: Some Observations on Piers Plowman B. XIV. 22-7." Medium Ævum 43, no. 2:133-38.
       The lines describing Haukyn's coat are a paraphrase of the Sermon on the Mount; Haukyn is the embodiment of what Christ preaches against, and Conscience rebukes him in B XIV 33 with Christ's words, "Ne solliciti sitis." Langland shows knowledge of the exegetical tradition on the Sermon, which contrasts earthly and heavenly treasures in terms of filth and cleanliness, and equates treasure and the heart. Haukyn's "wife" is his own flesh, for the "promise of renewal through penance includes the body as well as the soul."

2   BESTUL, THOMAS H. Satire and Allegory in Wynnere and Wastoure. Lincoln: University of Nebraska Press, passim.
       Wynnere and Wastoure is compared to Piers Plowman with reference to such topics as the multiplicity of genres both poems exhibit (see Bloomfield, 1961.3), formal complexities of the dream vision genre, realistic portrayal of the vices in the fourteenth century, social and apocalyptic issues, prophecies, and the topicality of social satire.

*3 BIRNES, WILLIAM JACK. "Patterns of Legality in Piers Plowman." Dissertation, New York University, 159 pp.
       Abstracted: DAI 35:1040A. See Birnes, 1975.5.

1974

*4 BOND, RONALD BRUCE. "A Study of Invidia in Medieval and Renais-
    sance English Literature." Dissertation, Toronto.
    Abstracted: DAI 35:1087A.

5 BRINK, BERNHARD ten. Early English Literature (to Wiclif).
    Translated by Horace M. Kennedy. New York: AMS.
    Reprint of Brink, 1883.1.

6 DEMEDIS, PANDELIS. "Piers Plowman, Prologue B. 196." Explicator
    33, no. 3 (November):Item 27.
        In this line, takes mase as "a sceptre or staff of of-
    fice, resembling in shape the weapon of war, which is borne
    before (or was carried by) certain officials." Translates the
    line: "for better is a little less than a long sorrow/ [Bet-
    ter] the mace among us all, though we miss a shrew-mouse."

7 DOOB, PENELOPE B.R. Nebuchadnezzar's Children: Conventions of
    Madness in Middle English Literature. New Haven and London:
    Yale University Press, pp. 226-28.
        The poem is compared with Hoccleve's Male Regle with
    regard to its confessional realism, the pretentious desire of
    some friars to be called "maister," and the confession of mad-
    ness made by the persona.

8 DWYER, RICHARD A. "The Appreciation of Handmade Literature."
    ChR 8, no. 3 (Winter):221-40, esp. pp. 224-25.
        MS. L (A-text) is briefly discussed as illustrating its
    scribe's free "improvement" of Langland's text by increasing
    the number of staves in the lines and introducing both second-
    ary alliteration and cross-alliteration. These changes in
    alliteration, as well as the inclusion of the poem in a MS
    otherwise comprised of romances, suggest that the scribe may
    have been "a conservative enthusiast for the old forms and
    stories . . . who may have been trying to bring Langland's
    novel use of those forms back into line."

9 FOWLER, DAVID C. "A New Interpretation of the A and B Texts of
    Piers Plowman." MP 71, no. 4 (May):393-404.
        A review-article on Kirk (1972.9) that praises the gen-
    eral deployment and disposition of the argument and its devel-
    opment and such individual topics of exposition as that of the
    Deadly Sins and the B-text poet's revision of the A-Vita.
    Criticizes, however, the notion that the Dreamer in the A-text
    undergoes a modification, as well as the notion, perhaps in-
    fluenced by Lawlor (1950.8), that the Visio ends with a dra-
    matic exposé of the inadequacy of Piers. Sees an effect of
    the writer's attention to the "difficulties" of the A-Vita,
    an analysis which "draws attention away from the poet's

satirical purpose--exposure of shortcomings in the attitudes
and behavior of various ranks of medieval society"; and concludes such that misreadings are derived "from the persistent
tendency of single-authorship criticism to link the A and B
texts together at the expense, always, of the A text, which is
alleged to lack structural clarity" and "to break off sharply
at the end." Calls for an analysis of the poem that pays
closer attention to historical circumstances of the fourteenth
century.

*10 HARPER, JAMES FARRELL. "Style in Medieval Art and Literature:
Three Essays in Criticism." Dissertation, State University of
New York, Stony Brook, 170 pp.
Abstracted: DAI 35:3682A.

11 HIGGS, ELTON D. "The Path to Involvement: The Centrality of the
Dreamer in Piers Plowman." TSE 21:1-34.
The poem is remarkable in its use of connected multiple
dreams, the dream-within-the-dream, and a highly individual-
ized Dreamer whose personality "gives coherency to the form
and the content of the visions." The Dreamer must learn the
legitimacy of doing good in an evil world. Will begins by refusing to participate in a world he self-righteously criticizes, but is brought by his successive dreams to understand
the relationship of truth and love, man and God, body and
spirit. Dreams 1-2 (the Visio) show Will refusing to participate in the world usefully through love; dreams 3-5 lead to an
understanding of charity, in a progression from presumption
through frustration to a better knowledge of himself. Dreams
6-8 show that Will comprehends Christ's mission and its per-
petuation on earth through the Church. Through Piers Plowman,
who is a correlative symbol of Will's changes through his
dreams, Will come to see that God uses imperfect mankind for
His own purposes.

12 HILL, THOMAS D. "Two Notes on Exegetical Allusion in Langland:
'Piers Plowman' B, XI, 161-67 and B, I, 115-24." NM 75,
no. 1:92-97.
B I 117-18 distinguishes between those angels who were
accomplices of Lucifer and those "whose commitment was more
tentative" and merely hoped his lies were true. Instead of to
Hell, these latter were sent, in Navigatio Sancti Brendani, to
earth and the air (erthe and eyre in Piers Plowman). With his
on fynger in B XI 163 ought to be taken literally, denoting
"one finger," and is a reference to the Holy Spirit, digitus
Dei, as explained by Hrabanus Maurus's De universo, I, 3.
Since the Holy Spirit's first attribute is love, Langland here

1974

provides a transition from the reference to law in Trajan's assertion that law without love is useless.

*13 HOLLOWAY, JULIA BOLTON. "The Figure of the Pilgrim in Medieval Poetry." Dissertation, University of California, Berkeley, 561 pp.
> Abstracted: <u>DAI</u> 35:2225A-26A.

14 KASKE, R.E. "Holy Church's Speech and the Structure of <u>Piers Plowman</u>." In <u>Chaucer and Middle English Studies in Honour of Rossell Hope Robbins</u>. Edited by Beryl Rowland. Kent, Ohio: Kent State University Press; London: Allen & Unwin, 1974, pp. 320-27.
> The speech of Holicherch (B Prol 11 ff.) first treats <u>bona temporalia</u>, divided between natural goods (clothing, food, and drink) and artificially contrived goods, and then the spiritual values of truth and love. Each subsection is introduced by a question of the Dreamer. These subdivisions are themselves treated in the poem: natural and artificial goods in the Visio (although in reverse order), and truth and love in the Vita. The reversal of natural and artificial goods is perhaps intended to stress the fact that reform is unsuccessful when up against mankind's "most instinctive and compelling appetites."

*15 KLEIN, M. "The Apocalyptic Configuration in Literature: A Study of Fragmentation and Contradiction in <u>Piers Plowman</u> and Its Implications for Modern Literature." Dissertation, Sussex.
> Source: <u>Index to Theses</u>, vol. 24, p. 5.

16 POOLE, ERIC. "The Computer in Determining Stemmatic Relationships." <u>Computers and the Humanities</u> 8 (July):207-16.
> Analyzes by computer A V 105-58 (Kane's edition), based on runs of material divided into lines 105-17, 117-29, 129-43, 143-58, and combinations of such material. Results suggest the affinities of MSS. TChH[2], RU, VH, AH[3], and WN. "On the whole, the groupings found by the computer vindicate the suggestions of Thomas A. Knott and David C. Fowler which were rejected by Professor Kane. It would, of course, hardly be safe to say, on the basis of such a small sample of 54 lines of text, that this judgment was incorrect."

*17 SCHWEITZER, EDWARD CHARLES, Jr. "<u>Kynde Love</u> and <u>Caritas</u> in the B-Text of <u>Piers Plowman</u>." Dissertation, Cornell, 229 pp.
> Abstracted: <u>DAI</u> 35:4555A-56A.

1975

18 SCHWEITZER, EDWARD C. "'Half a Laumpe Lyne in Latyne' and
    Patience's Riddle in Piers Plowman." JEGP 73, no. 3 (July):
    313-27.
        Interprets ex vi transicionis of B XIII 151 as equiva-
    lent to ex vi Paschæ, since transitus is used to gloss phase
    (Hebrew pesach) and pascha in the Vulgate Bible and its com-
    mentaries. The half a laumpe lyne comes from words of the
    baptismal liturgy, "Accipe lampadem ardentem et irreprehensi-
    bilem: custodi baptismum tuum: serua mandata, . . ." spoken
    when the priest presents a lighted candle, signifying spiri-
    tual illumination through caritas, to the neophyte. Dowel in
    the context of the riddle thus comes to mean fulfilling the
    obligation of caritas enjoined upon every Christian at bap-
    tism, the sacramental participation in the death and resurrec-
    tion of Christ and the moment of the Christian's passage from
    sin to grace. The saterday mentioned in line 153 refers to
    Holy Saturday, typologically suggesting the sacrament of con-
    firmation, which remains necessary even after baptism for its
    gift of the Holy Spirit.

19 TROWER, KATHERINE B. "Elizabeth D. Kirk's The Dream Thought of
    Piers Plowman." Costerus, n.s. 1:151-64.
        This review-essay praises the "new and exciting approach"
    of Kirk (1972.9) in viewing the poem as an exploration of the
    relationship of man and God in the face of God's omnipotence,
    but criticizes a lack of grounding in medieval tradition, a
    paucity of quotation from primary sources, and incomplete
    documentation.

                            1975

1   AERS, DAVID. Piers Plowman and Christian Allegory. London:
    Edward Arnold, ix + 141 pp.
        Criticizes scholarship on Piers Plowman that fails to
    subject the medieval practices of figural writing to close
    critical scrutiny and fails to draw the necessary distinctions
    between the theory and practice of exegesis. The allegorical
    interpretations of Robertson and Huppé are faulted for denying
    the theological commonplace of Christianity's essential his-
    toricism, and the approach of the critics of Robertson's
    methods is criticized for failing to take account of actual
    exegetical practice. Questions the conventional distinction
    between (Hellenistic) allegory and (Judaeo-Christian) typology,
    with regard in particular to Origen's essentially nonhistoric
    exegesis; and argues that the acceptance by an exegete of the
    historical truth of a text "does not enable a critic to make
    a priori assertions about the way the exegete handled the

1975

text." Traditional commentary on the stories of Rahab and the
fall of Jericho (Joshua 2:6) and David's adultery with Bath-
Sheba (II Kings 11), and on Genesis 3 shows the tendency of
medieval exegetes to "dissolve the literal and historical context, tone and nuance." Agrees with Beryl Smalley that the
late medieval period saw no increase of attention to the
literal.

Cites Deguilleville and Lydgate as representative of the
dominant traits of medieval figural writing: relying on
picture-models that are inadequate for developing religious
thought and language and ignoring the historical dimension.
The traditional critical model of the shell and kernel is
found to be inadequate in defending poetry against the charge
of Aquinas that what is figured is either subrational or could
have been better expressed in literal discourse. Sees an
alternative to this approach described in Dante's Letter to
Can Grande in which the image is intrinsic "to a whole process
of understanding" of sublime matters that cannot be adequately
described through conventional statement. Sees the idea of
the poet as vates without recourse to the conventional strate-
gies of shell/kernel in Langland's preoccupation with the
making of poetry as a subject, as well as in his re-creations
through figurative language that attempt to clarify through
the act of writing the perception of the vision.

Based on I Corinthians 9:22, Piers is to be seen as a
focusing point "for a range of perceptions and notions seen
through the characters' visions" and a saving agent appropriate to their own perception at a given time. The Tree of
Charity is discussed as an example of Langland's employment of
different modes of figural writing, in which the reader must
follow the Dreamer in the process of understanding the allegory, rather than merely reduce the allegory to an atemporal
set of propositions, as in a picture-model. Sees Langland's
use of plowing imagery (B V-VII; XIX) as meaningfully organic,
as Langland largely deprives such imagery of its traditional
spiritual implications until the career of Christ on earth and
the pentecostal gifts (B XVI) release the allegorical potential of such images: by B XIX Piers becomes the "figurative
lens" through which Langland allows us to see the effects in
history of Christ's victory. Reviewed by J.A. Burrow, TLS,
21 November 1975, p. 1380.

2 ALFORD, JOHN A. "Some Unidentified Quotations in Piers Plowman."
   MP 72, no. 4 (May):390-99.
        Advances possible sources or additional examples of the
   following quotations and their variants in the three versions:
        A X 92; A XI 238; A XI 303;

1975

B Prol 141-42; B Prol 144; B I 88-91; B I 139; B II 27;
B IV 120; B V 448; B V 612; B IX 181; B X 253; B X 259-60;
B XI 36-37; B XI 81; B XI 102; B XI 260; B XII 52; B XII 283;
B XIII 427; B XIV 59; B XIV 144; B XIV 169; B XIV 180; B XIV
275; B XV 59-60; B XV 62; B XVIII 237; B XVIII 390; B XVIII
407-8; B XIX 290; B XX 34;
C II 84-87; C II 140; C III 27; C V 188; C VII 257;
C VIII 87; C X 212; C X 265-66; C X 274; C XI 94; C XI 289;
C XII 160; C XII 296; C XII 304; C XIII 39; C XIII 152; C XV
208; C XVI 263; C XVII 116; C XVII 221; C XVIII 224; C XIX
242; C XXI 249; C XXI 453; and C XXII 295.

*3 ARN, MARY-JO. "The Function of Duality and Trinity in the
Structure of Piers Plowman." Dissertation, S.U.N.Y.,
Binghamton, 211 pp.
      Abstracted: DAI 35:6088A-89A.

*4 BAKER, DENISE NOWAKOWSKI. "Langland's Artistry: The Strategy
and Structure of Piers Plowman." Dissertation, Virginia,
170 pp.
      Abstracted: DAI 36:6109A.

5 BIRNES, WILLIAM J. "Christ as Advocate: The Legal Metaphor of
Piers Plowman." AM 16:71-93.
      Langland uses the contrast of English Common Law (which
had become in the fourteenth century an inflexible set of
precedents favoring the rich) and English Chancery Law, with
its emphasis on equity, as a metaphor for the contrast of the
Old and New Law, in which prohibition and punishment give way
to a sense of caritas. In B XVII we see the Old Law without
love as incapable of offering salvation (the Good Samaritan
scene), as well as the legal metaphor continued in Spes's
unsealed writ, which requires Christ's seal, His crucifixion
on the Cross. In the debate of the Four Daughters of God,
Mercy shows that the Old Law contains the justification of
her argument--guile engenders guile and man will ultimately
have grace--just as Christ argues in the Harrowing of Hell
scene. Piers argues with questions of conscience (the basis
of equity law) when Righteousness cites the "legal" precedent
of Adam's fall. Christ's speech (B XVIII 346 ff.) shows Him
fulfilling the law by offering Himself as surety and citing
statutory law, equity law, and royal prerogative. Thus, mankind is freed by law; and in the monarch's submitting to law,
the temporal and divine laws are fused, and law comes to be
seen as a reflection of divine power.

1975

6   BLAMIRES, ALCUIN G. "Mum & the Sothsegger and Langlandian
        Idiom." NM 76, no. 4:583-604.
            Describes similarities of Mum and the Sothsegger and
        Piers Plowman in terms of common interests and modes of
        expression, rather than in any attempt to reassert common
        authorship. Both poems value truth-telling in the face of
        intimidation by the powerful; both phrase the ideal of a rule
        that fearlessly upholds the law; both interrupt a line of
        argument to introduce new characters; both rely on a number
        of genres and modes--debate, sermon, encyclopedic satire,
        quest, and dream vision--to further the satire. Takes issue
        with Day and Steele (1936.1) that Mum and the Sothsegger shows
        a more authoritarian position with regard to the proper role
        of subjects.

7   BOWERS, A. JOAN. "The Tree of Charity in Piers Plowman: Its
        Allegorical and Structural Significance." In Literary Mono-
        graphs, edited by Eric Rothstein and Joseph Anthony Wittreich,
        Jr., vol. 6. Madison: University of Wisconsin Press,
        pp. 3-34, 157-60.
            Explores the imagistic unity of the B-text, centered on
        the traditional lignum vitæ, the tree of life. The structure
        of the B-text is cyclical, framed by sinful society and
        Antichrist's coming, with Holicherch instructing Will in
        passus I but the establishment of which is only described in
        passus XIX. Truth is described by her in a plant image sug-
        gestive of the Tree of Charity, and the plant of Truth is
        uprooted by Antichrist. Langland emphasizes the redemptive
        power of Christ and the importance of the true Church as
        aspects of the lignum vitæ with apocalyptic associations.
        The fall of man is that of choosing the lignum scientiæ boni
        et mali; the sins are in general described with tree imagery
        in B V; Adam becomes the fallen fruit of the tree gathered by
        the Devil in B XVI; then the Annunciation (XVI 92-96) and the
        Passion (XVIII 189-200) are likewise explained in such a
        fashion as to bring Adam and Eve almost full circle.
            The Church as an aspect of the lignum vitæ is seen in
        the description of Noah's ark (IX-X) and Piers's barn (XIX),
        on either side of the Tree of Charity. The ark symbolizes the
        apocalyptic Flood and Last Judgment, but also represents the
        saving role of the Church and the cross. Piers's barn is
        built by the Cross, in an image of the Church gathering to-
        gether the faithful during the reign of the Antichrist.
            The Tree of Charity subsumes interpretations as a tree
        of virtue, the Tree of Jesse, the three grades of chastity.
        As a tree of virtues, it is the antithesis of the trees repre-
        senting vices in B V. Langland's emphasis on mercy as root,
        pity as trunk, and Christ as fruit, sets the Tree in the

context of the Crucifixion; and the medicinal qualities of
charity and patience establish its significance of salvation
brought by Christ. The blossoms of Benygne-Lokinge may have
been suggested by the iconography of Synogoga/Ecclesia. Making the custodian of the Tree Liberum Arbitrium emphasizes, as
does Augustine, the gift of God's grace. Disagrees with
Bloomfield (1958.1) that the fruit of the three states corresponds to the progressive inner grades of perfection or point
toward a Joachimistic future Age of the Holy Spirit. The
fruit as a succession of prophets and patriarchs suggests the
Tree of Jesse, though of a more general or spiritualized
variety. Langland does not explicitly include Christ in
Piers's Tree, but he transforms the traditional flos into an
actual account of Christ's life, which follows the stealing of
the fruit.

8 HARWOOD, BRITTON J. "Imaginative in Piers Plowman." Medium Ævum
   44, no. 3:249-63.
        Imaginatif is a personification of the mind's power to
   make similitudes, phantasms "dwelt upon as such, as related or
   unrelated to sensation." The inner dream (B XI) is designed
   to lead the Dreamer to interpret similitudes of the phenomenal
   world. The C-text omits the discussion of Imaginatif's
   responsibility for simulacra in dreams, for though they are
   similitudes they are not clergye. Imaginatif does not satisfy
   the Dreamer's desire for a kynde knowyng of Christ because by
   definition it cannot supply the "first intentional knowledge
   of God."

9 HILL, THOMAS D. "A Liturgical Allusion in 'Piers Plowman'
   B.XVI.88: Filius, bi the Fader wille • and frenesse of
   Spiritus Sancti." N&Q, c.s. 220 (n.s. 22), no. 12 (December):
   531-32.
        B XVI 86-89 is translated: "Piers, out of pure anger,
   seized that one stave and hit after him [i.e., the Devil]
   recklessly, [with the stave] Filius by the Father's will and
   the free generosity of the Holy Spirit." The participation of
   all members of the Trinity in the Incarnation is paralleled in
   a Communion Prayer in the Sarum, York, Hereford, and Roman
   uses. Frenesse of Spiritus Sancti is considered sufficiently
   close to cooperante spiritu sancto.

*10 ISAACSON, MELANIE KELL. "The Unachieved Quest for Social Reform
    from the Roman de Carité to Piers Plowman." Dissertation,
    Stanford, 226 pp.
        Abstracted: DAI 36:6076A-77A.

1975

11 KIRK, ELIZABETH D. "Chaucer and His English Contemporaries." In
    Geoffrey Chaucer: A Collection of Original Articles. Edited
    by George D. Economou. New York: McGraw-Hill Book Co.,
    pp. 111-27, esp. pp. 115-18.
        Seemingly most unlike Chaucer's work, Piers Plowman
    offers an opportunity to see the effect on a writer's con-
    sciousness of aspects of the fourteenth century on which
    Chaucer avoids comment. Langland's attempts to combine social
    realism and the forms of allegorical analysis lead us to
    understand the formal elements in Chaucer, short of overt
    allegory, "which deflect us from participation to analysis and
    direct that analysis."

12 KROCHALIS, JEANNE, and PETERS, EDWARD, eds. and trans. The World
    of Piers Plowman. Philadelphia: University of Pennsylvania
    Press, xxi + 265 pp.
        A collection of historical documents and literary texts,
    presented in their entirety or in selections, that elucidate
    the social and intellectual context of the poem and its age.
    Latin and French texts and documents are translated. The
    introduction sets the poem in the context of growing dissent,
    satire, and complaint of the time after 1250. The material is
    drawn from those versions that circulated widely in the later
    Middle Ages, with attention to those MSS that also contained
    the poem. The material is organized under such headings as
    Microcosm and Macrocosm, Abuses in the Church and the World,
    The Voice of the Preacher and the Heretic, Instruction and
    Action, and so on. Includes introductions to the various
    selections, and bibliographies.

*13 KRUMME, RILEY DWANE. "Wealth and Reform in Piers Plowman."
    Dissertation, Claremont Graduate School, 183 pp.
        Abstracted: DAI 36:2848A.

14 [LANGLAND, WILLIAM.] Piers Plowman: The B Version. Will's
    Visions of Piers Plowman, Do-Well, Do-Better and Do-Best. An
    edition in the form of Trinity College Cambridge MS B.15.17,
    corrected and restored from the known evidence, with variant
    readings. Edited by George Kane and E. Talbot Donaldson.
    London: University of London, Athlone Press, vii + 681 pp.
        Describes the following MSS containing the second ver-
    sion of Piers Plowman: Bm, Bo, C, C^2, Cot, Cr [collated from
    Crowley's three impressions of 1550], F, G, H, Hm, Hm^2, L, M,
    O, R, W, and Y. Rejects MS. [Ht] as "sophisticated and with
    added spurious matter," and MS. S because of "the amount and
    character of its individual variation and because none of its
    readings helps with restoring the original text of the poem."

Working from smaller variational groups founded upon
agreements to larger ones, the editors identify two main
genetic groups of B-text MSS: RF and WHmCrGYOC^{2}CBmCotLMS.
RF as a genetic group is evidenced from the Prologue; the
other genetic group is established in passus III but in the
opinion of the editors also exists from the beginning of the
poem. MS. H may belong in the larger group or may represent
a third, distinct line of descent.   In the larger group, two
changing sets of MS relations are found: In V-VII there is
evidence of a family comprised of YOC^{2}CBmBoCot and in VIII-
XVII, of GYOC^{2}CBmBoCot; in XVIII-XX, the same MSS compose a
family in slightly different relation.   Moreover, in X-XV,
there is a family HmWCrS, and in XVII-XX, the same MSS, with
M, in an altered relation, compose a family.   The homogeneity
of the B-text MSS is demonstrated, regardless of the limited
genetic findings that collation yields; and the extreme
frequency of convergent variation in the transmission of the
poem is established.   MSS RF are shown not, as previously
believed (by Blackman, 1918.1), to relate genetically to LM,
and the absence of lines and passages present in RF from
WHmCrGYOC^{2}CBmBoCotLMS is explained as the consequence of
accidental omission from their exclusive common ancestor,
rather than as evidence that RF might preserve an authorial
form of the poem intermediate between the B-text and the
C-text, or that the larger group might incorporate changes
by the poet.

Establishes the order of composition of the three texts
of the poem as A-text, B-text, C-text through a comparison of
the content of the versions which shows that in its major
features, the B-text resembles the A-text more than does the
C-text, and also resembles the C-text more than does the
A-text; and through the hypothesis of authorial revision from
shortest to longest form, which accounts for the more extended
development of the B- and C-texts, as well as the various
omissions, reductions, rearrangements, and so on.   By compar-
ing the reconstructable B-text archetype with the text of the
A-version ([Langland], 1960.10) and a provisional text of the
C-version, notes numerous points where the reading of the
B-archetype is opposed by the reading of the two other texts,
and the B-archetype reading is clearly inferior.   Rejects the
hypothesis of vacillating authorial revision in such cases,
in favor of that of widespread scribal corruption in the
transmission of the B-text original down to the archetype of
all extant B-text MSS.   Notes also instances of the B-archetype
displaying a reading that is of scribal origin, where only the
A- and B-texts correspond, and in instances where only the
B- and C-texts correspond.   In this latter case, rejects the
probability of effective authorial revision and concludes that

in such instances the B- and C-texts had a common original reading which was preserved in the C-text, but which had been corrupted in the transmission of the B-text before the production of the B-text archetype.

Finds that although the MS used by Langland for the revision of the B-text to the C-text preserved in many instances original readings lost from the exclusive common ancestor of all extant B-text MSS, this B-text MS used by the poet was itself a corrupt scribal copy. This is suggested by the following classes of evidence: agreements between the B- and C-texts in readings which, in comparison with the A-text, appear scribal; agreements between the two later texts which on absolute editorial grounds appear scribal; instances where the readings of the archetypal B-text judged corrupt on comparison with the readings of the A-text are reflected in the revised C-text; instances of B-text readings judged corrupt on absolute editorial grounds are reflected in the revised C-text; and agreements in the last two (unrevised) passūs of the archetypal B- and C-texts in corrupt readings. Suggests that the unrevised nature of the end of the poem might mean that the poet was in no sense satisfied with his revision of Prol-XVIII when he stopped work, perhaps because he realized that "what lay before him was not as he had written it, was in an alien usus scribendi."

Edits the text through the comparison of variants viewed under the criteria of the common processes and effects of scribal debasement of texts, and the appropriateness of readings to the poet's style, sense, and versification. With respect to versification in particular, establishes descriptive rules governing Langland's use of rhymed letters, his occasional use of two staves in a single word, his use of a number of words to alliterate variously on one or another syllable, his use of "little" words as staves, his normative use of three staves per line, and his customary alliterative patterns. Illustrates the selection of original from scribal variants in such situations as those instances where the B-text has no recognizable equivalent in the other versions; and those in which the majority B-text readings appear scribal in comparison with the reading of the A-C-texts, or in comparison with the reading of either the A- or the C-text alone. Illustrates the restoration of original B-text readings "not actually preserved as such in any manuscript from the evidence of surviving variation." Finally, illustrates the method of conjectural emendation (see Kane, 1969.18); this involves the identification as unoriginal, unanimous, or unmistakably archetypal readings of the MSS and proposing in their place unattested, entirely hypothetical readings "as likely or possible originals."

1975

Views the resulting edition "as a theoretical structure,
a complex hypothesis designed to account for a body of phenomena in the light of knowledge about the circumstances which
generated them, that is, governed by a presumption of the
quality of Langland's art and by established information about
the effects of manuscript copying on the language, form and
meaning of texts." Insists that, because of the nature of the
textual problem and the methodology the editors were thus
forced to employ, the resulting text is of varying authority.
Chooses as a base MS W, largely for its consistent spelling
and systematic grammar. In an appendix to the introduction,
prints lines in various MSS judged to be unoriginal.
   Reviewed by David C. Fowler, YES 7 (1977):23-42 (see
Fowler, 1977.7); and E.G. Stanley, N&Q, n.s. 23 (1976):435-47
(see Stanley, 1976.20).

15 LUPAC, ALAN C. "Piers Plowman, B.VII.116." Explicator 34, no. 4
   (December):Item 31.
      For pure tene is glossed as "with righteous anger."
   Piers thus rejects the Priest's misinterpretation, based on
   the Priest's desire to receive forgiveness from words unsup-
   ported by works.

*16 MUSSETTER, SALLY ANN. "The Reformation of the Pilgrim to the
   Likeness of God: A Study of the Tropological Level of the
   Divine Comedy and Piers Plowman B." Dissertation, Cornell,
   207 pp.
      Abstracted: DAI 36:8035A.

*17 OIJI, TAKERO. "Langland Kenkyu no Senku, Ikuzo Iijima" [Pioneer
   of Langland studies, Ikuzo Iijima]. Eigo S 120:468-69.
      Source: MLA International Bibliography, 1975, p. 48,
   no. 2833.

*18 RADIGAN, JOHN D. "The Clouded Vision: Satire and the Way to
   God in Piers Plowman." Dissertation, Syracuse, 205 pp.
      Abstracted: DAI 36:6712A.

*19 STOCK, LORRAINE KOCHANSKE. "Patience and Sloth in Two Medieval
   English Works: Mankind and Piers Plowman C." Dissertation,
   Cornell, 150 pp.
      Abstracted: DAI 36:7446A.

20 TAITT, PETER S. Incubus and Ideal: Ecclesiastical Figures in
   Chaucer and Langland. Salzburg Studies in English Literature
   under the Direction of Professor Erwin A. Stürzl. Salzburg:
   Institüt für Englische Sprache und Literatur, Universität
   Salzburg, i + 228 pp.

1975

Langland's "uncompromising" attack on the friars is
based mainly on their covetousness, though in the course of
the poem all of the Deadly Sins are ascribed to them. The six
references to summoners in the poem do not individualize them:
they are mainly mentioned in the company of Lady Mede and in
connection with neglect of God's flock. Clerks are criticized
for their covetousness, lack of charity, and fault in learning.
There are only four references to pardoners, in which Langland
mainly contrasts the pardoners' abuses with the true pardon of
God. There are eleven references to monks in the B- and C-
texts, with the ratio of benevolent to derogatory allusions
of roughly 2:1: the monks are praised for controlling their
numbers (as opposed to the practices of the friars) and their
observance of claustration; they are criticized for their
lechery and avarice. Parsons and parish priests are criticized in the poem for their covetousness, ignorance of the
Bible and Divine Office, and their setting a bad example.
    In comparison with Chaucer, Langland is found to base
his characterizations on a critical examination of specific
abuses rather than on realistic portraits that depend on
salient details, and on an association of words with figures
rather than on dramatic interplay of characters. Langland's
irony is seldom specifically dramatic; his use of metaphor is
more Scriptural and didactic; his word-play has an "almost
structural importance." Finds the C-text no more moderate
than the previous versions in its treatment of ecclesiastical
figures. Includes as appendix an alphabetical index of references to ecclesiastical figures in the three texts.

21 WITTIG, JOSEPH S. "The Dramatic and Rhetorical Development of
     Long Will's Pilgrimage." NM 76, no. 1:52-76.
         The development of the poem is the result neither of
     confusion nor of "the working out of a series of dialectics
     whose outcome is constantly in doubt"; rather, there is a con-
     sistent pattern of narrative, intentionally structured by the
     poet. The Visio shows the disorder of society and suggests
     the impossibility of reforming it unless man uses his free
     will correctly. Passūs VIII-XII narrow the scope of the
     dramatic action from mankind-in-the-world to the Dreamer, or
     the individual will. Rather than a series of intellectual
     cruces, the early scenes of the Vita show the resistance of
     the individual will to the necessity of askesis. B XI and XII
     show his conversion, his affective awakening. His progress
     through the last eight passūs is conveyed through the five
     interludes that preface the five last dreams (B XIII 1-20,
     XV 1-11, XVIII 1-8, XVIII 425-XIX 4, XX 1-50), which show the
     relevance of Will's personal reform in the larger context of
     mankind's salvation history. The end of the poem insists on

the need of each individual's commitment of will to save the
world from corruption.

1976

1   ADAMS, ROBERT. "Langland and the Liturgy Revisited." SP 73,
     no. 3 (July):266-84.
          Sees no virtue in Kirk's theory (1972.9) that the Latin
     tags in B VII and XI are drawn from the Passion liturgy rather
     than directly from Scripture. Admits, with St-Jacques
     (1970.15) the circularity of the poem, but does not ascribe it
     to the liturgy; instead, sees the undeniable liturgical motifs
     of the final passūs as intended to show the audience that the
     circle of earthly time has been "punctuated by anniversaries
     of salvation history," and that only the Incarnation can break
     time's circularity and lead man toward salvation. Exposes
     errors in the methodology behind Hort's researches (1938.5)
     regarding Langland's use of the Breviary, and concludes that
     Langland was moderately familiar with the Divine Office, but
     apparently not much given to reading the Breviary.

2   ANDERSON, JUDITH H. The Growth of a Personal Voice: Piers
     Plowman and The Faerie Queene. New Haven and London: Yale
     University Press, x + 240 pp.
          Sees both Piers Plowman and The Faerie Queene as record-
     ing a parallel development of narrative consciousness mani-
     fested in the role of the poet, the characters, symbols,
     narrator, and story. Both poems begin with conventional
     settings, emphasizing in their familiarity awareness rather
     than instruction; but in both poems, the effect is to "bring
     the reader up sharply against the condition of mankind, a
     condition not to be separated simply from his own." This is
     accomplished in Piers Plowman through the interaction of the
     Dreamer, a representation of the narrator's confused state of
     mind and spirit, and Holicherch, whose speeches embody an act
     of perception; their dialogue shows the narrator of the Pro-
     logue reaching self-consciously toward "an act of creative
     recollection." The "touchstone" of love offered by Holicherch
     in her debate with the Dreamer is paralleled by the revela-
     tions of Contemplation to Redcrosse; and in the development of
     the relationship of these two characters, Spenser offers a
     paradigm of his own relation to the poem, though, as in
     Langland's poem, the poet at this point somewhat distances
     himself from this more personal involvement.
          In the Visio, the narrator and the Dreamer are in gen-
     eral more passive than in Prol-I. Problems in society (rather
     than in the particular self) are viewed from a vantage point

1976

between satiric observation and a more sympathetic involvement. So too in Book II of The Faerie Queene, where the
narrator is to a lesser extent inside the hero, and the Cave
of Mammon, portraying like the Visio the conflict of worldly
materialism and spiritual idealism, leads the central character to a heightened spiritual awareness.

The central passūs of Piers Plowman, beginning with the
Dreamer's discovery of Imaginatif and Conscience in the process of more fully understanding himself, are paralleled by
Books III and IV of Spenser's poem; in each work the poet
displays his awareness of "his own imaginative role in the
poem as shaper and actor, as creator and participant, . . .
and this action makes the form of the poem self-conscious-
ness."

Passūs XV-XX manifest a great awareness of personality,
conceived as the metaphysical, psychological, verbal, and
actual reality of a person, and viewed by Langland as both the
meaning of reality and the means whereby reality is actual-
ized. Passūs XIX-XX describe personality as the ultima
solitudo, as both affirmation and loss, triumph and loneli-
ness, in a way comparable to the latter portions of Spenser's
poem where, just as in Piers Plowman, personality becomes a
more self-conscious concern, and the unity of experience becomes more problematical. At the end of both poems the vision
is personalized, for just as Will wakes to find that the symbol of Piers must be realized in his own experience, the
Mutability Cantos present to the reader what was for Spenser
"Life perceived directly and whole." Similarly, in both poems
the vision is brought down to an individual realization of
faith in God, though Spenser's God seems "a more distanced
person and impersonal power than is Piers Plowman."

*3   ANHORN, JUDY SCHAAF. "Sermo Poematis: Homiletic Traditions of
     Purity and Piers Plowman." Dissertation, Yale, 280 pp.
          Abstracted: DAI 37:3605A.

*4   BALDWIN, A.P. "The Law of the King in the C-text of Piers
     Plowman." Dissertation, Cambridge.
          Source: Index to Theses, vol. 26, p. 6.

5   BENSON, C. DAVID. "An Augustinian Irony in 'Piers Plowman.'"
     N&Q, c.s. 221 (n.s. 23), no. 2 (February):51-54.
          The context of the Dreamer's citation of Augustine in
     B X 452-59 (Confessiones, Book 8) stresses the proper use and
     value of learning in achieving salvation. The Dreamer's view
     that Augustine denies the authority of learning is meant to
     be perceived by the audience as seriously flawed.

1976

*6   BROSAMER, JAMES JOSEPH. "The Personae of Piers Plowman:
     Narrator, Dreamer, and Will." Dissertation, Oregon, 247 pp.
     Abstracted: DAI 37:1559A-60A.

7   COVELLA, Sr. FRANCIS D. "Grammatical Evidence of Multiple
     Authorship in Piers Plowman." Language and Style 9 (Winter):
     3-16.
          Isolates seventeen major classes of grammatical struc-
     tures of the second half-lines, with the patterns thus iso-
     lated determined on the basis of frequency of occurrence. In
     comparing texts, the B-continuation and the C-interpolations
     were used. The B-text is found to show many significant
     variations, with many half-line structures showing corre-
     spondences of less than 51 percent. The limited number (483)
     of C-text interpolations makes conclusions less authoritative
     than for the B-text, though the results indicate that the C-
     text is closer to the A-text than is the B-text. The B-text
     is noted for its use of as it were (virtually unused in the
     A-text); and the C-text is remarkable for its extraordinary
     use of other (as the conjunction or) as an initial coordinate
     conjunction. An appendix lists the grammatical forms of the
     second half-lines.

8   DOBSON, R.J., and TAYLOR, J. Rymes of Robyn Hood: An Introduc-
     tion to the English Outlaw. London: Heinemann, pp. 1, 23,
     passim.
          Doubts the existence of any indisputable reference to
     Robin Hood earlier than that of B V 400-403, to which public
     attention was first drawn by [Percy], 1765.1. By the time of
     Piers Plowman, the legend had found expression in rymes or
     verses regarded by some as in bad taste--an attitude appar-
     ently not untypical of the fifteenth century. Declares it
     absolutely certain that the 1322 date of the Monkbretton
     Cartulary, noting a "stone of Robin Hode" lying near a spot
     later associated with Robin Hood's Well, is an error for 1422
     (cf. Smith, 1933.9).

9   HARWOOD, BRITTON J. "Langland's Kynde Wit." JEGP 75, no. 3
     (July):330-36.
          Develops the identification of Quirk (1953.6) of kynde
     wit as the vis cogitativa associated with the apprehension of
     the beneficial. Qualifies Quirk's ideas in suggesting that
     kynde wit is instinctual only to animals, but is learned
     through comparisons. The distinction between kynde wit and
     clergye is that, together with Imaginatif (the similitude-
     making faculty of the mind), kynde wit "can seize the bene-
     ficial in something represented only metonymically," while
     clergye "is a body of knowledge made possible by grace and

1976

built through allegorical interpretation;" they refer to the
two kinds of interpretations Christ associated with the
Pharisees and Sadduces, understanding one physical thing as
metonymic for another, and understanding the physical in light
of a belief in Christ. Whether viewed as leading to material
or spiritual satisfaction, kynde wit is never free from ego-
ism; and Piers's anger in the Pardon scene indicts the kynde
wit which had led him to what he thought to be truth.

10 HILL, THOMAS D. "Davidic Typology and the Characterization of
    Christ: 'Piers Plowman' B. XIX, 95-103." N&Q, c.s. 221
    (n.s. 23), no. 7 (July):291-94.
        The passage does not refer to Robert Bruce, as Skeat
    thought, but to David, the "fugitive king" who in the Middle
    Ages was considered on the basis of his vulnerability as a
    type of Christ. Notes that David is explicitly mentioned a
    few lines later (B XIX 128-32) in a passage that suggests
    parallelism of the two figures.

11 KING, JOHN N. "Robert Crowley's Editions of Piers Plowman: A
    Tudor Apocalypse." MP 73 (May):342-52.
        Crowley's introductory material and marginalia is
    interpreted as influenced by the millenarianism of Bale's
    Commentary on Revelation, as well as by the Wyclifite tradi-
    tion stretching back to Pierce the Plowman's Crede. Crowley
    aims in his editions of the poem to present an authoritative
    text that could be easily read by his contemporary audience.
    He introduces only a small number of substantive alterations
    of matters pertaining to doctrine, the veneration of Mary,
    and praise of the monastic ideal. His attack on clerical
    abuses is distinctly apocalyptic; he envisions Edward VI as
    the millenial Davidic ruler who will govern in reason and
    truth.

12 [LANGLAND, WILLIAM.] The Vision of Pierce Plowman, now fyrste
    imprynted by Roberte Crowley, dwellyng in Ely rentes in
    Holburne. Reprinted in facsimile. London: David Paradine
    Developments (in association with Magdalene College,
    Cambridge).
        A facsimile of Samuel Pepys's copy of the first impres-
    sion ([Langland], 1550.1), bearing a second title page (from
    the second impression) as well as "the printer to the reader"
    (from the second impression), and an afterword by J.A.W.
    Bennett.

*13 LEVY, LYNNE HUNT. "Piers Plowman and the Concept of Poverty."
    Dissertation, Oklahoma, 204 pp.
        Abstracted: DAI 37:7740A.

*14 McCULLY, JOHN RAYMOND. "Conceptions of Piers Plowman: 1550's
through 1970's." Dissertation, Rice, 386 pp.
    Abstracted: DAI 37:2164A.

*15 NEUFELDT, VICTORIA EMILIE. "The Metric of English Alliterative
Verse: Piers the Plowman and Beowulf." Dissertation,
Toronto.
    Abstracted: DAI 39:2226A.

*16 PRITCHARD, GRETCHEN WOLFF. "Law, Love and Incarnation: An
Interpretation of Piers Plowman." Dissertation, Yale, 265 pp.
    Abstracted: DAI 38:286A-87A.

 17 SEEHASE, GEORG. "Zu William Langlands Poem 'Peter der Pflüger.'"
Renaissanceliteratur und frühbürgerliche Revolution: Studien
zu den sozial- und ideologiegeschichtlichen Grundlagen euro-
päischer Nationalliteraturen. Edited by Robert Weimann,
Werner Lenk, and Joachim-Jürgen Slomka. Berlin and Weimar:
Aufbau-Verlag, pp. 106-11.
    The poet was presumably a member of the farmer-serf
faction of the priesthood; his sympathies were with the 1381
rebels, though he was no rebel himself. The antifeudal struggle for social equality is reflected in the poem in its descriptions, depiction of experiences, and evaluations. Sty-
listically, the poem combines the didactic sermon with folk
satire and the depiction of situations. The political meaning
is carried largely through anagrams: Piers, for instance, is
John Ball, although allegorically he stands for the exploited
workers, their leaders, and Christ. The description of Reason
in particular betrays Langland's Lollard sympathies, and
anticipates Thomas Müntzer's ideas of religious tolerance.

*18 SMITH, MACKLIN. "Piers Plowman and the Tradition of the Medieval
Life of Christ." Dissertation, Princeton, 482 pp.
    Abstracted: DAI 37:1571A-72A.

 19 SPEARING, A.C. Medieval Dream-Poetry. Cambridge: Cambridge
University Press, pp. 138-66, passim.
    In composing the A-text, Langland's original intention
was to write a poem like Wynnere and Wastoure, with a political solution to the economic and moral disorder of society.
By the end of the second dream, this proved impossible: a
visio had become an insomnium, as the Dreamer's own role in
the poem was called into question and the poet was forced to
realize that he, too, was a sinner. The poem became more
introspective, effectively coming to a halt on the topic of
predestination, with the suspicion that the quest for knowledge had no value for salvation. The B-text shows in the

1976

Trajan scene the value of human works; and the Dreamer realizes that he must change himself before he can change the
world. The difficulty of writing the poem becomes part of the
subject of the poem itself; and the inconclusive ending is
necessary from the standpoint of the Dreamer/poet, as fragmentary human expression is seen as the appropriate mode of
human apprehension of the transcendent. Notes similarities
of the Glutton scene (B V) with Wynnere and Wastoure, as well
as with Death and Liffe in the depiction of the Crucifixion
as a knightly tournament.

20 STANLEY, E.G. "The B Version of 'Piers Plowman': A New Edition." N&Q, c.s. 221 (n.s. 23), no. 10 (October):435-47.
Reviews [Langland], 1975.14. Highly praises Kane and
Donaldson for their justification of conjectural emendation,
with reservations expressed in regard to Langland's revisions
to make the poetry clearer rather than better, and the possibility that some of what the editors take to be scribal censorship is really authorial. Includes close analysis of Kane
and Donaldson's emendations in B V 218-23 and B X 30-58 of
their edition.

21 THOMPSON, CLAUD A. "Structural, Figurative, and Thematic Trinities in Piers Plowman." Mosaic 9, no. 2 (Winter):105-14.
Contends that the Holy Trinity is the organizing principle of the entire poem; and sees various triplets and
triplicities informed by the Trinity. The number of visions
in the three texts are three, ten (the trinity tripled, then
returned to unity), and nine; the triple alliteration of many
lines underscores thematic trinities in the poem; there are
numerous triads of metaphors and images; and the key dreams
are numbers three, six, and nine.

22 TRISTAM, PHILLIPA. Figures of Life and Death in Medieval English
Literature. New York: New York University Press, pp. 197-201,
passim.
Piers shows a medieval response that is contrary to the
perception of life as decay, that is, a passing out of time
and into eternity. Conversely, the joys of earth appear to
interest the poet largely as temptations. Langland's version
of the Harrowing of Hell assimilates the experience of the
Harrowing to that of Everyman through the identification of
Piers and Christ; for Piers, just like the human Christ, receives "no reassurance from divine omnipotence, but must, like
all men, seek through uncertainties, even to the suffering of
death itself, for the meaning of life."

23 WERTENBAKER, THOMAS J., Jr. "Piers Plowman, Prologue B. 196."
    Explicator 34, no. 7 (March):Item 51.
          Replies to Demedis (1974.6) and paraphrases the line as
    "For better is a little loss than a long sorrow, [to wit:]
    anarchy among us all, though we be freed of a despot."

24 WOODS, WILLIAM. England in the Age of Chaucer. New York: Stein
    & Day, pp. 164-68, passim.
          Langland was less well educated than Chaucer, "who had
    nothing original to propose." Though Langland lacks Chaucer's
    subtlety and acuity, he occasionally rises to a sublimity un-
    reached by his contemporary. The poem is used to illustrate
    such topics as spring, rural life, strip farming, peasant
    soldiers, the Black Death, and wage demands.

                              1977

1   ALFORD, JOHN A. "The Role of the Quotations in Piers Plowman."
    Speculum 52, no. 1 (January):80-99.
          Argues that Langland began with the Latin quotations in
    composing Piers Plowman and, using the standard aids of the
    medieval preacher in linking together verbally related texts
    from Scripture, derived from them the substance of the poem.
    In B XIV, the quotation after line 3, Uxorem duxy, et ideo non
    possum venire, serves as a tag for the Scriptural context,
    Luke 14:15-24, which provides the theme for the entire passus,
    as well as its two-part structuring on verbal concordance on
    the words bread and will, and rich and poor. Rather than an
    impulsive, impetuous artist, Langland thus emerges as a care-
    ful writer, "eking out his poem slowly, even tediously, while
    pouring over a variety of commentaries and preachers' aids."

2   ALFORD, JOHN A. "Literature and Law in Medieval England." PMLA
    92, no. 5 (October):941-51.
          Sees the extremely frequent use of legal forms and ter-
    minology in medieval literature as a reflection of a "profound
    faith in law as the tie that binds all things, in heaven and
    in earth." Reviews in this context the distinctions between
    divine (or eternal) law, the divine order or will of God;
    natural law, comprising the fundamental notions of right and
    wrong which would have been sufficient to govern man's conduct
    had he not sinned; and positive (or legislated) law, which
    guides mankind after the Fall and finds its validity in divine
    and natural law. Explains the Parliament of Devils (B XVIII
    270 ff.) in terms of Lucifer's false confidence in the legal
    notion of seisin, or possession, of the souls since the Fall,
    which is seemingly buttressed by the statute of limitations,

1977

but which is undercut by the notion of canon law (reflected in
B XVIII 294) that one must be in good faith for the entire
time of possession.

3   CLUTTERBUCK, CHARLOTTE. "Hope and Good Works: Leaute in the C-
    Text of Piers Plowman." RES, n.s. 28, no. 110 (May):129-40.
         Accepts Kean's identification of lewte and justice, but
    sees it also as implying hope, for lewte is justice in the
    sense of performing good works, and good works nourish hope.
    Lewte and its adjectival form leel are used in the context of
    heavenly reward for good works, and heaven is the object of
    hope; lewte is placed between "belief" and "love," represent-
    ing faith and charity, respectively. The appearance of the
    character lewte in C XIII signals the reawakening of hope in
    Will's heart, correcting despair and presumption, the two
    opposing sins against hope.

*4 COLAIANNE, ANTHONY JOSEPH. "A Companion to Piers Plowman
    Studies: Authorship, Editions, Backgrounds, and Critical
    Interpretation." Dissertation, Cincinnati, 318 pp.
         Abstracted: DAI 38:2106A-107A. See Colaianne, 1978.4.

*5 COTTER, MARY L. "Ties That Bind: Literature, Language, and the
    Idea of Man." Dissertation, Pennsylvania State University,
    234 pp.
         Abstracted: DAI 38:6139A.

*6 FINKEL, ANITA JANICE. "Language and Allegory in Piers Plowman."
    Dissertation, California, Los Angeles, 242 pp.
         Abstracted: DAI 38:4841A.

7   FOWLER, DAVID C. "A New Edition of the B text of Piers Plowman."
    YES 7:23-42.
         A review-article treating [Langland], 1975.14. Kane and
    Donaldson's edition is praised for its full explanation of
    procedure, its copious documentation of variants, and its
    remarkably accurate printing. Criticizes, however, the edi-
    tors' conclusion of widespread and extensive corruption in the
    B-text archetype, presumably determined through what the edi-
    tors detect as metrically defective, hence unoriginal lines.
    Remarks that of the 2200 lines of the A-text in the B-text,
    only 35 are judged to be in need of emendation on metrical
    grounds, while of the 1100 new lines in the B-text, 125 are so
    emended; this suggests that most of the metrically defective
    lines in the B-text represent simply the alliteration of the
    B-text poet, which he (a different man from the author of the
    A-text) improved in his C-version. Criticizes the editors'
    silence on the state of the A-text MS used by the author of

the B-version, as well as numerous instances of what Kane and
Donaldson took to be scribal censorship, but which is illustrated in the "undoubted work of the B poet retained in their
own edition." Remains unconvinced that MSS RF differ from all
other B-text MSS in what are only scribal additions or omissions rather than authorial revisions. An appendix classifies
and evaluates hundreds of emendations in the Kane-Donaldson
edition.

*8 JOHNSON, WALTER THOMAS. "The Prophecy of William Langland."
    Dissertation, California, Irvine, 275 pp.
        Abstracted: DAI 38:5451A.

9   KELLY, ROBERT L. "Hugh Latimer as Piers Plowman." SEL 17, no. 1
    (Winter):13-26.
        Latimer's "Sermon of the Plow," delivered January 1548
    at Paul's Cross, London, is shown to be an attempt by its
    author to establish a traditional sanction for Edwardian re-
    form measures, as well as to identify himself as a prophetic
    leader by placing the sermon in the "Piers Plowman tradition"
    as defined by White (1944.5). Latimer's use of the plowman
    metaphor allows him to enlist an orthodox tradition to sanc-
    tion nonconformity; and the satiric thrust of the sermon,
    directed against worldly clergy and greedy landowners, relies
    on the precedent evidenced in Piers Plowman of connecting
    religious and social reform. The sermon defines the ideal
    religious leader in terms of down-to-earth wisdom of the
    laboring classes, pastoral work, and a respect for the tradi-
    tional class structure.

10 LEWIS, C.S. The Allegory of Love. A Study in Medieval Tradi-
    tion. London, Oxford, and New York: Oxford University Press.
        A reprint of Lewis, 1936.4.

11 LINDEMANN, ERIKA C.D. "Analogues for Latin Quotations in
    Langland's Piers Plowman." NM 78, no. 4:359-61.
        Notes the occurrence of the following quotations:
    C X 265-66 and B XVIII 407-8 in Alanus de Lille's Liber
    parabolarum; B XVII 109 ff., B XV 62 ff., and B XI 36-37 in
    the works of Hugh of St. Cher. Eight other quotations in the
    poem are shown to be proverbial, as attested from MSS cited in
    Hans Walther's Proverbia Sententiæquæ Latinitatis Medii Ævi.

12 McLEOD, SUSAN. "The Tearing of the Pardon in Piers Plowman." PQ
    56, no. 1 (Winter):14-26.
        The key to the Tearing of the Pardon is to be found in
    the first part of B VII where Truth sends a message to Piers--
    in effect the Pardon itself--and sends a letter to the

1977

merchants, insisting on the necessity of doing well and on the
insufficiency of merely buying indulgences for one's sins.
Piers becomes angry when the Pardon appears not to be what
Truth has indicated it would be.

13 NOLAN, BARBARA. The Gothic Visionary Perspective. Princeton:
    Princeton University Press, pp. 205-58.
         Analyzes the poem as a series of seven interrelated
    readings (B Prol-IV, V-VII, VIII-X, XI-XII, XIII-XIV, XV-XVII,
    XVIII-XX) that aim for an examination of conscience. The
    basic form is that of the continental penitential quest, but
    Langland's enlarged field of vision goes beyond the mere
    individual soul to encompass fallen mankind moving toward "an
    imminent and much-needed eschaton." The various mnemonic
    devices of the poem--the Charter of Sin (II), the Manor House
    of Mercy (VI), the Castle of Caro (IX), and the Tree of
    Charity (XVI)--provide summary focus for the following narra-
    tive lessons. The poem can be said to herald the disappear-
    ance of medieval ideas of the vision, for although Langland
    draws upon vision-quest conventions throughout, he suggests
    at the same time their inability to bring Will to spiritual
    peace. Yet the poem ends in a vision of the possibility for
    mankind of the Age of the Spirit.

14 PEARSALL, DEREK. The Routledge History of English Poetry.
    Vol. 1, Old English and Middle English Poetry. London,
    Henley, and Boston: Routledge & Kegan Paul, pp. 177-83.
         Langland lacks the classical mannerisms of diction,
    syntax, and phraseology of the alliterative revival. No one
    kind of writing provides a framework adequate to describe the
    poem; its structure is associative and idiosyncratic, its
    handling of dream and allegory inconsistent; its apparent
    ordering structure (the Three Lives) "turns out to be a
    facade," its central theophonic character a mystery. Although
    by any standards other than its own the poem is close to
    artistic breakdown, it is able nonetheless to manifest organic
    growth and a purposive ordering of the material of its author's
    mind engaged in continuous intellectual and spiritual develop-
    ment. As opposed to Pearl where a transcendent order is
    superimposed upon a temporal, Piers Plowman shows the two
    orders inextricably combined: "the spiritual world is made
    concrete, the everyday world is spiritualized."

15 PEARSALL, DEREK. "Piers Plowman: The B Version." Medium Ævum
    46:278-85.
         Amidst general praise for the Kane-Donaldson edition of
    the B-text (1975.14), the work is criticized for the editors'
    "over-rigid assumptions" about Langland's metrical practices,

for example, determining Langland's "normative" patterns and
emending the text on the basis of these patterns where the
text as it stands is deficient in neither sense nor harmony,
as well as producing emendations that do not correspond with
natural speech stress.

16 St-JACQUES, RAYMOND. "Langland's Bells of the Resurrection and
    the Easter Liturgy." ESC 3, no. 2 (Summer):129-35.
        B XVIII 424-31 (Kane-Donaldson), in its depiction of
    awakening by the sound of the Easter bells, is an evocation of
    the Easter liturgy in its references to the bells of Resurrec-
    tion, creeping to the Cross, kissing the jeweled cross, and
    echoes of liturgical chants. The lectiones of Easter Matins
    proclaim Easter to be man's feast as well as God's; hence,
    what the Dreamer has witne-sed in his dream is made relevant
    to his waking reality.

17 St-JACQUES, RAYMOND. "Langland's 'Spes' the Spy and the Book of
    Numbers." N&Q, c.s. 222 (n.s. 24), no. 12 (December):483-85.
        The explanation of Hope as a "spy" in B XVII 1 ff.
    (Kane-Donaldson) is to be found in the commentary on Numbers
    13:1-27, in which the expedition of Moses' spies to view the
    promised Land is taken as a search for Christ. The grapes
    these spies bear back are understood by Cæsarius of Arles as
    the precepts to love God and neighbor, as echoed in B XVII 12.
    The association of Hope with the Levites (B XVII 62-65) is
    also seen in the commentary of Cæsarius.

18 SAPORA, ROBERT WILLIAM, Jr. A Theory of Middle English Allitera-
    tive Meter with Critical Applications. Speculum Anniversary
    Monographs, no. 1 [Cambridge, Mass.]: Mediaeval Academy of
    America, pp. 60-62, 76-79, 98-102.
        Applies to Piers Plowman and other alliterative poems a
    theory of meter developed from Samuel Jay Kaiser, "Old English
    Prosody," CE 30 (1969):331-56. Suggests that Langland learned
    his craft from poets who were nonconservative in metrical
    practice, and that the A-text poet was not a clumsy versifier.
    Lists the metrical forms of verses from the poem.

19 TURVILLE-PETRE, THORLAC. The Alliterative Revival. Cambridge:
    D.S. Brewer; Totowa, N.J.: Rowan & Littlefield, passim.
        The parallels between Piers Plowman and Wynnere and
    Wastoure may be merely the result of a common alliterative
    mode of expression and approach to themes, but the use in both
    of the dream-vision frame for satire shows that poems composed
    in the S.W. Midlands and the N.W. Midlands were not mutually
    exclusive. Piers Plowman differs from traditional allitera-
    tive practices in its spare use of alliterative vocabulary and

1977

its less formal style--perhaps designed to attract a wider
public (which it did). Unlike other alliterative poems, it
was read in most parts of the country; it greatly influenced
later S.W. poems, such as Pierce the Plowman's Crede, Mum and
the Sothsegger, and The Crowned King, all of which depicted
contemporary political, social, and religious conditions in
an unadorned style and with direct echoes of Piers Plowman.
Only Piers Plowman and Pierce the Plowman's Crede among all
the alliterative poems received widespread attention in the
sixteenth century. Remarks on the meter, style, and vocabulary of the poem.

1978

1   ADAMS, ROBERT. "The Nature of Need in Piers Plowman XX."
    Traditio 34:273-302.
            Need's moral allegories vary according to context. His
    appearance in B XX 6-50 (Kane-Donaldson) is a dramatization of
    the apocalyptic text, Job 41:13, and Gregory's comment upon it
    in Moralia in Iob, in which two needs are distinguished, and
    the speciousness of Need's insistence on the fallibility of
    prudence, justice, and fortitude is suggested. Need's urging
    theft is a dramatization of Proverbs 30:8-9, as it is affected
    by his knowledge of the use put to these verses in the anti-
    fraternal texts. The Parable of Need depicts the tribulation
    under the Antichrist, the beginning stages of which Langland
    feels are actual or imminent. The poet's apocalypticism is
    radical, historical, and literal; the Dreamer awakens to per-
    verted temperance, the fourth age of the Church in the Liber
    de Antichristo and other apocalyptic texts.

2   BOURQUIN, GUY. Piers Plowman: Études sur la génèse littéraire
    des trois versions. Thèse presentée devant la Faculté des
    Lettres et des Sciences Humaines de Paris, le 20 novembre
    1970. 2 vols. Paris: Honore Champion, 945 pp.
            Applying the criteria of semantic density, abstraction,
    and profundity of the allegory, suggests for the A-text a
    relative chronology beginning with VII (the least well inte-
    grated, the most prosaic), followed by a stage represented by
    Prol, V, VI 1-47; then a stage represented by II, IV, VIII,
    IX, X; then one represented by I, VI 48-end, XI; then III.
    The debate of Mede and Conscience shows the influence of the
    Voie de Povreté et de Richesse as well as of the Roman de
    Fauvel. The figure of Lewte may owe something to l'Histoire
    de Fauvain; l'Apocalypse versifée of William Gifford is per-
    haps the source of details relating the Whore of Babylon to
    the Antichrist; the Lamentationes de Matheolus exposes the

1978

corruption of society caused by money and contains a satire of
woman's pride; Nicholas Bozon's Char d'Orgueil describes the
Queen of sin as a daughter of Lucifer; La Plainte d'Amour
(attributed to Bozon) stresses the theme of the mastery of the
world by evil; the Lumière as Lais furnishes in the depiction
of the devil's charter an analogue for Mede's letter; and the
Roman des Romans emphasizes covetousness as a corrupter of the
social order in a fashion similar to Langland's depiction of
Mede. With regard to sources of political morality, suggests
the Chronique de Melrose, and the figure of Simon de Montfort
in particular, as the basis of the character Conscience; and
also puts forward such works as the Carmen de bello lewensi,
the Speculum regis, and the Secreta secretorum.

With regard to the B-text, separates the poem into three
zones, corresponding to that which faithfully reproduces the
A-text, enlargments of it, and the continuation of it (B XI-
XX). B XIX-XX show both the most numerous and precise connections in the B-text to the first version of the poem, and the
influence of the same source used in the Visio, the De
interiori domi of Pseudo-Bernard. B XIX-XX are the first part
of the B-text composed by the poet. B X is anterior to B XI-
XV; B IX is shown to be contemporary with B XVI. B XVI-XVIII
(Dobet) were written after B XI-XV; they form an original
ensemble, independent of the Dowel section to which they were
later added. The Dobet section marks a development in the
poet, in which he informs themes already treated with a new
intelligence born of new sources. The poet identifies more
with the Dreamer in this section, and the visions are con-
formed to the rhythm of the liturgy. They attest to "un
etonnant syncretism" of diverse influences of theological
treatises, iconography, illuminations, liturgical texts,
themes from the drama, and so on. Sees the greater part of
those enlargements of the A-text in the B-version as posterior
to the continuation of the earlier version in the B-text.
They almost always reflect authorial preoccupations that were
brought out in the continuation.

Treats the most significant changes introduced in the
C-text as follows: C VI 1-110 stresses sincerity and perse-
verance of both creature and Creator that alone guarantees an
authentic charity; C I 139-58 shows the author has become
aware of Richard II's conflict with the nobles; C IV 338-76
show Langland's ideas of the perfect political body as a mani-
festation of the Mystical Body; C IV 377-96 and 317-35 define
the relationship between diverse elements of society and suggest that the perfect monarch is the conduit through which the
grace of God irrigates the Mystical Body; C IV 404-9 unites
the theme of Incarnation with that of deification; C IV 288-
337 introduces the new term mercede to stand for mesurable

1978

hire of the A-B-texts (mede now means mede mesureless, and
connotes purification and charity; mercede, the deformation of
the divine image in cupiditas); C VI 181-97 offer the essen-
tials of the C-poet's vision and may well be influenced by
events in Richard's reign; and the additions of C XVII 365-
XVIII stress the deviation of the Church from its original
mission and call for the strict observance of ne solliciti
sitis.

Strong Franciscan influence on Piers Plowman is noted in
its emphasis on the monastic ideal, as well as in the details
of the "autobiographical" passage of A IX 1-13, the fact that
many proposed sources are found in a MS of friar William
Herbert (B.M. Add 46919), similarities to works of Nicholas
Bozon, and similarities to Franciscan hagiography and ideas of
work in the characterization of Piers.

*3   BOWERS, JOHN MATHEWS. "Acedia and the Crisis of Will in
      Langland's Piers Plowman." Dissertation, Virginia, 475 pp.
            Abstracted: DAI 39:4930A.

4   COLAIANNE, A.J. Piers Plowman: An Annotated Bibliography of
      Editions and Criticism, 1550-1977. Garland Reference Library
      of the Humanities, vol. 121. New York and London: Garland
      Publishing, xii + 196 pp.
            An annotated bibliography devoted to Langland, divided
      into four chapters treating biography and authorship; text and
      editions/translations; interpretive studies; and language,
      style, and meter. Each chapter reviews problems in that spe-
      cific area and offers a general summary of relevant criticism
      before listing individual studies with annotations. Special
      emphasis is placed on critical studies written after 1875,
      although "significant items written prior to 1875 have been
      included as well." An epilogue suggests future investigations
      of the poem's structural and organizational problems in light
      of the principles of medieval literary composition, of the
      poem's affinities with the methods of medieval oral delivery,
      of the poet's use of rhetorical strategies of persuasion, of
      the political and economic backgrounds of the poem, and of the
      poem's debt to particular sermons, preaching manuals, and
      patristic sources available during Langland's time in London
      and the Malvern area. Reviewed by P.M. Kean, RES, n.s. 30
      (1979):457-58.

*5   CREWS, CHARLES DANIEL. "Piers Plowman and Fourteenth Century
      Ecclesiology." Dissertation, North Carolina, Greensboro,
      304 pp.
            Abstracted: DAI 39:4266A.

6   ERZGRÄBER, WILLI. Neues Handbuch der Literatur Wissenschaft.
     Vol. 8, Europäisches Spätmittelalter. Wiesbaden:
     Akademische Verlagsgesellschaft Athenaion, pp. 231–39.
          Sees the B-text as springing from the controversy over
     predestination and the implied questions regarding divine will
     and human freedom on which the A-text was interrupted, though
     Langland needed more than a decade before he felt able to re-
     work the text. Suggests the affinities of the poem to medi-
     eval debates on courtly love, and describes it as an ars
     amandi in the religious sense. Sees Lady Mede as representing
     the basic problem, a desire for bona temporalia instead of
     God, and in opposition to Reason and Kynde Witte and Conscience.
     The Confession of the Deadly Sins is a necessary first stage;
     the appearance of Piers the second stage, demanding observance
     of the law of life founded upon natural morality and responsi-
     ble work. The Dream-within-the-Dream shows the importance of
     Reason in creation, having a part in the sinfulness of mankind
     and carrying its burden in humility. The poem moves from an
     endorsement of patient poverty to charity, which comprises
     Dobet. In the Dobest section, Piers becomes the head of the
     Church. The last vision is apocalyptic, but expresses hope
     for the reform of the Church and state that is close to the
     ideas of Wyclif. The influence of mysticism is seen in
     Langland's different levels of the deification of man and the
     scala perfectionis, but the poet does not stress the mystical
     oneness with God, and sees the idea of Piers as one that
     transforms society as well as the individual.

7   HILL, THOMAS D. "Christ's 'Thre Clothes': 'Piers Plowman'
     C.XI.193." N&Q, c.s. 223 (n.s. 25), no. 6 (June):200-203.
          The reference to the "thre clothes" of C XI 193 is not
     "merely indefinite," as suggested by Skeat (1886.1), but
     rather reflects the efforts of exegetes such as Ambrose and
     Ludolf of Saxony to harmonize the Gospel accounts of the
     scarlet cloak, the purple tunic, and the white robe.

8   JENNINGS, MARGARET. "Piers Plowman and Holy Church." Viator 9:
     367-74.
          As a figure of the Church, Piers is "essentially tenta-
     tive, pointing to something that is in need of constant inter-
     pretation." Will is the device through which Langland shows
     the need of the Church's guidance, that is, Piers, who is
     defined by those whom he is guiding, rather than by his own
     spiritual nature. Holicherch in the initial passus deals only
     with the basic principles of the way to perfection; Piers, as
     God's coworker in salvation, deals with the moral steps toward
     union with truth.

1978

> Piers teaches Christ the art of healing (B XVI 104)
> since the Church has existed since Abel's sacrifice and Piers
> represents the community of believers in any age. Just as the
> Church is said to comprise laborers, knights, and clergy, the
> poem stresses Piers as the laboring plowman, Christ as a
> knight in Piers's armor, and Piers with priestly functions
> (B XIX 196 ff.).

9 KING, JOHN N. "Robert Crowley: A Tudor Gospelling Poet." YES
   8:220-37.
   > Because of its antimonastic stance, Piers Plowman was
   > the only medieval English model for satiric poetry acceptable
   > to the reformers. Langland's analysis of society as a hier-
   > archy of estates became the basis of Crowley's stewardship
   > theory of property ownership. He imitates Langland's alliter-
   > ative line in his One and thyrtie epigrammes; his Voyce of the
   > last trumpet blowen bi the seventh angel (1549), like his com-
   > ments on Piers Plowman, is related to Bale's commentary on
   > Revelations, the Image of both Churches; and Crowley's
   > Philargyrie of greate Britayne (1551) looks to the just king
   > of Piers Plowman as well as models Philargyrie on Lady Mede.

10 KIRK, ELIZABETH D. "'Who Suffreth More Than God?': Narrative
    Redefinition of Patience in Patience and Piers Plowman." In
    The Triumph of Patience. Edited by Gerald J. Schifforst.
    Orlando: University Presses of Florida, pp. 88-104.
    > Piers Plowman, like Patience (to which it may be en-
    > debted), treats patience in the context of patient poverty,
    > and both works manifest a development from an initial negative
    > view of the virtue to a widened perspective in which it is
    > seen as a positive imitatio dei. This more positive role is
    > seen in Piers Plowman in the opening of Patience's bundle
    > (B XIV 47-48) and in Anima's speech on Charity (B XV 253-59).
    > The distinction of the negative and positive senses of the
    > virtues is made in Aquinas's Summa theologica.

11 LANGLAND, WILLIAM. The Vision of William concerning Piers the
    Plowman, together with Vita de Dowel, Dobet, and Dobest,
    Secundum Wit et Resoun, by William Langland (about 1362-1393
    A.D.). Edited from Numerous Manuscripts, with Prefaces,
    Notes, and a Glossary, by the Reverend Walter W. Skeat.
    Vol. 3, The "Whitaker" Text; or Text C. Early English Text
    Society, o.s. 54. Millwood, N.Y.: Kraus Reprint Co.
    > Reprint of Langland, 1873.5.

12 LANGLAND, WILLIAM. Piers Plowman by William Langland. An Edi-
    tion of the C-text. Edited by Derek Pearsall. York Medieval
    Texts, 2d series. London: Edwin Arnold (Publishers), 416 pp.
        Accepts the 1360s as the date of the A-text, with the
    poem probably still being worked on in 1369-70; the 1370s as
    the date of the B-text, with much allusion to events of
    1376-79; and the completion of the C-text by 1387. Defends
    an edition of the C-text on the basis of Skeat's choice
    (Langland, 1886.1) of a scribally sophisticated MS on which
    to base his text, the fact that the C-text represents the
    author's latest thoughts on the poem, the intentional exci-
    sions and additions made in this version by a poet "who knows
    what he is doing," and the success of the C-version in its
    general purpose of clarifying and reshaping the B-text. Con-
    siders the poem as a reflection of conflicts in late medieval
    society, specifically the breakdown of the feudal order and
    the Church. Langland's response is that of a devout medieval
    Christian, understanding change as decay, and eager to assim-
    ilate or understand change in a traditional, hierarchic mode
    of thought. With respect to religion, Langland is part of the
    fourteenth-century spiritual movement that stressed a personal
    devotion and a ministry closer to that of the Gospels. Al-
    though he shares with the Lollards a hostility to church en-
    dowment and to friars, as well as a sense that secular leaders
    are responsible for the reform of religious orders, he is no
    Wyclifite, as his positions on the Eucharist and the pope
    show. He shows a varied use of allegorical techniques, but
    the poem draws its structural power from the use of the
    Dreamer, who "engages the reader in the experience of the
    poem, so that its urgencies are shared, its discoveries seen
    and felt to be won."
        Bases the edition of the poem on MS. X, corrected by
    MS. U. Makes no attempt to reconstruct the author's original
    from which these two MSS are derived, though corrects, on the
    basis of MSS. T and I, readings evidently defective. Con-
    tains, besides introduction and text, select bibliography,
    alphabetical reference list, and glossary. Also published as
    Langland, 1979.6. Reviewed by T. Turville-Petre, RES, n.s. 30
    (1979):454-57.

13 [LANGLAND, WILLIAM.] The Vision of Piers Plowman. A Complete
    Edition of the B-Text. Edited by A.V.C. Schmidt. Everyman's
    Universal Library. London, Melbourne, and Toronto: J.M. Dent
    & Sons; New York: E.P. Dutton & Co., xlviii + 364 pp.
        Reviews editions, and questions of authorship, audience
    and date, accepting with Kane (1965.12) the general truthful-
    ness of the portrait Langland gives of himself in the poem,
    especially in its external particulars, noting however that

1978

it stops short of true autobiography and is capable of poetic
distortion "in the interests of ironic or didactic purposes."
Sees the most telling differences between Langland's poetry
and other alliterative poems in the absence in Piers Plowman
of ornamental diction, the lack of interest in description for
its own sake, and an extraordinarily dense poetic texture
relying upon imaginative metaphor and multitudinous associations. Considers the main structural principles in the poem
the protagonist's quest and the dreams themselves. Isolates
four aspects of Langland's poetic art that distinguish
Langland and other alliterative poets from Chaucer and Gower:
"delicately expressive rhythms," word-play, use of expanded
metaphor and thematic imagery, and use of Latin words and
phrases as part of the English poetry.

Accepts the division of B-text MSS described by Kane and
Donaldson (1975.14) into two families, RF and LMHCrGYOC^{2}CB.
Constructs the archetype from the agreement of the two sub-
archetypes or from one subarchetype when that one appears
superior on intrinsic grounds or in light of the A- and/or
C-text readings. In a few cases, reconstructs the archetype
from the readings of individual MSS that are judged to preserve the reading of the subarchetype. Reconstructs the
archetype when neither subarchetype can be firmly established.
Finds approximately 750 readings in the archetype capable of
correction, along the lines described by Kane and Donaldson;
but leaves many more readings uncorrected because of lack of
evidence. Includes, besides introduction and text, bibliography, textual and lexical commentary, literary historical
commentary, an appendix treating Langland's alliterative
practices, and an index of proper names. Reviewed by
T. Turville-Petre, RES, n.s. 30 (1979):454-57.

14 MATHESON, LISTER M. "An Example of Ambiguity and Scribal Confusion in Piers Plowman." ELN 15, no. 4 (June):263-67.
The variants of A VIII 78 suggest that the scribes were
uncertain whether they were dealing with misshape, "cripple"
(a rare word), or the near-homophonous mishap, "mishap."

15 MURTAUGH, DANIEL MAHER. Piers Plowman and the Image of God.
Gainesville: University Presses of Florida, 129 pp.
The familiar notion of man having been created in the
image and likeness of God is used to explain the Augustinian
notions of memory, intellect, and will; epistemology; and the
proper ordering of society as a perfect image of man's rational nature analogous with the universe as the concrete
expression of the ideas of God. The imago dei clarifies such
structural aspects of the poem as the constant changes of
perspective and connections between seemingly disparate areas

of experience. The representation of the Incarnation is shown
to give value to human works; hence, Dowel comes to be defined
through the Person of Christ, "Whose Redemption is achieved
through the human nature the dreamer first knew as Piers."
The speech of Holicherch defines Truth as both transcendent
and imminent, cognitive and affective, and manifesting itself
in the world as good works in a way that reproduces the
Incarnation. Piers's directions to Truth show how the
Incarnation and the Redemption make grace available to turn
good deeds into supernatural acts. Inwit is considered in the
context of Aquinian "active intellect" (the <u>agens</u> aspect of
<u>intellectus</u>) in its mediating relationship to Anima, but akin
to the Augustinian-Bonaventuran tradition in its supernatu-
rally illuminative function. The Creation of Man (B IX 26-49)
is developed in terms of God's self-fulfillment in man in the
context of Christianized Platonic exemplarism. The importance
of Liberum Arbitrium in the Tree of Charity scene of the B-
text (B XVI 46-52) and even more in the C-version (where he
replaces Piers) has the effect of identifying this faculty
with the Holy Spirit.

Cupidity is viewed in the poem as the great obstacle to
reformation of the world, for cupidity is in effect man living
according to man, rather than to God, and for that reason im-
peding the emergence of the <u>corpus mysticum</u>. Reform of the
world in the image of God is described by the poet in the
elimination in the C-text of infinite, heavenly meed and the
opposition of measurable hire to earthly meed, as described in
the "grammatical metaphor" of C IV 346-53, which shows man's
"agreement in kind" with Christ, manifested in his agreement
with other men through charity.

Intellectualism, like Lady Mede, is ambivalent in the
poem. Langland views learning as a species of good works.
Passus X shows Langland vacillating between an Ockhamist
indeterminism (and its denial of the ontological status of
grace as an essential constituent of merit), and the deter-
minism of Bradwardine—both of which views render the cooperation of the will with grace problematic, as well as take
salvation out of man's control. The confession of forty-five
years of vice (B XI 34-41) represents the nadir of indeterminism and skepticism, which is reversed by Lewte, the "strict
regard for human and divine law which forms the matrix of
love."

The appearance of Trajan shows Langland's acceptance of
the optimistic side of Ockhamist indeterminism. The Vision of
Middle Earth manifests the order established by God and shows
the necessity of mankind's patient awaiting of God's next act.
Imaginatif resolves the Dreamer's dilemma: man is saved by
grace, and learning is related to grace as a "parallel

1978

emanation" of Christ. In light of the Epistle of James, the
emphasis of the Pardon must be placed on its first line--the
need and hence the efficacy, of good works; indeed, the
Pardon gives human goodness a power it does not of itself
possess. Piers is God's search for man; he "teaches" Christ
lechecraft that, taking on human nature capable of suffering,
He might "learn" how to cure His suffering creatures. Langland is compared to Wallace Stevens ("A Primitive Like an
Orb"), in that for both a coherence sought in external reality
that takes on human shape (Stevens' "Giant") is found after
all men come together. Reviewed by P.M. Kean, RES, n.s. 30
(1979):457-58.

16 REGAN, CHARLES LIONEL. "John Gower, John Barleycorn, and William
Langland." AN&Q 16, no. 3 (March):102.
    Sees Gower's Confessio Amantis, VI, 60, as an echo of
the description of the drunkard in A V 213.

17 RUSSELL, J. STEPHEN. "Meaningless Dreams and Meaningful Poems:
The Form of the Medieval Dream Vision." Massachusetts Studies
in English 7, no. 1:20-32.
    Piers Plowman is characteristic of medieval dream vi-
sions in that it begins as a somnium animale or an insomnium,
not a revelation. The progress of the poem is first to show
that the vision is not relevant to "normal people," then to
demonstrate that if we understand it, we are troubled in ways
like the Dreamer. The audience becomes involved; and at the
end of the poem we are where the Dreamer began.

1979

*1 BISSELL, BARRY LYNN. "The Community of the Folk on the Field:
Langland's Allegory of the Polity." Dissertation, C.U.N.Y.,
388 pp.
    Abstracted: DAI 40:839A.

*2 BONNER, JOSHUA HALL. "The Half Acre and the Barn: Structural
and Thematic Unity in the Visio and Vita of Piers Plowman."
Dissertation, Indiana, 90 pp.
    Abstracted: DAI 40:839A.

3   CLOPPER, LAWRENCE M. "Langland's Trinitarian Analogies as Key
to Meaning and Structure." Medievalia et Humanistica, n.s. 9:
87-110.
    Langland's hand analogy (B XVII 141-43) is perhaps
derived from Isaiah 40:12; his torch analogy is perhaps suggested by the symbolism of the Paschal calendar, as well as

by Bartholomeus's analysis of the properties of candles and other light analogies of the Fathers. The hand analogy stresses the involvement of each of the Persons of the Trinity in Creation, but is careful to suggest that the traditional characteristics of power, wisdom, and goodness are not reserved to one Person alone. The torch analogy emphasizes the importance of the Holy Spirit (and charity) as a link to the Father through the Son. Most of the definitions of the Three Lives are developed out of models of power, wisdom, and goodness, as well as faith, hope, and charity (also linked with the Persons of the Trinity). As with the Trinity, the Three Lives are distinct yet inhere in one another; their definitions can be grouped with two sets of categories: hierarchical, to suggest estates and functions or degrees of perfection, and progressive, to denote successive stages of an individual's development in moral perfection. The four-part structure of the poem (Visio plus the Three Lives) is governed by the image of Father/faith, Son/wisdom/hope, and Holy Spirit/grace/ charity; and Unity of Godhead and Dobest. Yet the last sections of the poem show that Langland has overlapped the Three Persons in a way that emphasizes the importance of the Holy Spirit in Dobest, as well as the necessity to perceive the Oneness of God, not merely His Threeness.

4   DAVLIN, MARY CLEMENTE. "A Genius-Kynde Illustration in Codex Vaticanus Palatinus Latinus 629." Manuscripta 23, no. 3 (November):149-58.
        Explains an illustrated male priestly figure in MS. Pal. lat. 629, standing behind an arbor consanguinitatis, as a representation of Genius. Shows that in B IX 26-29 (Kane-Donaldson), Kynde is identified with God in an unprecedented way, and suggests that in the poem the figures of Natura and Genius coalesce in Kynde. The illustration may represent the only known analogue to Langland's Kynde.

5   HOBSBAUM, PHILIP. "Piers Plowman through Modern Eyes." In Tradition and Experiment in English Poetry. Totowa, N.J.: Rowan & Littlefield, pp. 1-29.
        A slightly revised version of Hobsbaum, 1971.17.

6   LANGLAND, WILLIAM. Piers Plowman by William Langland. An Edition of the C-text. Edited by Derek Pearsall. Berkeley and Los Angeles: University of California Press, 416 pp.
        See Langland, 1978.12.

1979

7   LAWLER, TRAUGOTT. "The Gracious Imagining of Redemption in
     'Piers Plowman.'" English 38, no. 132 (Autumn):203-16.
          Langland's idea of Christ's redemptive grace is asso-
     ciated with vigorous action and represented through the imagery
     of birds, music, and grass, with lighthearted ease and confi-
     dent mobility. Although not ignoring the burdensome aspects
     of the holy life, the poem presents lightness and mobility as
     desirable, encumbrance as bad. Characters such as Christ, the
     Magi, Lazarus, Dismas, Longeus, St. Francis, Piers, and Will
     express the ideal of lighthearted freedom and the mood of joy-
     ful confidence.

8   MANDER, M.N.K. "Grammatical Analogy in Langland and Alan of
     Lille." N&Q, c.s. 224 (n.s. 26), no. 12 (December):501-4.
          In contrast to Schmidt (1969.37), who suggested a general
     resemblance of the grammatical metaphor of C IV 335-409 to
     Wyclif's discussion of modes of logical prediction, finds a
     more telling comparison with Alanus de Insulis's De planctu
     naturæ, in which actual grammatical relations are referred
     to. Similar to Langland's, Alanus's use of the grammatical/
     sexual analogy exhibits the connection of grammar and truth.
     B IX 38-39 and Prosa V of the De planctu naturæ both use the
     analogy of Nature/Kynde providing a pen so that man can cre-
     atively use his parchment. And the grammatical analysis of
     mede/mercede is similar to Alanus's analogy for sexual passion
     in Metrum I.

9   MANN, JILL. "Eating and Drinking in 'Piers Plowman.'" Essays
     and Studies 32:26-43.
          B VI shows society ruled ultimately by the laws of phys-
     ical nature which overlap moral laws but are not identical to
     them. Justice is shown to be an inherent part of the world,
     capable of being perverted by those who are gluttonous or win
     food by begging, though Hunger demonstrates that physical need
     takes precedence over moral laws. The importance of food is
     seen in the emphasis on food and drink in the account of the
     Deadly Sins, the Fall, and the Eucharist. The familiar
     monastic metaphor of eating and drinking for the contemplation
     of Scripture also applies to material in distinctiones, con-
     cordances of key words, as in the dinner party at Conscience's
     house (B XIII). The Debate of the Four Daughters of God shows
     that God Himself has an "appetite for knowledge" that leads to
     our redemption through the Incarnation.

10 MARTIN, PRISCILLA. The Field and the Tower. London and
    Basingstoke: Macmillan Press, 172 pp.
        Sees the many problematic features of the poem in ten-
    sion with its theological orthodoxy, as well as with the
    allegorical mode which depends on a received system of values
    and is not generally well suited to the exploration of an
    author's problems. Narrative and symbolic topics and motifs
    such as pilgrimages, ploughing, pardons, and quests raise more
    questions than they answer. All sections and versions of the
    poem are ended on notes of frustration and/or anticlimax.
    Langland questions our notions of reality, expectations of
    narrative, and the clarity of received knowledge through
    generic indistinctness, vague locations, mysterious entrances
    and exits, and the mixing of the allegorical and literal; yet
    the feeling produced is most often one of religious awe,
    rather than skepticism.
        Langland is concerned with the utility and value of
    writing his poem; but the sense of "true minstrelsy" as de-
    fined in B XIII 436-51 might well indict Langland's original-
    ity and his intrusiveness into the poem as dangerously self-
    interested. Disputes the suggestion of Peter (1956.9) that
    Langland is writing "complaint," for Langland clearly felt no
    unease (as in B XI 84 ff.) in his denunciation of others.
        Langland's use of abstract and concrete vocabulary sug-
    gests he felt both respect and contempt for the fallen world.
    Often the abstract vocabulary suggests a comprehensive view-
    point of the narrator, and the concrete evokes the author's
    distaste for the values of worldliness. The difficulties of
    understanding abstractions are stressed, yet the use of the
    concrete suggests its capacity to embody the ideal.
        Langland uses allegory to define, while he is aware that
    argument by analogy can mislead, that language is corruptible.
    He is self-conscious in the opposition of the allegorical
    mode, (emblematic of clear-cut moral distinctions) and the
    literal (suggestive of compromise and confusion): especially
    in the figure of Conscience, the allegorical mode is almost
    destroyed by the fact of the literal. Nevertheless, the end
    of the poem shows Langland's desire for the idealism and in-
    tellectual coherence assumed by allegory. Langland uses alle-
    gory functionally, in both senses of ænigma (as concealment)
    and apocalypse (as illumination).
        The Vita represents a progression from the Visio, but is
    in part a contradiction of it in its questioning of the value
    of worldly responsibility. The C-text excises Piers's re-
    nunciation of his former life along with the Tearing of the
    Pardon, but introduces moral ambiguity into the character of
    Recklessness. Miracles in the poem are seen as a mediation of
    "reckless" world-denying austerity and a responsible approach

to social reform based on <u>mesure</u>. The wariness of the spiri-
tualizing metaphors is shown clearly in the autobiographical
episode (C VI 1 ff.), in the Dreamer's defense of his life
that is neither accepted nor disproved.

*11 OVITT, GEORGE ODELL, Jr. "Time as a Structural Element in Medi-
eval Literature." Dissertation, Massachusetts, 279 pp.
Abstracted: <u>DAI</u> 40:4587A-88A.

12 ROBBINS, ROSSELL HOPE. "Dissent in Middle English Literature:
The Spirit of (Thirteen) Seventy-six." <u>Medievalia et
Humanistica</u>, n.s. 9:25-53.
Finds the most dangerous manifestations of dissent in
Middle English literature in the works of the pro-Establishment
writers like Langland and Wyclif, in their unconscious formulations of dissident positions that "only later moved from
philosophical criticism and genteel reform to open rebellion."
Langland overstresses the primacy of the king, but in general
upholds traditional social theory of the Three Estates, and
excepts knights and clergy from manual labor. But his sentimental picture of the poverty of the English family (C X
72-87) might have led some to doubt the morality of the
Establishment.

13 SALTER, ELIZABETH. "Langland and the Contents of 'Piers
Plowman.'" <u>Essays and Studies</u> 32:19-25.
The poem is viewed in a variety of literary contexts,
for example, work-a-day texts like the <u>Poema Morale</u>, the
<u>compilatio</u> genre, in which authors function as rearrangers of
material to make it more accessible to readers. Though the
use of personification is not enjoined upon compilers, this
figure was perhaps stimulated by Langland's reading of the New
Testament, with its "deep mystery at the centre of appear-
ances," as evidenced in Christ's mysterious identity made
known to the disciples (Matthew 16:14) and the account of His
appearance after the Resurrection (Luke 24:31).

Index

The Index includes authors and titles of the bibliographical entries, significant names, authors and works mentioned in the annotations, and selected subjects. Those studies concerned with biographical and authorship questions are indexed under Langland, William; other subject headings are to be found under Piers Plowman.

Index

345

Bersuire, Pierre, 1973.1
Bessinger, J.B., 1960.10
Bestul, Thomas H., 1974.2
Bethurum, Dorothy, 1960.4, 7
Bibliographia Poetica, 1802.1
Bibliotheca Britannico-
    Hibernica . . ., 1748.1
Biggar, Raymond George, 1961.1
Das Bild in Piers the Plowman,
    1904.1
A Biographical Register of the
    University of Oxford to
    A.D. 1500, 1580.1
Birnes, William Jack, 1974.3;
    1975.5
"Bishop Brunton and the Fable
    of the Rats," 1935.8
Bishop Percy's Folio Manuscript,
    1868.2
"Bishop Thomas Brunton and His
    Sermons," 1939.4
Bissell, Barry Lynn, 1979.1
Björkman, E., 1916.2
Blackman, Elsie, 1914.1; 1918.1;
    1928.6; 1934.2; 1938.6;
    1955.2; 1975.14
Black Prince, 1879.1; 1916.2;
    1932.3
Blake, William, 1966.6
Blamires, Alcuin G., 1975.6
Blanch, Robert, 1932.15; 1939.1;
    1944.1; 1949.8; 1957.7;
    1963.4; 1964.8; 1965.2
Bloomfield, Morton W., 1939.1;
    1943.3; 1951.9; 1956.1;
    1957.3; 1958.1; 1959.6;
    1960.10; 1961.2-3, 8;
    1962.4, 11; 1965.20;
    1968.18; 1969.4; 1970.4;
    1971.11; 1973.5; 1974.2
Blythe, Joan Heiges, 1971.3
"The Body Politic and the Lust
    of the Eyes: Piers Plowman,"
    1966.8
Boethius, 1895.3; 1954.5; 1972.16
Bolton, Edmund, 1618[?].1; 1722.1
Bolton, W.F., 1970.19
Bond, Ronald Bruce, 1974.4
Bonner, Joshua Hall, 1979.2
Bonsdorff, Ingrid von, 1928.1

Book of Martyrs . . .,
    1560-64[?].1
The Book of the Poets, 1871.1
"The Book of the Poets. Scott,
    Webster, & Geary," 1842.1
"The Book of the Poets (Second
    Notice)," 1842.2
Bosch, Hieronymous, 1958.2;
    1971.25
Bourquin, Guy, 1957.4; 1960.10;
    1961.3, 8; 1962.4; 1965.13,
    20; 1978.2
Bowers, A. Joan, 1975.7
Bowers, John Mathews, 1978.3
Bowers, R.H., 1959.1; 1961.4;
    1971.4
Bozon, Nicholas, 1931.4; 1961.12;
    1967.6; 1978.2
Bradley, Henry, 1887.3; 1906.2-3;
    1907.1; 1908.3; 1909.1-2, 5;
    1910.1-2, 4; 1911.1; 1912.1;
    1913.1
Brereton, Richard, 1558.1; 1857.1
Brett, Cyril, 1927.2
Breviary, 1922.3; 1927.1; 1934.4;
    1938.5; 1976.1
Brewer, D.S., 1962.4, 11
Brian, Beverly Dianne, 1969.5
Bridges, Robert, 1880.1; 1882.2;
    1935.5
Brigan, Nicholai. See Brigham,
    Nicholas
Brigham, Nicholas, post 1546.1;
    1925.1
Bright, Alan H., 1922.2; 1925.1-
    2; 1926.1; 1928.2; 1930.1-2,
    7; 1934.6; 1935.4; 1944.2;
    1949.10
Brink, Bernhard ten, 1877.1;
    1883.1; 1907.5; 1948.6;
    1974.5
Brinton, Thomas. See Brunton,
    Thomas
The British Librarian, 1737.2;
    1738.1
Brockbury, James de, 1928.2;
    1934.6
Bromfelde, William, 1941.8
Bromyard, John, 1961.12
Brook, Stella, 1951.9; 1952.6

Index

Index

Index

ANNUAL BIBLIOGRAPHY

1986

Vincent DiMarco
University of Massachusetts (Amherst)

1. Aers, David. "Reflections on the 'Allegory of the Theologians,' Ideology and *Piers Plowman.*" *Medieval Literature: Criticism, Ideology & History.* Ed. David Aers. Brighton: Harvester Press, 1986. 58–73.

Allegorical interpretation is seen as the tool of the Church, an entrenched social institution, to control the "diverse potentials" of the sacred text and contain imaginative activity within its own ideological framework. *PPl* asserts conventional formulations largely to problematize them; as opposed to Jacques de Vitry and Stephen Langton who allegorize agricultural activity imperialistically, Langland refuses standard clerical allegory in B.6 in favor of a densely social and political depiction of the breakdown of social order. Although B.19 shows Langland asserting traditional social ideology, his recourse to a "magical" dissolution of all conflict suggests that the orthodox social ideology was already doomed.

2. Barr, Helen. "The Use of Latin Quotations in *Piers Plowman* with Special Reference to Passus XVIII of the 'B' Text." *N&Q* ns 33 (1986): 440–48.

Until B.18 Latin quotations generally have a didactic function and stand apart from the text of the poem. But as the disparity of words and works is exposed, and Piers as a figure of Christ illustrates the need of mankind to act in order to be saved, Latin quotations are here more than elsewhere incorporated into the verse-form as part of the narrative action, with their various citations enacted and fulfilled.

The Yearbook of Langland Studies, Volume 1, 1987, pages 174–189.

3. Bennett, J. A. W. "Langland." *Middle English Literature*. Ed. and completed by Douglas Gray. *The Oxford History of English Literature*. Ed. John Buxton and Norman Davis, vol. 1, part 2. Oxford: Clarendon Press, 1986. 430–55.

The *persona* of *PPl* is not the autobiographical projection of the author, but the poet's partly fictional vehicle of ideas not necessarily his own. Likewise, there is no reason to think that the interruption of the A text and the commencement of the B version signals Langland's own experience, then resolution, of doctrinal or personal problems. Like Chaucer, and as opposed to continental predecessors in the dream-vision tradition, Langland is skeptical concerning the interpretation of actual dreams, which the dream of the poem resembles in its non-rational, fragmentary aspects. The poem develops in a spiral-like fashion around four important concepts: the field of folk (the material world), Holy Church, the pardon (linked to the capital sins and identified with Piers), and the crucifixion rood.

The poem is a series of allegories that are largely not accessible to the methods of fourfold exegesis. Images and ideas are often incompletely fused, and the line between allegory and actuality often blurred. Langland's alliterative line appears closer to speech rhythm than to that of *Winner and Waster* or the *Parliament of the Three Ages*. His style combines the sublime with the mundane; he is especially fond of kinetic verbs in unexpected contexts; his language is seldom consciously poetic. The poem shares allegorical characters and images with Deguileville's *Pèlerinage de la Vie Humaine*, but the character Piers is unique; *PPl* inherits the traditional triadic pattern exemplified in the Anglo-Norman *Lumière as lais*, but balances the Active and Contemplative with a mixed life similar to that of an active, devout bishop.

4. Bowers, John M. *The Crisis of Will in Piers Plowman*. Washington, DC: Catholic University of America Press, 1986.

PPl, written by an intellectual poet uncommitted to scholasticism who was probably educated in a cathedral school, is a depiction of the crisis of the fourteenth century in which, *inter alia*, theological and philosophical questions were raised regarding the place of reason and experience in God's plan and the power and freedom of God's will. Langland was neither systematic nor doctrinaire concerning the topics of the voluntarist debate, the issues of which were exaggerated and distorted as discussion of them spread outward to the laity through the sermons of the secular clergy: generally Augustinian in his outlook, he appears to have been influenced by Duns Scotus's emphasis on the operation of the will independent of reason and its freedom to suspend judgment in the face of contending alternatives. The complex, multifaceted and argumentative character Will may have been influenced by Ockham, who invested the will with powers of cognition and reason. *Acedia*, early conceived of in the monastic and eremitic traditions as a spiritual phenomenon involving laziness and somnolence, was broadened in the twelfth century to include allied psychological states of mental slackness, boredom, etc.; with the rise of popular theology after the Fourth Lateran Council worldly and social manifestations of the sin were explored. By dividing the poem into the Visio and Vitae, Langland is able to examine Sloth as a social sin whose roots stem from spiritual idleness and a lack of *caritas*. Langland avoids all standard orderings of the Seven Deadly Sins, but always places Pride first and Sloth last; of these two sins, sloth is more impressive in Langland's handling. Sloth's confession (B.5.385–460) emphasizes omissions relating to the sacrament of penance that are developed at the end of the poem in Sloth's assault of Castle Unity after Flattery has caused Contrition to fall asleep. The presentation here of Sloth as a fierce warrior is probably unprecedented. Elsewhere (C.7.70–119), Sloth is shown through a tree image as the vice towards which others move.

Will is described as slothful, either as an unholy hermit or as one who disguises himself as a hermit to avoid work. A superior will, embodied in the king, is shown to be necessary to compel individual wills to law and order. English writers in particular show the potential of the monarch's will to corrupt the law. Langland's king at first lacks the guidance of *ratio*, and is guilty of sloth in his lack of vigilance to corruption and his decision to marry Conscience to Meed. True reform requires that the king's good intentions be joined by all members of society, represented by Will.

Emphasis on Will's repeated falling asleep, the details of his sleeping, the suggestion of wilderness and fairies, Will's identification as a fool, his worldweariness and forgetfulness are all quite possibly evocative of sloth and suggestive that the dreamer does not profit from the teachings of his visions. The Dreamer's account of his life (C.5) is not an autobiographical confession by Langland so much as a fictional pose that gives insight into the dreamer's moral predicament, with reference to Langland only in terms of his potential for willfulness. The form of the "autobiography" is a conventional debate of Wit and Will.

Langland's anxiety over the act of "makyng" is perhaps never finally resolved. His constant revising may have served as a means to explore his slothful temperament; his neglect of poetic game-elements denies poetry's recreative function. Poetry-as-process accords with the notion of the poem that intentions count more than what is achieved, and perhaps is intended to justify the act of poetic composition.

5. Burrow, J. A. *The Ages of Man: A Study in Medieval Writing and Thought*. Oxford: Clarendon Press, 1986. 69–70, 143–46.

B.12.3–11 (Imaginatif's address to the Dreamer) is influenced by the Gregorian interpretation (*XL Homiliarum in Evang.*, Bk. 1, Hom. 13) of the three *vigiliae* of Luke 12:36–38 as *pueritia*, *adolescentia vel juventus*, and *senectus*, which finds in the approach of old age an urgent reason to amend one's life before death and judgment. B.19.26–199 shows a traditional concern with seeing the *iter humanitatis* in the life of Jesus, styled *filius Mariae* as late as the marriage feast at Cana; later "in his moder absence" he reaches full maturity as *filius David*. B.16.90 ff. casts the natural *cursus aetatis* as an unfamiliar discipline in which Jesus as a man was instructed by Piers, in a model of how the human soul is to proceed in an orderly and productive way. The proverb, "Soon ripe, soon rotten" (first attested in C.12.222) is a popular notice of traditional distrust of early maturity and unnatural precocity.

6. Donaldson, E. Talbot. "Langland, William." In *Dictionary of the Middle Ages*, Joseph R. Strayer, Editor in Chief. Vol. 7. New York: Scribner's, 1986. 329–37.

Admits that nothing definitive can be known of the poem's author and that Langland's authorship of the three versions is "not yet a wholly dead issue," but accepts as authoritative the note in Trinity College, Dublin, ms. D.4.1 regarding Stacy de Rokayle, father of William "de Longland," etc., as well as Bale's ascription to Langland. Finds the presumed order of composition of the three versions not capable of absolute proof, but comparison suggests that B is intermediate and A earlier. Dates the A text in late 1360s or early 1370s (allusions to Alice Perrers), B text 1376–79 (references to Good Parliament), C text before 1388 (death of Thomas Usk).

Offers an interpretative summary of the three versions which stresses the transformation of Will from passive to active in the Visio and Vita, the similarities of Visio and Vita in sharply satirizing the clergy, the poem's combination of homily and intense poetry, and its constant discussion of Christianity's basic tenets. Truth, visible at the beginning, proves elusive; Holy Church is human and fallible. The C text shows Langland dissatisfied with the earlier, ideal distinction of true meed and "meed mesureless." In general, Dowel refers to living in accord with Christian teaching in the active life; Dobet to living more contemplatively in patience and charity, helping and teaching others; Dobest to the life of an ecclesiastical executive. Imaginatif is Will's own reconstructive memory; Anima (Liberum Arbitrium in C), a model of the human psyche with all its functions. Surprisingly, the narrative of Christ's triumph does not conclude the poem on a hopeful note; instead, there is a true apocalypse in which, characteristic of the poem, Dobest (here, Piers as St. Peter and a type of the good pope) must be sought anew. Includes a bibliography of editions and major studies to 1980.

7. Donaldson, E. Talbot. "Long Will's Apology: A Translation." Kratzmann and Simpson (no. 19 below) 30–34.

Translation into Modern English alliterative verse, with introduction, of C.5.1–104 from Huntington Library ms. HM 143. Autobiography in the passage is impossible to prove, but the character here accords well with evidence from elsewhere in the three texts. Will's defense, following St. Paul in remaining in the vocation to which one has been called, is the same used by both Alice of Bath and Falstaff. Will shows himself aware of taking a chance with his salvation; his apology is at once specious and heartfelt.

8. Donner, Morton. "The Gerund in Middle English." *ES* 67 (1986): 394–400.

Based on *MED* citations of *-ing* nouns, this study casts doubt on the gerund as an established ME construction. Notes the extreme scarcity of gerunds functioning as subjects: besides two passages from *Kyng Alisaunder* and two uses in medical writings, finds one example each by Langland and Pecock, for both of whom the *-ing* subject is part of an elaborate compound subject.

9. Doyle, A. I. "Remarks on Surviving Manuscripts of *Piers Plowman*." Kratzmann and Simpson (no. 19 below) 35–48.

Drawing in part on researches by M. L. Samuels (later published *MÆ* 54 [1985]: 232–47), notes that of 54 mss. of *PPl* earlier than Crowley's *editio princeps*, only four are of the second half of the fifteenth century and only three of the first half of the sixteenth: demand apparently was met by mss. available by mid-fifteenth century. Earliest mss. are all or parts of B and C texts, rather than simple A text, which had been written two decades or more earlier; perhaps the earliest copies of the A text were lost when longer versions became available. No A-text mss. are linked with London, yet some were probably copied there by scribes who preserved the spelling of their exemplars. More B mss. than A mss. date before or slightly after 1400, and many show W. Midlands characteristics, although these mss., too, could have been copied in London. More early C mss. survive than for A and B, and with a greater concentration than of B of W. Midlands features. The C version was probably neither released by Langland in London nor got there early.

10. Duggan, Hoyt N. "Alliterative Patterning as a Basis for Emendation in Middle English Alliterative Poetry." *SAC* 8 (1986): 73–105.

Examining a corpus of approximately 13,000 lines (including *Death and Life* 1–459; *Mum and the Sothsegger* 1–431; *Parliament of the Three Ages*; *PPl* B.5.365–4.167; *Winner and Waster*, et al.), finds that with the exception of *PPl* and *PPCrede* the alliterative poets wrote exclusively in the pattern *aa/ax*, with the single ordered exception *aa/aa* appearing when alliteration was vocalic.

Regarding *Parliament of the Three Ages*, of 31 lines in which both mss. lack regular alliteration or appear to fail in alliteration, six are found to be regular, fifteen can be confidently emended to restore the poet's lost reading, six can be less confidently emended given the existence of more than one alliterating synonym, and only four remain for which emendations according to the alliterative pattern *aa/ax* do not suggest themselves.

During his career Langland appears to have moved away from traditional modes of composition in formulaic language and grammmetrical patterns consonant with those of other alliterative poets.

11. Duggan, Hoyt N. "The Shape of the B-Verse in Middle English Alliterative Poetry." *Speculum* 61 (1986): 564–92, esp. 577–83.

PPl is the largest exception to what appears to be the authorial (rather than merely scribal) practice in ME alliterative poetry in which the b-verse consists of two lifts and one to three dips, with a minimum of four and a maximum of nine syllables. *PPl* also a major exception to the distributional rule dictating that if two or three dips are filled only one can have two or more syllables.

12. Finlay, Alison. "The Warrior Christ and the Unarmed Hero." Kratzmann and Simpson (no. 19 below) 19–29.

Christ of B.18 is a warrior with the paradoxical weapons of humility and passivity, as in the OE *Dream of the Rood*, and is depicted as a young knight of untried potential, unarmed and about to be dubbed, as in romances. The motif of a king eschewing armor as a gesture of defiance appears to be echoed in *Dream of the Rood* 39a, and is found explicitly in Beowulf's fight with Grendel, *Guthlac A* 302–07, and various of the sagas which make up Snorri Sturluson's *Heimskringla*.

13. Fletcher, Alan J. "Line 30 of the Man of Law's Tale and the Medieval Malkyn." *ELN* 24 (1986): 15–20.

The name "Malkyn" (C.1.179–80) is stereotypical in ME of lowly rank, unsophistication, and unattractiveness, at least as judged according to courtly standards; and association with lechery (as in the Man of Law's Tale) represents an extension of the stereotype.

14. Gray, Nick. "The Clemency of Cobblers: A Reading of 'Glutton's Confession' in *Piers Plowman*." *LSE* ns 17 (1986): 61–75.

Invariably read as an example of social realism, Glutton's Confession (B.5.296–318, 336–56) is better considered metaphorically as a mock-confession, in which the tavern functions as the "devil's chapel" of pulpit tradition, drinking cups replace hymns, the ale-pot stands for the chalice, and Glutton's vomiting is meant to recall the metaphor of voiding one's sins in confession. Clement the Cobbler, whose name suggests a confessor's merciful disposition and whose profession was notorious for pretension, is a mock-confessor; the scene thus returns the audience to the idea of confession even when one of the sins appears to have turned away from repentance.

15. Gray, Nick. "Langland's Quotations from the Penitential Tradition." *MP* 84 (1986): 53–60.

Lists Latin quotations similar or identical to those used in confessional manuals and penitential sections of scholastic *summae*, and employed by Langland
in contexts that recall their use in the penitential tradition.

C.6.257a (Thomas of Chobham, *Summa confessorum* 7.6.11.1); B.13.426a,
C.7.87a (Thomas of Chobham, *Summa confessorum* 6.4.4); A.4.126–27,
B.4.143–44, C.4.140–41 (exactly paralleled in Paul of Hungary's *De confessione*
23 and Bruno Hostiensis, *Summa Aurea* 5); B.11.81a (Robert Courson, *Summa*
2, sec. h; Bruno Hostiensis, *Summa Aurea* 5); B.15.530a, C.17.280a (Alain de
Lille, *Liber poenitentialis* 4.18); B.10.281a (Alain de Lille, *Liber poenitentialis* 4.16,
simplified from Matt. 15:14); A.9.16a, B.8.20a, C.10.21 (exactly paralleled
as a simplification of Prov. 24:16 by Raymond of Pennafort, *Summa de Poenitentia*
3.34, sec. 6, et al.); B.18.149a, C.20.152a (exactly paralleled in John of
Freiburg, *Summa confessorum* 3.34, q. 168).

16. Groos, Arthur, ed., with Emerson Brown, Jr., Thomas D. Hill, Giuseppe
Mazzotta, and Joseph S. Wittig. *Magister Regis: Studies in Honor of Robert Earl
Kaske*. New York: Fordham University Press, 1986.
    See nos. 33, 41 below.

17. Harrington, David V. "Indeterminacy in *Winner and Waster* and *The Parliament of the Three Ages*." *ChauR* 20 (1986): 246–57.
    The appeal of *WW* and *P3A* derives from their ability to challenge and drama-
tize the inadequacies of commonplace didactic lessons, in a fashion that recalls
Wolfgang Iser's notion of a literary text's indeterminacy, which engages the
reader's imagination to "fill in the gaps." Indeterminacy is fostered in these two
poems through such conditions and devices as an alliterative verse-situation
that relies on a dramatic interplay between the poet/minstrel and audience,
irresponsible narrators, a dream vision form that may relate enigmatic dreams,
and personification allegory that exposes the limitations of particular characters' values. The audience is thus led to formulate more acceptable solutions
to problems posed by, and in, the poems.

18. Kane, George. "Some Fourteenth-Century 'Political' Poems." Kratzmann
and Simpson (no. 19 below) 82–91.
    Criticizes as unhistorical the familiar classification of a number of fourteenth-
century poems as "poems of protest and dissent"; such a classification does not
take into account the conservative nature of estates literature, which does not
question the general principle of authority and explains social and political evils
on the basis of human failure. *The Simonie* is a theodicy demonstrating that
present sufferings are divine visitations for sins. Although *PPCrede* complains
of the friars' persecution of Wyclif, it insists on the truth of the Apostles' Creed
and is unfazed by Wyclif's heterodoxy. *Mum and the Sothsegger* is really two in

complete poems, perhaps by a single author: one that aims to justify Richard's deposition through conventional recommendations (after the fact) for better government, another that argues for speaking out against abuses familiar to estates satire. Both fragments are royalist, authoritarian, and unrevolutionary.

19. Kratzmann, Gregory, and James Simpson, eds. *Medieval English Religious and Ethical Literature: Essays in Honour of G. H. Russell*. Cambridge: Brewer, 1986.
See nos. 7, 9, 12, 18, 29, 36, 37, 38.

20. Middleton, Anne. *"Piers Plowman." A Manual of the Writings in Middle English 1050-1500*. Albert E. Hartung, ed., Vol. 7. New Haven: Connecticut Academy of Arts and Sciences, 1986. 2211-34, 2419-48.

Describes the poem as existing in three versions, all of which were copied and circulated early after their creation as more or less complete versions of what was considered a single work, as is suggested by the *explicits* of all three versions and the testimony of John But, if the "other werkes" he refers to are the B and C continuations. The B text preserves the boundaries of the A Visio but adds new material to the two dreams; the Vitae in B (and C) generally show less distinct boundaries than the Visio, and do not always coincide with passus division. The C text is a thorough revision of B, less than 100 lines longer, but with shifts of large blocks of B-text material, omissions and additions, and closely re-worked passages (up until the last two passus).

Since the genetic history of the mss. is largely irrecoverable, finds it impossible to infer from stemmatic evidence the poet's native dialect or the place of composition of the poem, as opposed to the place of copying of individual mss. Approximately 70 per cent of the poem is written in *aa/ax* lines, but Langland's variations from the norm and his use of secondary patterning is found not to have been precisely described in critical commentary. Also calls for a thorough revaluation of the poem's verbal and prosodic techniques, following the lead of Kane's investigations of alliterative patterning and metrical accent. Recognizes the possible influence of cadenced prose, and calls for more work in ME on the "terrain in which prose and verse technique meet."

Regarding the authorship question, sees Manly's work reflective of late nineteenth-century attitudes towards long, amorphous aggregates of originally separate compositions. Finds Manly's arguments were not based on close textual study or on evidence from analogous works circulating in multiple versions during their authors' lifetimes.

Sees in the poem no certain borrowings from French allegories, French court lyrics or narrative, or other English alliterative poems, and finds the poem's closest resemblances in alliterative biblical paraphrase and didactic verse. No single explanation of the author's education is sufficient to account for the range of his literate references, traceable to the Psalms, Gospels, Epistles, *sententiae, compendia*, patristic writings, etc.

The poet's social and political views are orthodox, yet his fresh and impassioned presentation caused *PPl* to appeal to the heterodox, in a period when orthodox and Lollard moral teaching and private devotion were sometimes hard to distinguish. Criticizes the simplification that describes Chaucer and Langland in terms of "courtly" and "popular," and finds in literary modernism's interest in non-naturalistic modes the impetus toward elucidation of the poem's key terms and concepts.

Bibliography, pp. 2419–48, arranged under the following headings: Background books; (1) Manuscripts, (2) Editions, (3) Information about MSS, (4) Classification of MSS and Problems of Editing, (5) Selections, (6) Translations and Modernizations, (7) Textual Notes, (8) Language, (9) Versification, (10) Date, (11) Authorship, (12) Authorship Controversy, (13) Sources, (14) Comparisons and Later Relationships, (15) General Interpretation, (16) Discussion of Particular Problems, (17) Contemporary Relationships, Mainly Non-Literary, (18) General References, (19) Bibliography, (20) Miscellaneous.

21. Peck, Russell A. "Social Conscience and the Poets." *Social Unrest in the Late Middle Ages: Papers of the Fifteenth Annual Conference of the Center for Medieval and Early Renaissance Studies.* Ed. Francis X. Newman. Binghamton, NY: Medieval and Renaissance Texts and Studies, 1986. 113–48.

Sees the close relationship of Wycliffite reform and the larger penitential movement stressing individual conscience in a direct relationship to God reflected in *PPl* where Conscience joins Reason in advising the King concerning Meed, where Conscience guides Will on his journey to discover his soul, and where Conscience helps Will after the vision of the Passion to understand the degenerative processes within Christianity. Wyclif's defense of royal authority against the temporalities of nobility and clergy are noted especially in C-text revisions. Wycliffite elements of *PPCrede* include attacks on avarice, simony, and temporalities; the many points of satire which it shares with Chaucer's works suggest that by the early fifteenth century the separate literary traditions of Langland and Chaucer were being blended by penitential and political writers.

22. Peverett, Michael. " 'Quod' and 'Seide' in *Piers Plowman*." *NM* 87 (1986): 117–27.

Quod, always placed before the speaker (as grammatical subject), indicates in ME that the words of the speaker are being repeated; it is more restricted in use than the approximately synonymous *seide*, which can be used to ascribe indirect speech. When either word is grammatically possible, Langland uses *seide* only to fit the alliterative scheme or to avoid using *quod* near the end of a line. *Quod* tends to emphasize the act of speaking; *seide* draws attention to what is said. *Quod* in C.15.138 rules out the possibility that Clergy's speech continues beyond line 137. Kane-Donaldson's punctuation of B.11.34-41 is to be preferred over Schmidt's, since *quod* suggests Plato's actual appearance here and direct speech. B.11.171 is probably to be seen as part of Trajan's actual speech, which may extend from B.11.140 to 319 (as interpreted by Schmidt).

23. Rex, Richard. "Pastiche as Irony in the Prioress's Prologue and Tale." *Studies in Short Ficiton* 23 (1986): 1–8.

The definition of charity offered to Will by Anima (Skeat, B.15.145–46) helps to define the Prioress's "child-like rapture," which is intended as a measure of her *fauntelte* rather than her *fre liberal wille*. Besides Matt. 18:3-4 and Luke 18:16-17, Langland's formulation draws on 1 Cor. 13:10-11, 14:20, and Isaiah 65:20, which define the vices of adults acting foolishly as children.

24. Rex, Richard. "Wild Horses, Justice, and Charity in the Prioress's Tale." *PLL* 22 (1986): 339–51.

With respect to the Prioress, Chaucer would have accepted the common medieval argument that charity, or its primary element, patience, is to be preferred to vengeance, as is seen in Christ's Crucifixion. Chaucer also would have assumed, with Langland, that in the absence of charity no virtue is sufficient for salvation.

25. [Samuels, M. L.] "Corrigenda." *MÆ* 55 (1986): 40.

Correction of printing errors in M. L. Samuels, "Langland's Dialect," *MÆ* 54 (1985): 232–47.

26. Schmidt, A. V. C. "The Inner Dreams in *Piers Plowman*." *MÆ* 55 (1986): 24–40.

The apparent omission of the second "inner dream" in C.18 may be seen as resulting from Langland's attempt at theological clarification, but entails significant loss to the poem nonetheless. The substitution of Liberum-Arbitrium for Piers diminishes the power to communicate affectively the mysteries of faith as they have been experienced by the Dreamer's emotional discovery in the inner dream of B.16. The second inner dream in B stresses the primacy of inner conversion, a necessary preparation for the salvation of the world, and suggests that God's *suffrance* (in the two senses of enduring and tolerating), when approached affectively rather than intellectually, can resolve the dilemma posed by the first inner dream concerning the power of evil.

27. Simpson, James. " 'Et Vidit Cogitaciones Eorum': A Parallel Instance and

Possible Source for Langland's Use of a Biblical Formula at *Piers Plowman* B.XV.200a." *N&Q* ns 33 (1986): 9–13.

B.15.149–212 (Schmidt) probably shows the direct influence of Augustine, *De Trinitate* 15, which elucidates the Pauline *aenigma* (1 Cor. 13:4–5) as that through which mankind's imperfect understanding perceives in the soul the *imago Dei*. Augustine defines thought as inner speech (*locutiones cordis*) and sees in such unspoken words a likeness to the Word of God. To Augustine, Christ alone is able to perceive the words of the heart (see Matt. 9:24, Luke 5:21–22); Langland presents Piers as capable of such perception. In order to know charity in himself, Will must discover the principle by which he is known, "which is provisionally Piers, and ultimately Christ."

28. Simpson, James. "From Reason to Affective Knowledge: Modes of Thought and Poetic Form in *Piers Plowman*." *MÆ* 55 (1986): 1–23.

PPl reflects the Augustinian tradition, exemplified by Alexander of Hales and Robert Kilwardby, in which theology is seen as an affective mode of knowledge, a *sapientia*, rather than an intellectual mode, or *scientia*, and in which such cognitive categories are linked to rhetorical modes. The Meed narrative (B.2–4), concerned with intellectual comprehension and the problem of distinguishing meaning, exemplifies styles appropriate to the exercise of reason (e.g. *difinitivus*, *divisivus*, *collectivus*), whereas from passus 12 on, when Imaginatif declares grace beyond the cognitive reach of Clergy or Kind Wit, the modes of poetry employed (e.g. *symbolicus*, *metaphoricus*, *parabolicus*) aim to produce a sapiential knowledge of God, in appealing to the will.

29. Simpson, James. "The Role of *Scientia* in *Piers Plowman*." Kratzmann and Simpson (no. 19 above) 49–65.

Piers's disparagement of the knowledge gained through human instruction draws on a monastic tradition exemplified by the twelfth-century *Tractatus de Interiore Domo* and the *Meditationes Piisimae de Cognitione Humanae Conditionis* (cited at B.11.3). Classical and patristic treatments of the liberal arts recognize the possibility of an unlettered person achieving wisdom, but generally defend the necessary use of the liberal arts for most people. That Dame Study knows she cannot give a complete understanding of truth is consistent with medieval formulations that stress the incapacity of the arts to teach moral virtue. Augustinian *scientia*, derived from the trivium, quadrivium, and allied disciplines, prepared one for the pursuit of *sapientia*, gained through reading Scripture. Clergy also recognizes the limitations of his "sevene sonnes," and points toward a higher knowledge. Piers's knowledge of God is "kynde," or sapiential, but Langland recognizes the propaedeutic function of the acquired disciplines.

30. Simpson, James. "The Transformation of Meaning: A Figure of Thought in *Piers Plowman*." *RES* ns 37 (1986): 161–83.

Explores Langland's poetic habit of using words with earthly referents in situations that describe spiritual realities. Finds this in contexts of exhortation (e.g. the speech of Reason, B.4), where unexpected words are given a spiritual dimension; in contexts intended as satire (e.g. Schmidt, B.5.234) where the spiritual force of a word is deliberately contracted in favor of the negative force of the image; and in contexts intended neither for praise nor blame, but rather to designate a spiritual reality by transforming, rather than rejecting, the meaning of reality.

31. Swanson, R. N. "Langland and the Priest's Title." *N&Q* ns 33 (1986): 438–40.

C.13.100–13 (Pearsall), corresponding to B.11.287–302, shows Langland complaining not that the ordained misuse the name of priest, but that many are insufficiently "entitled" to become priests in the specific sense that at ordination they lack a "title," i.e. possession of a means of livelihood that will enable the individual to live as befits his order. Whoever provided title had the responsibility of ensuring its sufficiency, just as it was the responsibility of a king to make sure that those dubbed knights had sufficient means to maintain such status.

32. Szittya, Penn R. *The Antifraternal Tradition in Medieval Literature*. Princeton: Princeton University Press, 1986. 247–87.

In the B Prologue, friars are grouped among the "wanderers" and "wasters" guilty of faults of speech and works. Langland upsets the traditional Franciscan notion of friars as *ioculatores Domini* by making friars practitioners of false speech, to be distinguished from true "minstrels" who use the divine gift of speech properly. The association of friars with the faults of speech recalls William of St. Amour's description of the *pseudoapostoli*; in his designation of friars as dishonest beggars, Langland is close to the position of Thomas de Wilton who attacked the friars' interpretation of *Ne soliciti sitis* as rejecting manual labor. The speech of Need, a possible agent of Antichrist, ignores careful theological restrictions governing the suspension of property laws and perverts the notion of temperance. The assault of Antichrist serves on the personal level to define Need's temptation to Will, himself described as a wanderer, beggar, and minstrel, as that of saving one's life in purely physical terms. The second half of B.20 parallels the first on an institutional level, with the friar's institutionalized need as threatening to the Church as Will's personal need is to his salvation. Friars are seen as the symbolic opposites of Piers and Conscience; Sir Penetrans Domos is the embodiment of those prophesied in 2 Tim. 3:6 on the Last Days.

33. Szittya, Penn R. "The Trinity in Langland and Abelard." Groos et al. (no. 16 above) 207–16.

The figure of the writing lord, parchment, and pen of B.9.39–41 and that of B.16.191–93 are both trinitarian analogues that derive from the twelfth-century Victorine tradition of describing the Trinity with respect to the non-exclusive aspects of *Potentia*, *Sapientia*, and *Benignitas*. In particular, Abelard's figure of a lute player (*Intro. ad theol.*, *PL* 178:1068–75), in which music is created from art (the power of playing, or the Father's *Potentia*), hand (the instrumental agent, i.e. the Son's *Sapientia*), and the strings (musical effects of art and hands together, i.e. the *effecta* of the Spirit), provides a paradigm of Langland's figures. In B.16.191–93, *might* refers to the Father, *seruant* to Christ, *mene* to the Holy Spirit. In B.9.39–41 the lord's power of writing is the creative power of *Deus artifex*; the pen represents agency, or the Son; and the parchment with letters the effect of the combined action of Father and Son, or *Benignitas secundum effecta* of the Spirit.

34. Tavormina, M. Teresa. "A Liturgical Allusion in the *Scottish Legendary*: The Largesse of St. Lawrence." *N&Q* 33 (1986): 154–57.

B.15.326–31 and C.17.64–71 (Pearsall) quote the first clause of Psalm 111:9 (also translated in the *Scottish Legendary*), traditionally associated with St. Lawrence, and taken over at several points in the liturgy of the saint's vigil, feast, and octave. As in a homily once ascribed to Maximus of Turin and in the twelfth-century Anglo-Norman *De saint Laurent*, Langland stresses both Lawrence's enduring sanctity and the lasting reward such sanctity merits.

35. Thorne, J. R., and Marie-Claire Uhart. "Robert Crowley's *Piers Plowman*." *MÆ* 55 (1986): 248–54.

Although comparison of the annotations of Crowley's three impressions of 1550 with the annotations of Cambridge Univ. Lib. ms. Ll.iv.14 cannot definitively prove Skeat's suggestion that the glossator/annotator was Crowley (who almost invariably uses word-forms as they appear in this ms.), it certainly establishes him to be of Crowley's frame of mind; and annotations of the ms. might well be preparatory work for a new copy. Crowley's texts modernize spelling and grammar, but are remarkable in preserving the poem's "difficult vocabulary." Crowley's Protestant bias comes out clearly in the marginal commentary; the faithfulness of his text is due to the wide readership the poem had gained in manuscript for two centuries.

36. Trigg, Stephanie. "Israel Gollancz's 'Wynnere and Wastoure': Political Satire or Editorial Politics?" Kratzmann and Simpson (no. 19 above) 115–127.

Criticizes the theoretical and methodological presuppositions of Gollancz's dating of *WW* as the early 1350s. Gollancz's reliance on the supposedly topical nature of the satire is seen as a function of his own royalist loyalties and nationalism in post–World War I England. Argues against literal reading of economic and social reference as criticism of Edward III's policies, in favor of consideration of such tensions in primarily moral terms, with the poet suggesting generosity as a legitimate mean between the extreme vices of avarice and prodigality. The poem was probably written between 1352 and 1370, and thus may not be an immediate precursor of *PPl*.

37. Waldron, R. A. "Langland's Originality: The Christ-Knight and the Harrowing of Hell." Kratzmann and Simpson (no. 19 above) 66–81.

Langland's treatment of the theme of the Christ-Knight recalls that of Nicholas Bozon's *Vn rey esteit iadis ke aueit vne amye*, where the lady is abducted by *vn traitour* who takes her *par un acord*, the action is described as a *gylerye*, and the king's *dreit en li clame* is stressed. Langland's emphasis is on the triumphant rather than sacrificial aspects of the Crucifixion. He turns the debate of the Four Daughters of God from a court-disputation to an argument among the sisters themselves, who function somewhat like a chorus in commenting on the action rather than as active participants. Langland's probable use of Bozon's *Chasteau d'Amour* shows how the older notion of a ransom paid to the Devil for souls in Hell (the "Devil's rights") becomes more like Anselm's notion of Christ's satisfaction for sin.

38. Wall, John. "Penance as Poetry in the Late Fourteenth Century." Kratzmann and Simpson (no. 19 above) 179–91.

Explores how the *Gawain*-poet, Langland, and Chaucer deal poetically (rather than only theologically) with the penitential tradition. In both *PPl* and *SGGK* repentance operates on an individual and "helps him to grow from that existential point." In *PPl* switching from personified abstractions to naturalistic representations is necessary to portray the consistent action of grace in the world. Piers is the sign of regenerate man; the visions of Dowel, Dobet, and Dobest correspond with the judgments of Arthur, Bertilak, and Gawain, respectively; and at the end of these poems both Gawain and Conscience continue a spiritual quest that shows progress through penance.

39. Whatley, Gordon. "Heathens and Saints: *St. Erkenwald* in Its Legendary Context." *Speculum* 61 (1986): 330–63.

Notes significant differences between the salvation of the righteous judge of *St. Erkenwald* and that of Trajan in *PPl*. Trajan is saved by his own righteousness, without the mediation of sacraments and without even having been resuscitated and converted (as would have been expected of a pagan born after Christ who had lived in knowledge of Christianity). *St. Erkenwald's* treatment of the theme may seek to "correct" the anti-ecclesiastical bias of versions such as Langland's and Wyclif's by stressing the role and prestige of the bishop and the visible sacramental church.

40. White, Hugh. "Langland's Ymaginatif, Kynde and the *Benjamin Major.*" *MÆ* 55 (1986): 241–48.

The Benjamin Major (1.6) of Richard of St. Victor offers a description of the function of *imaginatio* that parallels B.13.14–20 (Schmidt) in stressing the mind's running over the multitude of sensible things, the sense of wonder this elicits, and a consideration of God's activity as Creator of the material world. But whereas for Richard imaginative contemplation of divine *potentia, sapientia,* and *munificentia* should lead to love of God, Will is shown to be unable to connect what he sees to Kynde and to come to love Kynde. For Richard, the contemplative process passes from imagination through reason to the intellect; for Langland, imagination without patience yields an intellectual pursuit of God that is problematic.

41. Wittig, Joseph S. "The Middle English 'Absolute Infinitive' and the 'Speech of Book.' " Groos et al. (no. 16 above) 217–40.

Determines the general characteristics of the absolute infinitive to be 1) the marker *to* (sometimes *for to*); 2) a pronominal, typically nominative subject (when expressed); 3) syntactic function as the verb of a subordinate clause; and 4) modality that derives from that of the main clause rather than from the infinitive clause itself. Finds unlikely Donaldson's interpretation of Book's speech in which *unioynen* and *unlouken* of 18.258 are taken as absolute infinitives, given the absence of the *to* marker and the need for the subject to be re-stated in line 258 after a series of conditional clauses. R. E. Kaske's reading of line 255 as *but Jesus [will] rise to life*, with all following verbs as infinitives parallel with *rise*, is considered possible, but the context would then be clarified only at 258. Suggests as a plausible reading *to lyue* in 255 as an infinitive with all subsequent verb forms as parallel infinitives.

42. Woolf, Rosemary. *Art and Doctrine: Essays on Medieval Literature.* Ed. Heather O'Donoghue. London and Ronceverte: Hambledon Press, 1986.

In a collection, with the editor's introduction, of previously published essays by the author, reprints "Some Non-Medieval Qualities of *Piers Plowman*" (*EIC* 12 [1962]: 111–25); "The Theme of Christ the Lover-Knight in Medieval English Literature" (*RES* ns 13 [1962]: 1–16); "The Tearing of the Pardon" (in *Piers Plowman: Critical Approaches,* ed. S. S. Hussey [London: Methuen; New York: Barnes and Noble, 1969]: 50–75).

BOOK REVIEWS

43. Burrow, J. A. *Essays on Medieval Literature.* Oxford: Clarendon Press, 1984. Rev. Robert B. Burlin, *Speculum* 61 (1986): 630–31; Joerg O. Fichte, *SAC* 8

(1986): 170-72; Alexander Murray, *TLS*, Oct. 10, 1986: 1127; A. V. C. S[chmidt], *MÆ* 55 (1986): 134-35.

44. Fowler, David C. *The Bible in Middle English Literature*. Seattle and London: University of Washington Press, 1984. Rev. G. H. Russell, *SAC* 8 (1986): 185-88.

45. Griffiths, Lavinia. *Personification in Piers Plowman*. Piers Plowman Studies 3. Woodbridge, Suffolk, and Dover, NH: Boydell and Brewer, 1985. Rev. Elizabeth D. Kirk, *SAC* 8 (1986): 195-96.

46. Norton-Smith, John. *William Langland*. Medieval and Renaissance Authors 6. Leiden: E. J. Brill, 1983. Rev. John A. Alford, *Speculum* 61 (1986): 192-95.

47. Salter, Elizabeth. *Fourteenth-Century English Poetry: Contexts and Readings*. Oxford: Clarendon Press, 1983. Rev. John C. Hirsch, *MÆ* 55 (1986): 291-92; Götz Schmitz, *Anglia* 104 (1986): 484-87.

48. Stokes, Myra. *Justice and Mercy in Piers Plowman: A Reading of the B Text Visio*. London and Canberra: Croom Helm, 1984. Rev. Anna Baldwin, *MÆ* 55 (1986): 290-91; P. M. Kean, *RES* ns 37 (1986): 79-80; A. V. C. Schmidt, *N&Q* ns 33 (1986): 211-12.